Voices of Authority

Education and Linguistic Difference

Voices of Authority

Education and Linguistic Difference

Edited by

Monica Heller
and
Marilyn Martin-Jones

Contemporary Studies in Linguistics and Education, Volume 1
David Bloome and Jay Lemke, Series Editors

Ablex Publishing
Westport, Connecticut • London

Library of Congress Cataloging-in-Publication Data

Voices of authority : education and linguistic difference / edited by Monica
Heller, Marilyn Martin-Jones.
    p. cm.—(Contemporary studies in linguistics and education,
  ISSN 1530-8359 ; v. 1)
  Includes bibliographical references and index.
  ISBN 1-56750-530-9 (alk. paper)—ISBN 1-56750-531-7 (pbk. : alk. paper)
    1. Language and education. 2. Sociolinguistics. 3. Multilingualism.
  I. Heller, Monica. II. Martin-Jones, Marilyn. III. Series.

P40.8.V65 2001
306.44—dc21

                            00-028874

British Library Cataloguing in Publication Data is available.

Library of Congress Catalog Card Number: 00-028874
ISBN: 1-56750-530-9
     1-56750-531-7 (pbk.)
ISSN: 1530-8359

First published in 2001

Ablex Publishing, 88 Post Road West, Westport, CT 06881
An imprint of Greenwood Publishing Group, Inc.
www.greenwood.com

Printed in the United States of America

The paper used in this book complies with the
Permanent Paper Standard issued by the National
Information Standards Organization (Z39.48-1984).

10 9 8 7 6 5 4 3 2 1

Contents

Preface

One of the major challenges of our day is the provision of effective, democratic education under conditions of increasing sociolinguistic diversity and change. Yet, most work on this subject focuses on linguistic, cognitive, pedagogical, or policy dimensions of education and linguistic diversity, failing to address social and political issues. This volume argues that these issues are central to understanding the significance and consequence both of educational policy and practices in multilingual settings and of language policy and practices as they manifest themselves through education. Specifically, we argue that language practices in these settings reveal struggles over the establishment of authority and legitimacy; they can be interpreted as voices expressing a variety of social positions and interests with respect to the resources distributed through educational institutions and processes. They reveal what is at stake and for whom in choices made at state, institutional, school, and other levels regarding both language of instruction and assessment, as well as regarding language teaching and learning and the evaluation of linguistic proficiency.

In putting together this collection, our aims have been (1) to highlight the role played by educational institutions in multilingual societies in the construction of cultural identities, in the production and distribution of prestigious cultural and linguistic resources, and in the reproduction of social inequalities and (2) to show that we can develop a fuller understanding of these processes of production and reproduction in education by investigating the communicative practices of learners and educators in the daily cycles of life in educational settings.

The chapters in this volume provide close ethnographic analyses of socially and historically situated cases from a wide range of settings. We argue that insights from such situated accounts are essential to theory building and to substantive generalization. The cases include a variety of educational sites in postcolonial, indigenous, and immigrant settings in Australia, Botswana, Brazil, Britain, Burundi, Canada, Corsica, Hong Kong, Jaffna, Kenya, Malta, Peru, South Africa, and Switzerland. Some of the chapters originally appeared in two separate issues of *Linguistics and Education* 8 (1 & 2), in 1996, which we edited. Some of these have been revised and updated for this book. In our introduction and conclusion to the book, we have attempted to bring these situated accounts together within a unifying frame.

This collection has been put together slowly and steadily over the course of nearly three years, and we owe a debt of gratitude to many people who have helped us bring it to fruition. First, we need to thank David Bloome and Jay Lemke for their initial expression of interest in the possibility of publishing such a collection in their series "Contemporary Studies in Linguistics and Education." We would also like to thank them for their patience and understanding as we have worked away at it over the past three years. Working with contributors scattered across several continents, while divided ourselves by the Atlantic Ocean, has proved to be challenging, but the Internet and goodwill on the part of the contributors have made our task much easier than it would otherwise have been. In addition, three groups of colleagues in Europe made it possible for us to enjoy some of the best working conditions we have ever experienced. Our thanks first go to the staff of the Fryske Akademy (Friesland, the Netherlands), and especially to Durk Gorter, who provided us with space, access to a computer, and an inspiring work environment. Richard Watts and the staff of the Department of English, University of Bern (Switzerland), also provided us with similar support on a later occasion. Most recently, Joan Pujolar and his colleagues at the Open University of Catalonia (Barcelona) gave us practical support and encouragement while we were working on the introduction and the conclusion to the book. We would also like to acknowledge the financial assistance we received from the University of Wales, Aberystwyth Research Fund, to cover the costs of preparing the final manuscript for publication. Finally, we would like to thank Tim Kaiser, who produced the map of Malta, and Ruthanna Barnett, Adriana Boogerman-Castejón, Sally Kedge, and especially Estêvão Cabral for their touches of brilliance in helping us to put the manuscript into shape.

MONICA HELLER and MARILYN MARTIN-JONES

Introduction: Symbolic Domination, Education, and Linguistic Difference

Monica Heller and Marilyn Martin-Jones

What kinds of multilingualism should be developed through schooling? What kinds of multilingualism can be developed through schooling? What language or languages should be used as media of education in multilingual communities? Should public education be responsible for teaching minority languages? Why do speakers of minority languages often do better or worse than other groups at school? These and other questions about education and linguistic difference have long exercised policymakers and educators, and they continue to surface in public debates in a large number of countries.

One way or another, all of us who have contributed to this book have been concerned with these issues. We have encountered educational inequality in multilingual settings as students, parents, teachers, teacher educators, community translators, and researchers or in other capacities. We have lived through different experiences of educational inequality in many arenas of our personal and professional lives. This collection of papers provides an account of the ways in which the research we have done has enabled us to reflect on specific dimensions of our experiences.

The societies that we live and work in are all shaped in some way by nineteenth- and twentieth-century colonialism and by new global forms of cultural, economic, and social domination. They are societies where English, French, Portuguese, and Spanish are the dominant languages. Some of them are colonies or former colonies, engaged in processes of post-independence nation building and facing the effects of neocolonialist drives toward globalization. Others are former colonial powers that have experienced considerable social and political changes as a result of labor migration from former colonies and the arrival of refugees. One or two are cases of internal colonialism or combine characteristics of several such situations. Specifically, the chapters in this book focus on multilingual settings in Australia, Botswana, Brazil, Burundi, Canada, Corsica, England, Hong Kong, Jaffna, Kenya, Malta, Peru, South Africa, and Switzerland. In all these settings, education is a key site for the construction of social identities and of unequal relations of power. We focus here on ideologies and struggles centering on bilingual education, first-language teaching, other uses of first-language resources, access to dominant-language varieties, language revitalization programs, and the continued use of a former colonial language as a medium of instruction.

Questions of multilingualism in education are usually seen as a matter of linguistic proficiency, as tied to taken-for-granted goals of economic or political development. In this book, we propose a quite different approach. Our argument is that in order to adequately address such issues, it is necessary to foreground the ways in which linguistic difference in education is a matter of symbolic domination (Bourdieu 1982). Linguistic practices are central to struggles over controlling the production and distribution of resources and over the legitimation of relations of power, which are, in the end, what such control amounts to. All our debates about who should speak what and how are really, we argue, debates over who gets to decide what counts as *legitimate language* (Bourdieu 1977; Blommaert 1999).

We focus on the concept of legitimate language (rather than, for example, the notion of standard language). We do this explicitly in order to emphasize that the issue is principally one of what ways of using language, what kinds of language practices, are valued and considered good, normal, appropriate, or correct in the framework of ideological orientations connected to social, economic, and political interests. By exercising control over the value of linguistic resources, we argue, groups simultaneously regulate access to other resources (such as knowledge, friendship, or material goods) and legitimate the social order that permits them to do so by masking (that is, naturalizing) their ability to do so. Debates over linguistic norms and practices are, in the end, debates over controlling resources.

These debates are particularly important in education, which is a key site for defining legitimate language. The reasons (which we discuss further hereafter) have to do with the ways in which education acts as a key site for constructing what counts as knowledge, what counts as displaying knowledge, and who may define and display knowledge and for evaluating forms of knowledge, their display, and their performers. Language is important as one way in which knowledge is constructed and displayed and as a resource that becomes important in and of itself as a means of gaining or controlling access to other resources. It is also important as a means for masking the relations of power embedded in these processes. At the same time, these relations of power must be understood in the context of historical processes such as colonialism, postcolonialism and neocolonialism, globalization, and nationalist and minority rights movements (Grillo 1989; Pennycook 1994; Phillipson 1992; Tollefson 1991, 1995).

The position we are putting forward in this volume has grown out of different lines of enquiry and, in some ways, from the bottom up. One, mainly ethnomethodological tradition, was concerned to understand the institutional order of schools by examining the interaction order of classrooms (Cicourel 1974; Mehan 1979; Sinclair and Coulthard 1975). This approach focused on understanding the nature of social order in education through the discovery of patterns of interaction in daily life at school. Some of this work (see for example Carrasco et al. 1981) happened to be undertaken in classrooms in which the students came from a variety of different backgrounds, and the management of multilingual resources in these classrooms had to be understood as part of the construction of social reality in those settings.

This approach joined a different tradition, one that focused explicitly on local, functional analyses of multilingual practices wherever they were found to occur; not surprisingly, schools were an obvious site for European and North American researchers, since schools are an evident public meeting ground for people of different language groups. The two began to merge as interactionist sociolinguists, especially those working in the tradition established by John Gumperz and Dell Hymes, aimed at connecting linguistic variability with the ways in which schools (along with other institutional sites) act as institutions of social selection (Erickson and Shultz 1981; Gumperz 1982, 1986; Hymes 1974; Philips 1972, 1983).

The 1980s saw the publication of numerous studies in the United States that adopted a "cultural difference" model to understand the relationship between ethnolinguistic and class difference and social selection in schools (Gumperz 1982, 1986; Michaels 1981; Au and Jordan 1981; Heath 1983; Erickson and Shultz 1981). The central argument of this body of work has been that members of different speech communities (whose boundaries are assumed to result from separate socialization and interaction patterns due to physical or social distance) develop culturally distinct linguistic practices that index distinct frames of reference, and hence they engage in distinct inferencing processes in interaction. These different practices and processes of indexicality are, it is argued, mutually unavailable to members of different groups, resulting in negative judgments about the competence of others. Gumperz has argued that it is this process that underlies the development of stereotypes and of social selection.

For example, Philips (1972, 1983) argued that the school failure of Native North American school children could be attributed to cultural incompatibility in ways of learning and of displaying knowledge. She focused on student nonparticipation in classroom talk as a site for examining the construction of school failure. She argued that students' silence resulted from a mismatch in cultural conventions. In her account, mainstream schooling places an emphasis on individual displays of knowledge at different points in the learning process, whereas Native communities understand knowledge as collective and to be performed publicly only once mastered.

This line of argument has been critiqued for ignoring the ways in which institutionally organized relations of power constrain what happens in interaction (Singh, Lele, and Martohardjono 1988; Ogbu 1987). Critics argue that it is naive to assume that participants from different backgrounds come together on a level playing field, which only gets tipped as a result of local interactional practices. It is also naive, they argue, to assume that differences are simply the result of separate experience; they point out that if practices are distinct, this is because social boundaries are the result, not the cause, of social inequality. In addition, social inequality produces practices and frames of reference that are related in ways far more complex than simple difference. Difference is, in some sense, a resource for constructing, leveling, contesting, and blurring boundaries in order to attempt to maintain, contest, or modify relations of power. This insight also comes from more recent work inspired by cultural studies and postmodern perspectives (cf. Rampton 1995; Heller 1999). Finally, the ways in which difference is made salient and the reasons for it are linked to both community and institutional ideologies and practices. There is no simple one-to-one link between social categories, social inequality, and interaction in education. Instead, these relations are mediated and produced in institutions that are fundamentally about producing and distributing different kinds of resources. The ways in which they do so are articulated in a complex fashion with other institutions and social networks and with respect to historical processes.

If one returns to the example of Philips's (1972, 1983) work, this shift of perspective opens up opportunities for understanding Native North American students' silence in the classroom in a broader context. One can also understand it as a manifestation of resistance to white institutions in the context of a wider history of domination.

Communicative practices in multilingual educational settings thus emerge as far more complex and far more illuminating than simple reflections of existing social boundaries or sources of school-reinforced social inequality. Instead, they can provide us with a window on education-based processes of social and cultural production and reproduction and on the linkages between local interactional practices and institutional processes. Of course, there is a large body of work that has explicitly attempted to understand the social selection and reproduction processes of education. With the obvious exception of Bernstein (1990) and other scholars such as Dannequin (1987), this work has rarely looked explicitly at linguistic difference or at linguistic practices more generally. It has paid even less attention to multilingual practices. Our position is that examining education through the lens of language, and particularly of linguistic difference, allows us to see ways in which social boundaries in local community contexts intersect with institutional categorization processes and ways in which social structure is articulated with human agency. This approach allows us to understand some fundamental things not only about how education operates but also about the relationship between interaction, institutions, and community and about difference and inequality.

What this approach does is to link social order to institutional and interactional order. Communitywide categories (such as race, ethnicity, class, gender) are tied to institutionally relevant ones (such as categories based on school performance). Relations of power are also tied to access to and control over resources distributed in a number of arenas (for example, school credentials are tied to positioning on the job market). Categories and relations in different arenas are interactionally accomplished and also concretely linked to each other in terms of their consequences for the development of social networks and for the circulation of resources.

The central theme of this book, then, is that education is a key site (of course, not the only site) of struggle over social inequality. We understand education to be an institution of social and cultural production and reproduction, that is, a discursive space in which groups with different interests struggle over access to symbolic and material resources and over ways of organizing that access that privilege some and marginalize others on the basis of criteria of evaluation that have collective applications and effects.

Following Bourdieu and Passeron (1977), we also understand education as a key site because of its possibilities for the construction and application of processes of symbolic domination, that is, domination that works because it masks its concrete sources, that works because it appears not to work, that works by convincing all participants in an activity that the rules that are, in fact, defined by one group are natural, normal, universal, and objective, and that it is in everyone's interests to accept those rules. One of the objectives of education, in this view, is to construct hegemonic discourses and to ensure their acceptance. Education is in this way deeply about social order.

However, Bourdieu's vision focuses primarily on the workings of symbolic domination, that is, on hegemonic discourses that saturate collective consciousness and remain relatively uncontested. One of our goals here is to widen the focus to examine symbolic domination in the light of the ethnomethodological insight that social order is always interactionally constructed and therefore always to some extent indeterminate. While there are clearly ways in which no interaction can be said to start from scratch, nonetheless there is always some possibility (the extent of which always remains to be empirically established) for challenging and modifying the social order.

We are also concerned to understand the agency behind social and cultural reproduction or the challenging of it. While ethnomethodology allows us to understand that social reality is locally constructed, it does not allow us to understand why people make the interactional moves that they make. Here we assume that actors are no more completely unconstrained (nor, of course, overdetermined) than action. Hence it becomes necessary to understand actors as engaging in social positioning in the face of the constraints and possibilities open to them (Giddens 1984) and the resources available to them and with respect to their interests in the production and distribution of the symbolic and material resources that they may possess or wish to possess.

But constraints and possibilities are rarely straightforward; they emerge from a variety of sources and may mutually reinforce, intersect with, or contradict each other. Social positioning can therefore be as much about neutralizing tensions or about constructing ambiguity and multiplicity as a way of coping with complexity and contradiction as it can be about clarifying and categorizing. How, where, why, and by whom the social order is quietly reproduced or vociferously challenged are therefore questions that lie at the heart of this book.

Language is central to these processes in two ways. First, as a key means of accomplishing interaction, language is a particularly important resource and terrain for reproducing or struggling over the reproduction of social difference and social inequality. For this reason, we have explicitly tried to include in this volume papers that examine different scenarios. We have grouped these papers into three sections. The first group of papers foreground what appears to be the successful exercise of symbolic domination, that is, the construction and imposition of legitimate language. The middle group addresses situations that begin to get muddied, that is, situations in which there is some form of contradiction that must be handled in interaction and therefore presents difficulties for the imposition of a unified discourse, and possibilities (which may or may not be taken up) for contestation. The last group addresses settings in which contestation is more or less overt.

The second way in which language is central to these processes is that linguistic differences also act as a means to apply principles of social categorization and social hierarchization, principles that are simultaneously tied to processes of categorization and hierarchization along the lines of gender, race, ethnicity, class, and other principles of social organization. Clearly, what we argue here is valid for any differentiated community, not just multilingual ones. But multilingualism has the advantage of rendering visible processes that may otherwise be harder to see. It also has the advantage of resulting from a number of different social, economic, and political processes germane to understanding the world around us today. For this reason, we have explicitly attempted to select sites that examine postcolonial and neocolonial settings, as well as situations involving migrant, indigenous, and regional minorities.

Our aim here is therefore to engage in three conversations. The first conversation is situated within the field of sociolinguistics. This field has always aimed at making a contribution to, not just drawing from, social theory. One way in which we believe we can contribute to that is through the empirical study of the ways in which structure and agency are articulated, through linking ideologies, discourses, and practices and by tying together interactional, institutional, and community order. Social order does not exist anywhere beyond what is observable, as ethnomethodology has taught us. At the same time, it is not captured wholly in any given interaction; interactions are linked together, as Giddens would argue, in problematic ways that are discoverable only through operationalizing and empirically accessing linkages among them. This is quite a methodological challenge, and one that we only begin to address.

Nonetheless, the articles collected here do set out some ways in which the operationalization of these linkages can be achieved, for example, through the choice of sites in which there are visible fault lines (notably those observable in linguistic difference) running in directions that can be followed across time and space. For example, the use of more than one language by certain speakers in certain ways reveals differences of interest and position with respect to the intersection of the interaction order of the classroom, the institutional order of the school, the social order of the community, and the circulation of symbolic and material resources in these arenas. Such fault lines are made visible in interactional processes that index multiple ideological frames and that also have observable short-term and long-term consequences. While we still need to know more about the ways in which organizing interaction in certain ways (marginalizing or foregrounding some speakers and some discourses, for instance) is tied to the organization of institutional practice (and hence for example to the institutional marginalization or success of groups of speakers), we can at least start working in the direction of linking agency and structure.

The second conversation more specifically engages the field of education. Here, as in much social science, language tends to be treated as transparent. Our purpose is therefore to show some of the ways in which it is necessary to problematize language in order to understand what it is that educational institutions really produce in the way of knowledge and in the way of social order. Here, we want to show that linguistic practices are a key form of social action and that linguistic resources are central to the production and distribution of the other kinds of resources at stake at school (for instance, what counts as knowledge or what the school grants in the way of credentials). We also want to show that, despite intense political pressure to respond rapidly to the kinds of public policy questions that we raised at the outset, there is no easy answer to the question of how to organize multilingual resources in schooling. The best we can do is to show what interests are at stake and who stands to gain or lose what by privileging certain practices and discourses over others.

In our third conversation, we explicitly want to engage the field of language planning and language policy. Much of the work in this area is either conducted within state and institutional structures oriented toward accomplishing specific objectives or devoted to the construction of comparative descriptive typologies. In both cases, we argue, this work runs the risk of providing legitimating ideologies for specific social interests, rather than the kind of critical examination of those interests and their consequences that we call for here. It may fail to engage with the relations of power represented by state intervention or with the complexities and ambiguities of life on the ground.

In what follows, we set out some of the general concepts that emerge from a comparison across the cases assembled here. We then provide an overview of the structure and contents of the book.

RITUALIZATION AND LANGUAGE CHOICE

Analysis of what goes on in multilingual educational settings shows a range of ways in which multilingual resources are managed. We can see a range of situations: First, there are those where the relationship among linguistic resources seems to be organized in a highly ritualized way; then, there are others where there are progressive degrees of contestation of established ritualizations or of attempts to establish such ritualizations. By employing the term *ritualization*, we mean to invoke a range of conventions that organize the place of linguistic varieties (and their speakers) in discursive space. These conventions involve the construction of *interactional floors* and *stages, participant structures, keying,* and *footing*.

The discursive construction of *floors* is part of the regulation of what gets to count as a display of knowledge, that is, what are to be considered legitimate practices. It can be understood in Goffman's terms as constructing a distinction between what counts as front stage or back stage (Goffman 1956, 1974). In this way, other discursive practices, while clearly present, and indeed in many ways essential to the accomplishment of front-stage business, can be ritually marginalized, hidden, placed "back stage," so as not to overtly contradict front-stage affairs, that is, in order for certain forms of social order to be reproduced through symbolic practices that mask their operation.

Participant structures are important because they organize who can get access to the floor and therefore whose performances are made visible and whose performances can contribute to the definition of resources and to their distribution. This is observable, for example, in the allocation of turns, through which (some) participants regulate who can speak, when, and how. Turn allocation is one resource for regulating control over what gets to count as legitimate knowledge in schools, including what gets to count as legitimate linguistic knowledge. It is also of course simultaneously a resource for regulating *who* gets to decide what counts as legitimate language.

Finally, these conventions involve forms of what Goffman called *keying* and *footing* (1974), which we understand here to concern ways in which speakers signal their position with respect to the conventions and forms of language being produced interactionally. Many of the conventions to which we refer are linguistic and include various forms of discourse devices ranging through metapragmatic and metalinguistic to epilinguistic commentary, that is, commentary on how meaning is accomplished through linguistic structures (metapragmatics), commentary on language forms and practices (metalinguistics), or commentary on the social significance of linguistic varieties (epilinguistics). Linguistic or paralinguistic devices, including lexicalized flagging, hesitations, pauses, self- and other repairs, prosody, and intonation, are usually also accompanied by nonlinguistic devices, such as the organization of time and space through the orientation of the body (gaze, gesture, movement, and so on) with respect to other bodies and to the material world. In this book, we pay by far the most attention to linguistic devices, largely because these are the most available and the ones for which sociolinguistics has developed the best tools of analysis. However, these are also in many ways the most salient ones for multilingual settings, especially as concerns the management of multilingual resources themselves. Here it is clear that *code selection*, or *codeswitching*, becomes particularly prominent in strategies for the management of multilingualism or for the exploitation of multilingualism in the service of the construction or contestation of symbolic domination. As Martin-Jones (1995, 1997) has noted, the force of such code-selection strategies can be reinforced by their combination with other conventions.

However, we want to argue here that it is possible to go beyond fine-grained analyses of language practices in educational settings in multilingual contexts. It is certainly fascinating to see the regularities in the ways in which linguistic resources are managed, but it is harder to explain them on the sole basis of data from specific educational sites. In order to explain why linguistic practices take the shape they do, it is necessary to link them to institutional and historical processes, that is, to understand the role of education as an institution of social and cultural production and reproduction, an institution that is in many ways about organizing the construction of social difference and social inequality through the construction of what counts as legitimate language and of who count as legitimate speakers.

What the cases studied in this volume show us is that it is possible to use ritualized practices to separate linguistic resources (e.g., French in the classroom, English in the corridor; Spanish in the text, Quechua in the commentary; English with the teacher, Panjabi with the classroom assistant) precisely because of the ways in which linguistic and institutional ideologies intersect in schools. First, in most cases, schools adopt a model of language as the property of a nation, that is, a whole and bounded entity that corresponds to a whole, homogeneous, and bounded people (and in many cases this is explicitly extended to a state and a territory). In this sense, schools are about perpetuating ideologies that link languages to nations and therefore reproduce ideologically motivated social categories (and which it is presumably in the interests of some segments of the population to preserve). Second, schools operate with a cultural model of knowledge as something contained within the individual mind that must therefore be overtly monitored by teachers. It is for this reason, we believe, that teachers tend to be accorded legitimate rights to turn allocation and also that educational practice tends to privilege unified floors and sequential turn-taking, and especially the canonical Initiation-Response-Evaluation sequence (Mehan 1979), which explicitly allows for evaluation and monitoring of student performances.

These two processes make it possible to construct front-stage, public floors and therefore to consign some resources (and their possessors) to the margins. They make it possible to reproduce dominant ideologies of language and therefore of social categorization. Most important, they make it possible to engage in symbolic domination, that is, to exercise power without seeming to do so. This is possible because ritualized management of multilingual discourses allows people to do two contradictory things at once, specifically to appear to be engaging in the egalitarian distribution of resources (including linguistic resources) while, in effect, sorting some of them as legitimate and others as marginal. Thus, ritualization has the consequence of permitting the construction of dominant discourses that reproduce relations of power through the interactional construction of social positioning and social categorization, and hence of the unequal distribution of resources, and that legitimize this process through the construction of normalizing ideologies of language and of knowledge.

However, we do not want to take the fatalist position that schools are only about reproducing relations of power and that the agents of schooling are somehow to blame for it. First, it is important to recognize that actors rarely act out of bad faith. What people do makes sense to them; part of our job as ethnographers and analysts is to discover the nature of that sense, its sources and its (usually unforeseen and unintended) consequences. Second, especially in settings such as those described here, agents are often caught having to manage very difficult contradictions, for example, teachers having to work in conditions that presuppose symbolic and material resources that do not exist or that are rare or in conditions (very common to multilingual settings) where somehow it is necessary to harmonize opposing and conflicting interests. Third, it is rare that institutional practices are so rigid and so total, that is, that hegemony is so completely established, that there is no room for change. At the very least, change is possible through the contestation of the interactional and hence of the institutional order (although the consequences may be hard to live with). Usually, because of the complexity of the social order, there are gaps, interstices, where it is possible to invent new ways of doing things and conditions in which the possibilities of change through contestation of established conventions does not result in disaster, but rather in critique and change. This raises the question of what conditions tend to facilitate either the construction or the contestation of legitimate language practices and the social order they contribute to building.

THEORY AND METHOD IN THE STUDY OF
MULTILINGUAL PRACTICES

The kind of approach we have outlined here has implications for how we think such studies might be carried out. We have a preference for studies that link analyses of interactional practices to what might more broadly be understood as ethnography. These studies fall into a field that may be labeled sociolinguistic ethnography (Green and Wallat 1981; Heller 1999). We mean by this that we assume that in order to understand the social order, we have to understand it as observable in two ways. The first way is to understand social order as constituted in the interactional order; this is a well-established ethnomethodological principle (Garfinkel 1967; Sacks, Schegloff, and Jefferson 1974). At the same time, we do not understand the two as commensurate; rather, following such sociologists as Giddens (1984) and Cicourel (1974), we understand interactional orders to be linked and hence to require methodologies that can apprehend those linkages. In this respect, the social order is understood to be a web of relations, in which what happens in one interaction is constrained by the consequences of others and in turn constrains other interactions separate from it in time and/or space. The final element concerns the ways in which these webs of relations are fundamentally about the production and distribution of symbolic and material resources, which are always contingent upon specific—albeit dynamic—social, historical, and environmental conditions. An adequate methodology thus has to be able to identify these resources, their origins, and the processes of their production and distribution.

For these reasons, we consider an interactionist perspective essential but inadequate. The tools of ethnomethodological and interactionist sociolinguistics must be brought together with the tools of ethnography, which allow us to situate interactions with respect to the webs and the resources we have just discussed. By the same token, an ethnography that does not problematize language, that does not see it as a central form of social action itself (rather than simply a transparent reflection of it), will not be able to address the ways in which social processes unfold, nor will it adequately explain why they do so. These methodological concerns are reflected in the book insofar as we have made an explicit attempt to include work that does not focus only on classroom processes but examines other kinds of educational sites as well. We have also attempted to ensure that the choice of sites is explained and that some attempt is made to situate the participants in the sites and the linguistic and other resources circulating there in terms of the relationship between schools and the communities in which they operate.

ORGANIZATION OF THIS BOOK

The chapters in this book examine in detail the workings of symbolic domination in different educational sites in different multilingual contexts. The research documented here represents a broad continuum, from studies that foreground practices that contribute to the imposition of legitimate language to studies that highlight the ways in which participants deal with contradictions and tensions and, last, to studies that focus primarily on different forms of contestation and struggle. We have therefore grouped the chapters into three sections to bring out these contrasts and to capture the range of scenarios analyzed here.

Constructing Legitimate Language: Ritualization and Safetalk

The chapter by Nancy H. Hornberger and J. Keith Chick (Chapter 2) presents a detailed analysis of classroom interactions in two postcolonial contexts where learners have no choice but to receive their schooling through the medium of a language not their own. It compares classroom interactions in one seventh-grade math lesson for Zulu-speaking students in South Africa, which was taught through the medium of English, and in one first/second-grade language lesson for Quechua- speaking children in Puno, Peru, which was taught through the medium of Spanish. The authors draw out similarities between the classroom interactions in both settings, focusing in particular on the teacher-dominated patterns of classroom talk and the highly ritualized and rhythmically coordinated teacher prompts and choral responses from the learners. They also note that the learners engaged in these recitation routines showed little understanding of the academic knowledge being constructed.

Building on earlier work by Chick (1996) on the collusive dimension of such teacher-learner interactions, they refer to these classroom routines as *safetalk*, that is, classroom talk that allows participation without any risk of loss of face for the teacher and for the learners and maintains an appearance of "doing the lesson" while, in fact, little learning is actually taking place. They argue that this particular style of interaction arises from teachers' attempts to cope with the problem of using a former colonial language, which is remote from the learners' experiences outside school, as the main medium of instruction and from teachers' efforts to overcome problems relating to class size, autocratic school management, and inadequate facilities for initial and in-service teacher education. All these problems stem, in turn, from the wider social and institutional order in the specific regions of Peru and South Africa where this research was carried out.

Cumulatively, ritualized safetalk practices contribute to the construction of *safetime*, that is, time within the daily cycles of school life where there is very little risk of public displays of lack of academic knowledge. Hornberger estimates that safetime accounted for over 90% of the overall time spent in school by the Quechua-speaking children in her study. She and Keith Chick then draw the conclusion that, over the years of schooling, safetalk coping strategies and the predominance of safetime can only serve to reproduce the established patterns of school failure for all but a small minority of children and to reinforce the long-term oppression and marginalization of children such as these in Peruvian and South African society. The last part of this chapter is devoted to a consideration of alternative pedagogies that have been introduced in both contexts and to a candid assessment of their limits and potential.

The chapter by Jo Arthur (Chapter 3) reveals similar processes at work in Botswana classrooms. There, English is the language of instruction, and Setswana the language of post-independence nation building. The national language is used as a language of instruction for the first few years of schooling, but this is followed by a switch to English in the later years of primary schooling. This is a clear manifestation of the tension or ambivalence prevailing in local ideologies of language and education. Setswana is the first language of the dominant ethnolinguistic group in Botswana, a country that also counts among its citizens indigenous groups with other languages. Drawing on an ethnographic study carried out in two English-medium (Grade 6) primary classrooms in Botswana, Arthur shows how patterns of bilingual interaction contribute to the local hierarchization of languages and to the reproduction of the relations of power between English, Setswana, and the even more marginalized other languages.

Like Chick and Hornberger, Arthur focuses her analysis on the recitation routines and the unequal distribution of talk in these classrooms and concludes that Chick's (1996) notion of "safetalk" is also applicable in this context. There are powerful resonances between the practices she observed in these Botswana primary schools and the schools described in Chapter 2. Arthur also shows how the pressure on both teachers and learners to produce monolingual, "on-stage" English performances created real obstacles to learning, thereby reproducing asymmetric relations of power between English-speaking representatives of the new "aid" and "development" imperialism and the indigenous population, between the local elite that already masters English and the rest of the country, and between speakers of Setswana and speakers of other languages.

Chapter 4, by Grace Bunyi, contrasts rural and urban educational contexts in Kenya. Here, again, English has been established as a medium of instruction since the colonial era, and it remains the main medium of education from Standard 4 onwards (from the fourth year of primary schooling). In this chapter, Grace Bunyi unpacks the myth that social equality can be achieved in Kenya through the development of equal opportunities for all children. She does this by drawing on ethnographic research carried out in two settings: a rural area where most people are speakers of Gikuyu, a local indigenous Kenyan language, and an elite urban neighborhood in Nairobi, the capital city, where the *lingua franca* is English. In this project, she carried out interviews with parents in these two settings and did ethnographic work in two local schools, audiorecording classroom interactions. Her focus was on the teaching of reading in the early years, first in Standard 1 and then in Standard 4, when English was introduced. Drawing on this ethnographic material, she shows how the learners in these two communities were differentially positioned in relation to access to English and to school literacies, with the learners from the elite urban neighborhood having greater access and thereby being equipped with greater cultural capital on entry to school.

Grace Bunyi also highlights the substantial differences in the teaching and learning experiences of the children in the rural and urban schools. The learners in the rural classes were, for the most part, involved in repetitive chorusing routines of the type referred to by Hornberger and Chick and by Arthur as "safetalk." In contrast, the pupils in the urban schools were discouraged from providing unthinking choral responses. They also engaged in a range of purposeful activities, and the teacher's style was more interactive and scaffolding. Drawing on her interviews with the teachers and other staff in the school, Grace Bunyi shows that the children in the rural school were seen as lacking in the linguistic and cultural capital required for school success, while the children in the urban school were perceived as likely to benefit from their school experience. These views of the children's capabilities, coupled with particular pedagogic ideologies, were clearly shaping the day-to-day classroom practices in the contexts described in this chapter.

Lin Ndayipfukamiye's chapter (Chapter 5) makes similar observations about schools in rural and urban areas of Burundi, where Kirundi is central to post-independence nation building, while French is the language of power mastered by the urban elite. He describes in illuminating detail specific episodes in two classrooms where code contrast helps construct a distinction between knowledge of the world in rural and urban settings and between knowledge of the world outside and inside school. These distinctions orient students to the value of French, the legitimate language of the later years of schooling, and have the inevitable consequence of marginalizing Kirundi. As in South Africa, Peru, Botswana, and Kenya, these distinctions serve to reinforce the dominance of the former colonial language and hence the urban elite who speak that language.

The chapter by Marilyn Martin-Jones and Mukul Saxena (Chapter 6) focuses on primary classrooms in Lancashire (England), where a majority of learners are speakers of Panjabi, Gujarati, and Urdu, from areas of South Asia that were formerly British colonies. Educational policy in England regarding the languages of minorities of migrant origin is primarily assimilative, but provides for what is called "bilingual support" in the early years of primary education as a means of facilitating minority language students' social transition to school and eventual access to an English-medium education. In a number of areas such as Lancashire, this support is provided by bilingual teaching assistants who speak both English and the language of the minority students. Practices vary, but for the most part, these bilingual teaching assistants are often positioned as marginal to the "main action" of the classroom, which is defined and orchestrated by monolingual English-speaking teachers. Martin-Jones and Saxena show that fine-grained analysis of interaction in such classrooms provides insights into the discursive and organizational practices that construct this marginalization in everyday life, notably through ways in which the monolingual teachers control turns at talk, frame topics, and otherwise occupy center stage. Bilingual assistants use codeswitching to manage their role as brokers, in ways that make linkages for the students between their knowledge and the knowledge of the school, but these discourse practices ultimately serve to reinforce the symbolic dominance of English.

Angel M. Y. Lin's chapter (Chapter 7) focuses on Hong Kong schools where English is the language of instruction, although teachers and learners all have Cantonese as a first language. She explains why English came to be valued by the Hong Kong elite, not only as a reflection of British colonial power but more importantly as a means of maintaining Hong Kong's privileged position in world markets and as a means of access for individuals to economic and educational resources in English-speaking countries. She then goes on to demonstrate that the linguistic market in Hong Kong has remained largely unchanged in the post-1997 postcolonial situation. The new Chinese administration introduced a linguistic streaming system in 1998 that retained a tier of over one hundred elite English-medium schools, along with the general Chinese-medium provision. The same values are still associated with English, and the elite English-medium schools in Hong Kong are still seen as key sites for access to English and, eventually, to the predominantly English-medium higher education institutions.

In addition, Lin describes the force of pervasive ideologies of language that devalue mixed codes. This ideology heightens pressure for a particular way of using English in the classroom, that is, in ways that mirror English-language education in monolingual settings. Drawing on classroom-based research conducted in English-medium schools during the colonial era, Lin describes the consequences of these ideological pressures for teachers and learners and for language use in Hong Kong classrooms, demonstrating how students of the dominant group who already have knowledge of English from outside school are positioned advantageously in comparison to poorer students who do not have this access. Again, the codeswitching practices of these classrooms reproduce existing relations of dominance.

All the chapters in Part I show how important it is to examine the discursive practices of everyday life at school in order to arrive at a critical understanding of how those practices serve to maintain prevailing constructions of cultural identity and to reinforce asymmetric relations of power among linguistic groups. But they also show that in order to understand the significance of these practices, it is necessary to link them to the institutional arrangements and social, economic, and political interests that act as constraints on what can be said or written at school, by whom, and in what ways.

We turn now to chapters that foreground the contradictions and tensions inherent in educational policies, ideologies, and practices in particular multilingual settings and the ways in which teachers and learners respond to such contradictions and tensions.

Coping with Contradiction and Creating Ambiguity

The chapter by Celia Roberts and Srikant Sarangi (Chapter 8) focuses on further education classes in multiethnic contexts in England and draws on a joint ethnographic project conducted in the early 1990s. The classes they describe and analyze were part of ongoing vocational programs designed to prepare students for the job market and for the world of work. Almost all the students enrolled in these classes were from minority ethnic groups, some being of South Asian origin and some of Afro-Caribbean origin. They were returning to study after having left school without obtaining sufficient qualifications for securing employment. The two teachers were white, and they were from the dominant majority group.

These classes were chosen by Roberts and Sarangi as the site for their study because they have a crucial part to play in shaping the life chances of minority students. One of the main goals of their research was to investigate the ways in which the teachers managed the contradictions of the role that they assumed. Both teachers had a commitment to constructing a positive learning environment and to maximizing opportunities for the students in their classes. At the same time, they were under pressure to orient the students to the world of work, to transmit the "skills" required in the workplace (including both spoken and written communication), and to assess the students as they progressed through the vocationally defined curriculum.

As Roberts and Sarangi show, the teachers responded to these contradictions in different ways, thereby creating different conditions for learning. Applying Bourdieu's (1977, 1982) idea of "the rules of the game" in their analysis of the interactional dynamics of these classrooms, they describe in detail the discursive practices and the interactional styles of the two teachers and the students' responses. The main contrast between the two classrooms lay in the way the teachers defined and deployed the rules of the game. In one class, the game had to be played by the rules all the time, whereas in the other, the teacher openly acknowledged the illusion of the game from time to time, thereby allowing the students to expose and challenge it. In the latter class, there was not a single controlling voice of authority but a juggling of different discourses and a more active negotiation of the ritualized activities of teaching and learning, which allowed the students to display different identities and forms of knowledge.

The chapter by Suresh Canagarajah (Chapter 9) focuses on a very different context: that of classes in Jaffna where English is taught as a second language (ESL). Canagarajah demonstrates that, in this context, there is a tension between two opposing monolingual ideologies and policies and that this tension is played out in the language practices of these classrooms. First, there is a Tamil-only ideology and *de facto* policy, which has been imposed by the militant nationalist organization LTTE (Liberation Tigers of Tamil Eelam). This ideology has its roots in the Sri Lankan language politics of the 1950s and in earlier religiolinguistic movements, and it has underpinned attempts to define an authentic, traditional Tamil culture. This Tamil-only ideology predominates in most public institutions in Jaffna, including the local schools. Second, there is an English-only ideology, espoused by local English teachers in their English language classes. These teachers are influenced by pedagogical orthodoxies that have their origins in the Anglo-American world of English language teaching (ELT). Although the LTTE had established a separate Tamil-medium educational system in Jaffna by the time that Canagarajah carried out his research, the ESL program he describes here was broadly the same as that administered by the Sri Lankan government and was guided by the same pedagogical principles. Local teachers were dependent on the program for the supply of textbooks and assessment materials. In addition, they were involved in joint in-service programs with ELT teachers from Sri Lanka and with foreign ELT consultants.

Drawing on the classroom-based research he carried out in this context, Canagarajah shows how the English teachers and learners managed the tension between the Tamil-only and English-only ideologies in their day-to-day classroom interactions. Codeswitching between Jaffna Tamil and Tamilized English served as a key communicative resource for learners and for teachers, despite the commitment expressed by the latter to the principle of sole use of the target language in the language classroom. Teachers codeswitched as they moved in and out of episodes framed as pedagogical, as they distinguished the textbook material from talk about it, and as they evoked worlds beyond the classroom and the identities associated with those worlds. Learners switched into Tamil in secretive exchanges to help each other to make sense of the lesson content or to negotiate their relationship with the teacher. Canagarajah emphasizes that these classroom codeswitching practices were congruent with the multilingual lifeworlds outside the classroom. His chapter reveals the contradictions inherent in the imposition of essentializing monolingual agendas in educational contexts and draws attention to the complex nature of the responses that people make to such agendas in postcolonial settings such as Jaffna.

In the Maltese situation described by Antoinette Camilleri Grima in Chapter 10, there is no official policy requiring English monolingual practices at school. Instead, use of both Maltese and English is officially encouraged. However, English is still more powerful and more prestigious than standard Maltese, which is in turn more prestigious than regional varieties of Maltese. The social hierarchy tends to be dominated by an urban elite who are either monolingual in English or, more frequently, bilingual in English and standard Maltese. English derives its value from its role as a former colonial language and from its importance in tourism. Because of former colonial links, Malta draws large numbers of travelers from Britain. English is also highly valued in the linguistic market because of the access it provides to higher education in Britain or other English-speaking countries. Maltese derives its value from its position as the language of post-independence state nationalism. While the use of both Maltese and English at school is encouraged, there is a great deal of ambiguity as to how bilingual teaching and learning should be conducted in practice. Camilleri shows that because of the real relations of power between English and Maltese, which are masked behind an official rhetoric of equality, what happens in the classroom bears some resemblance to the classrooms of Botswana, Kenya, and Hong Kong. That is, English dominance is reflected in both the material and symbolic conditions of Maltese education, notably in the paucity of teaching materials in Maltese, as a result of which teachers pervasively use codeswitching between Maltese and English, particularly when classes are organized around monolingual English texts. These practices symbolically orient students toward the value of

English. Once again, classroom codeswitching serves to reproduce re-lations of power, despite official efforts to redress the balance.

Chapter 11, by Lorenza Mondada and Laurent Gajo, draws on joint research carried out in *classes d'accueil* (reception classes—literally, "welcome classes") in a French-speaking region of Switzerland, that is, in classes where French, math, and German (the three core subjects) are taught to groups of children who are, for the most part, of migrant and refugee origin. This research centered on classrooms that included Portuguese-speaking children, the largest linguistic minority group in the *classes d'accueil*. The aim was to identify classroom learning condi-tions that were (or were not) conducive to the use of the learners' home language and to the development of their communicative resources.

Mondada and Gajo draw attention to the contradictory goals of transitional forms of educational provision such as the *classes d'accueil*. On the one hand, such classes aim to affirm and value linguistic and cultural diversity and to open up dialogue across cultural worlds, while, on the other hand, the day-to-day communicative rituals and organization of such classes have a homogenizing and normative effect. In their detailed study of two of these classes, Mondada and Gajo focus on (1) the ways in which different groups of learners were categorized in the discourse and in the practices of the teachers and (2) the ways in which the learners' patterns of codeswitching and home language use were evaluated and categorized by the teachers.

Using audiorecorded data from the two classes, they identify three broad types of classroom learning situations: first, situations (most frequently observed in smaller classes) where the teachers allowed the learners ample scope for using their home language and even opened up opportunities for incorporating talk about the language as part of the lesson content; second, situations characterized by greater ambigu-ity where the norms for classroom language choice had to be continu-ally negotiated between teacher and learners; and third, situations (most frequently observed in larger classes) where the teachers explic-itly discouraged or disallowed home language use in the classroom. In these situations, French, the legitimate language of the school, was used to assert the teacher's authority and keep learners "on task." The research reported in this chapter demonstrates the value of adopting an interactionist approach to the study of language education provision in multilingual classrooms. It provides a window on processes of catego-rization as they are practically accomplished in the daily cycles of life in such classrooms. It also provides a means of charting learners' responses to such processes, responses that, in the long run, are likely to shape their commitment to language learning.

Chapter 12, by Alexandra Jaffe, presents a detailed analysis of con-temporary debates in Corsica about compulsory Corsican language education. Her chapter opens with a brief account of the sociolinguistic history of Corsica, which demonstrates the key role that schooling has played in the imposition of French and in the incorporation of Corsica into the French nation-state. It then traces the development of the Corsican language revitalization movement (from the 1970s onwards) and shows how attempts at linguistic intervention centered on the schools. Initially, these interventions led to some institutional gains: Corsican was introduced as an optional subject within the school curriculum and taught for three hours a week. The gains were of considerable importance symbolically, but their practical importance was limited. Language activists and nationalist politicians then attempted to strengthen the position of the language through further language legislation. The creation of a new Regional Assembly in 1982 provided a new forum for debating language issues, but since then, few attempts at introducing language planning measures have been successful. Attempts to introduce mandatory Corsican language education have fared particularly badly and have generated considerable debate and controversy.

The chapter provides a penetrating analysis of the different discourses that have surfaced in the debates about the mandatory teaching of Corsican in schools. Jaffe looks at both popular and political discourses about French/Corsican bilingual education, drawing on ethnographic and textual material gathered in Corsica. This includes a corpus of survey and interview data, official documents, nationalist manifestos, and legislative material. She considers in turn the arguments fielded in favor of compulsory Corsican teaching and the arguments fielded against it.

In her analysis of arguments fielded in favor of mandatory Corsican instruction, Jaffe reveals contradictory views about the bases of the legitimacy and value of the Corsican language as an emblem of identity and competing ideas about the ways in which language mediates relations of power and authority in the Corsican context. She also draws attention to the fact that, in formulating their arguments in favor of the promotion of the language, Corsican nationalists have appropriated dominant discourses about the relationship between language, nation, and territory, discourses that have underpinned the growth of nationalism in Europe since the nineteenth century. In analyzing the arguments fielded against the introduction of Corsican as a compulsory subject, she identifies a rhetoric of "freedom from coercion." She also identifies a deeper oppositional essentialism and an oppositional romanticism that seek to distance Corsican from the school domain and that make the primary use of the language in the lifeworlds outside of public instititutions its main source of authenticity. The chapter provides us with valuable insights into the contradictions inherent in educational interventions in minority language settings. It also draws our attention to the complex and ambiguous nature of popular and political responses to such interventions.

The last chapter in this section is that by Donna Patrick (Chapter 13). This chapter details recent political, economic, and cultural changes in Arctic Québec and examines the implications of these changes for Inuit children attending local schools. She shows how the relative status of the languages spoken in Nunavik (the Inuit name for Arctic Québec) has changed in tandem with the changes in political and economic conditions. Inuktitut remains the language of home and local community for most Inuit; English has long been used in the region as a result of colonization and the dominance of English as a medium of instruction in the schools; and French has been used since the 1960s, with its status being considerably enhanced by the rise of Québec nationalism. Now, it is increasingly associated with the world of work and of commerce. Most recently, the status of Inuktitut has changed, as a result of the political mobilization of the Inuit in the 1970s.

The Inuit eventually gained the right to administer their own school board and to make decisions about the medium of instruction. They opted for a trilingual educational policy, with Inuktitut being used in the first three years of schooling and then either French or English thereafter. Parents have to choose a French-medium or an English-medium stream for their children. Donna Patrick provides us with a detailed analysis of the issues confronting Inuit adults when they choose between French and English for their children and when they make their own language learning decisions. Drawing on fieldwork in one Nunavik settlement, she demonstrates that most Inuit adults there were aware of the benefits that would accrue from learning French but that few took up opportunities to study the language, preferring instead to continue speaking English, in addition to Inuktitut. Some parents were adopting a long-term strategy and investing in French-medium education for their children, though as she shows, several factors weighed against this option: They were unable to provide home support for their children's learning of French since they did not speak the language themselves, and there were few opportunities for using the language outside school, since English was long established as the language of intercultural communication. This chapter illustrates very clearly the ways in which the legitimacy and value of different languages are shaped by political and economic conditions. It also demonstrates the need to take account of local language practices, and the contradictions and constraints associated with them, in the implementation of new language education policies.

The six chapters in this second part of the book illustrate how important it is to investigate the interactional order of the classroom to gain insight into how teachers and learners manage the contradictions inherent in language ideologies, policies, and forms of educational provision within the daily cycles of classroom life. The chapters also show that, at the same time, analyses of bilingual classroom interaction and of different local conditions for classroom learning need to be embedded in a broader account of the political, ideological, and historical context and of the asymmetrical relations of power between ethnolinguistic groups.

Contestation and Struggle

The chapters in Part III extend the perspectives of the two previous sections by examining both the construction and the contestation of legitimacy in specific school sites.

Marilda Cavalcanti's chapter (Chapter 14) introduces the notion of reflexivity, which is then echoed in the chapter by Ben Rampton (Chapter 17). Cavalcanti reports on the experience of a team of Brazilian teacher educators invited by a Guarani-speaking community in the region of São Paulo to develop a teacher education course for a group of young people in their village. These young Guarani speakers were to become teachers in a local school soon to be opened where Portuguese would be the language of instruction. Since the teacher educators spoke no Guarani, the interactions took place in Portuguese. These are all significant facts in and of themselves. Cavalcanti then tells us about the problems the teacher educator team came up against while working with the young Guarani teachers and in their face-to-face interactions with them. These problems included "cross-cultural" misunderstandings that occurred in meetings between the teacher educators and the Guarani teachers. She goes on to argue that these misunderstandings were not simply due to differences in styles of working or in cultural conventions of communication; rather, she argues, they were manifestations of deeper underlying differences in participants' views of what the agenda of collaboration should be. In addition, Cavalcanti shows that the differing agendas needed to be understood with reference to the Guarani teachers' attempts to ensure that what they learned would be used to further their own community priorities, priorities defined in part by the community's need to resist Brazilian Portuguese domination. As Cavalcanti puts it, the Guarani have learned to say "no" by saying "yes."

Chapter 15, by Helen Moore, uses Bourdieu's concepts of legitimacy, habitus, mystification, and symbolic domination to examine the ideological underpinnings and political goals of Australian discourse concerning English as a Second Language (ESL) language assessment. The chapter is based on a comparison of two separate sets of guidelines for

ESL assessment, developed at about the same time by two different groups. She shows how the discourse and structures of the texts of these guidelines themselves reveal very different orientations to multilingualism in Australian education. One orientation places English in the context of other language varieties that learners master, and hence views it as part of a repertoire of knowledge and skills drawn from many sources. This orientation places individual multilingualism at the center of how it defines ESL and the assessment of language skills. The second frames the assessment of the English language skills of multilingual learners in terms of the acquisition of a monolingual-type competence in English. It therefore relegates other kinds of language knowledge to the margins and places the display of English monolingualism at the center. Moore also shows the political and historical context from which these two orientations stem and analyzes them as manifestations of a deep underlying debate in Australian society about the construction of Australian identity. Currently, it is the monolingual view that prevails, but the existence of different kinds of assessment guidelines with different orientations shows that there are locations in which contestatory visions can be framed and expressed, if not widely diffused or officially sanctioned.

Monica Heller's chapter (Chapter 16) uses Bourdieu's notion of legitimate language (Bourdieu 1982) to analyze the sources and consequences of ideologies of legitimate language in a French-language minority school in Ontario (Canada). She first examines the interactional means by which teachers in the school define what counts as good French, showing that the social organization of the school, and in particular the Initiation-Response-Feedback structure of teacher-centered classroom talk, provides occasions for the definition of legitimate language as the monolingual practice of standard French. She then shows how students in university-bound streams collude through their own practices with those of the school, while those in streams oriented towards the job market contest either their placement or the content of what school is trying to teach them. By refusing to collude either with the interaction order or with legitimate language practices, these students lay bare what the underlying ideology of the school is and how it positions them at a disadvantage. They also lay bare some contradictions that school language practices are meant to contain, such as a contradiction between pedagogical values of serving students' needs and pedagogical and institutional practices of streaming and concomitant differential treatment (cf. Collins 1988). In addition, they reveal a contradiction between the value of Canadian French codeswitching vernacular as a source of authenticity, solidarity, and legitimation of the type of school examined here as the backbone of mobilization and that accorded to the practice and symbolic display of standard monolingual

French as central to achieving the goal of mobilization, namely, access to mainstream institutions and global economic and political networks.

Ben Rampton's chapter, the last in the volume (Chapter 17), examines the issue of legitimate language in school from the perspective of Panjabi-speaking students in a school in England. Rampton argues that such students regularly encounter liminal zones in a number of sites in school, that is, sites where students must manage their relationship with English-speaking whites in a position of authority, in the absence of already established conventions of interracial interaction that exist elsewhere, such as in the classroom. It is here, he argues, that the issue of institutional inclusion and exclusion becomes inescapable. Rampton shows that the students manage these interactions through the adoption of what he calls "Stylised Asian English," a form that adopts, and turns back onto whites, the colonial stereotypes of slow-witted obsequious Asians. At one level, this practice can be understood as the students' way of testing the extent of true inclusiveness within the school, since uncritical reactions on the part of white teachers display their unconscious adherence to racist principles. Rampton argues that provoking this display is primarily aimed at showing other students how things are. But at another level, this practice can also be read as one way in which Asian students make a move toward opening themselves toward white educators, that is, toward displaying their own positioning, a move that can be returned by white educators in ways that can lay the foundations of amicable and maybe even, in the long term, transformative relations and interactional practices at school.

Like the earlier chapters, these four chapters demonstrate the importance of understanding the policies and practices of language and education in terms of the wider interests they serve and in terms of their consequences for differentially positioned groups of learners. They also show that policies and educational practices need to be understood in terms of the vision of society that underpins them and of the vision of education's role in producing or reproducing the forms of social organization, the relations of power, and the cultural identities that different groups may favor. Finally, they point to the institutional and interactional locations where legitimacy is constructed and may be contested, as well as to the practices that intentionally or unintentionally contribute to maintaining or undermining the social and symbolic order.

CONCLUSION

As we have shown, the chapters in this volume range over a wide variety of historical and educational sites and therefore provide a basis for formulating some general questions about the role of education in the production and reproduction of cultural identity and social inequality in multilingual settings. For us, the most important of these questions include the following:

1. In whose interests is it to be bilingual or multilingual or to master certain language varieties? Who is bilingual? or multilingual? Who masters which language varieties? Who wants to? Who says people should learn which language varieties and why?
2. What is the link between language and pedagogical ideologies, institutional arrangements, pedagogical practices and conventions of language use in educational settings? What views of education and what views of language learning underpin different ways of organizing educational structures, programs, materials, and activities? What views underpin legitimized or stigmatized language practices? For example, does codeswitching occur? Is it tolerated? Who is considered a legitimate user of legitimate language? Why?
3. How conventional are the practices observable in specific historical locations? What has to be invented?
4. How do participants use discursive strategies to position themselves and others with respect to ethnolinguistic, class, and institutional structures? What kinds of social identities are being constructed?
5. What role do spoken and written texts play in the construction of monolingual or bilingual learning environments? To what extent and how are texts (especially as authoritative representations of dominant ideologies) mediated by monolingual or bilingual language practices?
6. How are performances of teachers and learners evaluated against specific ideal versions of monolingual or bilingual speakers and writers?

Certainly many other questions can, and should, be asked. Our hope is that the chapters in this volume will help push research in this area forward by framing some ways in which to further elaborate and define questions that will help address our shared concerns, but that we ourselves have not yet imagined.

REFERENCES

Au, K. H., and Jordan, C. (1981). Teaching reading to Hawaiian children: Finding a culturally appropriate solution. In H. T. Trueba, G. P. Guthrie, and K. H. Au (Eds.), *Culture and the bilingual classroom: Studies in classroom ethnography*. Rowley, Mass.: Newbury House.

Bernstein, B. (1990). *The structuring of pedagogic discourse*. London: Routledge.
Blommaert, J. (Ed). (1999). *Language ideological debates*. Berlin/New York: Mouton de Gruyter.
Bourdieu, P. (1977). L'économie des échanges linguistiques [The economy of linguistic exchanges]. *Langue française, 34*, 17–34.
Bourdieu, P. (1982). *Ce que parler veut dire* [What speaking means]. Paris: Fayard.
Bourdieu, P., and Passeron, J. C. (1977). *Reproduction in education, society and culture*. London: Sage.
Carrasco, R. L., Vera, A., and Cazden, C. B. (1981). Aspects of bilingual students' communicative competence in the classroom. In R. Duran (Ed.), *Latino language and communicative behavior* (pp. 237–249). Norwood, N.J.: Ablex.
Chick, J. K. (1996). Safetalk: Collusion in apartheid education. In H. Coleman (Ed.) *Society and the language classroom* (pp. 21–29). Cambridge: Cambridge University Press.
Cicourel, A. V. (Ed.) (1974). *Language use and school performance*. New York: Academic Press.
Collins, J. (1988). Language and class in minority education. *Anthropology and Education Quarterly, 19*, 236–326.
Dannequin, C. (1987). Les enfants baillonnés (gagged children): The teaching of French as a mother tongue in elementary school. *Language and Education, 1(1)*, 15–31.
Erickson, F., and Shultz, J. (1981). When is a context? Some issues and methods in the analysis of social competence. In J. Green and C. Wallat (Eds.), Ethnography and language in educational settings. Norwood, N.J.: Ablex.
Garfinkel, H. (1967). *Studies in ethnomethodology*. Oxford: Polity Press.
Giddens, A. (1984). *The constitution of society*. Berkeley and Los Angeles: University of California Press.
Goffman, E. (1956). *The presentation of self in everyday life*. New York: Doubleday.
Goffman, E. (1974). *Frame analysis*. Harmondsworth: Penguin.
Green, J., and Wallat, C. (Eds.). (1981). *Ethnography and language in educational settings*. Norwood, N.J.: Ablex.
Grillo, R. (1989). *Dominant languages: Language and hierarchy in Britain and France*. Cambridge: Cambridge University Press.
Gumperz, J. J. (1982). *Discourse strategies*. Cambridge: Cambridge University Press.
Gumperz, J. J. (1986). Interactional sociolinguistics in the study of schooling. In J. Cook-Gumperz (Ed.), *The social construction of literacy*. Cambridge: Cambridge University Press.
Heath, S. B. (1983). *Ways with words: Language, life, and work in communities and classrooms*. Cambridge: Cambridge University Press.
Heller, M. (1999). *Linguistic minorities and modernity*. London: Longman.
Hymes, D. (1974). *Foundations in Sociolinguistics*. Philadelphia, Pa.: University of Pennsylvania Press.
Martin-Jones, M. (1995). Codeswitching in the classroom: Two decades of research. In L. Milroy and P. Muysken (Eds.), *One speaker, two languages: Cross-disciplinary perspectives on code-switching*. Cambridge: Cambridge University Press.
Martin-Jones, M. (1997). Bilingual classroom discourse: Changing research approaches and diversification of research sites. In N. Hornberger and D. Corson (Eds.), *Encyclopedia of language and education: Vol. 8. Research methods in education*. Dordrecht, The Netherlands: Kluwer.

Mehan, H. (1979). *Learning lessons: Social organization in the classroom*. Cambridge, Mass: Harvard University Press.

Michaels, S. (1981). "Sharing time": Children's narrative styles and differential access to literacy. *Language in Society, 10*, 423–442.

Ogbu, J. (1987). Variability in minority school performance: A problem in search of an explanation. *Anthropology and Education Quarterly, 12 (1)*, 2–29.

Pennycook, A. (1994). *The cultural politics of English as an international language*. London: Longman.

Philips, S. (1972). Participant structure and communicative competence: Warm Springs children in community and classroom. In C. B. Cazden, V. John, and D. Hymes (Eds.), *Functions of language in the classroom*. New York: Teachers College Press.

Philips, S. (1983). *The invisible culture: Communication in classroom and community on the Warm Springs Indian reservation*. New York: Longman.

Phillipson, R. (1992). *Linguistic imperialism*. Oxford: Oxford University Press.

Rampton, B. (1995). *Crossing: Language and ethnicity among adolescents*. London: Longman.

Sacks, H., Schegloff, E., and Jefferson, G. (1974). A simplest systematics for the organisation of turn-taking in conversation. *Language, 50*, 696–735.

Sinclair, J. McH., and Coulthard, R. M. (1975). *Towards an analysis of discourse: The English used by teachers and pupils*. London: Oxford University Press.

Singh, R., Lele, J. K., and Martohardjono, G. (1988). Communication in a multi-lingual society: Some missed opportunities. *Language in Society, 17*, 43–59.

Tollefson, J. (1991). *Planning language, planning inequality*. London: Longman.

Tollefson, J. (Ed.). (1995). *Power and inequality in language education*. Cambridge: Cambridge University Press.

Constructing Legitimate Language: Ritualization and Safetalk

2

Co-Constructing School Safetime: Safetalk Practices in Peruvian and South African Classrooms

Nancy H. Hornberger and J. Keith Chick

INTRODUCTION

Like other oppressed and marginalized language minorities around the world, Zulu-speaking students in South Africa and Quechua-speaking students in Peru have long experienced schooling through the medium of a language not their own. While such a circumstance is so common worldwide that it is taken for granted, it undeniably poses a challenge to both teacher and pupil in accomplishing the teaching and learning tasks of education. This chapter takes a close look at language practices in two classrooms, a first-second grade for Quechua-speaking pupils in Puno, Peru, and a seventh grade for Zulu-speakers in Durban, South Africa, seeking to understand how teachers and pupils confront this challenge and what kind of learning appears to take place.

Our analyses of lessons in these two classrooms suggest that they are exemplars of what Chick has termed safetalk (Chick 1996), in which teachers and students preserve their dignity by hiding the fact that little or no learning is taking place. We argue in the course of the chapter that the origins of this particular type of classroom interaction lie in the social and policy context of language minority education in these countries (we use minority here in the sense of nondominant and not necessarily in the numerical sense), that is, in the systematic discrimination Zulu- and Quechua-speaking students and teachers experience in their respective educational systems and societies at large. We outline some of the salient features of the Peruvian and South African contexts that lead to schools being arranged such that children and teachers can get through without getting caught "not knowing," that is, so that there can be safetime. We argue that the principal interest of the safetalk evident in the lessons analyzed is that it illustrates the process through which the victims of oppression interactionally accomplish school safetime.

In both Peru and South Africa, new language-related pedagogies with the potential to radically alter the picture of traditional classroom interaction described here have been introduced either preceding or accompanying changes in national language education policy. After outlining these changes and their impact on interactional and instructional practices in these two societies, we conclude with speculations on what the notion of school safetime and the role of safetalk in constructing it have to contribute to the understanding of the role and limits of new pedagogies.

NATURE AND FUNCTIONS OF TALK IN TWO CLASSROOMS

In order to investigate the language practices of teachers and students from marginalized communities and how these facilitate or inhibit learning, we examined lessons displaying "typical" interaction in two classrooms located in very different parts of the world. In the Peruvian case, we considered a representative, audiotaped lesson from among many observed and recorded in the course of a two-year ethnographic study; in the South African case, we analyzed a videotaped lesson that the participants and informants identified as a "typical" lesson. Next we present selected episodes from those lessons. (Following Tannen 1984, we define episodes as interactional sequences bounded by change of activity or topic.)

A South African Math Lesson

We examined a math lesson taught through the medium of English by a native Zulu-speaking teacher to a seventh-grade class of 38 students, also all native Zulu-speakers. The average age of the class was fourteen years. In the lesson analyzed here, which took place in 1985, their teacher, whom we shall refer to as Mrs. Gumbi, conducted the entire lesson from the front of the classroom, making considerable use of the chalkboard. The students were crowded into multiple-seat wooden desks (five or six pupils to a desk), arranged in rows facing the board.

As the transcript of the following episode shows (Extract 1), the focus of the lesson was "elements which form the union set." At the start of the lesson Mrs. Gumbi had introduced the notion of elements of a union set and had written elements on the chalkboard and pointed to common elements. She asked one student to name one of the elements she had written on the board. The few subsequent student contributions took the form of teacher-initiated group chorusing. The lesson continued as follows:

Extract 1

(T = teacher; Ss = students, in chorus; S = individual student)[1]

1　T: but I know that these two elements are common because
2　　　they are found in set B as well as in set C do you get that　Ss: yes
3　T: now now a let us form the universal set the
4　　　universe I mean sorry union set the union set is the
5　　　set which has the elements of both sets get it B *and* *C　Ss: *C
6　T: collect the elements of those two sets and
7　　　write them together all them they will form *union* *set　Ss: *set
8　T: can you try to to list the elements of the union set　Ss: two three
9　T: that is *two*　Ss: three
10 T: *three*　Ss: four
11 T: *four*　Ss: five
12 T: *five*　Ss: six
13 T: *six*　Ss: seven
14 T: *seven*　Ss: eight
15 T: *eight* and eight . . .
16　what type of set is this now . . . it is *a* *union set　Ss: *union set
17　it is a union set because we have been listing now
18　the elements of set B together with the elements of *set* *C　Ss: *C
19　to form one set which called what . . . . a *union* *set　Ss: *set
20 T: but remember when you list the union set the elements
21　for the union set do not repeat those elements which are
22　written twice do you get that　Ss: yes
23 T: do not repeat them list them once O.K.　Ss: yes
24 T: do you understand this　Ss: yes
25 T: do you understand this　Ss: yes

Most people who viewed the recording of this lesson found two characteristics noteworthy: the coincidence of teacher volubility with student taciturnity, and the rhythmically coordinated chorusing behavior (cf. Watson-Gegeo 1992, 59, who comments on the special prosodic characteristics of teachers' English in Kwara'ae: exaggerated pitch, excessive stress, and chant-like rhythm).

We considered but discarded the explanation that these behaviors could be traced to the culture of the teacher and pupils. It is true that many observers have commented (mostly unfavorably) on the teacher volubility and student taciturnity of interactions in segregated schools for black people in apartheid South Africa (see, for example, Schlemmer and Bot 1986; Thembela 1986; and Macdonald 1988). We also considered the explanation that these behaviors could be traced to particular characteristics of third-world contexts, especially in light of the fact that they were also observed in the Peruvian case that follows. However, it is also true that studies of classroom discourse in many parts of the world, including middle-class European (see, for example, Sinclair and Coulthard 1975) and U.S. classrooms (see, for example, Mehan 1979), have shown that the unequal distribution of talk, if not universal, is very pervasive. This suggests that this feature can be traced mostly to the asymmetrical distribution of social power and knowledge between teachers and students evident in most educational institutions throughout the world.

Our examination of how Mrs. Gumbi and her students accomplished the rhythmically coordinated chorusing behavior revealed that what was critical was the provision and recognition of two kinds of contextualization cue (Gumperz 1982a). The first kind includes various yes/no questions: "do you understand this?" (lines 24 & 25); "do you get that?" (lines 2 & 22); "O.K." (line 23); and "isn't it?", "do you see that?", and "can I go on?" (elsewhere in the lesson). The second kind of cue is a rising tone on accented syllables, which the teacher provided in lines 5, 7, 9, 10, 11, 12, 13, 14, 15, 16, 18, and 19. Further examination revealed that the chorusing prompted by both kinds of cue serves a social rather than academic function.

We considered the possibility that the chorusing elicited by the first kind of cue (the set of questions) serves the academic function of enabling Mrs. Gumbi to access the level of her students' understanding so that she can know whether or not to recycle her explanation at a lower level of abstraction. However, we found that the chorused responses were without exception "yes." This suggests that the questions are not really open questions and that their function is to signal participation rather than level of understanding. Similarly, we considered the possibility that the chorusing elicited by the second kind of cue (rising tone) serves the academic function of reinforcing certain key information items and, perhaps, helping the students to become more familiar with (to memorize?) technical terms (e.g., line 16). However we found that it was not *new* information that students were asked to chorus, but information already available to them before the lesson (e.g., in lines 7 & 19 the students were required to supply the word SET rather than the name of the set that they had learned about in the lesson). Elsewhere in the lesson the rising tone prompted them merely to complete words (e.g., intersecTION; we are looking for the unKNOWN). Moreover, we discovered that throughout the lesson, students, in response to both kinds of cue, provided mainly confirmative one- or two-word responses, or responses that repeated information on the board, or information that had been recycled again and again by Mrs. Gumbi. We concluded that the chorusing, here as in the Peruvian case, functions principally to give students opportunities to participate in ways that reduce the possibility of the loss of face associated with providing incorrect responses to teacher elicitations or not being able to provide responses. It is interesting to note that the chorusing was more evident at the beginning of the lesson than later on. Once responses had been well rehearsed, so that the chance of being wrong publicly was reduced, more individual responses were elicited, and at the end students were even invited to leave their desks and carry out the very public act of writing their responses on the board.

A Peruvian Language Lesson

We also examined a language *lenguaje* lesson, taught through the medium of Spanish, in a combined first-second-grade class of 36 native Quechua-speaking students ranging from six to thirteen years of age, in a rural community of Puno, Peru. The teacher, Sra. Sara, was a native Spanish speaker who also spoke Quechua, having learned it as an adult.

In the lesson analyzed here, which occurred in 1983, Sra. Sara opened with a series of questions, using objects in the classroom (e.g., chair, table, chalk, sticks, notebook, her fingers, her hand) to elicit student responses as to whether there was one or more than one item in what she was holding or indicating. The students provided choral one-word answers, as in the opening exchanges[2] of the lesson, shown in Extract 2.

Extract 2

(T = teacher; Ss = students, in chorus; S = individual student)[3]

1   T: *Ya ... este, tus compañeros del primer grado ¿están sentados en qué?*

2   Ss: *Si..lla, silla.*

3   T: *Silla. ¿Y sobre qué escriben?*   Ss: *Mesa.*

4   T: *Mesa. ¿Cuántas mesas tenemos?*   Ss: *Tres.*

1 T: Now . . . your companions in the first grade, what are they sitting on?
2   Ss: Cha..ir, chair.
3 T: Chair. And what do they write on top of?   Ss: Table.
4 T: Table. How many tables do we have?   Ss: Three.

After several exchanges in the same vein, Sra. Sara began to use the blackboard, drawing figures to represent the sticks *palos* she had earlier held in her hand, singular and plural, and writing the name next to each one, *palo* and *palos*, respectively. At this point, she explicitly introduced the concepts of singular and plural and the letter "s" (both spoken and written) that signals plural in Spanish (Extract 3).

Extract 3

5 T: *Entonces, hoy día.. vamos a aprender que las palabras o los nombres..*
6   *no siempre es igual.. A veces hablamos solamente de uno, otras veces*
7   *hablamos de varios, ¿sí o no?*   Ss: *Sí.*
8 T: *Pero Uds. tienen la mala costumbre. "Señorita, ¡me ha quitado mi*
9   *mi cuaderno!" dicen a veces, cuando les ha quitado todo. O+*
       les ha
10   *quitado un lapicito, y "señorita, me ha quitado mis lapices!" dicen.*
11   *Cuando se les está quitando uno..*
12   *¿Qué estamos viendo? [T. levanta un palo.]*   Ss: *Palo.*
13 T: *¿Ahora?*   Ss: *Palos.*
14 T: *Cuando yo digo esto, ¿qué cosa estoy diciendo?*   Ss: *Palo.*
15 T: *Palo. ¿Aquí?*   Ss: *Palos.*
16 T: *Entonces, cuando yo hablo de una cos, ¿estoy diciendo?* Ss: *Palo.*
17 T: *¿Y cuando yo hablo de varios, digo?*   Ss: *Palos.*
18 T: *Clemencia [T. llama la atencion a una niña]. Entonces, esto que*
19   *estamos hablando es.. una palabra, es una parte del lenguaje que*
20   *nosotros debemos entender para saber hablar, para*
21   *saber escribir. Lidia [T. llama la atención a una niña]. Van a darse*
22   *cuenta Uds. que es diferente. ¿Yo estoy agarrando cómo?* Ss: *Palo.*
23 T: *Palo. Pa..lo*   Ss: *...lo*
24 T: *Ahora, ¿estoy agarrando?*   Ss: *Palo, palo,*
25   *pa..los.*
26 T: *¿Es igualito la letra, a ver? [T. indica las palabras en*
       la pizarra]   Ss: *No.*
27 T: *No. ¿Por qué a ver? ¿Por qué no es igual? ¿Qué le falta aquí?*
28   *Este es la s que se ve.. a ver vamos a dibujar ese palito.. ahí.*
29   *Aquí, el otro ..*   Ss: *Palos, palos.*
5 T: So, today .. we are going to learn that words, or names .. are not
6   always the same. Sometimes we talk about only one, other times we

7	talk about several, yes or no?	Ss: Yes.
8	T: But you (all) have a bad habit. "Miss, somebody took my notebook!"	
9	you sometimes say, even when somebody has taken them all.	
10	Or someone takes your pencil and you say, "Miss, somebody took my	
11	pencils!" When they have only taken one..	
12	What is this you see here? [T. holds up a stick.]	Ss: Stick.
13	T: And now?	Ss: Sticks.
14	T: When I say this, what am I saying?	Ss: Stick.
15	T: Stick. And here?	Ss: Sticks.
16	T: So, when I speak of one thing, what do I say?	Ss: Stick.
17	T: And when I speak of several, I say?	Ss: Sticks.
18	T: Clemencia [T. calls her to attention]. So, what we are talking	
19	about is .. a word, is a part of language that we need to understand	
20	in order to know how to speak and to write. Lidia [T. calls her to	
21	attention]. You (all) need to realize that they are different.	
22	Now I am holding what?	Ss: Stick.
23	T: Stick. Sti..ck.	Ss: ...ck.
24	T: And now, I am holding?	Ss: Stick, stick,
25		sti..cks.
26	T: Are they written the same? Look. [T. points to words	Ss: No.
	on board.]	
27	T: No. Why? Why isn't it the same? What's missing here?	
28	This is the 's' that you see . . . look, let's draw this stick . . . there.	
29	Here, the other.	Ss: Sticks, sticks.

After following a similar procedure with the nouns table *mesa* and chicken *pollito*, also drawing them on the board with their names, in singular and plural, Sra. Sara continued to practice the concept of singular and plural with the children, this time asking various children to come forward and themselves serve as representative "nouns"; for example, she differentiated between plural girls *niñas* and singular boy *niño*, and between singular and plural sweater(s) *chompa(s)*, using the physical objects or persons to make the point.

Next, she introduced the terms "singular" and "plural" (Extract 4). At one point, Sra. Sara noticed that the students were mistakenly pronouncing "pr" for "pl," and she focused on that (Extract 4, lines 43–53).

Extract 4

30 T: *Hoy día esto que estamos trabajando en esta clase, se va a llamar*
31 *el número del sustantivo. El número puede ser.. cuando yo hablo de uno,*

32   *¿esto se va llamar? Sin.. gu..lar, ya. ¿Cuando yo hablo*   S: *Plural.*
      de varios?

33 T: *A ver, ¿este niñito está en . . . ?*   Ss: *Singular.*

34 T: *Esta niñita está en singular. ¿Por qué le voy a decir singular?*

35 .. *¿Porque solamente es . . . ?*   S: *Una.*

36 T: **Ch'ullallamanta parlanchis**, *ya? Eso se llama* sin..gu..lar. Ss: *...lar.*

37 T: **Ch'ullallamanta parlanchis, ima sutin?** *Singu*...lar.

38   **Ashkamanta parlasun**, *a ver,* **askha p'asñitamanta parlasun?**

39   *Etonces, ¿eso se va llamar?* Plu..ral. *A ver.* plu   Ss: *ral*

40 T: *Plu..ral.*   Ss: *Plu..ral.*

41 T: *Repetimos.*   Ss: *Prural.*

42 T: *Plu..ral.*   Ss: *...ral.*

30 T: What we are working on here today in this class, is called the

31   number of the noun. Number means... when I talk about one,

32   it is called? Sin..gu..lar, ok. And when I talk about several? S: Plural.

33 T: Look, this little boy is in the ...?   Ss: Singular.

34 T: This little girl is in the singular. Why do I say singular?

35   Because she is only....?   S: One.

36 T: **When we talk about just one,** ok? That's called   Ss: ...lar
       sin..gu..lar.

37 T: **When we talk about just one, what do we call it?** Singu...lar.

38   **When we talk about many,** look here, **when we talk about many girls?**

39   Then, that's called? Plu...ral. Look, plu...   Ss: ...ral.

40 T: Plu..ral.   Ss: Plu..ral.

41 T: Let's repeat.   Ss: Prural.

42 T: Plu..ral.   Ss: ...ral.

43 T: *Todos los chiquitos no repiten igualito. ¿A ver? ¿Número?* Ss: *...ral.*
       Plu...

44 T: *A ver* plu...

45 T: *A ver,, digan planta. Todos a ver, plan..ta.*   Ss: *Planta.*

46 T: *No escucho. Yo repito y después Uds., a ver. Plan..ta.*   Ss: *Plan..ta.*

47 T: *Ahora van a decir* plu..ral.   Ss: Pru..ral.

48 T: *A ver, escúchenme bien.* Plu..ral.   Ss: Pru..ral.

49 T: *Están diciendo, yo escucho, están diciendo pru..ral.*

50   *No es pru, si*no *plu.*   Ss: *Plu.*

51 T: *Otra vez.*   Ss: *Plu..ral,*

52   *plural.*

53 T: *No es pru, sino plu.*   Ss: *Plu..ral.*

43 T: Not everyone is repeating the same. Look? Number? Plu.. Ss: ...ral.

44 T: Look here now, plu...   Ss: ...ral.

45 T: Okay, look, say plant. Everyone now, pla..nt.	Ss: Plant.
46 T: I can't hear. I'll repeat, and then you (all), ok. Pla..nt.	Ss: Pla..nt.
47 T: Now, say plu..ral.	Ss: Pru..ral.
48 T: Let's see, listen carefully to me. Plu..ral.	Ss: Pru..ral.
49 T: You're saying, I hear you saying pru..ral.	
50 It's not pru, but plu.	Ss: Plu.
51 T: Again.	Ss: Plu..ral,
52	Plural.
53 T: It's not pru, but plu.	Ss: Plu..ral.

Finally, she summarized the lesson once more and charged the children to copy what was on the board into their notebooks (Extract 5).

Extract 5

54 T: *Cuando hablamos de uno solo, estamos hablando en..*
55   *sin..gu..*lar.   Ss: *...lar*
56 T: *Cuando hablamos de varios, ¿estamos hablando en ...? Plu..ral*
57   *Entonces, hoy día vamos a hacer el género, el número del*
58   *sustantivo,* o sea la palabra escribirse de diferentes
59   *formas. No siempre* es igual... *todos pueden copiar, todos,*
60   *todos. Luego, dibujan esto de acá..en su cuaderno de lenguaje.*
54 T: When we talk about just one, we are speaking of ..
55   sin..gu..lar.   Ss: ...lar.
56 T: When we talk about several, we are speaking of ...?
57   Plu..ral.
58   So, today we are going to do the gender, the number of
59   the noun, or in other words the word can be written in a
60   different form. It's not always the same... you can all copy
61   now, all of you, everybody. Then, draw this here... in your
62   language notebook.

As the children proceeded to copy, there was evidence in nearly every child's notebook that they had no idea what they were writing, as the following examples illustrate. On the board, the teacher had written:

El sustantivo singular
nombra a una sola person-
a animal o cosa.

One student copied only as much of each line as fit onto his page, one letter at a time:

Elsustantivosin
nombraaunasolape
a a n i m a l o c a s a

Similarly, what the teacher wrote as "El sustantivo plural indica," a student copied as "Elsustantivopluralindica." It seemed that pupils were getting practice at forming the shapes of the letters, but with no understanding of any meaning in the shapes.

As in the South African lesson analyzed earlier, oral participation in this lesson is characterized by a pattern of teacher prompt and choral response. Although in this case there is less use of yes/no questions (the exception is line 7) and less evidence of rhythmic coordination, still there is a notable pattern of teacher volubility and pupil taciturnity: The teacher asks a series of questions, to which the students respond in chorus, usually with one word (see lines 2–4, 12–17, 22, 24); or the teacher leaves a sentence, phrase, or word incomplete and the students fill in the missing piece, again most often in chorus and with one word (lines 33, 35) or even part of a word (lines 23, 36, 39, 42, 55), as we also saw in the South African case. As in the South African case too, this Peruvian teacher uses a rising tone on stressed syllables to prompt students to complete or repeat words (lines 23, 36, 39, 43, 44); she also uses this stressed rising tone to draw attention to a syllable or word she is introducing (lines 47, 48, 49) and to elicit students to repeat information she has just taught them (lines 33, 35). Interestingly, in Sra. Sara's case, the rising tone sometimes serves a double purpose as student prompt and teacher emphasis; in other words, the teacher uses a rising tone to prompt or invite students' response, but if a response is not forthcoming, the rising tone instead provides emphasis to what the teacher is about to say (lines 54, 56). Given these interactional practices of teacher prompt and student choral response, oral interaction in this lesson creates space for the students to participate, but without necessarily much real understanding.

Since schools are about literacy and since literacies are embedded in talk, it should come as no surprise that reading and writing practices in this lesson also allow students to participate while not necessarily learning academic content. Reading in this lesson consisted of repeating aloud what the teacher read from the board (not shown here). In most cases, pupils were not even looking at the words they were reading. Writing consisted of pupils being asked to copy from the board (see lines 59–60). Unfortunately, the nature of copying is such that pupils can copy into their notebooks without understanding what they are copying, which is what appeared to be happening in this classroom. Pupils could look and feel busy, yet little learning was going on since there was little understanding.

On the whole, characteristics of the oral interaction, reading, and writing in this lesson point to a failure in the learning of academic content in this class (and in others of which it is representative). It is our contention that the emphasis on copying as writing, on repetition (and correct pronunciation) as reading, and on teacher prompt–choral response as interaction, are all practices that have arisen over time in an attempt to create a learning atmosphere against great odds produced by, among other unfavorable contextual circumstances, the gap between the language of instruction (Spanish) and the language the children speak and understand (Quechua). In this regard, it is not purely coincidental that Sra. Sara switches into Quechua in order to explain the essence of the concept of singular and plural at a crucial point in the lesson (lines 33–35). As has been shown in other multilingual settings around the world, this is a case of "the use of codeswitching to scaffold knowledge building, or, to put it differently, to bridge the gap between the knowledge acquired by students through the medium of their first language(s) and the knowledge of the school mediated through . . . the language of instruction" (Martin-Jones and Heller 1996, 9).

It is often said that Quechua children—and indigenous or marginalized children in many parts of the world, for that matter—are naturally shy and reticent and that that is why they rarely speak in school; therefore, we should not interfere with their cultural practices by encouraging them to speak out more. In light of observations such as those just outlined here, however, we think we should ask ourselves whether at least some of that reticence is due to the fact that the school language in many of these cases is a language entirely foreign to the child. Of course, more may be involved than language per se; at issue too may be culturally or institutionally specific language practices. In some parts of the world, children are shy in school even though the home language and the school language are the same. Philips (1983) has shown that, for the case of the Native American children at Warm Springs, who speak English at home and at school, it is in fact classroom language practices that are key to the children's participation. Given participation structures and language practices that are more congruent with their own cultural practices, Warm Springs children do participate more in school. Participation structures and language practices may also be a factor in the case of Quechua children. Nevertheless, an even more fundamental issue seems to be language itself. Who, after all, can speak out in a language that they do not know?

Safetalk and Safetime

On the basis of our analysis of the preceding two lessons, as well as observation of many other lessons in these contexts and the observations of other commentators, we contend that in unfavorable social and policy contexts teachers and students may opt for interactional practices that serve important social functions but do not necessarily facilitate learning. For example, taciturnity and chorusing helped the students in Mrs. Gumbi's class avoid the loss of face associated with being wrong "publicly" in the classroom; while in the Peruvian case, teacher prompt–choral response as oral interaction, reading consisting of repeating after the teacher, and writing consisting of copying from the blackboard served the same purpose. They no doubt also provided teacher and students with a sense of purpose and accomplishment despite the fact that little learning took place. Such interactional practices could also help teachers avoid loss of face associated with displays of incompetence. They ensure that the lesson develops along predetermined lines and that opportunities for students to raise issues and problems that teachers may not be competent to handle are few. Because these interactional practices serve such social functions, we refer to them as safetalk practices (cf. Chick 1996).

As Lemke (1990, 17) explains, every move in classroom discourse has meaning as part of an activity (participant) structure and a thematic (semantic) pattern, that is, it has both social meaning and academic content. He explains, further, that because it is not always possible to successfully carry out both a thematic development pattern and a social interaction pattern, the participants must sometimes choose between them. Thus, for example, a teacher may accept a contribution "called out" if it advances thematic development. On the other hand, a teacher may delay thematic development because she feels the need to reinforce an activity structure that requires learners to be recognized before they can legitimately answer. Our data suggest that where social and policy contexts make teaching and learning a hazardous experience for teachers and learners, they tend consistently to give priority to the social function of discourse over the academic function. We argue that teachers make such a (conscious or unconscious) choice because, where teachers are poorly educated, classes large, classrooms overcrowded, educational bureaucracy authoritarian, school management autocratic, and the language of instruction an ex-colonial one, displays of academic incompetence occur easily, and the consequences for the participants are grave. Such displays can jeopardize teachers' jobs and their prospects of advancement, while school failure can cut off learners' access to the limited opportunities for further education or employment that tend to be available in such contexts. We argue that in response to such circumstances, participants often resort to safetalk, which is classroom discourse that affords few opportunities for displays of academic incompetence. In other words, through engaging in safetalk practices, they co-construct school safetime.

Our thinking about the function of safetalk was strongly influenced by two studies that attempt to trace the relationship between the form classroom discourse takes and the social and policy contexts in which it occurs. In the first of these studies, Collins (1987) argues that the ideology of ability grouping promoted in school systems in the United States leads students in low-ability groups and their teachers to socialize one another into systematic departures from the normative model of classroom interaction, which, though hierarchical, allows opportunities for reading practice. Since these departures provide less opportunity for practice, low-ability groups tend to fall progressively further behind high-ability groups in their acquisition of literacies valued in the school system.

In the second of these studies, McDermott and Tylbor (1987) analyze an episode in which teachers and students, in response to the institutional requirement that students' reading ability be constantly evaluated, do interactional work to make the illiteracy of one of the students, Rosa, not noticeable. They show that while evaluation is constantly taking place, teachers and students collude in evaluating overtly only when the evaluation is positive. This means that students like Rosa are continuously denied reading practice, that is, opportunities to acquire schooled literacies.

These two studies show how wider social and policy contexts constrain what takes place at a microlevel of classroom interaction. They show participants working together to socialize one another into sets of sociolinguistic norms that enable them to preserve their dignity in the face of oppressive discriminatory policies, structures, and practices, but with unfortunate consequences for their learning. As Collins (1987, 313) puts it, "Institutional ideologies and bureaucratic organization forms do not entirely constrain participants; people still strive to make sense of their situation, to avoid or resist that which is demeaning or oppressive. But the solutions achieved to local problems may have unfortunate consequences which are quite damaging."

These insights suggest that safetalk is an interactional practice that minority groups socialize one another into as a means of coping with the overwhelming odds they face in social and policy contexts such as the two we describe here, that is, contexts of long-term oppression and marginalization where children are taught through the medium of a language not their own. They suggest, further, that, through safetalk, the impotent collude with their oppressors in reinforcing the inequalities that led to widespread use of such practices in the first place.

These insights apply to other means of co-constructing school safetime as well, that is, the ways in which schooltime and classtime are organized so that very little schooltime is devoted to the academic learning that school is supposed to be about. We refer here not to inroads into schooltime resulting from explicit student or teacher resistance to conditions of oppression and inequality. One such example, a response to the repressive structures of South African apartheid society that cannot be characterized as an instance of co-construction of school safetime but one that drastically eroded teaching time and undermined the morale of teachers, was the recruitment of students by liberation forces to engage in protest and other political activities. This sometimes took the form of attacks on the persons and property of teachers and the destruction of school property. In the latter years of the apartheid regime the academic program was further disrupted by chalkdowns by teachers, expressing their frustration of being caught between the authoritarian bureaucracy of the educational system and the anger of their students about the inadequacy of the education offered to them. Such direct and intentional disruptions of schooltime are not the focus of our attention here.

Instead, what we are highlighting here are the more hidden ways in which teachers and students may co-construct practices that erode academic learning time at school. In the South African case, even when schools were operating "normally," classroom time was severely reduced by chronic student and teacher absenteeism; by sports meetings organized during school hours; and by extended study breaks for staff engaged in upgrading their qualifications, during which classes were left to their own devices. In the Puno case, only about 6% of schooltime was devoted to academic learning time[4]; overall schooltime was reduced because of pupil absences to attend to family agricultural or childcare needs and teacher absences due to problems with transportation or living accommodations, emergency family situations, conflicting districtwide and "functional group" meetings, and teacher reassignments or strikes; classtime was reduced because of abundant nonclassroom duties and activities such as working in the school garden, preparing for special events, extended recess periods, or school-parent meetings held during school hours; and finally, academic learning time in class was reduced by hours of busywork or by an emphasis on behavioral as opposed to intellectual development. Seen in this light, safetalk in the classroom appears to be but one piece of a larger picture of school safetime, in which schools themselves appear to be arranged to help children and teachers get through school without getting caught "not knowing" (Hornberger 1987b).

CHANGING CONTEXTS AND NEW PEDAGOGIES

In both Peru and South Africa there have been marked changes in the social and policy contexts that teachers and students responded to by engaging in safetalk and other means of co-constructing school safetime. The nature and direction of change has in many ways been different in each case. However, in both societies such change has been preceded or accompanied by the introduction of new language-related pedagogies with the potential to change traditional classroom interactional practices. Accordingly, we concluded that we could learn more about the relationship between social and policy contexts and classroom interactional practices and especially about the role and limitation of innovative pedagogies by comparing the changes that have occurred in the two societies and how these have had an impact on learning.

The Rise and Fall of Official Bilingual Education in Peru

In Peru, the role of the school in Quechua communities has been highly ambiguous, beginning from early in this century when schools were first introduced in the communities and continuing up to the present. Quechua-speaking communities have survived through centuries of exploitation and dominance by developing strategies of internal cohesion and exclusion of the larger, Spanish-speaking society; historically, they have not been inclined to easily permit within their midst an institution (the school) representing that larger society. Only when they have perceived that Spanish literacy might be to their advantage in maintaining themselves against the abuses of the larger society have they sought to have schools. Thus, from the point of view of Quechua community members, the role of the school is to confer Spanish literacy and with it a possible avenue to social mobility.

In this context, the Experimental Bilingual Education Project of Puno (PEEB) introduced and implemented Quechua as medium of instruction in selected classrooms and schools of Puno throughout the decade of the 1980s. What became clear as a result of PEEB is that safetalk practices and other means of co-constructing school safetime could be contested and interrupted when the pupils' own language was used in the classroom. In PEEB classrooms, teachers still used copying from the board as a pedagogical technique; but there, it more often occurred as a reinforcement at the conclusion of a lesson, rather than as a substitute for a lesson. In PEEB classrooms, pupils could read, and read with understanding. For example, pupils in first grade read words from the board, obviously associating pictures above the word with what they were saying, rather than simply memorizing the sounds in order and "reading" them without even looking at the board, as so often happened in traditional non-PEEB classrooms. In contrast to non-PEEB classes, the PEEB teachers often asked summary-and-review questions about what the children were reading and got appropriate responses. Finally, in PEEB classrooms, the traditional teacher volubility and student taciturnity were interrupted; in other words, when pupils were encouraged to speak Quechua instead of Spanish, they usually said more and said it with more variety of expression (see Hornberger 1988a for more detail).

Nevertheless, despite the successes of the PEEB in changing interactional practices within PEEB classrooms, the larger social and policy context in Peru at the close of the 1980s was such that not only the PEEB but also official bilingual education more generally was eventually dismantled (see van Lier 1996, 385–386, on the PEEB as yet one more ghost of projects past). On the one hand, the PEEB suffered at the local level from having been introduced in a top-down manner, which meant that it occasionally ran into resistance from Quechua-speaking communities for the very reason just outlined (instruction in Quechua was incongruent with the perceived role of the school as conferring literacy in Spanish); on the other, it suffered from a shifting policy climate and a deteriorating economy at the national level (see also Hornberger 1987a).

The PEEB had arisen out of a socially progressive policy context that included the 1972 National Educational Reform and the 1975 Officialization of Quechua. Ironically, as the PEEB moved during the 1980s from a language-as-problem toward a language-as-right orientation (Ruiz 1984) and the concomitant maintenance model of bilingual education (Hornberger 1991), official language policy in Peru moved in the opposite direction, away from the understanding of language-as-resource that had been evident in the 1975 Quechua Officialization, back toward a view of language-as-problem (Ruiz 1984; Hornberger 1988b). By the end of the 1980s, referred to by social scientists as the "lost decade" because of the economic failure and social decomposition Peru experienced under the APRA government of Alan García (von Gleich 1992, 60), the official climate for bilingual education had steadily worsened and PEEB was eventually dismantled in 1990.

As a result, official bilingual education in Peru was severely affected, since the public sector did not have either the financial resources or the professional personnel and expertise to go on with bilingual education experiments. In 1992, the national Bilingual Education Directorate, which in 1988 had succeeded the Bilingual Education Unit created in 1973, was dismantled under the restructuring of the Ministry of Education. This occurred in spite of the fact that a year earlier a new and thoroughly updated Bilingual Education Policy, which to a large extent reflected PEEB's orientation and influence, had been approved. A new institutional transformation of the Ministry of Education in 1996 reestablished a Bilingual Education Unit as part of the National Directorate of Primary Education, implying that intercultural bilingual education should restrict itself to primary education. Gone are the days when Peruvian academicians thought bilingual education could become an important cross-sectional component of the Peruvian educational system and permeate all levels and modalities of Peruvian education. PEEB's admirable record of success in overcoming numerous technical challenges to present a panorama of new possibilities in indigenous bilingual education was not enough to overcome the weight of political failure (Hornberger 1987a).

At the same time, however, more than a dozen bilingual education projects have arisen in southern Andean Peru out of private initiatives and as a result of the involvement of both local and international nongovernmental organizations and foundations. The new projects emerged both in Puno and in other Quechua-speaking areas, such as Apurimac, Cuzco, and Huancavelica. Although of minor scope and coverage, such initiatives have generated more local attention and have to a certain extent offered better and more realistic possibilities for the development of bilingual education in the Quechua-speaking areas of Peru. A major bilingual education initiative has also been incorporated in Bolivia's National Education Reform of 1994 (see Hornberger and López 1998 for more detail) and, as of 1997, a renewed effort has been evident in Peru's Ministry as well. These new projects draw on the experience and knowledge accumulated and generated by the PEEB. The Puno legacy has been a key determinant for the present and future of bilingual education in Peru (and beyond) and may yet prove to have been a wedge for dislodging school safetalk and safetime practices in indigenous Andean contexts.

The Advent of Nonracial Democracy and Multilingual Language Policy in South Africa

In South Africa, school safetalk and safetime are set against the backdrop of systematic discrimination under the apartheid policy implemented by the Nationalist Party beginning in 1948 (and lasting until the defeat of the Nationalists by the African National Congress in the early 1990s)—a massive program of social engineering based on the rigid segregation of black, white, Indian, and colored population groups. In education, the apartheid system was evident in the differentiated per capita expenditure on education for the different groups; in differentiated teacher-pupil ratios; in differentiated levels of professional qualification of teachers; and in a medium of instruction policy that black people perceived as promoting division among them and as limiting their life chances. Before Nationalist rule, the medium in senior primary schools and beyond had been English, but "Bantu education" dictated mother-tongue instruction throughout the primary school (thus setting apart speakers of Zulu, Sotho, Xhosa, and other indigenous African languages). It also required Afrikaans and English as media of instruction in secondary school on a fifty-fifty basis, thus dramatically reducing the opportunity of black students to become proficient in English, the language widely perceived, then as now, as the key to social mobility and economic advancement.

The 1976 Soweto uprising, sparked by resistance to the policy of Afrikaans as medium of instruction in high schools, marked a watershed in South Africa's sociopolitical history. It led to the regime's making a number of concessions, one of which was to grant black communities their choice of medium of instruction. The result was an abrupt return to the practice of using exclusively English as medium after the first three years of schooling. The uprising also prompted the setting up of a range of nongovernmental organizations (NGOs). Together these NGOs constituted a civil society in waiting, offering, as they did, a range of services to black communities to compensate for the injustices and discrimination they had received at the hand of the apartheid regime. One example was the intervention by NGOs when the state instituted no special measures to assist primary teachers, most of whom were ill-equipped linguistically and pedagogically, when they had to make the abrupt shift in 1979 from teaching all subjects through one of the indigenous languages, to teaching through English. Initially the main focus of their intervention was inducting teachers into the pedagogy of communicative language teaching (CLT). CLT appealed to these NGOs and to the applied linguists who assisted them because of the respect CLT shows for learners and for the linguistic resources they bring to the classrooms. As Holliday (1994, 167) explains, the genesis of CLT can be traced to the revolutionary realization within the notion of communicative competence that the language learners, rather than having a deficit, already have "certain competences, either in the mother tongue or other tongues, or in the experience they [have] already gained of the target language, which must be capitalized or built upon." This is, of course, particularly true of learners from marginalized groups in South Africa, many of whom enter the classroom already competent in a number of languages and varieties. Not least, CLT appealed to NGOs because its emphasis on group work and learner choice challenged traditional classroom interactional practices.

One measure of the progress these NGOs made in promoting CLT is that state education authorities subsequently initiated curriculum reform, which led to communicative competence being identified as the principal goal of language teaching. However, such evidence as is available suggests that neither the efforts of NGOs nor the implementation of new core syllabi for the teaching of languages in state schools led to widespread changes in the traditional classroom interactional practices in English-language classrooms, let alone in the various content subjects. There are no doubt many reasons, including the limited resources of NGOs and teachers' feelings of alienation, which made it difficult for them to respond to state education initiatives with enthusiasm. Our belief, though, is that one of the main reasons is that, in the absence of any fundamental change to the discriminatory social and policy context, safetalk had still too great a "payoff" for teachers and pupils for them to readily abandon it. It was still necessary for teachers and learners to use safetalk to avoid displays of academic incompetence that might jeopardize teachers' jobs and reduce learners' opportunities for further education and employment.

Since then there have been two developments with potential to change traditional classroom interactional practices. The first is an attempt at further innovation in English-language teaching in the form of critical language awareness (CLA) materials. This development was in part a reaction to the state's promotion of CLT, which some critics viewed as an attempt to co-opt teachers in the maintenance of the status quo. As Peirce (1989, 411) put it, "in a society in which racism, sexism, and elitism are considered appropriate in many communities, the teaching of rules in these communities would simply perpetuate inequality." Janks (1991) explains that CLA materials were written in response to proposals drafted by the National Education Crisis Committee for People's English. This committee envisaged the study of English as empowering students and serving as a vehicle for liberation. CLA materials (see, for example, the series edited by Janks 1993) focus on the relationship between language and power. By focusing attention on the verbal and nonverbal choices the speakers and writers have made in constructing their discourses, they attempt to raise awareness of how those in power use language to defend the status quo. They also attempt to teach students through a process of deconstructing texts to contest the language practices that disempower them and to use language in ways that do not disempower others.

It will be apparent from this short description that the roles that CLA calls for students to take up are at odds with the social relations of power implicit in the traditional classroom interactional practices. However, the impact of CLA to date has been even less than that of CLT. Its association with the National Education Crisis Committee for People's English means that it enjoys considerable credibility with those African teachers aware of this association. However, partly because CLA materials in South Africa became freely available only very late in the struggle against apartheid and partly because the advocates of CLA had even fewer resources than the NGOs who promote CLT, most teachers outside the Johannesburg area are not familiar with the materials and the rationale for them. What may also be inhibiting the impact these materials make on classroom interactional practices is that teachers see CLA as having served its historical function and as being no longer relevant in the context of a democratic South Africa, that is, as having usefully served to politicize education at the height of the liberation struggle but as, now that liberation has been attained, perhaps no longer required. Not least, what may be limiting the impact of CLA materials on classroom interactional practices is that they place the burden of contesting dominant practices and discourses on the shoulders of students among whom are some of the most disempowered members of society.

However, we believe that the chief reason that CLA and CLT have not served to change traditional classroom interactional practices on any large scale is that they both focus on the teaching of English and call for a high level of proficiency in it. Further, even if they lead to the abandonment of traditional interactional practices in English classes, there is no guarantee that these will be adopted in other subjects. More telling is the fact that teachers and students with limited proficiency in English experience difficulty in negotiating the more symmetrical social relations associated with both approaches. It is because it opens up the possibility of students and teachers negotiating social relations in the classroom in their mother tongues that the third new pedagogical development is of particular interest to us.

This development is South Africa's new multilingual language policy, which represents a dramatic shift from a language-as-problem to a language-as-right orientation (Ruiz 1984). This policy raises to official status eleven major languages, these being nine indigenous African languages and the two ex-colonial languages English and Afrikaans (N.B., there is some dispute about the status of Afrikaans, which some have argued is an indigenous African language). The section in the constitution on human rights includes clauses that ensure that all people have the right to use the language of their choice and that no person shall be discriminated against on grounds of language. It also requires the establishment of a Pan South African Language Board specifically to foster multilingualism.

This development is but one of many changes ushered in with the advent of a nonracial democracy in South Africa that, together, are beginning to constitute a social and policy context that may be less conducive to the construction of school safetalk than that which obtained before. For example, desegregated schooling has brought to an end differentiated per capita expenditure on education for different groups. However, apartheid continues to cast a long shadow. Mother-tongue instruction is still viewed with deep suspicion, and English is still the overwhelming preference for language of instruction. This is borne out by the responses of over 500 Zulu-first-language tertiary and senior high school students to a questionnaire administered in March 1996 (see Chick and Wade 1997). As many as 63% of the respondents indicated that, if they were given the choice, they would introduce English as the language of instruction and learning as early as grade one, while a further 7.2% indicated that they would introduce it as early as the pre-school level. Evidence of the continued widespread perception that English is the key to social mobility and economic advancement is that the vast majority of respondents also indicated that they anticipated using mostly English in their future professions (81%) and in interacting with public servants (68%). The elevation to high political office of speakers of indigenous languages and their growing importance as consumers has increased the economic value of proficiency in such languages. The indications, though, are that, in the short term at least, speakers of indigenous languages are unlikely to be easily persuaded that their own mother tongues should be widely used as media of instruction.

Ironically, this choice may do more to prevent the mass of the people from enjoying significant social and economic advancement than to help them to achieve this goal. Samuels (1995, 80) has pointed out that "in almost all the countries of Anglophone Africa only a thin layer of between 5% and 20% of people have ever gained a passable measure of proficiency in English." As South Africa has greater resources and a larger number of native-speaker models than many Anglophone African states, it should be more successful in developing English proficiency among its citizens. However, this strategy seems more likely to contribute to the emergence of a small English-speaking elite than to the economic and social advancement of the mass of the people.

Our examination of the relationship between unfavorable social and policy contexts and the kind of learning that takes place for marginalized language minorities (especially the handicap of having to teach and learn through a language not their own) suggests why in the South African case the overwhelming choice of English is likely to have such unfortunate consequences. Without denying the need for promoting widespread proficiency in English, we believe that this should not be accomplished primarily through making English the sole medium of instruction. If this practice continues, there is a danger that most South

African teachers and pupils, especially those most marginalized, will continue to use up too much of their academic learning time engaging in safetalk and other means of constructing school safetime.

GETTING BEYOND SAFETIME

We have provided examples of lessons in two classrooms on opposite sides of the world, and we have argued that teacher and students in these classrooms co-constructed interactional practices characterized as safetalk, talk that creates a space where teacher and students know more or less what to expect and how to behave in class, but where a high price is paid in terms of (a lack of) learning. We have suggested that in the Peruvian and South African cases, at least, safetalk is one piece of a larger co-construction of school safetime that contributes to the continuing marginalization of language minorities in social and policy contexts of long-term oppression. We have also briefly reviewed recent initiatives in both contexts that attempt to introduce new language-related pedagogies in classrooms such as those we analyzed here. We conclude now with thoughts on the potential of these (or other) new pedagogies to radically alter school safetalk and safetime practices in such contexts.

We believe that pedagogical innovation for marginalized language minorities cannot advance very far so long as the larger social and policy contexts remain unfavorable to those minorities. In the Peruvian case, we have seen that shifting language-planning orientations and bilingual education policies interrupted advances made in bilingual education for Quechua speakers in the 1980s. In the South African case, we have suggested that the lack of headway made in introducing communicative language teaching (CLT) and critical language awareness (CLA) approaches in English language teaching in the 1980s is in large part attributable to the absence of any fundamental change to the discriminatory education system and language-medium policy.

Even in favorable social and policy circumstances, moreover, we suggest that pedagogical innovation takes time, on the order of years and decades, not weeks and months. This is because true pedagogical innovation involves more than the simple introduction of a new language of instruction (e.g., bilingual education) or a new language-teaching method (e.g., CLT or CLA). We believe that the lessons we have analyzed show that safetalk language and literacy practices and participation structures are somewhat hidden and self-sustaining, anchored in larger social and policy structures and relationships. It requires more than a new method or medium of instruction to dislodge such practices. Reflecting on the impact of the PEEB, one consultant noted his realization that "the use of L1 as the medium of instruction would only bear its promised fruit if at the same time one could effect a change in basic teaching habits. It would not, automatically or easily, bring about such a change by itself" (van Lier 1996, 384). Although there were signs that such changes were underway as a result of sustained efforts in some PEEB classrooms and schools, progress was cut short when the official policy climate shifted away from the progressive social reforms that had been undertaken in the 1970s. In the South African case, the advent of a nonracial democracy and a multilingual language policy in the 1990s provides a new and promising social and policy context in which teachers and students may be able to negotiate new classroom practices and relationships. Only time will tell, however, if favorable contexts and new pedagogies can assert and sustain themselves for long enough to fundamentally alter safetalk and safetime practices in South African and Peruvian classrooms and schools.

NOTES

1. Notes on transcription conventions: Underline (_) indicates rising tone on a stressed syllable. Asterisk (*) indicates simultaneous talk by two or more speakers.

2. We use exchange here in the sense in which Sinclair and Coulthard (1975) define it, that is, as the basic unit of interaction, consisting of two or more moves, and in classrooms usually three—an initiating move, a response, and a follow-up move. This parallels Mehan's (1979) IRE sequence: initiation—response—evaluation.

3. Notes on transcription conventions: *Italics* indicate Spanish language. ***Bold italics*** indicate Quechua language. Brackets [ ] enclose nonverbal information. Underline (_) indicates rising tone on a stressed syllable.

4. Tikunoff and Vazquez-Faria (1982, 249; following Fisher et al. 1978) define academic learning time in terms of a combination of allocated time, student engagement, and student accuracy rate, thus using a stricter definition of academic learning time (ALT) than our use here. For our purposes, we define ALT as the portion of classtime in which students and teachers work collaboratively on an academic lesson; this encompasses allocated time, student engagement, and at least some degree of student accuracy (as monitored by the teacher). We exclude from ALT, for example, periods when pupils copy from the board or are on their own with no apparent instruction. It is possible that some academic learning occurs under these two participant structures; however, since our observations indicated that student responses were usually not accurate during these times, it seems likely that very little academic learning was going on.

REFERENCES

Chick, J. K. (1996). Safe-talk: Collusion in apartheid education. In H. Coleman (Ed.), *Society and the Language Classroom* (pp. 21–39). Cambridge: Cambridge University Press.

Chick, J. K., and Wade, R. (1997). Restandardization in the direction of a new English: Implications for access and equity. *Journal of Multicultural and Multilingual Development, 18(4)*, 271–284.

Collins, J. (1987). Conversation and knowledge in bureaucratic settings. *Discourse Processes 10*, 303–319.

Fisher et al. (1978). *Teaching behaviors, academic learning time and student achievement: Final report of phase III-B, beginning teacher evaluation study.* San Francisco: Far West Laboratory for Educational Research and Development.

Gumperz, J. (1982a). *Discourse strategies.* Cambridge: Cambridge University Press.

Gumperz, J. (1982b). *Language and social identity.* Cambridge: Cambridge University Press.

Holliday, A. (1994). *Appropriate methodology and social context.* Cambridge: Cambridge University Press.

Hornberger, N. H. (1987a). Bilingual education success but policy failure. *Language in Society 16(2)*, 205–226.

Hornberger, N. H. (1987b). Schooltime, classtime, and academic learning time in rural highland Puno, Peru. *Anthropology and Education Quarterly, 18(3)*, 207–221.

Hornberger, N. H. (1988a). *Bilingual education and language maintenance: A southern Peruvian Quechua case.* Berlin: Mouton de Gruyter.

Hornberger, N. H. (1988b). Language planning orientations and bilingual education in Peru. *Language Problems and Language Planning, 12 (1)*, 14–29.

Hornberger, N. H. (1991). Extending enrichment bilingual education: Revisiting typologies and redirecting policy. In O. García (Ed.), *Bilingual education: Focusschrift in honor of Joshua A. Fishman*, volume 1 (pp. 215–234). Philadelphia: John Benjamins Publishers.

Hornberger, N. H., and López, L. E. (1998). Policy, possibility, and paradox: Indigenous multilingualism and education in Peru and Bolivia. In J. Cenoz and F. Genesee (Eds.), *Beyond bilingualism: Multilingualism and multilingual education*, 206–242. Clevedon, U.K.: Multilingual Matters.

Janks, H. (1991). *Critical language awareness and People's English.* Paper presented at the international conference on Language and Literacy, University of East Anglia, Norwich, 6–10 April. Unpublished manuscript.

Janks, H. (Ed.) (1993). *The critical language awareness series.* Johannesburg: Hodder and Stoughton.

Lemke, J. (1990). *Talking science: Language, learning and values.* Norwood, N.J.: Ablex.

Macdonald, C. (1988). Teaching primary science in a second language: Two teaching styles and their cognitive concomitants. In A. Weideman (Ed.), *Styles of teaching and styles of learning* (pp. 115–127). Bloemfontein: SAALA.

Martin-Jones, M., and Heller, M. (1996). Education in multilingual settings: Discourse, identities, and power. *Linguistics and Education, 8(1 & 2)*.

McDermott, R., and Tylbor, H. (1987). On the necessity of collusion in conversation. In L. Kedar (Ed.), *Power through discourse* (pp. 153–170). Norwood, N.J.: Ablex.

Mehan, H. (1979). *Learning lessons: Social organization in the classroom.* Cambridge, Mass.: Harvard University Press.

Peirce, B. (1989). Toward a pedagogy of possibility in the teaching of English internationally: People's English in South Africa. *TESOL Quarterly, 23(3)*, 401–445.

Philips, S. U. (1983). *The invisible culture: Communication in classroom and community on the Warm Springs Indian reservation.* New York: Longman.

Ruiz, R. (1984). Orientations in language planning. *NABE Journal, 8(2)*, 15–34.

Samuels, J. (1995). Multilingualism in the emerging educational dispensation. In C. Le Roux, (Ed.), *Constitutionally enshrined multilingualism: Challenges and responses. Proceedings of the 15th Annual Conference of the Southern African Applied Linguistics Association* (pp. 75–84). University of Stellenbosch.

Schlemmer, L., and Bot, M. (1986). Education and race relations in South Africa. In G. Kendall (Ed.), *Education and the diversity of cultures* (pp. 75–85). Pietermaritzburg: University of Natal.

Sinclair, J., and Coulthard, R. M. (1975). *Towards an analysis of discourse*. London: Oxford University Press.

Tannen, D. (1984). *Conversational style: Analyzing talk among friends*. Norwood, N.J.: Ablex.

Thembela, A. (1986). Some cultural factors which affect school education for blacks in South Africa. In G. Kendall (Ed.), *Education and the diversity of cultures* (pp. 37–43). Pietermaritzburg: University of Natal.

Tikunoff, W. J., and Vazquez-Faria, J. A. (1982). Successful instruction for bilingual schooling. *Peabody Journal of Education, 59(4)*, 234–271.

van Lier, L. (1996). Conflicting voices: Language, classrooms, and bilingual education in Puno. In K. M. Bailey and D. Nunan (Eds.), *Voices from the language classroom: Qualitative research in second language education* (pp. 363–387). Cambridge: Cambridge University Press.

von Gleich, U. (1992). Changes in the status and functions of Quechua. In U. Ammon and M. Hellinger (Eds.), *Status Change of Languages* (pp. 43–64). Berlin: Walter de Gruyter.

Watson-Gegeo, K. A. (1992). Thick explanation in the ethnographic study of child socialization: A longitudinal study of the problem of schooling for Kwara'ae (Solomon Islands) children. *New Directions for Child Development, 58*, 51–66.

3

Codeswitching and Collusion: Classroom Interaction in Botswana Primary Schools

Jo Arthur

INTRODUCTION

This chapter is based on an ethnographic study of interaction be-tween teachers and pupils in Standard (Grade) 6 classes in two primary schools in northeastern Botswana. I shall begin by describing the hier-archical values attached to languages in Botswana: English occupies a prestigious position as the language of education beyond Standard 4; the medium of instruction during the first four years of primary educa-tion is the national language, Setswana; the other languages of Botswa-na, spoken by a minority of up to 20% of the population, are officially accorded no classroom role. The linguistic resources at the disposal of the teachers and pupils I observed are then described. While acknowl-edging the occurrence of discourse-related codeswitching (Auer 1984) by teachers, I shall focus on their more frequent use of participant-related codeswitching.

One of the functions of participant-related codeswitching by teachers was encouraging participation by pupils. However, a ground rule of discourse in these classrooms was that pupils answering teachers were not free to switch from English, the officially approved classroom language, to Setswana. I relate this finding to the asymmetrical roles of teachers and pupils in the joint "staging" of ritualized question-and-answer performances, which were typical of the lessons observed; while pupils are merely performers, teachers have access to Setswana as the "backstage" language because they are directors as well as co-actors.

Accounts of the institutionalized phenomenon of recitation routines in the context of education in Botswana (Prophet and Rowell 1993) and elsewhere, for example, in Kenya (Cleghorn et al. 1989), have hypothesized that its origins lie in traditional cultural patterns of interaction. I shall argue instead, in agreement with Ellis (1987), that it derives from conventions imposed during colonial rule, including the requirement to use a foreign language as the medium of instruction. The final instances of teachers' codeswitching from English into Setswana that I cite below offer, in my view, insights into the collusion of teachers and pupils in mutual face-saving over the adequacy of their classroom interaction for the achievement of teaching and learning. This collusive interpretation draws on the approach to conversation analysis of McDermott and Tylbor (1987) and on Chick's (1996) analysis of teacher-dominated routines in Zulu-English classrooms in South Africa.

Context of the Study

The data in this chapter is drawn from audiorecordings of classroom interaction in Standard (Grade) 6 classes in two primary schools in semirural locations in northeastern Botswana. I spent three weeks in 1990 as a participant observer in each school, compiling field notes and audiorecording English, math, and science lessons for subsequent analysis.

School 1 is located in an area where Ikalanga (the mother tongue of an estimated 10% to 20% of the national population) is the language of the local community; School 2 is in an area where the national language, Setswana, is spoken by almost all as a first language. In Standard (Grade) 6 classrooms, English, the official language of Botswana, is the medium of instruction.

The Hierarchy of Languages

Ndayipfukamiye points out that the curriculum to which schoolchildren are exposed goes beyond the knowledge set out in syllabi to encompass "concepts, actions, events, relations, beliefs, values" (1994, 81). Extracts 1 and 2 are records of exchanges that make visible a usually hidden curriculum of hierarchical language values in Botswana. They took place during English lessons in classrooms where the pupils' first language was Ikalanga (also known as Sekalaka), and the teacher's first language was Setswana. (In the extracts, T = teacher, P = pupil, Ps = pupils in chorus. Pupils' names have been deleted from all transcripts.)

Extract 1

	T	Which language is spoken in your country? Which language is spoken in your country? . . . . Which language do we speak? (Pupil's name)
	P1	I sp – I speak Setswana and Sekalaka.
5	T	The people of our country speak Setswana and they . . . and what? Do they all speak Sekalaka?
	Ps	No.
	T	No. Only the Kalangas speak Sekalaka, but (the majority) speak Setswana and English. Most of them spoke speak
10		Setswana and English . . . Who can point to the map of Botswana on that map of Southern Africa? . . (Pupil's name)
	P2	This is Botswana.
	T	Good boy. This is our country, Botswana.

In Extract 1 the hierarchical values attached to languages in Botswana emerge clearly and are explicitly conveyed to children as an uncontested reality. Ikalanga, the mother tongue of the children, is denied any national legitimacy, and their complicity in this denial is the price they must pay for the right of inclusion as citizens of "our country, Botswana." (The teacher's use of pronouns also reflects this theme of inclusive versus exclusive identity.) On a chart of pupils' writing about themselves on the classroom wall there was, however, encouraging evidence of some resistance to such powerful messages; perhaps half of the pupils claimed to speak Ikalanga in addition to Setswana and English.

In the same lesson it was made explicit to children that Setswana, the national language that they have struggled to learn since entering primary school, is of little status or consequence internationally, where the so-called metropolitan languages or codes of wider communication such as French or the official language of Botswana, English, hold sway.

Extract 2

| | T | What is the capital of the USA? (Pupil's name) |
| | P1 | The capital of USA is Washington |

> T Good boy. [WRITES ON BOARD] Which city does Gary
> live in? Which city does Gary live in? (Pupil's name)
> 5 P2 He lives, he lives in (   )
> P3 He lives in New York.
> T Good. [WRITES ON BOARD] Which language does he
> P4 He speaks English.
> T He speaks English [WRITES ON BOARD] And which one
> 10   does he learn at school? . Which language does Gary
> speak at, learn at school? (Pupil's name)
> P5 He learn Setswana in school.
> T He learns Setswana in school. In America! Do they learn
> Setswana? (Pupil's name)
> 15 P6 He learns French at school
> T He learns French at school. Good.

The hierarchy of language values in Botswana reflects a social order in which the dominant elite have greatest access to English and are therefore concerned to maintain its prestige. Setswana is the mother tongue of the majority of the elite, as well as a *lingua franca* throughout the country, which accounts for its accepted position as secondary in prestige only to English. The lack of prestige or even official acknowl-edgment of the existence of the other languages of Botswana, includ-ing Ikalanga, reflects the exclusion of minority groups, apart from a few individuals who assimilate to the dominant Setswana culture, from social or political power. According to Bourdieu (1977), symbolic domination, that is, the consent of subordinated groups to the legit-imacy of those in power, is normally secured and reproduced through the institutions of state, primarily through schools. The social order in Botswana is, in my view, embodied and reinforced by the interac-tional classroom order, which I shall describe in this paper in terms both of the languages in which the interaction is encoded and of the differential discourse rules that govern participation by teachers and pupils.

Language Repertoires of Pupils and Teachers

In only one of the four classrooms I observed did the teacher and pupils share a first language, as can be seen from the following table:

SCHOOL 1	SCHOOL 2
(in Ikalanga-speaking area)	(in Setswana-speaking area)
Teacher A - Setswana speaker	Teacher C - Setswana speaker
Teacher B - Setswana speaker	Teacher D - Ikalanga speaker

In School 1, Teacher A was a newly appointed headteacher from the south of Botswana, who claimed to know no Ikalanga, while Teacher B, who had taught there for several years, was married to a Kalanga and was a fluent speaker of Ikalanga. In School 2, Teacher C claimed to know a number of second languages in addition to English: She alone was heard during a lesson to make a few interjections in Ikalanga, as well as several in Afrikaans. Teacher D, the only male, made no use of his native Ikalanga. There appeared to be no clear correlation between the extent of overlap between the linguistic repertoires of teacher and pupils in any given classroom and the amount of codeswitching by teachers. Teacher A was the most consistent English-user. Although Teacher B codeswitched between Setswana and English much more frequently than Teacher A, she was never observed using Ikalanga in the classroom. Teacher C made frequent use of tag switches into Setswana, mainly by appending the invariant **ga ke re?** (equivalent to canonical variations on the English *isn't it?*) to her statements or through the interactional particle **lo a bona?** (*do you see?*); otherwise, she did not appear to switch more than Teacher D, the native Ikalanga speaker.

Such variation between teachers in the use of codeswitching is to be expected and is in line with the observations of other researchers such as Zentella (1981) and De Mejia (1993). There were also more general differences in teaching style, for example, in how teachers preferred to position themselves while teaching, whether they moved around the classroom, and in the way seating for pupils was arranged in the classrooms. One likely important factor in teaching style and in the way teachers related to pupils was length of service of the teachers, which ranged from nearly twenty years in the case of Teacher C, who had qualified as a mature entrant to the profession more than a decade before, to two years in the case of Teacher D, who was the most recently qualified.

TEACHERS' USE OF CODESWITCHING

Attitudes Toward Codeswitching

The teachers I observed operated under conditions of tension between institutional pressure to adhere to language policy, that is, the exclusive use of English in the classroom, and their professional and personal instincts to codeswitch in response to the communicative needs of their pupils. My survey data from interviews and questionnaires and my experience of six years as a teacher educator in Botswana confirm that, like the Zulu-speaking teachers observed by Adendorff (1993) in South Africa, many Botswana teachers are ambivalent in their views of codeswitching and reluctant or even ashamed to admit to its part in their classroom practice. The educational climate can be characterized as prescriptive, with nationally published syllabi and teachers' guides and a central agenda of preparing pupils for the predominantly English Primary School Leaving Examination. Thus teachers are unlikely to advertise personal initiatives, including codeswitching, that could be interpreted as deviations from official policy.

Discourse-Related Switching

Although not the central focus of this paper, it is important to acknowledge the remarkably creative language use of teachers under such adverse conditions as I have described. The teachers I observed at times used code contrast to fulfill such pragmatic functions (Gumperz 1982) as addressee specification, where they wished to give encouragement or praise or reproof to individual pupils. Code contrast also served as a framing device, typically to get pupils' attention when moving on to the next stage of a lesson or back to the central agenda. Teachers thus used discourse-related codeswitching (Auer 1984) in order to provide contextualization cues that enabled them to refine the meanings they conveyed to their pupils.

Participant-Related Switching: Facilitative Strategies

Participant-related code alternation is defined by Auer (1984) as hearer-oriented. Martin-Jones (1995) has drawn attention to its salience in classrooms, such as those in Hong Kong studied by Lin (1990), where retention of a foreign language as a medium has led to communication difficulties for learners. In the two following sections I shall focus in turn on each aspect of the dual role I observed teachers to play as facilitators: how they managed and encouraged participation by learners and how they tried to ensure understanding.

Encouraging Participation by Pupils. Holmes (1984) points out that tag questions may be used as markers of positive politeness, one of their functions being to facilitate contributions from others. The tag-switches used with varying degrees of frequency by all the teachers I observed were of this type, eliciting a chorus of minimal responses (usually a mixture of English *yes* and Setswana *ee*) to punctuate a continuing teacher monologue of statements such as "That is why we say plants are living things, *ga ke re?*." Ndayipfukamiye (1994) has observed that the same phenomenon in primary classrooms in Burundi is likewise not intended by teachers as a genuine check on pupils' understanding.

Rather, it constitutes a ritualistic pseudo-checking, with the concomitant convention that the only possible response is affirmative.

The switches from English into Setswana that teachers used to encourage individual pupils to speak were, by contrast, more varied. Often the Setswana terms employed explicitly expressed solidarity, as in **Buela go godimo tsala ya me** (*Speak up, my friend*) from Teacher D. All the teachers were also observed to use to individual pupils the Setswana polite forms of address **mma** and **rra**, which are habitual in Botswana when addressing adults either in Setswana or in English. An example from Teacher B is **Leka mma. Re utlwe.** (*Try madam. We are listening.*). Since the pragmatic force of these forms is normally conveyed in English by prosody rather than by lexis, it is difficult to translate them into English without giving an impression—sometimes but not always misleading—of sarcasm.

The aim of the teachers in the examples I have given was to facilitate contributions by pupils in English. The option of codeswitching was not available to pupils, at least while the public performance of the lesson was underway and the pupil was, so to speak, center-stage. In contrast to the "follow-the-leader" principle of code choice identified by Zentella (1981) in bilingual classrooms in New York, a strict asymmetry applies in these Botswana classrooms. The pupil in Extract 3, from a science lesson with Teacher B, apparently mistook the signal sent by her teacher's switch into Setswana for a genuine invitation to reply in Setswana. The pupil's response in Setswana in line 6 is therefore rejected:

Extract 3

    T   Now give me a list of the water supplies with clean water.
           A list of water supplies with clean water. . Yes, (Pupil's
           name). . . **Mafelo a re gelelang metsi mogo one.** (Pupil's
           name)!
           Places where we fetch water from.
           A a nang le metsi a a senang leswe.   **A a senang**
           Those with clean water.   *Which don't*
    5   **malwetse ape.**
           have diseases.
    P   **sediba**
           well
    T   In English. Uhuh. [Nominates another pupil.]

Extract 4 is from an English lesson in which the topic is storytelling, and pupils have heard the traditional story of the scorpion and the chameleon. Teacher B's switch in line 15 is unusual in that she uses it to explicitly invite pupils to contribute in Setswana from the cultural knowledge she knows they possess.

Extract 4

T My chart has got pictures. . By just looking at those
pictures what do you think is happening there?. . Oh, do
you want me to begin first?. . I think lizards and insects
are going to school and the scorpion does not want to go
5   to school so it is hiding itself under a big rock because it
does not want to go to school. What do you think?
Because we don't think in the same way do we?

Ps No

T No we don't. Yes (Pupil's name). What do you think is
10   happening there?

P1 I think that they want to choose a king

T Uhuh. You think they want to choose a king. Uhuh. What
do you think? We have different thoughts. . We have
different thoughts. Do you mean you are not thinking?
15   **A ko eme rra.**
Stand up, rra.
Tlhe mma a ko o mpolelele gore wena o bona o kare go a
Please mma tell   me   how   you   see what is going on.
reng. Lefa e le ka Setswana mpolelele. O akanye
Even in Setswana tell me.   Think of
sengwe fela. Se o ka akanyang gore go ka dirafala.
anything.   Think of any that could be happening.
Okay. What creature is this, what is it? Yes (Pupil's name)

20 P2 Chameleon.

T It's a chameleon. Good. It's a chameleon.

There is a clear contrast in Extract 4 between the teacher's open-ended questioning and prompting in Setswana, which fail to elicit pupil responses, and her subsequent reversion to a closed question in English, which is "successful" insofar as a one-word answer is elicited. Setswana, although the second language of these pupils, would allow them much greater possibilities of self-expression than English. The pupils do not appear, however, to give credence to their teacher's explicit legitimizing of responses in Setswana. In this they differ, for example, from those observed in Tanzanian secondary schools (Rubagumya 1993), who switched to Kiswahili where it was condoned by their teacher on the grounds of their difficulty in English expression. However, it is perhaps not surprising that the Botswana pupils in Extract 4 do not accept their teacher's invitation to speak so publicly in Setswana during an English lesson, despite her attempts earlier in the lesson to construe the topic as the telling of stories from any source. To do so would involve breaking a ground rule of discourse in their classroom, which, as Extract 3 demonstrated, is at other times strictly enforced.

Intercomprehension Strategies. Bilingual classrooms, as character-ized by Nussbaum (1990), are sites of exolingual communication, in which the high degree of divergence between the linguistic repertoires of the participants leads to a need for intercomprehension strategies, of which codeswitching is one. Such switching is further usefully classi-fied by Nussbaum as either hetero-facilitative on the part of teachers, that is, anticipating and intended to preempt learners' comprehension difficulties, or self-facilitative on the part of learners, that is, resorting to the L1 to fill in gaps in knowledge of target language vocabulary or to prevent errors. I shall discuss each of these strategies in turn in the following sections.

Codeswitching by Teachers as a Hetero-Facilitative Strategy. Inter-lingual reformulations occur in my data like those identified by Cambra-Giné (1991) in French as a foreign language classrooms in Catalonia and by De Mejia (1993) in early English immersion class-rooms in Colombia. There are examples of literal translations juxta-posed, of equivalence explicitly marked, and of paraphrase where an equivalent lexical item is not available in Setswana. All are examples of what is termed reiteration by Gumperz (1982) and pseudotransla-tion by Auer (1984); no new information is added, the purpose in each case being facilitative repetition rather than repair or qualifica-tion of meaning.

The Absence of Codeswitching by Pupils as a Self-Facilitative Strategy. In my data, codeswitching from English into Setswana as a facilita-tive strategy is used exclusively by teachers. It is not available as a self-facilitative strategy to the learners I observed, unlike those, for example, in the classrooms studied by Lin (1990) in Hong Kong or Nussbaum (1990) in Catalonia. In only one instance in my data did a nominated pupil appear to break the rule of responding in English to a teacher's question posed in English. Having stood to answer, as is the convention in Botswana classrooms, he averted his eyes and said in a subdued tone almost too low for the tape recorder to catch: **Ke ne ke ke re ke bua yone.** The Setswana translates into English as *I was going to say that,* and refers to the previous pupil's answer. Setswana was, therefore, the language of apology for failure to re-spond acceptably. Other pupils unable to answer tended to remain silent and might be left standing in ignominy until later in the lesson when their teacher gave them permission to sit down or when they judged that they might be able to do so unnoticed. The discourse rules internalized by learners in Botswana classrooms deny them the freedom to use their first language as a means to increase their participation, either quantitatively or through negotiating the lesson agenda at any given moment.

Why Don't Teachers Make More Use of Codeswitching as a Hetero-Facilitative Strategy? Nussbaum (1990) points out that hetero-facilitative switching is just one of a range of intercomprehension strategies available to teachers; others include intralingual repetition or simplification, and the use of gesture. The teachers I observed appeared to prefer such alternatives, particularly that of repetition. Although there was a significant incidence of codeswitching in lessons I observed across three subject areas, my presence as a native English speaker undoubtedly evoked an observer effect that inhibited the use of codeswitching. In my view there are, however, other factors that help to explain why more codeswitching, particularly of a facilitative kind, was not observed. Subject syllabi are in many cases designed to progress on a spiral model by revisiting the same topics in each standard. The intention is that more in-depth understanding should be progressively developed, but the result in practice is often a great deal of re-presentation and revision of previously introduced material. Moreover, English is exemplified and practiced but seldom used communicatively in the teacher-dominated routines common in these classrooms. The following section focuses on the roles of teachers and pupils in these routines and suggests insights into their nature that are offered by teachers' code alternation.

"STAGING" THE LESSON

In most of the lessons I observed, the main activity was whole-class teaching, often focused on a chalkboard or wall-chart picture. The dominant recitation pattern of teacher questioning and group or individual response was one that had become familiar to me over several years of visiting Botswana primary schools as a teacher trainer. In describing the lessons, I find their similarity to stage performances striking: Pupils are called upon to say their lines, by a teacher who is not only their co-actor but fulfills a number of backstage roles such as director, prompt, and stage manager. Cambra-Giné (1991) has recourse to a similar metaphor when she describes what goes on in the French as a foreign language classrooms she observed in Catalonia. She said they were reminiscent of a film scenario that is being rehearsed. In their study of upper primary and junior secondary classrooms in Botswana, Fuller and Snyder (1991) refer to "the scripts that teachers follow," concluding that these have little to do with the age or developmental character of their pupils.

Center-Stage Language Use

In the setting of traditional teacher-fronted classrooms, which are in themselves reminiscent of a stage, the convention in Botswana that nominated pupils stand to answer a teacher's question enhances the impression of public performance. Also, teachers often exhort pupils to project their voices, as if to reach an audience, such as by telling them in Setswana **Bua go godimo** or in English *Speak aloud, my boy*. As even these two utterances show, English was not used exclusively during recitation routines. However, English predominated as the language of onstage public performance, and Setswana as the language of offstage or backstage dealings. The juxtaposition of the two codes was clearly imbued with social meanings that reverberated beyond the classroom.

Pupils as Performers

The questions put by teachers were overwhelmingly of the closed type, often designed to elicit English vocabulary items—a genre of classroom language use described by Heath (1986) as a label quest. In cognitive terms most questions were undemanding, requiring merely recall of previously introduced material. Chorus completion of teacher statements offered a kind of gap-filling exercise, in which pupils' understanding was little probed and the risk of their responding unacceptably was minimized.

By contrast, where pupils were individually nominated by teachers, they were normally expected to answer in full English sentences, and feedback on their answers was often bedeviled by a dual focus on content on the one hand and on form on the other. Pupils at times seemed confused over which of the dual agendas of communication and language learning was being pursued at a given moment. In Extract 5, from an English grammar lesson on tags, Teacher A was finally explicit about her requirements, reinforcing her *Don't answer the question* in line 16 with a tag-switch into Setswana.

Extract 5

	T	Good girl. The wedding will be held in Gantsi, won't it? The wedding will be held in Gantsi, won't it? People didn't read, huh? (Pupil's name)
	P1	Yes it won't
5	T	Do we say "Yes, it won't"? The wedding is not yet held. It is still going to be. So, we say "Yes, it . . ."? We are still waiting for the wedding to come so now do we say it? "Yes, it . . ." ? (Pupil's name)
	P2	Yes, it is . . . . do.

[PUPILS GASP]

10 T   Which word words do we use to show the future? The
         two words that we we use to express the future?
    P3   Yes, it won't
    T   Listen. Give me those two words that we use when we
         want to express the future tense
15 P4   Yes, it was
    T   Don't answer the question. **Ke a utlwana ?** Give me the
                                    Is it understood?
         two words that we use to express the future, that we use
         when we talk about things still to happen. We use the two
         words which are . . . ?

In Extract 6, from another English lesson, Teacher B similarly attempts to clarify her focus by codeswitching into Setswana: She gives
a literal Setswana translation of the English sentence offered earlier by
a pupil, thus signaling that she has accepted the content but now
requires correction of the grammatical form.

Extract 6

    T   When do you think this happened? Is it still happening?
         Has it happened already or in the past? When do you
         think this happened?. (   ) somebody try. The lizards
         and the insects met to choose a king. When do you think
5   this happened? . . (Pupil's name)
    P1   It already happened
    T   It has already happened. When do you think it has
         happened? Yes. . (Pupil's name)
    P2   It has happened on the past
10 T   Yes, in the past. In the.. this is a story that happened some
         years back in the past. It can be that year, it can be some
         years back but it is in the past. So it is correct to say they
         choose chameleon they choose chameleon? Is it correct to
         say that?
15   What's wrong with this sentence? What is it supposed to
         be? They choose the chameleon. Yes. The the the insects and
         the lizards met to choose a king. **Ba ile ba tlhope** chameleon
                                            They chose the chameleon
         but I want the correct sentence. (Pupil's name)
    P   (chose) They chose a chameleon
20 T   Good. It should be they chose a chameleon. They chose a
         chameleon.

Grammatically correct English is clearly the only legitimate language
of onstage pupil performance in these classrooms.

Backstage Language Use

Conversations between pupils and teachers outside the classroom, in any other part of the school compound, took place in Setswana or, depending on the participants' repertoires and preferences, in Ikalanga. A child arriving at a classroom door while a lesson was underway would invariably state her or his business in Setswana; the teacher then switched from English, in which she was conducting the lesson, to attend to the visitor in Setswana.

Juxtaposition of the two codes was also a means of distinguishing between "doing lessons" and talking about them. On several occasions references to past or future lessons or learning events involved a switch by the teacher from English to the 'backstage' language, Setswana. For example, in Extract 7, from an English lesson with Teacher B, this "stepping out" of the pedagogic frame of the current lesson is signaled by the code switch from English to Setswana. (The teacher's revision lecture then proceeds by means of English grammar rules stated in Setswana and reiterated in English.)

Extract 7

p   The scorpion hid under the rock, didn't it?
T   Good. The scorpion hid under the rock, didn't it? Now
    this time if you look at my sentences, huh? **Ke ne ke ntse**
    I have always
    ke le bolelela gore . . I was telling you that **fa re dirisetse**
    been telling you that   if we have put
5   'are' **fa le fa o nna teng. Fa re dirisetse** 'is' even in here
    'are' here, it goes here too.   If we have put the
    'is' is going to appear

Extract 8 is from a math lesson on decimals. In line 5 this same teacher cuts into her English explanation of tenths and hundredths to comment parenthetically in Setswana on pupils' prior learning when she notices how many pupils are putting their hands up to show eagerness to contribute.

Extract 8

T   So it is eight tenths. When you write it I know you will
    write   eight   tenths.   [MOVES   TO   ANOTHER
    CALCULATION ON THE BOARD] We get onto this one
    here. This one is not tenths, it is hundreds. Oh. [LAUGHS]
5   **Bokhutshwane ga ke re le a itse** hundreds. How do we
    write it here?
    In short,   you know
5   **le a itse** hundreds. How do we write it here?

In line 7 of Extract 9, from a science lesson, Teacher C switches from English to Setswana in order to indicate an activity planned for later.

Extract 9

	T	Now the roots feed the parts of the plant of the plant **ga ke re** ?
	Ps	**Eemm**
	T	They keep it safe. They keep the plant firm to the ground.
5		**Gakere, o a bona?**
		You see, don't you?
	Ps	Yes
	T	We shall go outside **kgantelenyana, ga ke re?**
		later, okay?
	Ps	**Eemm**
	T	So that we can pick out the plants and see how the roots
10		are, **ga ke re?**
	Ps	**Eemm**

Code contrast thus allows a distinction between a pedagogic focus on knowledge to be gained and displayed, accomplished through English, and occasional references in Setswana to the processes by which that knowledge is to be gained.

A COLLUSIVE INTERPRETATION OF THE JOINT PERFORMANCE

In teacher-dominated procedures such as those I am describing, the asymmetrical distribution of talk, in terms of both number and duration of speaker turns, is obvious. Unequal access to English, that is, a much higher level of competence on the part of the teacher, constrains pupils into a minor role in the interaction. However, the performance I have alluded to is above all a joint one: Pupils and teacher play asymmetrical but synchronized roles to the best of their ability. Recitation routines are reported to be typical of many teacher-centered classrooms throughout the world, but seem to be particularly salient in large classes in poor countries (Coleman 1989). Cleghorn and associates (1989) offer an explanation of the phenomenon in Kenya in terms of "traditionally rooted interaction patterns such as those that are characterized by a rhythmic questioning and group response" (p. 37). A similar view emerges from statements by educational researchers in Botswana such as Prophet and Rowell: "It may be that the dominant teaching style originates out of the African respect for tradition and authority" (1993, 208).

The study of Zulu-English classrooms in South Africa by Chick (1996), mentioned in the introduction to this chapter, proposes a less obvious—and less convenient—explanation: Teachers and pupils are, it is argued, adhering to institutional conventions imposed during colonial rule rather than by wider cultural norms. This view is supported by Ndayipfukamiye (1993), who argues that the routines he observed in French-Kirundi classrooms in Burundi were those that had been internalized by teachers when they themselves were pupils. Likewise, Ellis (1987) comments on the balance between interpretation and transmission that characterized informal African education, whereas the tradition of formal education that has developed in African schools in this century "has derived from the kind of classroom practices common in pre-war European schools" (p. 87).

In his South African study, Chick focuses on chorusing of responses within recitation routines in English. He points to the apparently random nature of the chorus and the low information value of many items chorused as evidence that its primary function is social rather than academic. Drawing on the collusive approach to conversation analysis of McDermott and Tylbor (1987), Chick coins the term "safetalk" for the interactional style of which chorusing forms part. Safetalk allows participation without loss of face on the part of either teacher or pupils, whether through lack of knowledge or through language errors. By resorting to safetalk, black teachers and pupils collude with each other to maintain at least an appearance of getting on with the proper classroom business of teaching and learning; they are thus able to deny to themselves, to each other, and to onlookers the realities of the lack of appropriate materials and skills that are the legacy of institutionalized oppression and segregated schooling under apartheid.

Severely underresourced primary schools in many African countries have been termed "'facade institutions' where little learning takes place" (Foster 1989). In Botswana, however, textbooks and materials are in reasonable supply, relative to African though not to European or North American norms, and the vast majority of the teaching force has undergone a two-year training course. The crucial common constraint on learning that operates in many classrooms throughout the continent, including those I observed in Botswana, is the requirement to use a foreign language as the medium of instruction. Particularly in rural areas of Botswana, teachers and pupils have limited access to English, which is, for them, a foreign language transmitted almost exclusively through the school. Thus one way to interpret certain instances in my data of feedback in Setswana from teachers to their classes is as a means of achieving mutual face-saving over the adequacy of the classroom interaction in which they are involved and the degree of pupil understanding that could reasonably be expected to result.

Extract 10 comes from the end of a sequence during an English lesson in which Teacher B has attempted with little success to elicit retelling in English of a previously introduced story.

Extract 10

	T	OK, good. Sit down. good. So it means that some people were really listening at me yesterday when I was telling the story. I know that you could all tell the story if you had chance, **ga ke re? Ga ke re rotlhe re ne re ka bua, huh?**
		we would all speak, huh?
5	Ps	Yes
	T	Yes. But let us look at this sentence this sentence.
		Tse dingwe re tla nna re di bona. They choose a chameleon
		We shall relate others later.
		they choose a chameleon

In Extract 11 Teacher C is rounding off an English lesson. Pupils are putting hands up to indicate how many sentences they wrote correctly. I was able to observe that many pupils had clearly found the exercise difficult and made a lot of mistakes.

Extract 11

	T	Uhuh. Those who got ten. There are only two mhm nine .. ( ) mhm eight .. Where are your hands if you have got eight **Ee, ke rile** ( ). You write the answers in short.
		Yes, I said
		They are correct. **Ee, tshwara jaana.** Correct, (Pupil's
		Yes, now you understand
5		name). ( ) one two three four. seven. . three. mhm. six. . Okay sit down. five. Those who got five upwards. five six seven eight nine ten stand up. . . . Okay sit down.
		Le lona lo tla tshwara kamoso, ga ke re?
		You will also understand tomorrow, won't you?

In exchanges such as those represented by Extracts 10 and 11, I would suggest that Setswana functions as the language of complicity. By this I do not mean that Setswana signals solidarity—the "we-code" in contrast to the English "they-code"; as Martin-Jones (1995) points out, this kind of opposition is too simplistic. It does not advance our understanding of the complex relationship between code choice and speaker identity. Also, code choice of itself tells us little about the teacher-pupil relationship: In my data, switches by teachers into Setswana to give feedback to individual pupils were invariably accompanied by other prosodic or nonverbal contextualization cues, so that their effect ranged from a softening of criticism to its sharpening by means of sarcasm. Rather, teacher and pupils are mutually interdependent in that all need to keep up the appearance of effective activity in the classroom and of fulfillment of their respective roles. Any problems that arise must, therefore, be glossed over or kept backstage, and that is what is often accomplished by switching to Setswana.

CONCLUDING COMMENTS

In this chapter, I have attempted to demonstrate that the variation in the content and structure of teaching and learning events across the classrooms I observed occurred within a constraining framework of institutionalized and institutionalizing pressures. The familiar ease of routinized interactional patterns is one such pressure. My experience as a teacher educator in Botswana allows me to confirm that these patterns characterized much teaching across the curriculum, including the teaching of Setswana as a subject. However, it is the combination of routinized teacher-dominated performances of teaching and learning with the internalized discourse rules of English-medium instruction that most powerfully inhibits attempts by teachers and pupils to pursue more challenging and culturally congruent learning: Pupils are, in effect, prevented from meaningful and critical engagement with the curriculum. Rowell and Prophet (1990) observed similarly limited and limiting patterns of interaction in lessons in Junior Secondary Schools in Botswana. "What is missing from most classroom interactions is any recognition of the beliefs and values which students bring with them or even acknowledgment that students have constructed cognitive schemes for interpreting the world" (p. 24). Learning of this culturally congruent kind would, I conclude, conflict with the social values that are embodied and perpetuated through the classroom discourse I have investigated.

APPENDIX: TRANSCRIPTION CONVENTIONS

Normal sentence punctuation has been used as far as possible, in order to make the transcripts accessible to lay readers. Commas have, however, been avoided in favor of full stops (one or several) to indicate hesitations and pauses.

Plain font: English

Bold: **Setswana**

Italics: *Translation of Setswana into English*

( ) indicates unclear speech.

[BLOCK CAPITALS] indicates commentary on what is happening in the classroom.

{indicates overlapping speech}

There is no translation of the following:

- frequently used Setswana tags: **Ga ke re?** Is it? (Are they? Do we? etc.)
  (L)o a bona? Do you (singular o, plural lo) see?
- polite forms of address for females (**mma**) or for males (**rra**)
- the short responses **ee** (yes) and **nnyaa** (no). **Eemm** is a contracted form of **Ee mma**.

REFERENCES

Adendorff, R. (1993). Codeswitching amongst Zulu-speaking teachers and their pupils: Its functions and implications for teacher education. *Language and Education, 7(3)*, 141–162.

Auer, P. (1984). *Bilingual conversation.* Amsterdam: John Benjamins.

Bourdieu, P. (1977). The economics of linguistic exchanges. *Social Science Information, 6 (6)*, 645–668.

Cambra i Giné, M. (1991). Les changements de langue en classe de langue étrangère, révelateurs d'une certaine organisation du discours. In *Papers from the Symposium on Code-Switching in Bilingual Studies: Theory, significance and perspectives.* (Vol. 2). Strasbourg: European Science Foundation Network on Code-Switching and Language Contact.

Chick, J. K. (1996). Safetalk: Collusion in apartheid education. In H. Coleman (Ed.), *Society and the language classroom.* Cambridge: Cambridge University Press, 21–39.

Cleghorn, A., Merritt, M., and Obagi, J. O. (1989). Language policy and science instruction in Kenyan primary schools. *Comparative Education Review, 33(1)*, 21–39.

Coleman, H. (1989). *Approaches to the management of large classes.* Project Report No 11. Universities of Lancaster and Leeds, Language Learning in Large Classes Research Project.

De Mejia, A. (1993, July). *Two early immersion classes in Colombia: The role of reformulation in bilingual story-telling.* Paper presented at the British Association for Applied Linguistics Symposium on Bilingual Classroom Discourse, University of Lancaster.

Ellis, R. (1987). Using the English medium in African schools. In D. Young (Ed.), *Bridging the gap between theory and practice in English second language teaching.* Cape Town: Maskew Millar Longman.

Foster, P. (1989). Some hard choices to be made. *Comparative Education Review, 33*, 104–110.

Fuller, B., and Snyder, C. W. (1991). Vocal teachers, silent pupils? Life in Botswana classrooms. *Comparative Education Review, 35*, 274–293.

Gumperz, J. J. (1982). *Discourse Strategies.* Cambridge: Cambridge University Press.

Heath, S. B. (1986). Sociocultural contexts of language development. In D. Holt (Ed.), *Beyond language: Social and cultural factors in schooling language minority students*. Los Angeles Evaluation, Dissemination and Assessment Center, California State University.

Holmes, J. (1984). Hedging your bets and sitting on the fence: Some evidence for hedges as support structures. *Te Reo, 27*, 47–62.

Lin, A. (1990). *Teaching in two tongues: Language alternation in foreign language classrooms*. Research Report No. 3, City Polytechnic of Hong Kong.

Martin-Jones, M. (1995). Code-switching in the classroom: two decades of research. In L. Milroy and P. Mysken (Eds.), *One speaker, two languages: Cross-disciplinary perspectives on code-switching* (pp. 90–111). Cambridge: Cambridge University Press.

McDermott, R. P., and Tylbor, H. (1987). On the necessity of collusion in conversation. In L. Kedar (Ed.), *Power through discourse*. Norwood, N.J.: Ablex.

Ndayipfukamiye, L. (1993). *Teaching/learning bilingually: The case of grade five in Burundi primary schools*. Unpublished Ph.D. thesis, University of Lancaster.

Ndayipfukamiye, L. (1994). Code-switching in Burundi primary classrooms. In C. Rubagumya (Ed.), *Teaching and researching language in African classrooms*. Clevedon, Avon: Multilingual Matters, pp. 79–95.

Nussbaum, L. (1990). Plurilingualism in foreign language classrooms in Catalonia. In *Papers from the Workshop on the Impact and Consequences of Code-Switching*. Strasbourg: European Science Foundation Network on Code-Switching and Language Contact.

Prophet, R., and Rowell, P. M. (1993). Coping and control: Science teaching strategies in Botswana. *Qualitative Studies in Education, 6 (3)*, 197–209.

Rowell, P. M., and Prophet, R. (1990). Curriculum-in-action: The "practical" dimension in Botswana classrooms. *International Journal of Educational Development, 10(1)*, 17–24.

Rubagumya, C. M. (1993). *The language values of Tanzanian secondary school pupils: A case study in the Dar-Es-Salaam region*. Unpublished Ph.D. thesis, Lancaster University.

Zentella, A. C. (1981). Ta bien, you could answer me en cualquier idioma: Puerto Rican code-switching in bilingual classrooms. In R. Duran (Ed.), *Latino language and communicative behaviour*, 109–132. Norwood, N.J.: Ablex.

4

Language and Educational Inequality in Primary Classrooms in Kenya

Grace Bunyi

INTRODUCTION

Political ideology in Kenya posits that Kenya is an egalitarian society or at least that it aims at egalitarianism. According to the Ministry of Education (1987), one of the national concerns on the attainment of independence in 1963 was "more equitable distribution of national income" (p. 3). Indeed, National Goal of Education number 4 in Kenya states: "Education *should promote social equality* and foster a sense of social responsibility *within an education system which provides equal educational opportunities for all*" (emphasis added) (Ministry of Education 1994, p. v). Consequently, education is seen to be an important player in the leveling of socioeconomic and political differences in Kenyan society. It is widely believed that social equality can be achieved through the provision of equal educational opportunities for all children.

Does the education system in Kenya actually provide equal educational opportunities for children from different socioeconomic backgrounds? Does education in Kenya actually lead to social equality? Can children from all socioeconomic backgrounds in Kenya use education to get ahead? In this chapter, I advance the argument that, because of the use of English as the medium of instruction, the educational system in Kenya does not provide equal educational opportunities for children from different socioeconomic backgrounds. I also argue that current educational practice and, in particular, the differential educational treatment of children in rural and some urban schools in Kenya contributes to the reproduction of unequal power relations in Kenyan society.

EDUCATION AND SOCIAL REPRODUCTION

Educational research in the developed world, especially North America and Europe, has shown that the educational achievement of children from different socioeconomic backgrounds is not the same. In these countries, children from mainstream middle-class backgrounds often do much better in school than children from working-class and ethnic minority backgrounds. Consequently, the search for an explanation for and a solution to the problem of the underachievement of working-class and ethnic minority children has engaged researchers there since the 1960s.

Among those who have contributed to this debate is anthropologist John Ogbu. Ogbu (1981, 1987) argues that explanations for the school failure of some minority and immigrant children have to be sought with reference to broader socioeconomic and political processes. Ogbu posits that to know the causes of what goes on in school and thus to be able to suggest solutions, we must look into "the interrelation between schooling and other social institutions and how such relationships may affect classroom processes" (Ogbu 1981, 13). Taking the case of African Americans and Mexican Americans in the United States, Ogbu argues that minorities have been discriminated against in schools and in the job market for so many generations that they no longer believe that educational credentials will provide them with a chance of upward social mobility. Consequently, these students resist school authority and reject its values. Unfortunately, this only leads to their failing in school and therefore to their being relegated to working-class jobs. This, in turn, leads to the reproduction of unequal relations in North American society. Ogbu's theory underscores the importance of probing the power relations in the wider society and demonstrating how these are both involved in and a consequence of what goes on in school.

Writing on the dialectical relationship between broad social processes and everyday local activities, Giddens (1984) states, "The day-to-day activity of social actors draws upon and reproduces structural features of wider social systems" (p. 24). According to Giddens, language plays a central role in social activities. He states, "Language use is embedded in the concrete activities of day-to-day life and is in some sense partly constitutive of those activities" (Giddens 1984, p. xvi). Therefore, according to Giddens, the verbal interactions that accompany everyday activities constitute the doing of social processes, while the social processes provide the social context within which the interactions take place and therefore have an impact on the interactions.

Giddens' proposal for a unified theoretical approach to social phenomena has been applied by Heller (1996) to the study of language practices in multilingual contexts. She draws on and extends the work of John Ogbu and Pierre Bourdieu, highlighting the role of language in social reproduction in bilingual and multilingual settings. Although Ogbu does not talk of the role of language *per se*, Heller (1996) argues that a sufficient analysis of social reproduction in the school, based on Ogbu's ideas, must take language into consideration. It is through discourse that students learn what school expects or does not expect of them, and it is through discourse that they contest or collaborate with school values and authority. Consequently, I believe that to find out how language and education contribute (or do not contribute) to social reproduction in Kenya today, it is important (1) to explore the links between language, education, and social mobility in Kenyan society and (2) to examine how these links are played out in the day-to-day, face-to-face language practices of different socioeconomic and political groups in Kenyan society. At the same time, I believe that current social processes are the result of past social, economic, and political processes. In the next section, I therefore explore the social, economic, and political roots of the links among education, English, and social mobility in Kenya.

LANGUAGE, EDUCATION, AND UPWARD SOCIAL MOBILITY IN KENYA: A HISTORICAL PERSPECTIVE

Kenya is a highly multilingual society. There are over 40 indigenous languages (Abdulaziz 1982). In addition, Kiswahili is the national language and English is the official language. Nearly everyone in Kenya speaks an indigenous language. It has been estimated that 75% of the population have varying degrees of competence in Kiswahili and that only 15% of the population know English well enough to use it effectively in all areas of life (Abdulaziz 1982). The percentage of English speakers must now have increased, because of the massive expansion in educational provision since Independence. As the official language and the mandated medium of instruction from Standard 4 upward, English is the language of education and is clearly associated with upward social mobility in Kenya.

The Colonial Period

Education (in the Western sense) and upward social mobility in Kenya have been linked since the introduction of Western education by missionaries in the colonial period. In the same period, the English language and education were so closely associated that they were at times seen as synonymous. Writing on the situation in Africa in general, Mazrui (1975) says, "A command of the English language was often used as a criterion of one's level of education" (p. 55). In British colonial Africa in general and in Kenya in particular, English was the language of the socially, economically, and politically powerful white colonial officers, settlers, businessmen/women, and missionaries. Consequently, ever since its introduction into Kenya through missionary education, English has been associated with power. Writing about the situation in Nigeria, in particular, and British colonial Africa, in general, Goke-Pariola (1993) states, "to speak that language in itself was power . . . the local person who understood the White man's language increased his own power dramatically: he became a man before whom others stood in awe" (1993, 223). At the same time, those Africans who acquired English language skills gained access to the institutions where colonial power was vested. According to Ngugi, in Kenya, "English was the official vehicle and magic formula to colonial elitedom" (Ngugi 1985, 115). During this period, some Africans gained employment in the colonial administration, but only in junior positions.

However, in much of the colonial period in Kenya, very few African children had the opportunity to learn English. The 1937 Commission on Higher Education in East Africa, for example, suggested that those children selected by the Education Department for further education should be taught English not later than the end of the third year, but that for those who would not continue into secondary classes, English should not come into question even as a subject (Gorman 1974). Before 1949, African children's educational opportunities beyond the primary school were very restricted. Even the 1949 Beecher Report, which has been much acclaimed for liberalizing education for African children (Sheffield 1973), recommended that only 10% of African children should receive an education beyond the primary school and that only 1% should enter high school (Weeks 1967). Therefore, going by the recommendations of the Commission on Higher Education, less than 10% of African children were to get some exposure to English and less than 1% were to have meaningful exposure to the language in high schools. The privileged few came to constitute the new elite.

After 1945, because of intensified pressures from nationalistic movements and from the international community, the British government realized that the days of colonialism were numbered. In preparation for handing over power to the Africans, opportunities for higher education were expanded, especially at the intermediate and secondary school level (Sheffield 1973). Education beyond the primary school level being available to more Africans meant that more of them could now learn English. Ngugi (1981) has argued that, during this period, the colonial government found it necessary to ensure that, in its absence, its interests would be served by those who took over power. The colonial government therefore expanded the teaching of English as a way of ensuring that the incoming African leaders, educated in English, were acculturated into the British value system and that they would therefore continue to serve British interests as they sought to serve their own.

At the same time, colonial language in education policy leaned more towards the teaching of English at lower and lower levels of education. For example, the 1953–1955 East African Royal Commission Report stated that the teaching of English should begin at as low a level as possible and that it should become the medium of instruction as early as possible. In 1962, English was introduced in African schools as the medium of instruction from Standard 1 as part of what came to be known as the New Primary Approach.

The Postcolonial Period

On the attainment of independence in 1963, the political and economic structures of the colonial regime, cast in a capitalist mold, were transferred to the new regime. The African elite that took over power retained the language policies of the colonial regime since these policies bestowed considerable socioeconomic and political advantages upon them. When the first post-independence Education Commission was appointed in 1963, it endorsed the English-medium policy for the entire nation, from Standard 1 onward. This decision was amended in 1976 by the second post-independence Education Commission. The second Commission recommended that English should only become the medium of instruction in all schools from Standard 4 onward. This is still the operative language in education policy in Kenya today. English is the sole official medium of instruction from Standard 4 onward, and since 1985, Kiswahili, the national language, has become a compulsory subject in the school curriculum, from Standard 4 onward. The indigenous language of each region of Kenya is used as the instructional medium only in the first three years of primary school and only in linguistically homogeneous areas. In areas where there is considerable linguistic diversity, Kiswahili and English are used as instructional media in these first few years.

This brief historical overview of the links between the English language, education, and social mobility in Kenya reveals that the introduction of Western education and English in Kenya in the colonial days led to social stratification with education and the English language as symbols of elite class membership. Through the retention of English as the official language and the language of education in Kenya, this English-based process of social reproduction has been perpetuated.

This medium of instruction policy in Kenya has legitimized standard English as the language of authority. The value of the language on the local linguistic market derives, in the main, from the fact that it is still difficult to gain access to it. As Bourdieu (1977) and Bourdieu and Passeron (1977) have shown so well, the crucial question to ask in any educational site is about access to the legitimate language. Learners have "differential chances of access to the instruments for producing the legitimate competence" (Bourdieu 1977, 654). In the case of Kenya, the key questions are: Who has access to English? What are the educational consequences of inadequate access to English? By extension, what are the lifelong consequences of this?

In the rest of this chapter, I will consider in further detail how language and education influence social reproduction in Kenya today. I will do this (1) by exploring how children from different socioeconomic backgrounds are positioned with respect to access to English and to the school and (2) by examining the educational treatment that children from different socioeconomic backgrounds receive in the school as a result of their differential positioning. To achieve these two goals, I will use ethnographic data from two primary schools and their communities:[1] Gicagi and Park View.[2] In both schools, Standards 1 and 4 were the focus of my study. In the following section, I focus on the Gicagi and Park View communities' differential positioning in relation to access to English and to the school.

THE POSITIONING OF THE GICAGI AND PARK VIEW COMMUNITIES IN RELATION TO ACCESS TO ENGLISH AND TO SCHOOLING

The Gicagi Community

The Gicagi community and school are located in Kiambu district, a rural district adjacent to Nairobi, the capital city of Kenya. Gicagi is a homogeneous Gikuyu-speaking community. Although most people in the community claim to have different levels of competence in Kiswahili and English, Gikuyu is virtually the only language spoken in Gicagi. Even those Gicagi people, such as teachers, who know English and use it at work told me they do not speak English at home. Mrs. Muhoro, the Standard 4 teacher, explained, **"Twakinya mucii riu tutwikaga aciari Githungu gikamba guthira"** {*When we get home, we become parents and English comes to an end*}. When Gicagi people find themselves constrained to speak another language, as when on a visit to Nairobi, they choose to speak Kiswahili. A woman, whose son, Nderi, was in Standard 1, made the following observation: **"Ndathii Nairobi ngore mukabira ndikiaragia Githweri o giki gitu kia Mashambani"** {*If I go to Nairobi and meet a non-Gikuyu speaker, I speak in our village Kiswahili*}. Many Gicagi people have radios, and they listen to Gikuyu broadcasts more often than to English or Kiswahili ones. Very few people in Gicagi have television. Consequently, Gicagi children have almost no access to English in their homes and community.

However, even in Gicagi school itself, Gicagi children have very limited access to English. Gikuyu is the first language of everyone in the school, and it dominates the out-of-class communication of both the teachers and the students. Although there is a rule that prohibits Standard 4–8 children speaking Gikuyu in the school compound, according to the headmaster, it is very difficult to enforce the rule. The teachers themselves break the rule and start speaking Gikuyu to the students. There are also lower-primary schoolchildren who have had very little contact with English or Kiswahili and who therefore cannot speak these languages. Consequently, the no-Gikuyu-in-the-school-compound rule remains dormant most of the time, only to be resurrected when poor examination results come. Believing poor English competence to be one of the reasons for the poor results, the teachers enforce the rule with dedication for a while.

Inside the classroom in Gicagi school, in Standard 1, Gikuyu is the medium of instruction. It is also the dominant language of all non-curriculum activities. However, in their English language and content subject lessons, words or phrases that the children are expected to remember and recognize in the examinations are repeated several times after the teacher in English (and in Kiswahili in the Kiswahili lessons). They are written on the blackboard and in the children's exercise books in the same language. At the same time, the children use Kiswahili and English in participating in the performance of a few linguistic routines such as exchanging greetings with the teacher, singing, and reciting the end of morning prayers.

In Standard 4, Gikuyu remains the dominant language of non-curriculum activities. In the delivery of the curriculum, the teachers make a definite attempt to use English. However, the teachers also use strategies such as codeswitching between English and Gikuyu, translating number problems into word problems in the math lessons, reading passages aloud themselves, and asking one-word-answer questions, thereby attempting to help the students understand or cope with the impossibility of working in English. My argument is that these strategies may make the lessons more comprehensible in the short term, but in the long term they hold the children back in the learning of English, the language to which they need to gain access in order to be able to build school knowledge.

From the foregoing discussion of linguistic practices in the Gicagi community and school, it is evident that, as regards access to English, Gicagi children are caught up in what Bourdieu (1977) has called the "double paradox." They have no access to the language in their homes and community, and Gicagi school provides them with very limited access to the language. This limited access to English puts Gicagi children at a disadvantage with regard to participating in school life.

At the same time, Gicagi children have little access to written language and to the literacy practices associated with schooling. Gicagi people's physical work on the farms does not involve literacy, and Gicagi is not a reading community. There are few children's schoolbooks available, and the only reading materials in many Gicagi homes are the Gikuyu bible and hymnbook. Consequently, not only are Gicagi children negatively positioned as regards access to spoken English, but they are also negatively positioned in respect to literacy in either English or Gikuyu, an important aspect of school life.

Life in Gicagi is an economic struggle, and for most people, money is hard to come by. Most families in Gicagi depend solely on subsistence farming. Returns from these farming activities depend to a great extent on natural weather conditions, and crop failure is not uncommon. When I arrived in Gicagi for my fieldwork, the community had just come out of a protracted drought that had caused near famine. Working as laborers on coffee plantations (formerly owned by white settlers and by the time I carried out my study by individual Africans or local cooperatives) was the most easily available form of employment for people in Gicagi. Wages from such work were, and still are, very low. At the time of my fieldwork, the daily wage was Ksh. 47.40. At the same time, one 2-kilogram packet of maize flour (enough for a meal for a family of 6) cost Ksh. 45.00. (Many Gicagi families actually have more than 6 members). The English textbook for Standard 1 cost Ksh. 119 or approximately $2\frac{1}{2}$ days' wages. Few Gicagi parents were able to provide for the school needs of their children. As a result, there was a dearth of teaching-learning resources in Gicagi school. When I asked the parents why they sent their children to school, the reply I often received was: **"guthoma"** {to read/learn}, but there was not much to read in Gicagi school. Many children came to school without any textbooks and with no pencils or paper to write on. Hence, in every lesson, children scrounged for learning resources.

Almost 100% of the children in Gicagi were attending school when I carried out my study; however, the majority of the adult population in Gicagi had very low levels of education. Many older adults, such as grandparents and some of the parents of the Gicagi schoolchildren, had not attended school themselves, while others had dropped out in the primary school or in the early years of secondary school. Many attributed their disadvantaged position to their lack of educational success and to their lack of English language competence. One woman, whose daughter, Wangari, was in Standard 4, put it this way: **"korwo ni ndathomire na menye Githungu kiu onanii ingiri handu. Ndingirathinika uu. Kwi miikarire i thinjo nene muno teno tuikaraga"** {*If I had got an education and known English, I would also be somewhere. I would not be struggling this hard. Some lives, like the ones we lead, require a lot of sacrifice*}.

A number of the Gicagi parents I interviewed had tried schooling, but it had not worked for them, while it had worked for others they knew. For example, Nderi's mother (cited earlier) told me the story of one of her girlfriends in school who had continued with her education and had ended up working as a secretary in the Central Bank in Nairobi: **"na riu arathii na ngari ici njeru"** {*and now she drives the latest cars*}. To the extent that Gicagi parents have seen school work for others, they recognize the potential benefits of schooling for their children. However, school represents personal failure for them. It has left them powerless in relation to those for whom it worked and in dealing with it for their children.

At the same time, the Gicagi people I became acquainted with had positive attitudes toward education. They wanted their children to go to school, get an education, and then leave Gicagi for work in Nairobi and/or other urban areas. Herein lay a contradiction: Gicagi people were subsistence farmers and their lives were tied to the land. They lived monolingual lives and did all right without much use of literacy in their daily lives. That was the life they knew, and they passed on specialized forms of knowledge and values shaped by their life experiences to their children. All the parents I talked to told me they thought it was important for children to learn to farm and for girls to learn to do domestic work. Although most Gicagi parents were sending their children to school, they were also giving them contradictory messages and passing on two sets of values: those based on their lived experiences and those related to their investment in education for their children.

However, few parents were confident that their children would do well in school. They talked about the poor examination results of the local school and saw this as preventing their children from going on to good high schools. At the same time, Gicagi parents were not confident that educational credentials would buy their children social mobility. Another participant in my study, the mother of a boy called Manyeki, who was in Standard 1, put this point to me as follows:

Aria mena mahinya ringi nimekuoya mwana ucio wao makamucariria wira. Makamwandikithia handu tondu ena mbia cia kuhakana handu riu mwana ucio akona wira. A gathii akona wega. No riu utari na mahinya ma mwana waku, no nginya mwana ucio agaikara mucii.

{*Those with means will take that child and look for a job for him/her. They get him/her employed because they have the money to bribe somebody and that child finds a job and does well. But if you do not have the means for your child, that child must stay at home.*}

Indeed, some Gicagi parents saw a risk element in schooling for their children. Again, in the words of Manyeki's mother:

Riu nikurathi uguo. Ukona mundu ni athomire onaongorwo ni kinya form four, ukona e mucii niagire wira riu akorwo ni mucii ucio ona aheo ibuti, ndangiruta. Tondu riu arona ena githomo kia form four ndagiriirwo gukorwo akiruta wira wa mucii. Riu agaikara uguo tondu ona wira wa mucii ndangiruta.

{*That is how it is nowadays. You see somebody has gone to school up to form four and you find he/she is at home. He/she has failed to get a job. Now at home, even if he is given a contract to dig some place, he will not do it because he feels since he has form four education he should not be working at home. So he/she stays just like that because he/she cannot work at home.*}

According to Manyeki's mother, schooling for some Gicagi children leads to disillusionment since they cease to value the way of life and work of their parents, yet what schooling they are able to get does not enable them to enter into other ways of life and work either because it is too limited, compared to that of others, or because their parents lack other resources like connections and/or money to bribe gatekeepers to provide jobs for their children.

From the foregoing discussion, it is clear that some of the age-mates of the parents of Gicagi children used education and an accompanying knowledge of English to move up the socioeconomic ladder and therefore to go and live in neighborhoods of Nairobi such as the one I will describe in the next section. However, it is extremely difficult for the current generation of Gicagi children to make the same transition. This is because the parents' generation was more or less the first generation of educated Africans and therefore did not face competition from children of elite family background. At the same time, there were more opportunities for those with an education since they went into the job market just before and soon after Independence, when many positions in the civil service and elsewhere fell vacant on the departure of colonial officers and when new positions were created. Unfortunately for them, the current generation of Gicagi children has to compete with more privileged children for far fewer opportunities. To make matters worse, as Manyeki's mother explained, because of corruption, educational credentials alone are not enough to get one a job in Kenya. One needs money and/or powerful connections. Gicagi parents and their children have little command of these two resources. In addition to lack of access to the linguistic resources valued in the school, Gicagi children's attendance at school takes place under difficult and sometimes contradictory conditions. Consequently, Gicagi children's attitude to school is ambivalent. The reverse is the case in Park View, the neighborhood I will now go on to describe.

The Park View Community

Park View school and community are situated in one of the more prestigious residential areas of Nairobi. During the colonial era, Park View was a Whites-only area. The only Africans living there were those working as domestic servants for the Whites. Today, upper-middle-class African, European, and Indian families live in Park View.

The Park View community is made up of people from different ethnolinguistic backgrounds. Most of the African members of this community grew up in rural communities like the Gicagi one just described. They grew up speaking an indigenous language and only learned English and Kiswahili in school or, in the case of Kiswahili, through daily use after moving into Nairobi. Broadly speaking, Park View people speak their indigenous languages in their immediate families or with other relatives on visits to their rural areas. In addition, Park View people from the same ethnolinguistic background use their indigenous languages in conversation with one another.

Park View adults speak Kiswahili in two situations: in speaking to their juniors at work and in speaking to those people from ethnolinguistic communities other than their own who they think do not have much education and therefore do not know how to speak English. Such people include the elderly, domestic workers, security guards, shop attendants, market women, and people working on the public transport. English is the language of work for the Park Viewers. English is also the *lingua franca* for Park Viewers from different ethnolinguistic groups. Park Viewers say this is because they do not know Kiswahili well enough and because they are fluent in English and can express themselves better in English. At the same time, Park View parents speak English with their children, especially after the first child goes to an English nursery school and starts to use some English words. Park View children therefore grow up in a multilingual environment and come to school with some experience of bilingualism or trilingualism. Most important, they come to school with English, the language of education and social mobility in Kenya.

English is the language of the school in Park View. This was a Whites-only school in the colonial days. Park View has retained many of the traditions of the British education system, but the most important for our purpose here is the use of the English language. English is the main language for all out-of-class teacher activities and the sole language of the curriculum from Pre-primary. Outside the classrooms, the students speak English, Kiswahili, and Sheng[3] among themselves. As a result, as far as language development in English is concerned, acquisition and use are occurring in a natural fashion with Park View children, as part of everyday living. Therefore, the children are developing a familiarity with the language that allows them to use it unself-consciously. They are therefore becoming fairly fluent speakers of the language. This means that Park View students approach the curriculum from a position of confidence.

At the same time, the work and lifestyle of adult members of the Park View community is literacy-related, and literacy resources such as books, newspapers, and magazines are readily available in their homes. Therefore, unlike Gicagi children, Park View children are exposed to literacy in English, and they encounter a range of literacy practices in their homes. Therefore, in their homes and community and in their school, Park View children are positively positioned in relation to access to English and literacy.

Unlike the adult members of the Gicagi community, Park View adults were, on the whole, successful in school and therefore acquired the necessary educational and English-language resources that enabled them to leave the rural areas for well-paid jobs in the urban areas. Park View community members include high school graduates, people with some years of training, and people with college and even higher education. Most have fairly high incomes from their jobs and/or businesses. In many families, both husband and wife are in paid employment. The men hold managerial or professional jobs, whereas most of the women work as clerks/junior administrators, teachers, nurses, or secretaries. As a result, Park View parents have no problems providing educational resources for their children. At the same time, because of their personal success in school, Park View parents have confidence in dealing with the school on behalf of their children.

Park View people owe their advantaged position to their education, to their structural advantage and historical privileges. The covert and overt messages they pass on to their children about education are clear: "Education is good for you." They themselves succeeded in school, and therefore another message they pass on to their children is: "School success is possible." Indeed, everything points to Park View children succeeding in school, and their parents look to their going to university and taking up professional careers in fields such as medicine, dentistry, and law.

The material resources available to Park Viewers, the symbolic resources such as access to English and literacy, and the noncontradictory messages about school that Park View children receive from their parents and community combine to put Park View children in a positive position in relation to the school.

In the foregoing contrastive account, I have tried to demonstrate that the children from the Gicagi and Park View communities are differentially positioned in relation to access to English and to school literacies. What remains to be seen then is whether these differential positions shape the interactions that take place between teachers and learners in Gicagi and Park View schools and what impact they have on teaching/learning processes, particularly in contexts where teachers have differing views about pedagogy. In the next two sections of this chapter, I will present interactional data from Standard 1 reading lessons in Gicagi and Park View schools to provide my reader with insights into the contrasting educational experiences of Gicagi and Park View children.

EDUCATIONAL EXPERIENCES IN GICAGI AND PARK VIEW SCHOOLS

Learning to Read in Gicagi School

Mrs. Wambaa, the Standard 1 teacher, appeared to have a somewhat behaviorist view of teaching and learning. On one occasion, she explicitly stated this view as she addressed the children in her class:

Na ndakwirire atiriri, hingo ciothe hindi iria urerwo uge undu ukageragia gutumura kanua gaku ukauga ni tondo waga kuuga ruciu ndukamenya undu ucio. No wahingura kanua gaku uge niuriuririkanaga.

{I told you that each time you are told to say something, you should try to open your mouth and say because if you do not say, tomorrow you will not know that thing. But if you open your mouth and say, you will be remembering it.}

According to Mrs. Wambaa, "knowing" is remembering discrete pieces of information that the teacher passes on to the students, and the only way for the students to ensure that they will remember is to say the same thing over and over again. Consequently, in all the lessons I observed, she relied on a "pattern and drill" approach to teaching and learning. She had the children repeat over and over again words or phrases that she wanted them to learn. Extract 1 below is an example of how Mrs. Wambaa's pattern-and-drill approach was enacted in a reading lesson in English.

The reading text for the day was taken from the book *Hello, Children*, which was Book One in the *Progressive Peak English Course*. The reading texts in the book mainly described the activities of a family of five: Mr. Kamau, the father; Mrs. Kamau, the mother; and the children, Tom and Mary and the baby. The book extended an audiolingual approach to second-language learning to early reading activities. This was evident in the way the same names and the same sentence constructions appeared over and over again in the different sections of the book.

Mrs. Wambaa drew the learners' attention to page 17 of this book. The words "riding," "bean-bag" and "reading" were presented in a box at the top of the page. The first letter "i" in the word "riding" was highlighted by the use of the color black. The rest of the letters in this word were in red. In the words "bean-bag" and "reading," the letters "e" and "a" were highlighted in blue, while the rest of the words were in black and red respectively. The focus of the words in the box was thus on the contrasting sounds associated with the graphemes "i" and "ea." The words "riding" and "bean-bag" had appeared on previous pages, but the word "reading" had not.

Below the box were two balloons containing the words spoken by the two children, Tom and Mary. Tom was seated on a stool on the left, and Mary was seated on a stool on the right. Tom was saying, "I'm reading a book," and Mary was saying, "I'm reading a book too." These images and this text were followed by the sentences that were set in the middle of the page: "Tom has a book and Mary has a book too," "Tom is reading his book and Mary is reading her book," and "Tom's book is green and Mary's book is green too." The three words highlighted in the box and these three sentences constituted the principal reading text for the lesson.

The learners could not make sense of this reading text. They responded to the activity with enthusiasm to begin with. The enthusiasm seemed to derive more from the opportunity afforded to them to shout out loud the unfamiliar English sounds. Many of the children were not even looking at the reading text as they chanted. However, after a while, their enthusiasm waned, and some children only participated when Mrs. Wambaa was watching them. I have included in Extract 1 a fairly long extract from this lesson to illustrate the ritualized nature of the exchanges that took place around this text.

Extract 1

T	:	So let us first of all read the new word. The new words are on page seventeen. **Na uthikiririe riu.** {*and you listen now*}. Okay, the first word here is ride. Say riding.
SS	:	Riding.
T	:	Riding.
SS	:	Riding.
T	:	Again.
SS	:	Riding.
T	:	Again.
SS	:	Riding.
T	:	Once again.
SS	:	Riding.
T	:	Okay. Now the second word is bean-bag. Say bean-bag.
SS	:	Bean-bag.
T	:	Again.
SS	:	Bean-bag.
T	:	Bean-bag.
SS	:	Bean-bag.
T	:	Bean-bag.
SS	:	Bean-bag.
T	:	Bean-bag.
SS	:	Bean-bag.
T	:	Again.
SS	:	Bean-bag.
T	:	Spell the word bean-bag.
T&SS	:	B E A N B A G bean-bag [reading the spelling from the book].
T	:	Bean-bag.
SS	:	Bean-bag.
T	:	Bean-bag.
SS	:	Bean-bag.
T	:	Now, the next word is reading. Say reading.
SS	:	Reading.
T	:	Again.
SS	:	Reading.
T	:	Reading.
SS	:	Reading.
T	:	Again.
SS	:	Reading.
T	:	Again.
SS	:	Reading.
T	:	Reading.
SS	:	Reading.

T	:	The first words are in the box. The three words are in the box and the first word is riding. Say riding.
SS	:	Riding.
T	:	Riding.
T	:	Again.
SS	:	Riding.

[At this point, Mrs. Wambaa stopped to tell the children to look at the book as they read.]

T	:	Riding.
SS	:	Riding.
T	:	Riding.
SS	:	Riding.
T	:	Bean-bag.
SS	:	Bean-bag.
T	:	Bean-bag.
SS	:	Bean-bag.
T	:	Reading.
SS	:	Reading.
T	:	Reading.
SS	:	Reading.

[The reading then proceeded to the sentences.]

T	:	Tom has a book and Mary has a book too.
T&SS	:	Tom has a book and Mary has a book too.
T	:	Tom has a book and Mary has a book too.
SS&T	:	Tom has a book and Mary has a book too.
T	:	Tom has a book and Mary has a book too.
SS&T	:	Tom has a book and Mary has a book too.
T	:	Again.
SS&T	:	Tom has a book and Mary has a book too.

The class was divided into three groups: the lion group, the leopard group, and the zebra group. Mrs. Wambaa then asked the different groups to read the sentence, after which she asked individual children to read. Those who read correctly were complimented and applauded. When children could not read, the others laughed at them. Mrs. Wambaa then asked the whole class to read the same sentences all over again, as in Extract 2.

Extract 2

T	:	...Okay everybody read...Tom has a book and Mary has a book too. Everybody read.
SS	:	Tom has a book and Mary has a book too.
T	:	Yes.... Let's go to the next line. Tom is reading his book and Mary is reading her book. We have got HIS and HERS. His is for Tom and hers is for Mary. His is for Tom and hers is for

T&S	:	Mary.
T	:	Tom is reading his book and Mary is reading her book. Now read
SS	:	Tom has....
T	:	Tom is reading his book.
SS&T	:	Tom is reading his book.
T	:	and Mary is reading her book.
S&T	:	And Mary is reading her book.
T	:	**Raini iyo ina kahinya no tihinya munene kwoguo ngwenda uthikiririe niguo uhote guthomera wiwiki.** {*That line is a little hard but not very hard so I want you to listen so that you can read for me on your own.*} Tom is reading his book. Read up to there.
T&SS	:	Tom is reading hi book.
T	:	Tom is reading HIS book
SS	:	Tom is
T [Joins in]		reading his book
T	:	Again.
SS	:	Tom is
T [Joins in]		reading his book
T	:	Tom is reading his book.
SS	:	Tom is reading his book.
T	:	Tom is reading his book.
SS	:	Tom is reading his book
T [Joins in]		reading his book.
T	:	Again
SS	:	Tom is reading his book
T [Joins in]		reading his book and Mary is reading her book
SS	:	and.
T [Joins in]	:	Mary is reading her book...Okay...Tom is reading his book and Mary is reading her book.
SS&T	:	Tom is reading his book and Mary is reading her book.
T	:	Tom is reading his book and Mary is reading her book.
SS&T	:	Tom is reading his book and Mary is reading her book.

The reading aloud was then organized in groups, where again there was a lot of repeating after the teacher. Problems arose with *his* and *her*. However, Mrs. Wambaa did not draw the children's attention to the differences in the spellings of these words as they read them aloud. The children concentrated on listening and repeating after her, and to that extent it looked as if Mrs. Wambaa was teaching them to repeat what they heard rather than to sound out what they saw on the page. The children got rather confused by the two words.

After the reading in groups, Mrs. Wambaa asked for volunteers to read the next sentence in the book. A few children volunteered. She then got the whole class to read the new sentence after her two more times, as shown in Extract 3.

Extract 3

T	:	Okay, everybody read, Tom's book is green and Mary's book is green too
SS&T	:	Tom's book is green and Mary's book is green too
T	:	Tom's book is green and Mary's book is green too
SS	:	Tom's book is green and Mary's book is green too

Mrs. Wambaa then got the children to read the three keywords of the lesson aloud in chorus after. She did this twice and then moved on to rehearse with them the sentences they had encountered in the reading passage. This brief exchange is captured in Extract 4:

Extract 4

T	:	Riding
SS	:	Riding
T	:	Riding
SS	:	Riding
T	:	Bean-bag
SS	:	Bean-bag
T	:	Bean-bag
SS	:	Bean-bag
T	:	Reading
SS	:	Reading
T	:	Reading
SS	:	Reading
T	:	Tom has a book and Mary has a book too
T&SS	:	Tom has a book and Mary has a book too
T	:	Tom is reading his book
SS	:	Tom is reading his book
T (Joins in)	:	reading his book
T	:	and Mary is reading her book
SS	:	and Mary is reading her book
T (Joins in)	:	reading her book
T	:	Tom's book is green
S	:	Tom book is green
T	:	Tom's book is green
SS	:	Tom's book is green
T (Joins in)	:	book is green
T	:	And Mary's book is green too
SS&T	:	And Mary's book is green too

At the end of the lesson, Mrs. Wambaa told the children to go home and practice reading the text aloud over and over again. They were advised to do this in the evening and over the weekend so that they could read it for her the following Monday with no effort.

This is how Gicagi children were learning how to read, by repeating individual words and sentences in chorus after the teacher from texts they barely understood and from texts that had little relevance to their lives. In every reading lesson, Mrs. Wambaa got the children to repeat bits of the textbook several times after her. Indeed, the children did not need to look at what was being read to participate in the reading and many of them did not, either because they did not have the textbook or because they did not bother to look at the book. Mrs. Wambaa had to constantly remind them to look at their books. On their part, the children showed their resistance to this kind of teaching and learning activity by quietly playing with their friends, by refusing to participate in the chanting when Mrs. Wambaa was not looking, and by injecting fun in the responses. When Mrs. Wambaa was looking, they would repeat each successive response louder than the one before and by the third and fourth responses, they would be shouting at the top of their voices.

Learning to Read in Park View School

Mrs. Mwangi was the Standard 1 teacher in Park View. I would describe Mrs. Mwangi's approach to teaching and learning as being more interactive and scaffolding than that of Mrs. Wambaa. This seemed to stem from a commitment to a view of children as active, reflective learners. Her ideas about teaching and learning were evident in the things Mrs. Mwangi told the children and in her day-to-day classroom practice. Mrs. Mwangi often told the children to think about what they were doing so that they would understand and learn. In one lesson, she said, "If I had a way, I would stick a needle with all the knowledge in your head, but I can only teach you the ways of learning."

Here, she was representing knowledge to the children as something that learners need to know how to acquire, not as something that some knowing person passes on ready-made to them. Mrs Mwangi clearly believed that for children to understand, they must be intellectually engaged. For example, in one English lesson, she made the following observation to the children about reading for meaning: "Another important thing about language is that you must understand what you read. You read those words for me, do you know their meaning?"

The students in her class were occasionally involved in reading aloud in chorus, but she discouraged mindless choral responses and chanting, as in Extract 5.

Extract 5

T	:	Read for me. Touch the word.
SS	:	If you blow into a balloon, the air goes inside.
T	:	Read again.
SS	:	If you blow into a balloon, the air goes inside.
T	:	Again.
SS	:	[Shouting] If you blow into a balloon, the air goes inside.
T	:	[Very cross] Don't shout. I know why I am asking you to read many times. There is a type of writing which is darker [i.e., on the word air]. That means it is very important.

Here, Mrs. Mwangi's reason for asking the children to read the same thing again and again was to draw their attention to the different characteristics of the printed words on the page and to the use of bold print for highlighting words. Because she wanted to get them to understand the meanings associated with these distinctions, she got very cross when the children started to chant louder and louder without thinking about what they were doing.

In teaching reading, Mrs. Mwangi employed a phonic approach but, again, she attempted to make this as interactive as possible and checked from time to time on the children's understanding. She started the reading lessons by telling the children what sound they were going to focus on. She then wrote the graphic symbol(s) for the sound on the blackboard and asked the children to read after her once or twice. After this, she asked the children to give her examples of words that had that sound. When the children supplied words, they were asked to spell them out loud while she wrote them on the blackboard. In most of the reading lessons I observed, the children came up with a lot of words and Mrs. Mwangi wrote them all on the blackboard. Sometimes, she asked the children to make sentences with the words that came up or even questions, using interrogative forms like "whose," "when," "where." If a word came up that Mrs. Mwangi thought might be difficult for the children, she dealt with it by asking the class to say what it meant or by prompting. For example, in one lesson, when she was eliciting words with the diphthong / oi / at the end, the word "employ" came up. She proceeded as shown in Extract 6.

Extract 6

S	:	Employ.
T	:	Employ. Spell it for me.
S	:	E M P L O Y
T	:	Good. Employ. What is to employ somebody?
S	:	To get somebody to do some work.
T	:	With payment or without payment?
SS	:	With payment.

At the end of this exchange, Mrs. Mwangi asked the children to write the words in their reading exercise books and to read them silently to themselves. She then sat at her table and began working with the children individually as they brought their reading books to her for marking. The children were expected to work individually on various exercises from different textbooks. When the children came to Mrs. Mwangi asking her how to do the various exercises, she encouraged them to read the instructions in the book. Take Extract 7 as an example:

Extract 7

T   :   Read what the teacher is saying. That line [the instructions] is the teacher telling you what to do, so read and do what the teacher is saying.

Consequently, in the reading lessons in Park View, the children were reading for different purposes and engaging in purposeful activities. This would help them read in other contexts beyond the classroom. The children also got exposed to a wide range of vocabulary and got used to dealing with real texts. The children were clearly being intellectually challenged. The children also got exposed to a wide range of exercises and did many exercises on their own. They were being introduced to working on their own and taking responsibility for their work. All these things were important in preparing students for the heavily examination-oriented system that required them to study and do a lot of work on their own in preparation for the examinations by which their academic success would be judged.

THE IMPLICATIONS OF THESE CONTRASTING EXPERIENCES AT PRIMARY SCHOOL

In the foregoing description of the teaching-learning processes in Gicagi and Park View Standard 1 English reading lessons, I have illustrated the differences between the early reading experiences of learners in Gicagi and Park View primary schools. While the Gicagi children were engaged in limited, repetitive classroom routines, Park View children had relatively challenging reading lessons and were encouraged to work alone and to engage in a range of purposeful activities. I would like to argue that these differential educational treatments were, in part, due to the teachers' perceptions of the linguistic and cultural resources that the children brought to school.

A combination of factors led Mrs. Wambaa, the teacher in Gicagi school, to construct the reading lesson as she did. Among these factors were her teacher training and her own experience as a student. However, her teaching and learning approach was also shaped by her perception of the children and the values that she associated with English. Because the Gicagi children did not have English as a resource as part of their communicative repertoire on entering school, they were seen as lacking in what it takes to be good students.

In Gicagi school, the children's lack of English was indeed a major concern for the teachers. The headmaster identified the children's lack of English on arrival in school as a problem, during the interview I conducted with him. He said,

> **Guku thina ungi tukoragwo naguo ni wa** language. Especially **kuria** lower **tondu ciaana itikoragwo ciui Githungu. Mangikamenya matuike ati nimara**understand **na makahota gu**communicate **ni maikaraga muno.**

> *{Language is another problem we have here especially in lower [lower primary] because the children come without any knowledge of English. They take a long time before they can understand and communicate [in English]}.*

Mrs. Wambaa often said to me: **"Aya me thina muno. Matiguaga. Matinyitaga narua"** *{these ones [children] pose real problems. They do not understand. They do not learn easily}.* Mrs. Wambaa explained that she therefore had to do the same thing over and over again so that the children would learn. The result of the repetitious nature of the routines in her classroom was that very little curriculum content was covered. At the same time, the children soon lost interest in what was going on and did not become intellectually engaged in the learning since all that was required of them was to repeat what the teacher had just said. With this experience of primary schooling behind them, Gicagi children were not likely to achieve academic success. Indeed, Gicagi school children performed poorly overall in national examinations.

However, in Park View, the children were not seen as having any problems. Park View teachers did not see themselves as working in a problematic situation. Unlike Gicagi teachers, they did not volunteer comments on their students' learning problems. In fact, Park View teachers had only positive things to say about their students. Talking about what the other teachers had told her when she came to Park View, Mrs. Ngoma, the Standard 4 teacher, said, "The teachers told me that the children in this school are very clever and that they don't need much teaching. All they need is for you to show them how to do something and they will do it."

Her own experience with the children had proved the other teachers right. She said, "It is true. These children are very clever. . . . These children are clever and they do their work. They learn very quickly and even if you test them on things that you did long ago, they pass."

On one occasion, Mrs. Mwangi said to me, **"Ici ni ciana njugi muno. Mandutithagia wira muingi muno tondu niogi muno"** {*These are very clever children. They make me work very hard because they are very clever*}. She made other similar comments on other occasions.

The broader point I want to draw out here is that schools in Kenya define children on the basis of the linguistic and cultural resources that they bring from home. Because of the mismatch between the language and the cultural practices of the school and the language and cultural background of Gicagi children, the school defines Gicagi children as deficient in the linguistic and intellectual attributes required for academic success. In line with that definition, the school offers Gicagi children limited and limiting educational experiences.

Because English is the legitimate language within the Kenyan education system, children's knowledge of English and their ability to speak and write it has become the norm on which teachers' expectations are based. Gicagi children have no access to English and therefore fail to meet this criterion. The school's response is to treat the children as non-knowers. Teachers are seen as the only source of legitimate school knowledge, which they pass on to the children in small doses. Owing to the limiting and limited educational experiences they have, few Gicagi children are likely to attain academic success. They are therefore unlikely to fulfil their parents' dreams of social mobility. The reverse is true for Park View children.

TRANSCRIPTION CONVENTIONS

The transcription conventions I have adopted in this paper are: bold for all Gikuyu words; capital letters for all Kiswahili words, for sudden increase in volume, and when words are being spelled out; and regular typeface for all English words. Translations are within {} brackets in italics. T=teacher; S=student; SS=students; SS&T=students and teacher.

NOTES

1. The research on which this chapter is based was carried out as part of my doctoral studies at the Ontario Institute for Studies in Education, University of Toronto, Canada. It was supported by a full scholarship awarded by the International Development Research Center.

2. For the sake of anonymity, Gicagi and Park View are pseudonyms, as are all personal names in the chapter.

3. Sheng is an urban youth language that is characterized by frequent codeswitching between English and Kiswahili and by code-mixing. Sheng incorporates lexis and grammatical structures from English, Kiswahili, and indigenous languages.

REFERENCES

Abdulaziz, M. H. (1982). Patterns of language acquisition and use in Kenya: Rural-urban differences. *International Journal of the Sociology of Language, 34*, 95–120.

Bourdieu, P. (1977). The economics of linguistic exchanges. *Social Science Information 16(6)*, 645–668.

Bourdieu, P., and Passeron, J. (1977). *Reproduction in education, society and culture*. London: Sage Publications.

Giddens, A. (1984). *The constitution of society: Outline of the theory of structuration*. Berkeley: University of California Press.

Goke-Pariola, A. (1993). Language and symbolic power: Bourdieu and the legacy of Euro-American colonialism in an African society. *Language & Communication, 13(3)*, 219–234.

Gorman, T. P. (1974). The development of language policy in Kenya with particular reference to the educational system. In W. H. Whiteley (Ed.), *Language in Kenya* (pp. 397–454). Nairobi: Oxford University Press.

Heller, M. (1996). Legitimate language in a multilingual school. *Linguistics and Education 8(2)*: 139–157.

Mazrui, A. (1975). *The political sociology of the English language: An African perspective*. The Hague: Mouton.

Ministry of Education. (1987). *Education in Kenya*. Information handbook. Nairobi: Jomo Kenyatta Foundation.

Ministry of Education. (1994). *Primary education syllabus*, Vol. 1. Nairobi: Kenya Literature Bureau.

Ngugi wa Thiong'o. (1985, April–June). The language of African literature. *New Left Review*, 109–127.

Ngugi wa Thiong'o. (1981). *Writers in politics: Essays*. London: Heinemann.

Ogbu, J. (1981). School ethnography: A multilevel approach. *Anthropology and Education Quarterly 12(1)*, 3–29.

Ogbu, J. (1987). Variability in minority school performance: A problem in search of an explanation. *Anthropology and Education Quarterly, 18(4)*, 312–334.

Sheffield, L. (1973). *Education in the Republic of Kenya*. Washington: U.S. Government Printing Office.

Weeks, S. (1967). *Divergence in educational development: The case of Kenya and Uganda*. New York: Teachers College Press.

5

The Contradictions of Teaching Bilingually in Postcolonial Burundi: From <u>Nyakatsi</u> to *Maisons en Étages*

Lin Ndayipfukamiye

INTRODUCTION

In this chapter, I focus on data gathered as part of a wider study of bilingual classroom discourse carried out in primary schools in Burundi in 1991 (Ndayipfukamiye 1993, 1994). The data consists of teacher/learner interactions during French language classes audiorecorded in two schools: one in an urban setting and one in a rural school. The two languages used in these classes were Kirundi and French; as I will show, the languages are associated with very different social and cultural values in Burundian society.

During these French language lessons, both the teachers and the students codeswitched between Kirundi and French. Codeswitching practices such as these, at the local level of lessons, need to be understood with reference to relationships and ideological forces operating at a broader societal level. The primary function of the codeswitching was to provide a means of resolving the immediate communicative difficulties encountered by the teachers and students, difficulties that stemmed from the use of French as a medium of instruction. Codeswitching was thus a resource for managing the local communicative demands of the classroom situation but, as in some of the other postcolonial contexts described in this volume, it also served to reinforce the social and linguistic order in Burundi society.

This chapter has three main parts: In the first part, I sketch the context in which my study was carried out; in the second part, I give a brief description of the sociolinguistic situation in Burundi, focusing in particular on the values assigned to French and to Kirundi in educational circles; and, in the third part, I will provide an account of the ways in which two teachers used codeswitching in their French language lessons to co-construct knowledge with the learners. The focus of the lessons was on vocabulary relating to the construction of different types of buildings in Burundi: The first type of building was the traditional dwellings typically found in villages in the rural areas of Burundi that have **nyakatsi** 'thatched roofs'; the second type of building was *maisons en étages* 'houses with more than one floor.' This second type is mostly found in urban environments.

I focus on two samples of classroom discourse in which the teachers are discussing **nyakatsi**: One sample is from a French lesson in the urban school and one from the rural school. My account will contrast the ways in which urban and rural perspectives on the topic are constructed in the bilingual interactions of the teachers and learners. I then go on to look at the way in which the urban phenomenon of *maisons en étages* is taken up in the bilingual discourse of the teacher in the rural class. In all three of these lessons, the teachers codeswitched frequently in order to facilitate the learners' access to the curriculum content. But their codeswitching also echoed their concern about complying with the centrally imposed educational policy of employing French as a medium of instruction.

THE CONTEXT FOR THE STUDY

Kirundi is spoken by most of the population of Burundi (approximately 6 million people in a territory covering 28,000 square kilometers). It is the national and official language along with French, though French is used as an official language in most institutional contexts.

When I carried out the research on which this chapter is based, students in government schools were taught in Kirundi during the first four years of primary school. They were then taught in French, starting with grade 5. Up to that level, French was taught as a subject for two years, in grades 3 and 4. The extracts that I am focusing on here are instances of bilingual discourse audiorecorded in two grade 5 classes:

one class in a rural school and one class in an urban school. The working conditions of the teachers and learners in these two schools were quite different. The urban classroom was relatively well off with regard to infrastructure and teaching materials. Although the number of students who attended lessons in the two daily shifts was relatively high (some 50 students), there was enough room to move around and to store materials. The classroom in the rural area had much more difficult working conditions. Building materials, cement, glass, and iron sheets, had been in short supply at the moment of construction; for example, there was just a corrugated iron roof, which increased the noise level when there were heavy downpours of rain.

Each class that I observed was the responsibility of one teacher. Each of the two teachers had had five years of secondary school education, which included a two-year teacher-training program. Regular in-service training sessions were organized for teacher trainees during the summer holidays. The teacher in the urban class had had more than ten years' teaching experience, while the one in the rural class had had six.

There were differences between students relating to their socioeconomic backgrounds. The students in the urban school were on the whole much younger than their counterparts in the rural schools; they started school younger and had repeated the school years less often. The grade 5 students in the urban school had parents whose backgrounds were different from those of the parents of the students in the rural school. These parents were either civil servants (people who worked for the government, the army, or paragovernmental agencies) or people in small businesses (self-employed people or small traders). In the rural school, most of the parents were peasants working on small farms. The students in the urban and rural schools were oriented to different social and cultural worlds. However, in the classroom, this polarization was blurred by obvious commonalities: the same languages, French and Kirundi, were being used to convey the same curriculum content, which was couched in centrally produced learning materials. Moreover, students and teachers in both the rural and urban schools were pursuing the same agenda: overcoming curriculum hurdles that blocked their way to socioeconomic mobility.

EDUCATION AND LANGUAGE VALUES IN BURUNDI

Language and Educational Policy

Bourdieu and Passeron (1970) and Bourdieu (1979, 1982) have argued that schools play a central role as agencies for the legitimation of the cultural capital of dominant groups. This is primarily achieved through the mechanisms of certification and reward that underpin education systems. In Burundi, a small French-speaking elite ensures that the school plays an important role in the legitimization of the dominant form of linguistic capital, French. They are able to do so because of the control they exert over state structures.

Views about Language Policy

When I carried out this study in Burundi in 1991, four contradictory views about language were being articulated by teachers, educational administrators, and commentators on educational policy. The first three of these four views legitimized the continued dominance of French within education:

1. Burundi needs an international language to achieve "modern" development.
2. Kirundi is not suitable for teaching science and technology.
3. Functional bilingualism needs to be established between Kirundi and French.
4. Kirundi is essential to the project of nation-building

Recent survey evidence from Burundi provides insights into teachers' views about language policies. Sabushimike-Ndayizeye (1992) carried out a survey of primary school teachers and drew attention to the contradictions implicit in the teachers' responses. As she put it:

> *Parmi ces aspects contradictoires, les enseignants insistent sur l'option politique de Kirundisation et la passation du concours national en Français, l'absence d'une orthographie officielle du Kirundi, l'enseignement des matières scientifiques et techniques en Kirundi qui ne facilite pas les acquisitions des élèves.* (Sabushimike-Ndayizeye 1992, 19)

> One of these contradictory aspects is the teachers' insistence on the political option of Kirundisation and [at the same time] on passing the secondary entrance examination in French, on the absence of an official Kirundi orthography, on [the claim that] the teaching of scientific and technical subjects in Kirundi does not facilitate students' learning.

In a colloquium on "Education in Burundi" (held in Bujumbura, the capital, in August 1989), participants deplored the absence of an official Kirundi orthography and recommended the creation of an academy that would be charged with initiating, centralizing, and coordinating research on the Kirundi language. While the recommendation was a positive one—the establishment of a National Language Academy is long overdue—it also has to be said that behind the recommendation lay the assumption that Kirundi is not yet ready to be used for educational purposes, that it needs "language treatment" (in the terminology of language planners) in a "laboratory" environment away from the mainstream of language use until it is ready for general use. In the discourse of a number of the participants at this colloquium, the relationship between Kirundi and French was characterized in terms of complementarity. In fact, it is often emphasized in debates within the public arena in Burundi that there is no competition or conflict between the two languages. Educational experts argue that both languages have official recognition and are ascribed complementary functions:

> *Le Kirundi est la langue nationale et officielle, le Français est la langue officielle, langue de travail et d'ouverture sur le monde. La complémentarité des deux instruments de communication est donc garantie officiellement.* (ANADIL 1986, 4)

> Kirundi is the national and official language, French is the official language, the language of work and access to the world. Complementarity between the two means of communication is thus guaranteed officially.

Another commonly expressed view is that this complementarity actually contributes to the improvement of the quality of education provided in Burundian schools:

> *Les rapports entre la langue nationale et le français ne sont pas en termes de choix exclusifs ni de conflit, mais de complémentarité active devant conduire à une amélioration qualitative du système éducatif fondé sur un enrichissement mutuel des cultures.* (ANADIL 1986, 4)

> The relationships between the national language and French are not to be seen in terms of exclusive or conflictual choices, but in terms of active complementarity leading to a qualitative improvement of the educational system based on a mutual enrichment of cultures.

Contradictions within the Language Policy and Curricular Guidelines

The contradictions in the language and educational policies implemented in Burundi result from the fact that policymakers do not take stock of classroom realities when they formulate policies. The educational objectives and teaching methods proposed are often unrealistic. The levels of achievement expected are unattainable given the conditions in which teaching and learning take place. Codeswitching is not officially acknowledged, yet it is an unavoidable reality in lessons in

Burundi primary schools, particularly in grade 5, the year in which students first make the transition from Kirundi-medium to French-medium instruction. All is done as if the lessons were conducted solely in French, as prescribed in curriculum guidelines.

Another feature of educational practice in Burundi is that the status and roles of Kirundi and French are blurred in ways that ultimately benefit French. Curricular guidelines are skillfully formulated. Precedence is given to the French language without overtly confronting the advocates of Kirundisation policy. The guidelines reflect the subtle accommodating practices of those who formulate them. Such practices ensure that the contradictory nature of the language education policy is not readily detected. The consequence is that Kirundi is placed in a secondary position, where it is seen merely as a means of facilitating the transition to the use of French for the transmission of knowledge across the curriculum.

Many program designers recognize that the existence of Kirundi as the main national language presents a considerable advantage. The 1973 education reform built on this advantage by stipulating that Kirundi should be the main language taught in primary schools and the medium used to teach all the subjects (Eisemon et al. 1989). The best course of action should then have been to translate these recommendations into reality instead of hesitating, double-talking, and eventually reversing the Kirundisation policy.

In 1991, the curricular guidelines noted that, among other things, the teachers should tap the learners' personal experience, ensure their active participation in learning events, and enhance the communicative use of the French language. These objectives are unrealistic given the sociolinguistic situation in Burundi. The authors of these guidelines seem to have been ignoring the fact that the learners' first experiences of the world had been through the medium of Kirundi and that their learning was still being consolidated through this language. Therefore, the best way to tap their experiences was through the use of the mother tongue, not through French, no matter how hard the teachers tried.

Student participation is now seen by educators around the world as crucial to effective language learning. However, that is difficult to achieve in Burundi primary school classes. There are far too many students in each class for language practice to be organized in a useful way. Teaching aids are inadequate and, because of the pressures stemming from the examination system, French-language lessons accord too much emphasis to the grammatical structure of language and vocabulary acquisition. The communicative use of the French language cannot be achieved in these circumstances.

The establishing of links between classroom activities and the worlds of experience beyond the local school is also made very difficult by the centralizing nature of the curriculum. In particular, the curriculum fails to take account of the differences between rural and urban learning contexts. As a result, the bias in favor of the French language is pervasive in the curriculum. To start with, the curriculum objectives are written in French. There is no equivalent booklet in Kirundi and no bilingual version. Less space is devoted in the statements of curriculum objectives to topics and activities associated with the teaching of Kirundi than to those recommended for French: just two pages as opposed to six. Moreover, as shown the following chart, the amount of time allocated to the two languages in the school time table is not balanced.

Hours devoted to each language per week

Grades:	one	two	three	four	five	six
Kirundi	10	10	7	5	4	4
French	10	11	12	12	13	13

The views and practices that I have described reveal a clear weighting in favor of French. Within the education system in Burundi, French is seen as a more important language, worth more time and investment than Kirundi. While positive views *are* expressed about both languages, the use of French actually predominates in day-to-day educational practice. This asymmetry is ideologically sustained and ultimately serves the interests of the French-speaking elite.

CONSTRUCTING KNOWLEDGE BILINGUALLY: NYAKATSI AND *MAISONS EN ÉTAGES*

I have taken three extracts from lessons by the two teachers: the one in the urban class and the one in the rural class. The lessons were about different types of buildings and the ways they are constructed. The focus of two of the lessons was on the building of traditional houses (with thatched roofs or **nyakatsi**) in rural areas and on the construction of different sections of the houses. The focus of the third lesson was on the construction of houses in urban areas: houses with more than one story (*maisons en étages*). The extracts illustrate the ways in which new items of French vocabulary and culturally specific curriculum contents were discussed bilingually.

The Content and Vocabulary of French Lessons

When this study was being carried out, curriculum and textbook designers in Burundi had been trying to place the teaching of vocabulary in French classes in a wider social context. In the lessons discussed here, the curriculum content was clearly influenced by a growing awareness about the environment and by a campaign about forest conservation that had been going on in Burundi. But, as the classroom data below reveals, there were constraints on the extent to which the target language could be used to refer to wider social and environmental issues.

Constraints on the Sole Use of the Target Language

The two teachers in the classes I observed were unable to make sole use of the target language. They codeswitched frequently between French and Kirundi. A close analysis of their codeswitching shows that code contrast was being used to distinguish talk about the lesson content and learner-oriented talk addressed to the learners that refers to their experience beyond the school. Extract 1 was recorded during a lesson led by the teacher in the urban school (Teacher A); Extracts 2 and 3 were recorded in a class in the rural school (Teacher B). The lesson is about Nyakatsi roofing.

Extract 1 (Teacher A).

T: *on dit qu'on prend ses feuilles pour faire des . pour faire les toits .. vous avez été à l'intérieur?* **hanyuma hari ivyo bariko barwaganya vyitwa** *hein. donc* **eh ubu biriko birahera mugabo kera ugiye wasanga inzu zose zisakaje ivyatsi . ivyatsi . hamwe wasanga ari ubgatsi vyo mw ishamba . ahandi ugasanga ari ubgatsi?**

P: **ari ibihubahuba.**

T: **ibihubahuba** . *par exemple* . **canke?**

P: **ibibabi**

T: **ibibabi vy ibitoke . vy ibitoke. ariko ubu kenshi iyo** ( ) *vous voyez qu'on n'utilise plus les feuilles . de . de quoi?* **iyo badafashe birya bintu bashobora gufata**

T: it is said that its leaves [the leaves of a tree] are used to cover roofs . have you already been in the countryside? **there is a practice that is being combated called thatched roofing** er . and so . **the practice is now receding but in the past all the houses were covered in thatch . thatch . it was forest foliage and in other instances what could you find?**

P: **there were banana leaves**

T: **banana leaves** for example . **or?**

P: **leaves**

T: **banana leaves but now you often get** ( ) you see they no longer use leaves . which leaves? **if they do not use leaves they could do** like in Zaire for example **you've** nko muri *Zaire par exemple* . mwarigeze kubi bona muri *film* . mu muri *télévision* . hariho ahantu bafata ibibabi ibintuze vy imyembe bagakoresha bagasakaz inzu . bagashira ku nzu . rero urumva ko badafise ibitoke badafise ivyatsi vyo mw ishamba . vya vyatsi vy imikenke. arik urumva barashobora kubikoresha {*pauses and clears her voice*} *on prend ses fruit*s

seen some time back in a film on the television there are places where they use mango tree leaves to cover houses . it is because they don't have banana leaves . or forest foliage . they then use mango tree leaves {*pauses and clears her voice*} they take its fruits

Extract 2 (Teacher B)

T: *la majorité des maisons portent des toits hein . en paille . compréhensible? bon* ... izo nzu ziba zisakajwe n iki ? . . har akajambo baharay ubu . ic ari ico cose bakunda kuvuga ngw iki ikintu cose *qui n'est pas* ... *la mode actuellement* . bavuga ngo nyakatsi nyakatsi . no kw iradiyo ngo turwanye nyakatsi . n ibikoko biri mu mazi . muramaze kuvyumva . ntimwiyumvire ngo n abantu bagize nte . baba basiganye . kubera ivyatsi biba vyaboreye hejuru . ibikogoshi bigakorokera mu ki . mu mazi . *ainsi de suite. la paille. en général* bavuga ko ari ivyakatsi . *n'est ce pas* . ivyatsi *la paille*

T: most houses have roofs . right? thatched ones . understandable? right . how are those houses covered? there is a popular word they use nowadays to refer to something which is not in fashion at the moment they say thatched roofs, thatched roofs, even on the radio, they say "let's fight thatched roofs". even insects in the water disapprove of nyakatsi roofing . have you already heard that? don't think it's [just] people who . who are discussing [it] . because the thatch has gone rotten on the roof . in general insects fall into . into drinking water . and so on . thatch .generally speaking . thatch means foliage, doesn't it? thatch thatch

In Extracts 1 and 2, both Teacher A (the teacher in the urban area) and Teacher B (the teacher in the rural school) codeswitched frequently between French and Kirundi while they were explaining one particular aspect of traditional housebuilding practices: the use of **nyakatsi** 'thatched roofing'. **Nyakatsi** has been used for centuries in Burundi instead of tiles or corrugated-iron sheets. The teachers were discussing a cultural practice associated with rural life in classes where the main purpose was to teach French vocabulary. The teachers alternated between Kirundi and French throughout this part of the lesson.

Both teachers began by reporting the textbook information in French. They then addressed the pupils in French. Teacher A inquired about the students' experience. Teacher B checked on the students' understanding. In both extracts, the teachers then went on to comment in Kirundi on the information given in the textbook. They talked about the traditional practice of covering houses with thatch, using the term **nyakatsi** (or the morphological variant **ivyatsi**). The use of this term was interesting because of the negative connotations it had in public discourse in Burundi at that time: a vigorous campaign against covering houses with thatching was under way.

The two teachers also used Kirundi to help the learners to understand the French word *paille* 'straw or thatching'. They did this in different ways. Teacher A realized that some explanation was needed: The statement in the textbook referred to a way of constructing houses that was remote from the experience of students in the city. She mentioned the various types of foliage used to cover roofs, including the mango tree leaves used in Zaire. She referred to a television documentary on different uses of tree leaves that some of the children had seen. In the urban context, the students had had less direct experience of the use of thatching; the practice is still widespread in rural areas. Teacher B contextualized the lexical item *paille* 'thatching' in a different way. He made reference to the frequent messages broadcast on the radio in Burundi at that time with the purpose of discouraging the use of thatch in building rural houses. He referred indirectly to sketches on the radio in which animal characters criticized those who build **nyakatsi** 'thatched roofs,' drawing attention to the fact that insects drop from thatched roofs into drinking water.

Teacher B also provided the French equivalents of Kirundi words by codeswitching. These were the key words to be taught that day. The last utterance of Extract 2 is **ivyatsi** . *la paille* '[literally] **thatching** . thatching': The concept is first labeled in Kirundi and then, immediately afterward, in French. In both extracts, there is codeswitching into French on a number of discourse markers, tags, or adverbials: *donc* 'then'; *par exemple* 'for example'; *ainsi de suite* 'and so on'; *en général* 'in general'; *n'est-ce pas?* 'don't they?'; *bon* 'right'. This suggests that both teachers were operating within a frame of "doing lessons in French." Further evidence for this interpretation comes from the fact that the exchanges in both extracts opened and closed in French. The teachers were mindful of the official medium of instruction.

By codeswitching in this way the teachers were endeavoring to bridge the gap between the world of the textbook and the students' existing knowledge about house building in Burundi. This bridging could not have been done solely through the medium of French. Both teachers opened the teaching/learning exchanges in French but then switched into Kirundi to elaborate on the information in the textbook. The explanations in Kirundi were quite long, but they were interspersed with switches into French, as shown, creating an overall impression of teaching in French. Extract 3 is from the lesson in the rural class at the point where the focus is on *maisons en étages* 'multistory houses,' a phrase that the students have difficulty understanding and saying.

Extract 3 (Teacher B)

T: *au rez de chaussée . qui sont déja entrés dans une maison en étages? levez le doigt . personne? ou*

P: ... **Bujumbura.**

T: *à* **Bujumbura** . *ou?*

P: **Bujumbura.**

T: ... **Bujumbura** . *bon . vous l'avez déjà constaté . ici dans notre province . je ne dirais pas qu'il y a beaucoup de maisons en étages .n'est-ce pas? . mais au lycée de* **Bururi** *je pense qu'il y a . hmm . les dortoirs sont en étages .* **ni bande bamaze kuja kuri** *lycée de* **Bururi . murimwebge . aba abakobga mwabonye barara amaja hehe . hein . hariho abarara hejuru n'abandi barara munsi .** *n'est-ce pas? . bon . ce sont des maisons en étages . c'est expliqué maintenant . bon . normalement une maison en étages est divisée en plusieurs salles superposées ... vous comprenez? s'il vous plaît* **zigerekerana . bagenda barashi ramwo . ivyumba . inzu bakayigaburamwo ntuze ivy-umba vyinshi . biduga bigere-keranye** *vous comprenez? s'il vous plaît . bon . alors . la première salle .* **iri hasi nyene hagaca haza . dufate aha duhagaze iyoba hari** *étage .* **aha niho twinjirira nta yindi nzu iri munsi .** *alors . cette première salle est appelée le rez ...*

T: on the ground floor . who has already been in a multistory house? raise your hands . no-body? . where?

P: ... **Bujumbura**

T: in **Bujumbura** . where?

P: **Bujumbura**

T: **Bujumbura** . right . you've already seen it here in our province . I can't say that there are many multistory houses, can I? but in **Bururi** secondary school I think that there are . hmm .the dormitories are on more than one floor . **who has already visited Bururi** secondary school? **who amongst you? did you see where the girls sleep? there are some who sleep upstairs and others who sleep downstairs,** aren't there . right . those are multistory houses . it's explained now okay normally a multistory house is divided into many superposed rooms ... please, do you understand? **superposed . they build rooms . they build a house with many rooms . the rooms are superposed** . please, do you understand? right . then . the first room **the one that is on the ground floor and then we have ... if we consider this floor where we are standing ... if we had a multistory house it**

PS: *de chaussée*

T: *le rez de chaussée. le rez de chaussée . le rez de chaussée . bon . à partir maintenant du rez de chaussée on commence maintenant . compter le nombre d'étages . ici nous disons . on dit*

PS: *premier étage.*

T: *premier étage . et puis?*

PS: *deuxième étage.*

T: *deuxième étage . et puis?*

PS: *troisième étage*

T: *troisième étage ainsi de suite . tout dépendra .eh . des nombre de salles . qui s'y trouvent . vous comprenez? s'il vous plaît . alors disons par exemple .* **kugira ngo uduge muri** *étage* **. hari ico bita ntuzee** *on peut l'appeler* **ascenseur ahandi naho bagashiramwo ingazi zigenda ziraduuga .** *n'est-ce pas? ascenseur* **ngo n akuma badagamwo bagafuny amabuto . kagaca kakudugana muri** *étage* **ugomvye . gushika aho ugomba .** *n'est-ce pas? . étage* **ushikako .** *vous avez bien compris? . bon .* **ahomuzigir i Bujumbura muzobibona .** *bon . je pense que le mot est expliqué . on continue . on continue . toujours dans l'introduction*

would be **through this room that we would enter the house .. ..there would be no other house underneath ...** then this first room is called the ground ...

PS: ground floor

T: the ground floor . the ground floor . the ground floor . right . now . from the ground floor upwards we start . counting the number of floors...here we say...people say...

PS: first floor

T: first floor . and then?

PS: second floor

T: second floor . and then?

PS: third floor

T: third floor . and so on . all will depend on er . the number of rooms we find there. please, do you understand? . then let's say for example **to go up from one** floor **to the next there is something called** . we can call it a lift . **in some buildings you find stairs** right? a lift **is a box you go up in and you press a button ... it takes you to the** floor **you want** right? the floor **that you reach** . have you really understood this? okay **you'll see them when you go to Bujumbura** . okay . I think that the word has been explained . let's go on . let's continue . still in the introduction

In this exchange about multistory houses, the teacher faced the difficulty of explaining lexical items that had no equivalent in Kirundi: *étage* 'floor,' *rez de chaussée* 'ground floor,' *ascenseur* 'lift,' *dortoirs*, 'dormitories.' Moreover, the grade 5 students in the rural school had no knowledge of the features of "modern" buildings. The teacher switched into Kirundi because of the problems he encountered trying to explain the terms in French, but even the explanation in Kirundi posed a challenge for him because the concepts were remote from the experience of the learners. He resorted to comparisons. I observed this exchange as it took place, and it was not clear whether the students had understood these lexical items. The teacher's final remark in Kirundi, **ahomuzigir i Bujumbura muzobibona** 'you'll see them when you go to Bujumbura,' suggests that he was not sure whether all the pupils had understood.

The teacher alternated frequently between the two languages in attempting to deal with these communicative challenges and to check on understanding. The new terms were presented in French; then, the teacher provided explanations and commentary in Kirundi and compared the new concepts to those that he felt were familiar to the students. As the extracts show, the teacher talk here was predominantly monologic. One student intervened with a brief utterance, **Bujumbura** (the name of the capital city of Burundi), to indicate where he had seen multistory houses. Otherwise the students all repeated in chorus: *rez de chausée* 'ground floor,' *premier étage* 'first floor,' *deuxième étage* 'second floor,' and *troisième étage* 'third floor.'

The exchange unfolded as follows: Starting off in French, the teacher first drew attention to the word *rez de chaussée* 'ground floor' in the textbook. He then asked the class if anyone had even been in a multistory house. He urged those who had to raise their hands. Only one student had. Still in French, the teacher asked him where he had seen a multistory house. The student said that he had seen one in the capital city. The teacher continued in French with a comment to the effect that there were not many multistory houses in the province where the school was. He added that there were some multistory dormitories in the secondary school in Bururi, the town that served as the administrative center of the province, some 15 km away. The teacher then switched to Kirundi to check whether he could use the secondary school as an example. He asked how many students had already visited the school. My fieldnotes tell me that at this point a substantial number of students raised their hands. The secondary school was a boarding school, so the teacher then explained that some students had their sleeping quarters upstairs and some downstairs.

He resumed the use of French to formulate a definition of a multistory house. He said: *normalement une maison en étages est divisée en plusieurs salles superposées* 'normally a multistory house is made up of many rooms one on top of another.' However, this definition included French words that the students could not readily understand. The teacher reformulated the definition in Kirundi. At this point, he switched into French and, instead of the word *rez de chaussée* 'ground floor,' he used the phrase *la première salle* 'the first room'. He switched back again to Kirundi to give a fuller explanation of the concept of "ground floor," saying that it is the space you enter when you first go into a building. He reinforced the explanation by getting the children to think of their classroom as if it were a multistory building. He then reintroduced the term *rez de chaussée* 'ground floor' in French and continued in French with a counting routine that had a clear Initiation/Response/Feedback structure. By means of this routine, he elicited from the students, in chorus, the names for first, second, and third floors.

After this, the teacher explained how one moves from one floor to the other. The French term *ascenseur* 'lift' and the Kirundi term **ingazi** 'stairs' were used in this codeswitched utterance. The teacher concluded the exchange about *maisons en étages* 'multistory houses' in French, noting that the concept had now been explained, and he then moved the students on to the next part of the introduction in the textbook.

CONCLUSION

The codeswitching of teachers such as these in urban and rural primary classrooms in Burundi can only be fully understood if we take account of the wider social and linguistic order and the value assigned to Kirundi and to French within local institutions and within the national arena. Teachers play a key role in mediating the forces that contribute to the reproduction of the dominance of French. In these extracts from French vocabulary lessons with grade 5 students, we saw the two teachers codeswitching between French and Kirundi in their attempts to bridge the students' worlds and the world of the textbook and the national curriculum. Codeswitching serves as an important resource for teachers in managing the communicative demands placed upon them by the French-medium provision introduced in grade 5. However, these bilingual discursive practices serve ultimately to reinforce the dominance of French and the French-speaking elite.

TRANSCRIPTION CONVENTIONS

Bold   Kirundi utterances

                  English translation of Kirundi utterances (in the data extracts)

Italics	French utterances
Normal font	English translations
T	Teacher
P	Pupil
PS	Pupils

Note: In Extracts 1–3 in this chapter, the transcription of the audio-recorded classroom data is in the left-hand column and the English translation is in the right-hand column. The English translation of the Kirundi is shown in bold font and the English translation of the French is shown in normal font to reflect the code contrasts in the left-hand column.

In the main body of this chapter, the English translations of Kirundi and French utterances appear between single quotation marks. Here, the English translations of Kirundi utterances are not in bold face but in normal font.

REFERENCES

Atelier National de la Didactique des Langues (ANADIL). (1986). *L'enseignement des langues nationales et du français en Afrique francophone: Experience du Burundi*. Proceedings of a conference held in Bujumbura, Burundi, September 1986. Bujumbura: Ministère de l'Éducation Nationale, Burundi.

Bourdieu, P. (1979). "The economics of linguistic exchanges." *Social Science Information, 16(6)*, 645–668.

Bourdieu, P. (1982). *Ce que parler veut dire*. Paris: Fayard.

Bourdieu, P., and Passeron, J.-C. (1970). *La reproduction: Éléments pour une théorie du système d'enseignement*. Paris: Les Éditions de Minuit.

Eisemon, T. O., Prouty, R., and Schwille, J. (1989). What language should be used for teaching?: Language policy and school reform in Burundi. *Journal of Multilingual and Multicultural Development, 10(6)*.

Ndayipfukamiye, L. (1993). *Teaching/learning bilingually: The case of grade five classrooms in Burundi primary schools*. Unpublished Ph.D. thesis, Department of Linguistics and Modern English Language, Lancaster University, U.K.

Ndayipfukamiye, L. (1994). Codeswitching in Burundi Primary Classrooms. In C. Rubagumya (Ed.), *Teaching and researching language in African classrooms* (pp. 79–95). Clevedon: Multilingual Matters.

Sabushimike-Ndayizeye, J. (1992). *Situation de l'enseignement du Français à l'école primaire au Burundi: à partir des observations des difficultés éprouvées en lecture et en écriture par l'écolier*. Unpublished doctoral thesis, University of Bordeaux, France.

6

Turn-Taking and the Positioning of Bilingual Participants in Classroom Discourse: Insights from Primary Schools in England

Marilyn Martin-Jones and Mukul Saxena

INTRODUCTION

Since the mid-1980s, a new form of educational provision has gradually been put in place in some schools and local education authorities in Britain. It has come to be known as "bilingual support," and it has been developed for bilingual learners from minority ethnic groups, primarily in schools in multilingual urban areas of England. There is considerable variation in practice from school to school, but, generally speaking, bilingual support involves occasional use of the learners' home and/or community language along with English in teaching/learning events across the curriculum. The vast majority of provision is organized in the early years of primary education and is overtly transitional in its goals: The main aim is to provide access to the curriculum until the learners have acquired sufficient English to make the transition to monolingual education through the medium of English.

A new category of staffing has also been defined to facilitate the delivery of this new (and minimal) form of bilingual education provision. From the mid-1980s onwards, members of local minority communities began to be appointed to schools in their areas as "bilingual aides" or "bilingual assistants." For some, this meant official recognition for a role they had already assumed on a voluntary basis. They included speakers of a range of languages, including Panjabi, Gujarati, Urdu, Sylheti, Bengali, Chinese, and Somali. Many were appointed to low-status posts, with ill-defined job descriptions. In the early 1990s, as severe cuts began to be made in local budgets, we also saw fully qualified bilingual teachers being redeployed into bilingual support work.

In the first part of this chapter, we begin by tracing the way in which this category of staffing first came to be constructed in British educational discourse about provision for bilingual learners of migrant and refugee origin from the 1960s to the 1990s. We will also show how bilingual support came to be organized, focusing in particular on the way in which bilingual support staff have been positioned as brokers between the mainstream schools and local minority ethnic groups while at the same time being structurally marginalized.

In the main body of the chapter, we go on to examine the ways in which asymmetric working relationships between monolingual class teachers and bilingual classroom assistants were being constructed in two settings in the early 1990s. Here, we will be drawing on ethnographic work we carried out over a three-year period, from 1989 to 1992, in inner-city primary schools in the Northwest of England. This work was undertaken as part of a wider project conducted with colleagues at Lancaster.[1] The project documented the implementation of a local educational scheme that involved the creation of the equivalent of forty full-time posts in local schools for bilingual classroom assistants. The majority of the children in these schools spoke Panjabi, Urdu, or Gujarati at home. The bilingual assistants appointed by the local education authority were all women of South Asian origin who spoke one or more of the children's languages in addition to English. Our aim was to investigate the ways in which the idea of providing bilingual support was being translated into classroom practice in this local context. We therefore focused on teaching/learning events in which the bilingual assistants had some opportunity to use the children's home and/or community language.

CHANGING DISCOURSES ABOUT BILINGUAL LEARNERS IN BRITAIN, 1960s–1990s

Official, Classificatory Discourses

Categories of teaching staff, of learners, and of forms of provision are products of educational policies and "official pedagogic discourses"

(Bernstein 1991). Such discourses serve the key institutional function of creating social classifications. Classificatory discourses are transmitted through teacher education and through academic and popular debates about education and eventually get taken up by local education administrators, by schools, and by teachers. At the level of the school, these classificatory discourses have two main effects: They position subjects within the social hierarchy of the school, and they constrain them to engage in discourse practices associated with that positioning. Subjects within schools cannot take on *any* voices, only those associated with the way they are positioned.

Categories of Learners in British Schools

Bourne (1993) has charted in detail the changes that have taken place in the classification of learners in official pedagogic discourses in Britain since the 1960s. She has shown that a sharp distinction was drawn between monolingual and bilingual children in the discourse of several educational reports in the 1960s and 1970s. In this period, monolingual and bilingual learners came to be characterized as having different competencies and therefore different educational "needs." This categorization of pupils coincided with the emergence of a new discipline of teaching English as a Second Language (ESL) with its own discourses about the nature of language learning.

These official discourses about bilingual learners from minority ethnic groups in British schools were then translated into a specific form of educational provision: that of withdrawing pupils from the mainstream classroom into special language classes where they were taught English through the audiolingual method. In these withdrawal classes, there was a strong emphasis on the forms of language and on drilling in the correct use of language forms, while monolingual English speakers experienced more child-centered, discovery-type pedagogies. This differentiation of provision was underpinned by funding arrangements. From 1966 onwards, Section 11 funds were made available from the central government to local education authorities (LEAs) specifically as a response to immigration and to the increase in the numbers of bilingual pupils in inner-city schools (for further details, see Bourne 1989).

Changing Discourses about Bilingual Learners, Changing Forms of Provision

A major change in official pedagogic discourses about bilingual children came with the Swann Report (DES 1985). This is the closest we have ever come in Britain to an official policy statement on the education of bilingual learners from minority ethnic groups. As Bourne (1993) shows, in this report, there was a weakening of the distinction between monolingual and bilingual learners and a new emphasis on provision of the same education for all. Withdrawal now came to be viewed as discriminatory, and it was recommended that educational provision for bilingual children should be organized within the mainstream class-room (for further details, see Martin-Jones and Saxena 1995).

A New Category of Bilingual Staff

The Swann Committee explicitly rejected the idea of developing bilingual education programs. The rationale given was that they were anxious about recommending specific forms of provision that would result in the segregation or marginalization of Black and Asian pupils in a climate of increasing institutional racism. However, they made one concession: They suggested that there might be a new means of providing "language support" within the mainstream classroom. This recommendation was formulated in rather vague terms. The view expressed by the committee was that each school with a large intake of bilingual learners from minority ethnic groups should have "a bilingual resource," someone who could "help with the transitional needs of non-English speaking children starting school" (DES 1985, 407). They went on to give examples of people who might be called upon to be a bilingual resource: The inventory included bilingual staff already appointed to a school (e.g., a bilingual teacher, a non-teaching assistant, or a nursery nurse); bilingual parents or even older children from local secondary schools involved in community service programs or child care courses. Bilingual support as a form of educational provision was clearly seen as an optional extra that would not have any major implications in staffing terms.

The members of the committee described the role of the person acting as a bilingual resource as follows:

> We would see such a resource as providing a degree of continuity between the home and school environment by offering psychological and social support for the child, as well as being able to explain simple educational concepts in a child's mother tongue, if the need arises, but always working within the mainstream classroom and alongside the class teacher. (DES 1985, 407)

The emphasis in this chapter of the Swann Report was on easing the bilingual child's transition to school. There was, however, considerable lack of clarity about what bilingual support might entail in practice. Since the mid-1980s, educationalists have, on a number of occasions, drawn attention to the fact that the main function of the bilingual resource person in many primary classes is to provide support for the class teacher. Bourne (1993), for example, has noted that, in primary classes where a child-centered exploratory approach predominates, the role of a bilingual teacher or bilingual assistant in providing bilingual support is often defined as "extending the monitoring gaze of the teacher" and supporting the teacher in keeping track of children's performance.

The move toward the mainstreaming of bilingual pupils was well already underway in Britain by the mid-1980s. The Swann Report (DES 1985) merely endorsed this trend. The move toward the appointment of bilingual classroom assistants gathered pace soon afterward. There is still considerable variation in the ways in which the role and status of bilingual support staff are defined from one LEA to another and from one school to another, but very few bilinguals working within the educational system in Britain are appointed to mainstream teaching posts. For the most part, they occupy low-status positions that have become even more precarious as funding has been cut back.

ONE LOCAL BILINGUAL ASSISTANT SCHEME

We will now briefly describe the way in which this new category of bilingual staff was being defined in the inner-city schools where we carried out our project. A range of practices was observable in the schools we visited in the local area. Many teachers were uncertain about the official job description of the bilingual assistants. They were seen as similar in status to other ancillary workers in the classroom, such as nursery nurses. However, among nursery nurses, there was considerable resentment about the arrival of bilingual assistants in the schools. The nursery nurses saw them as being appointed to do the same work but with less training. When the scheme was first implemented in September 1989, there was little guidance for the predominantly monolingual class teachers who had begun working with the bilingual assistants. There was virtually no in-service support for them and no forum for discussing ways of working in the classroom that would facilitate the use of the children's home language. The main recipients of training during this period were the bilingual assistants.

The newly appointed bilingual assistants were positioned as low-status staff in the schools to which they were appointed. This positioning took different forms in different schools, but it included decisions about the amount of playground duty they were required to do, the extent to which they were involved in curriculum planning meetings, and the way in which the scope of their work was defined within the school. For example, in most schools (85%), the bilingual assistants worked in more than one class and were primarily expected to work with individual children on the margins of the class to provide support rather than working "alongside" the class teacher. As very few bilingual assistants were involved in joint planning of classroom activities with the teacher, they could not anticipate the demands that might be placed on them from day to day. When bilingual assistants were involved in staff meetings, patterns of turn-taking and the use of names, titles, and terms of address also served to position them as low-status staff. The bilingual assistants were commonly addressed by their first names only, both in staffroom conversations and, in some schools, in front of the children in class. In contrast, the established convention was for teachers to address or refer to each other in front of the children using titles and last names.

TWO SCHOOLS, TWO RECEPTION CLASSES

We turn now to our account of the specific ways in which the notion of bilingual support was being taken up by the teachers in our study and translated into classroom practice. In the second year of the project, we based our observations in the reception classes of two schools. The schools were located in two different inner-city areas of Blackburn, an industrial town in the Northwest of England. The catchment areas of the schools included new council estates and rows of Victorian terraced houses where the residents were primarily of Pakistani or Indian origin. The local education authority operated a policy of parental choice of primary school rather than a tight catchment area system. However, most parents in these two minority groups in Blackburn preferred to send their children to the local school. As a result, a majority of children in both schools were of South Asian origin when we undertook this research. A substantial proportion of the children in the reception classes of both schools had spent the previous year in a nursery class, but for some of the children, this was their first year at school. They ranged from 4 to 5 years in age.

THE ORGANIZATION OF BILINGUAL SUPPORT IN THE TWO CLASSES

Class A: The Staff, the Children, and the Teacher's Views about Bilingual Support

Mrs. Anwar,[2] the bilingual assistant appointed to this class, was a mature woman who had been educated in Pakistan. She spoke Panjabi,

Urdu, and English (with a Pakistani accent). She was also biliterate in English and Urdu. Before moving into classroom-based work with bilingual children, she had had considerable work experience as an interpreter in a local hospital. She had already been working in the class for a year when we began our observations. When addressing individual children, she almost always used Panjabi or Urdu. On these occasions, she also made frequent use of terms of endearment such as *beTe* (my child). The children reciprocated by addressing her as "auntie" when they spoke Panjabi.

Mrs. Talbot, the class teacher, was a young woman who already had several years' experience of primary school teaching behind her. She spoke only English and spoke it with a Lancashire accent. Her response to the bilingual assistant scheme had been a positive one from the outset. Soon after we began visiting the class, she set aside time one afternoon after school to give a talk to other local teachers about the bilingual support strategies being developed in her class. Later, in conversation with us, she went into more detail about her views on the bilingual support work. Echoing the discourse of the Swann Report, she indicated that she felt that the role of the bilingual assistant was to help children to gain access to the curriculum while they were still at a developmental stage with English. She believed that new concepts should be introduced in English and then explained in Panjabi if the learners found it difficult to understand.

In this class, it was only the children who were perceived to have the greatest difficulties with English who had access to support from Mrs. Anwar. The children were grouped according to their English-language abilities. Each group was labeled by color—there were red, orange, blue, green, yellow, and purple groups—but it was clear to all in the class which the "low ability" groups were: the red and orange groups. Mrs. Anwar always worked with these two groups. In fact, the teacher occasionally slipped into calling these groups "Mrs. Anwar's children."

There were four children in the red group, three boys and one girl. There were five children in the orange group, three boys and two girls. Most were 5 years old, though a couple of children were still 4. All the children in the orange group were speakers of Panjabi. The red group were nearly all children who spoke Gujarati at home. One boy spoke Urdu at home, and Mrs. Anwar often codeswitched from Panjabi to Urdu when addressing this child.

Twice a week Mrs. Digby, the English language support teacher, visited the class. She worked on a peripatetic basis, sharing her time between this and other schools. When she came to the class, she always worked in tandem with the bilingual assistant, guiding the children in the orange and red groups through a series of preplanned activities. As a trained teacher, she had higher status than the bilingual assistant, but as a member of the language support staff, she was expected to fit in to the pattern of language support work organized for this class by Mrs. Talbot.

The pattern of work was organized at weekly meetings. At these meetings, Mrs. Talbot indicated what the timetable of activities would be for each member of staff working in the class and which groups of children they would be working with. She then explained how she wanted these activities to be tied in to the topic work that was currently being developed in the class and to different areas of the curriculum: language, math, science, craft/design and technology, artwork, music, drama, and so on. Mrs. Anwar, the bilingual assistant, was sometimes assigned to work alone with just one small group (either the red group or the orange group), and sometimes she was asked to work with *both* the orange and red group, "alongside" a monolingual teacher.

In this local context, Mrs. Talbot stood out as a teacher who had more commitment than most to exploring ways of incorporating bilingual support work into the planning of teaching/learning activities in her reception class. Mrs. Anwar had more scope than many other bilingual assistants appointed to the local schools to use the children's home language in the classroom. Nevertheless, Mrs. Talbot retained control over the definition and organization of bilingual support in the ways in which we have just described. Mrs. Anwar was positioned as a bilingual *assistant* through these organizational practices. The practices stemmed from Mrs. Talbot's views about the value and purpose of bilingual support work. These ideas were not idiosyncratic inventions of her own but, as we have shown, they had their origin in official educational discourse about provision for bilingual learners from minority ethnic groups.

Doing Bilingual Support Work: One Primary Science Activity

We will now give a brief description of one teaching/learning event in which Mrs. Anwar was asked to work in tandem with Mrs. Talbot. This teaching/learning event was observed through the lens of a video camera. We have chosen it because it is a telling example. As Mitchell (1984, 239) suggests, focusing on telling cases is more fruitful in ethnographic work than searching for typical cases. The particular circumstances observed in this event served to draw our attention to the need to take account of the different ways in which this and other bilingual assistants were being positioned by the discourse practices of the monolingual teachers.

On the day when we visited the class, Mrs. Talbot had planned a primary science activity with two groups of bilingual children, the red

and the orange groups. She had asked Mrs. Anwar to work with her.
The activity was to be one of several science activities built around the
topic "lights." The class had just completed a series of activities focusing on "traffic lights" and the purpose of this new activity was to focus
on "electricity and electric lighting." The event unfolded as follows:
First, the bilingual assistant sat alone with the children in one corner of
the classroom. She reminded the children of the work they had done
that week on traffic lights. She then talked about electric lighting in the
children's homes and asked them if they knew how to switch lights on
and off. Most of this exchange took place in Panjabi, though occasionally the bilingual assistant switched into Urdu when addressing the one
child who spoke Urdu at home (Extract 1).

Extract 1, Class A[3]

1 BA: <P>ākkhaā vand kariye.te anheraa ho= aaj Mrs. T dassegii:
         If we close our eyes, it {becomes=} dark. Today Mrs. T will

         saanuu~ ke<E>light<P>jeRii heggii aa. o kis taraā bal dii
         tell us how the light *comes on,*

         aa. kis taraā bujdii aa.. taar kii hondii aa.. <E>[vallab]
         how it goes off, what a wire is, {and} what

         <P>kii hondaa e. hum
         a bulb is. OK?

5 BA: <U>Suhail Thiik se baiThoo.. aaj hamne kaunse? rang sikhe
         Suhail sit properly. What colors did we learn today?

         the subhaa kaun kaun? se<E>color<U>dekhe the?
         What colors did we see in the morning?

The class teacher then came over to join the bilingual assistant and
the two groups of children. She immediately assumed the main speaking rights and began addressing the children in English. She led them
through a presentation of the concept of electricity. She pointed to
illustrations in a book. She also provided English labels for abstract
concepts and for concrete objects like a lamp, a bulb, and a plug visible
in the immediate vicinity. She then gave a demonstration using a table
lamp, switching it on and off, sometimes enlisting the children's help.
From time to time, she paused to allow Mrs. Anwar an opportunity to
reformulate in Panjabi for the children what she had just said in English.
The allocation of these turns was accomplished through a change in eye

gaze direction toward the bilingual assistant and/or through the use of overt turn-giving cues, as in Extract 2.

Extract 2, Class A

1 CT: electricity comes through here.. and it makes it light up.. it comes
           from the socket in the wall.. you want to explain

   BA: \<P>edde~ viccõ. e dekkho e\<E>plug\<P>lagaayaa naã.. e
           Through this, see this, when we put the plug in, where

           \<E>plug\<P>kitthe? lagaayaa.\<U>idhar dekho Yusuf..\<E>plug
           did we put the plug in? Look here, Yusuf. The plug

5   \<P>edde vic lagaayaa.. e heggaa\<E>socket\<P>edde viccõ.
           is inserted in it. This is the socket. Through this

           edde vic aayii\<E>electric.. electricity\<P>jeRii heggii aa
           Through this came the electric. the electricity, it came

           o edde vic aayii. edde viccõ es taar de vic aayii. es taar de
           through this through this, it came through this wire traveling

           viccõ hondii huyii. e saare taar de vic eddrõ hondii huyii
           through this wire, through this whole cable, through here,

           hondii hoyii hondii hoyii edde anddar aayii
           through here, through here, it came inside this

Here, the cue is given directly to Mrs. Anwar. On other occasions, the cue came in the form of an utterance addressed to the children, in an explicit statement about the discourse role the bilingual assistant was performing as in line 10, Extract 3.

Extract 3, Class A

1 CT: \<E>right. do you know what this is called.

   L?:   wire

   L?:   + wire

   CT: + wire

5 LL: wire

CT: and these clips on the end are called crocodile clips. ('cause they go){ } like a crocodile like that

L?:   like a dog

CT: like a dog ([nauu]) crocodile clip

10 CT: Mrs. A she'll tell you..

BA: <U>kyaa hai ye<E>clip<U>jo hai~. ye<E>wire<U>hai...
      What is this? This clip= *This is a* wire.

      ye kyaa hai ye<E>wire<U>hai aur jo iske uupar<E>clip
      What's this? This is a wire. *And look at the* shape *of*

      <U>hai uskii<E>shape<U>aage se dekho.<E>crocodile
      the clip *in front of it. Look from the front. Have you seen a*

      <U>dekhaa hai jo paanii mai~ hotaa hai. uske jaisii<E>shape
      crocodile *{which/it} is found in water? The* shape *looks like*

15   <U>hai ye dekho. uskaa muuh kaise khultaa hai<E>crocodile
      that. ok here, see, it opens like a crocodile's *mouth*

      <U>kaa aise. [wo:~a] {making sound}
      Like this.

L?:   [wo:~a]

BA: [wo:~a] {CT laughing?}

L?:   [wo:~a]

20 BA: <P>e dekh aise..<E>crocodile<U>kii tarah wo:~a. hai
      Look, like this. 'wo:~a' like a crocodile, *isn't*

      naã. kyoõ kii aise khultaa hai. ye hai<E>crocodile clip..=
      it? Because it opens like this. This is a crocodile clip.

After this initial presentation phase of the activity, the two adults and the children moved over to a small table in another part of the classroom. There, Mrs. Talbot began showing the children how to test out simple electricity circuits built on individual boards with batteries and bulbs. Very soon, this part of the activity was interrupted by the arrival of another member of staff, who informed Mrs. Talbot that a child from another group in the class had had an accident. The teacher had to leave the classroom. She asked Mrs. Anwar to carry on without her, (Extract 4).

Extract 4, Class A

1 CT: <E>there's a child who has had an accident.. I'll have to go and sort it out can you start this with them can you start it with them or do you not feel confident. do you feel all right {talking to BA}

 BA: yeah I'll do it and=

5 CT: this is a real wire. this is what happens.. I think I could be about five minutes. and I'll come back. like that and then you touch.. by the side of the battery... touch that and there. OK all right.. just explain about the light and the bulb.. and there is a magnifying glass there so you can... wait a minute. give everybody a bulb
10   let them look at the filament with the magnifying glass. OK

 BA: OK....

 BA: right<U>Thiik se baiTho..<U/P>acchaa<P>e mai~ dasyaa
        Right! Sit properly. I told you {about}

       siggaa e kii? heggaa vaa!.
       this. What is this?

15 L?:   <E>wire

 L?:   wire

 BA: wire<P>**heggii e**
        This is a wire.

Mrs. Anwar suddenly found herself positioned quite differently, she was now leading the teaching/learning activity. She could choose what language to use, she could assume the responsibility for allocating turns to the children. This is not what we had expected to happen, but we left the video camera on and continued to record the rest of the activity. Mrs. Anwar switched into Panjabi and continued with the demonstration of the electricity circuits until the teacher returned. As she had done earlier, she switched occasionally from Panjabi to Urdu when addressing the child whose home language was Urdu.

This episode illustrates the two main ways in which Mrs. Anwar was positioned as a participant in the teaching/learning events that took place in this classroom: (1) doing group work "alongside" Mrs. Talbot (or "alongside" Mrs. Digby, the other monolingual member of staff who worked regularly in this classroom) and (2) working alone with a small group of bilingual learners. In teaching/learning activities of the first type, Mrs. Anwar was positioned as an interpreter and the monolingual teacher controlled the distribution of turns. The patterns of codeswitching across turns in teaching/learning activities of this type provided illuminating insights into the ways in which asymmetrical relations of power and authority were being constituted in this classroom. In teaching/learning activities of the second type, Mrs. Anwar controlled the allocation of turns. She therefore had more scope for responding to contributions from learners in their home language(s) and for addressing them in what she knew to be their preferred language.

Class B: The Staff, the Children, and the Organization of Bilingual Support

Miss Khan, the bilingual assistant appointed to this class, was a younger woman who had spent most of her life in Blackburn. She spoke Panjabi and Urdu and had learned a little Gujarati from Gujarati-speaking friends. She spoke English with a Lancashire accent. She lived in the local neighborhood and had actually attended the same school when she was a child. She had brothers and sisters the same age as the children she was working with, and she knew several of the children's families. When speaking Panjabi to the children, she generally used the most intimate second person singular pronoun *tu* and had clearly established a warm and playful relationship with the children by the time we began visiting the class.

There were 36 children in the class in the year we carried out our observations. They were all between the ages of 4 and 5. Eight children spoke Gujarati at home, one spoke Katchi (a regional language spoken in the Indian state of Gujarat), and the rest came from local households where Pakistani varieties of Panjabi were spoken.

Mrs. Howe, the class teacher, was several years older than the bilingual assistant and had had considerable experience of primary-level teaching in inner-city schools. She spoke English with a standard Southern accent. Mrs. Howe's response to the experience of working with a bilingual assistant was a very positive one. She said she felt that the bilingual assistant had an important pastoral role to play. She was also one of the few teachers we met who took the view that new concepts should first be introduced in the children's home language and then recycled in English. For example, on one of our visits to the class, she asked the bilingual assistant to tell a story in Panjabi to small groups of children. The bilingual assistant took each group in turn to a small quiet room adjacent to the class to read the story to them. After this, each group of children retold the story to the class teacher in English while she did drawings of their accounts on a flip chart.

Although the children were divided into groups in this class, the groupings were quite flexible. Groups worked together, and sometimes individual members of groups worked with other groups. Mrs. Howe explained that there were two reasons for this: She wanted to create opportunities for children to work together in mixed ability groupings, and she also felt that all the children should have the opportunity to work with the bilingual assistant. The teacher drew up the plans for the week, but she also checked with the bilingual assistant on a daily basis to see how things were working out and sometimes reorganized the activities. She consulted the bilingual assistant about the progress of individual children, and she also gave her status in the eyes of the pupils by such practices as asking her to sit beside her in front of the whole class at moments such as the taking of the register or joint storytelling sessions. The two women addressed each other in a fairly formal manner in front of the children, using each other's title and last name. However, in the staffroom, they addressed each other by first name only.

Doing Bilingual Support Work: One Storytelling Event

We will now show how Mrs. Howe's views about bilingual support were being translated into practice in this classroom. We will look at one storytelling event where Miss Khan was working "in tandem with" Mrs. Howe. The event took place one afternoon in early February. It was planned by Mrs. Howe as part of the cross-curricular work developed around the topic "winter." The story was titled "The Two Snowmen." It had been written in English by teachers working in the local resource center, which produced teaching materials with a multicultural content. The two snowmen in the story were made by two boys called Yasim and Nasser. One was tall and thin, and the other was short and fat. Each boy made a snowman that had the bodily dimensions of the other boy. At the end of the story, as the two boys began to ask other people to judge which of the two snowmen was the best, but, perhaps predictably, the two snowmen melted before any judgment could be made. Mrs. Howe's decision to choose this particular story was motivated by the fact that there had recently been a snowfall and the snow was now melting in the sun outside the window of the classroom.

In her daily lesson plan, Mrs. Howe had written: "Story to be read by Miss Khan in mother tongue with some discussion to follow." The actual storytelling event unfolded as follows: The two women sat together on chairs placed on either side of the board with the children seated on the carpet in front of them. Mrs. Howe initiated the event by turning to Miss Khan and giving her the cue to begin (see line 1 of Extract 5). She said, "Shall we have Yasim and Nasser?" Miss Khan then switched into Panjabi and began telling the story in Panjabi, pointing to the pictures in the book as the story unfolded. Since the storyline was actually written in English, she re-created it in Panjabi as she went along.

Extract 5, Class B

1 CT   <E>shall we have Yasim and Nasser? {addressing BA}

   BA: yeh<P>**e jeRii**<E>story {addressing children}<P>**e.**
         This story, *you know,*

         naa? eda. naã ve<E>The Two Snowmen OK?
         it's called "The Two Snowmen" OK?

A few minutes later, Mrs. Howe picked up a felt-tip pen, turned to the board, and began drawing the outlines of two snowmen on the board. She then interrupted the storyline as it unfolded in Panjabi, to ask Miss Khan for clarification about the names of the boys in the story. There was a pause. She stopped drawing for a moment, and her eye gaze returned in the direction of the bilingual assistant. This was Miss Khan's cue to resume in Panjabi.

The flow of the storytelling was interrupted again when Mrs. Howe called to a girl who was sitting near Miss Khan but could not see the book she was holding. Mrs. Howe then retained the floor and turned to the drawings she had done on the board. She asked the children what she should draw next. Eyes, nose, and teeth were added to the drawings. About halfway through this series of exchanges in English, she stood up and assumed the most physically dominant position in the class.

The end of Mrs. Howe's contribution was signaled with the discourse marker: "right" (line 4 of Extract 6). This was followed by an explicit turn-giving cue addressed to the bilingual assistant: "Thank you. Miss Khan" (line 6 of Extract 6).

Extract 6, Class B

1 CT: anything else. Nargis

   L1:   not yet

   L2:   buttons {whispers}

      CT: buttons. one two three .. right

5 LL: one two three

      CT: thank you Miss K

      BA: <P>**fer one ... jeRaa patlaa ... Yasim e. naa? one**
            Then he, the thin one, that's Yasim, isn't it? He

            moTaa. nikkaa te moTaa<E>snowman<P>**banaayaa sii.**
            made a fat, small and fat, snowman.

            fer naa? moTe Nasser ne. naa? aapne<E>snowman<P>**noõ.**
            And then fat Nasser   put a red colored *hat on his*

10   **naa?**<E>red color<P>**dii Topii paaii [siis] te patle**
            snowman.   *And thin*

            Yasim ne. naa? aapne aapne<E>snowman<P>**noõ nikkii**
            Yasim   put a small

            <E>blue hat<P>**paaii sii.**
            blue hat *on his own* snowman.

      CT: {points to board}<E>now then. the FAT snowman what am I
            going to give the FAT snowman? what did the fat snowman (have)

15 LL: hat

      CT: a hat. what color?

      LL: blue .. blue

Mrs. Howe took over again (see line 13 of Extract 6) to initiate another brief exchange with the learners about the blackboard drawings. The rest of the storytelling event then continued in this vein. Miss Khan revealed the story line in Panjabi, bit by bit. She was interrupted from time to time by Mrs. Howe, whose contributions took the form of a series of brief exchanges with the children in English. Each time she interrupted Miss Khan, Mrs. Howe's switches into English were accompanied by a nonverbal cue such as pointing to the pictures on the board or gesturing to a particular child. Each time she allocated a turn to Miss Khan, she used an explicit turn-giving cue or a nonverbal cue. Later examples included "Okay. Carry on, Miss Khan!" or nonverbal cues such as pausing, sitting down, and directing her eye gaze towards Miss Khan.

There was just one occasion when Miss Khan took the floor without first being invited to do so (see Extract 7). She intervened in a series of exchanges in English between Mrs. Howe and the learners. Mrs. Howe had asked a closed question: "What did the thin snowman have?" The answer she anticipated was, "a pipe." But one learner volunteered "glasses" instead. At this point, Miss Khan took the floor in Panjabi to explain what a pipe was and how it was different from cigarettes. When discussing this event with us later, she said that she had realized that the children were not familiar with the practice of putting pipes in the mouths of snowmen and were also unlikely to have seen anyone in their immediate family smoking a pipe. One child then introduced a point in English about a cousin of hers who smoked cigarettes. Again, the bilingual assistant picked up on the significance of this point for the child because smoking was frowned upon in the local Muslim community. Not realizing the significance of the child's point, Mrs. Howe assumed the floor again, cutting across this exchange between the learner and the bilingual assistant and directing everyone's attention to the board.

Extract 7, Class B

1 CT: and what did the thin snowman have?

   L1: (I know?) glasses

   BA: no<P>**enoõ ... enoõ** {points to book} **e**
       What's this (called)? This

   CT: <E>(not glasses)

5 L: ([Tailifoon])

   BA: **enoõ aaxde ne**<E>**pipe**<P>**jeRe**<E>**[sigrat]**<P>**hunde**
       This is called a pipe. Do you know cigarettes?

       naa? ik hundaa .. e jeRaa lakRii
       There's a- this- that's made of wood.

       {BA mimes action of holding a pipe, filling with tobacco, and smoking pipe}

       daa banyaa hundaa e . ede vic tabako paãde naa? fer onoõ
       They put tobacco in this, then they

<E>light<P>**karde, naa? taã fer enoõ piinde naa?**<E>[sigrat]
light *this.* And then they smoke this like cigarettes

10   <P>( ) **piinde**<E>[sigrat] ( )<P>**aa**
smoke like cigarettes. *This is called*

<E>pipe<P>**aaxde. kii e?**
a pipe. What is it?

LL: <E>pipe ... pipe ... a pipe

BA: [sigrat]<P>**piinde?**
{They/he} smoke cigarettes?

L: <E>do you know my cousin

15 BA: he's got a pipe?

L: he not got a pipe he's got ... he .. he (smokes cigarettes) everyday

BA: he smokes everyday?

CT: shall we give one to this snowman then? like that. put it in his
mouth? oh he ... is that alright?

20 LL: yeh

CT: OK

Mrs. Howe and Miss Khan had not worked out in detail how this storytelling event was to be organized, and they had not at any point talked
about the specific nature of the contributions that they would each
make to the event. Mrs. Howe's interventions in English directed the
learners' attention to specific vocabulary items. In generic terms, the exchanges initiated by her in this particular teaching/learning event were
primarily "label quests" (Heath 1986). The tenor of the discourse was
quite playful, because it was based on the teacher's sketches on the
board. The exchanges with the children were very much teacher-led,
with closed questions and a good deal of teacher evaluation. The learners made minimal contributions. In contrast, Miss Khan acted as narra-
tor for most of the event, taking turns in Panjabi when they were
assigned to her, with just one brief intervention to explain to the children in Panjabi what a pipe is. The pattern of codeswitching across
turns was consistent with Mrs. Howe's view that all teaching/learning
activities and all new concepts should be introduced in Panjabi. This

was the way in which she had interpreted official pedagogic discourses about the value and purpose of bilingual support work with young bilingual learners. But, despite her stated commitment to maximizing opportunities for the use of the children's home and/or community language in teaching/learning events across the curriculum, in this and in other teaching/learning events we observed she retained control over the distribution of turns and generally orchestrated the enactment of the event by both verbal and nonverbal means.

What "Working Alongside the Class Teacher" Meant in Practice

What was common to both teaching/learning events described in detail here was that the monolingual teachers assumed the principal speaking rights. They took the floor whenever they deemed it to be appropriate. They allocated turns to the bilingual assistants and shaped the patterns of codeswitching across turns. Although both teachers were committed to developing ways of working bilingually in class that would have concrete benefits for the bilingual children, they were actually constraining the contributions that the bilingual assistants were able to make in such joint teaching/learning activities. A close analysis of the transcripts from these and other teaching/learning events shows that the bilingual practitioners were being positioned *as assistants*, while at the same time quite clear messages were being given to the children about the relative value of the languages being used and about the status of the bilingual assistant within the class hierarchy.

As we have shown, the teachers differed to some extent in their approach to the organization of bilingual support. Mrs. Howe believed that concepts should first be introduced in Panjabi, while Mrs. Talbot felt that this should be done in English, with explanations in Panjabi given later if necessary. These views represented slightly different interpretations of official pedagogic discourses about the education of bilingual learners in Britain. But both agreed that the main purpose of using the children's home language was to provide access to the curriculum until the children had developed sufficient confidence with English to switch over to English as the sole medium of instruction.

CONCLUDING COMMENTS

Studies of language policy changes and educational policy developments typically focus on the political and historical processes involved in the formulation of the policies, or they chart changes over time in official discourses. It is also necessary to observe and describe the ways in which policy changes impinge on the working lives of people in different institutional contexts. As Heller (1995) has argued, we need to turn our attention to "the interstices in which strategies of implementation have to be invented" (p. 70). This paper has attempted to provide a glimpse at two educational sites where strategies of policy implementation were still being invented. Crucially, these processes of invention involved the definition and negotiation of pedagogic practices that brought two or more languages into play. We have shown how these processes were shaped by power asymmetries and by monolingual teachers' views about "bilingual support." We have also shown that the teachers' views had their origins in official pedagogic discourses where this particular category of staffing for delivery of the curriculum was first defined. The discourse practices and the forms of classroom organization that we observed in these two classes contributed to the positioning of the bilingual assistants as marginal to the main action of the class; at the same time, the bilingual resources they brought to the classes were contained within a primarily monolingual order of discourse.

TRANSCRIPTION CONVENTIONS

Character Format

italics	*translation of Urdu/Panjabi into English*
normal	transcription for English utterances
bold	**transcription for U/P utterances**
UPPER CASE	indicates louder speech than usual
Capital Letters	initial capitals (only used for proper names, language names, place names, titles, and months/days of the week)

Symbols

< >   marks the beginning of an utterance in a different language, that is, a codeswitch, for example:

    <U> marks the beginning of an utterance in Urdu.

    <E> marks the beginning of an utterance in English.

    <P/U> indicates

        a) that the utterance could be in either language

        b) that there is a word internal switch, that is, across morpheme boundaries.

( )   indicates an unclear item. Sometimes an attempt was made to transcribe the item, for example, (let him speak); (**bo::laa**);

empty brackets indicate completely unintelligible stretches and their approximate length.

{   }   (a) curly brackets in the line of speech represent additional information, such as nonverbal actions, for example, {hesitation}; or comments about the utterance transcribed, for example, regional language variants like 'rollin{g}.'

(b) curly brackets in the line of translation are used to mark a literal gloss, additional words, or the researcher's comments.

[   ]   marks phonetic transcription.

Representation of Simultaneous Speech

/ /   indicates that two people are speaking simultaneously, but only one can be heard, the one whose utterance has been transcribed.

/ / / /   indicates that more than two people are speaking simultaneously, but only one can be heard. This speaker's utterance has been transcribed.

L1:+   The plus sign represents simultaneous speech, for example,
L2:+   when two (or more) people start speaking at exactly the same
BA:+   time and can be heard clearly. Their utterances have been transcribed on different lines.

Representation of Other Features

=   indicates that the turn continues below, at the next identical symbol, or is interrupted by other participant(s).

...   pause: the number of dots indicates the relative length of each pause.

bo::la one or more colons indicate marked lengthening of the preceding sound.

?   rising intonation

!   emphasis: marked prominence through pitch or increase in volume

Participants

L?   unidentified learner

L1,L2 (etc.)   learners identified, but not by name

LL   several learners or all learners simultaneously

BA   bilingual assistant

CT	class teacher
NN	nursery nurse
ST	monolingual support teacher

NOTES

1. This project was based at Lancaster University from 1989 to 1992. It was entitled "Bilingual Resources in Primary Classroom Interaction." Funding was provided by the Economic and Social Research Council (ESRC) as part of a broader ESRC Initiative on "Education for a Multicultural Society." Our colleagues in the research team were David Barton and Roz Ivanic.

2. Fictitious names have been adopted in this paper to preserve confidentiality.

3. This data was transcribed by Mukul Saxena.

REFERENCES

Bernstein, B. (1991). *The structuring of pedagogic discourse*. London: Routledge.

Bourne, J. (1989) *Moving into the mainstream: LEA provision for bilingual pupils*. Windsor, Berkshire: NFER/Nelson.

Bourne, J. (1993). *Inside a multilingual primary classroom: A teacher, children and theories at work*. Unpublished Ph.D. thesis, University of Southampton.

Department of Education and Science (DES). (1985). *Education for all (The Swann Report)*. London: HMSO.

Heath, S. B. (1986). Socio-cultural contexts of language development. In D. Holt (Ed.), *Beyond language: Social and cultural factors in schooling language minority students* (pp. 143–186). Los Angeles: Evaluation, Dissemination and Assessment Center.

Heller, M. (1995). Language choice, social institutions and symbolic domination. *Language in Society 24(3)*, 373–405.

Martin-Jones, M., and Saxena, M. (1995). Supporting or containing bilingualism? Policies, power asymmetries and pedagogic practices in mainstream primary schools. In J. Tollefson (Ed.), *Power and inequality in language education* (pp. 73–90). Cambridge: Cambridge University Press.

Mitchell, J. C. (1984). Typicality and the case study. In R. F. Ellen (Ed.), *Ethnographic research* (pp. 237–241). London: Academic Press.

7

Symbolic Domination and Bilingual Classroom Practices in Hong Kong[1]

Angel M. Y. Lin

INTRODUCTION: BILINGUAL INTERACTION AND THE MEDIUM OF INSTRUCTION IN HONG KONG

"What we don't want is for young people to be taught in Chinglish rather than either English or Chinese and that's what we are trying to avoid at the moment." (former governor Chris Patten, cited in the *South China Morning Post*, May 13, 1994)

"What we must ban in the classroom is mixed-code, commonly known as 'Chinglish'—that's not language at all." (former director of education Helen Yu Lai Ching-ping, cited in the *South China Morning Post*, March 14, 1998)

"Efforts will be stepped up to ensure schools teaching in English do not use a mixture of Chinese and English to boost standards. . . . If they are found to be teaching in a mixture of languages, we will ask them to switch to teach in the mother tongue." (Secretary for Education and Manpower Joseph Wong Wing-Ping, cited in the *South China Morning Post*, March 15, 1998)

The word . . . and all the stereotyped or ritual forms of expression are programs of perception and different, more or less ritualized strategies for the symbolic struggles of everyday life. (Bourdieu 1991, 106)

The former colonial Hong Kong governor appropriated a derogatory word to *name* bilingual interaction. He referred to the Cantonese-English bilingual medium of instruction in many Hong Kong schools as *Chinglish*—a word historically associated with the contact variety of English spoken by Chinese merchants to Westerners in China's coastal cities in the nineteenth century (termed "Chinese Pidgin English" by linguists, see Hall 1944). Although few specific written records have been available about the usage of the word (e.g., the word is not listed in dictionaries), members of the bilingual speech community in Hong Kong remember the word being used in the early 1970s by some school-masters or English teachers to describe in disparaging tones spoken or written English that shows a heavy syntactic or stylistic influence from Chinese. For instance, a sentence such as "He like listen music" (instead of "He likes listening to music") might be described by some people disparagingly as an instance of Chinglish. However, the pejorative word "Chinglish" is today rarely heard among the English teaching professionals in the territory, possibly because of the spread of the second language acquisition concept of *interlanguage* (Selinker 1972) among Hong Kong English teachers in recent years. However, the former colonial Hong Kong governor was probably not alone in appro-priating a derogatory word from the past to speak of bilingual interac-tion (the post-1997 government officials sounded exactly like him; see statements quoted at the beginning of the article).

Speaking bilingually, as will be shown, is quite different from speak-ing a pidgin or an interlanguage. The 1980s and 1990s witnessed the increasing visibility in the society (e.g., in movies, popular fiction, and magazines) of a Cantonese-English bilingual mode of communication (characterized by the insertion of English lexical items in an otherwise Cantonese sentence, e.g., **Neih take gei fo?**, meaning "You take how many subjects?"). This mode of communication has become especially visible among English-educated Cantonese such as university students and professionals (Gibbons 1979, 1987) and has occasionally come under attack from language purists, who also use words like Chinglish or **jung-ying-gaapjaahp** (meaning "Chinese-English-mixing") to speak disparagingly of this widespread bilingual phenomenon in the society. Typically, they view this pervasive aspect of bilingualism in Hong Kong society disapprovingly and argue that it is both evidence for and the cause of *semilingualism*, or deteriorating language abilities, among young people in Hong Kong (see Fu's 1987 review of this position, p. 37, and a review by Luke 1990; see Martin-Jones and Romaine 1986 for a critique of the notion of semilingualism).

This stance towards bilingual language practices in the society is more normatively based than research based and conveys little more than the speaker's or writer's normative claims about what counts as standard or legitimate language use. The work of sociolinguists in Hong Kong (Cheung 1984; Gibbons 1979, 1987; Luke 1984) has helped us to build a more accurate picture of bilingualism in Hong Kong. They have also drawn attention to the complex and subtle social meanings that social actors are negotiating when they are interacting bilingually.

For instance, Luke (1984) noted that bilingual language use in Hong Kong is not merely a necessary way of talking about new experiences (e.g., when no native term exists for a Western term), but also, more important, it is a linguistic reflection of how different social groups in the society respond to them. More specifically, Luke showed that a Hong Kong person may insert English words in an otherwise Cantonese sentence both to negotiate an informal situation and to reflect his or her reaction to Westernism by virtue of his or her social group membership. For example when a Hong Kong Cantonese chooses to use the word "billiard" instead of the existing native equivalents—the "high" Cantonese word, "cheuk kauh" (signaling a formal, native situation) or the "low" Cantonese word, "toi bo" (signaling an informal, native situation)—he or she is using the bilingual code to indicate his or her English-educated, Western quality while at the same time maintaining an informal, friendly atmosphere.

It seems that the linguistic purist's argument at best misrepresents and at worst totally ignores the sociolinguistic reality of Hong Kong society. This sociolinguistic reality has been aptly summarized by Cheung (1984): "While English in Hong Kong divides people into those who know the language (the middle class) and those who don't (the working class), Cantonese unites the general public and mixed-code[2] the middle class" (p. 15).

Recent research on codeswitching in popular local magazines (Lee 1999) shows that the use of Chinese, English, and other languages (e.g., Japanese, French) in popular media texts reflects the identity construction processes of people in Hong Kong. However, in using the term "Chinglish" or the derogative phrase "a mixture of languages" in the statements cited at the beginning of this chapter, the former colonial governor and the postcolonial Hong Kong officials alike seemed to be not so much concerned with using words to provide an explicit, empirically checkable representation of the sociolinguistic reality as with using words to implicitly impose an official theory about bilingual interaction. Because they were used by officials, the words had the effect of announcing that bilingual interaction was equivalent to speaking a pidginized variety or not speaking any acceptable language at all, and that was in turn implied as logical grounds for the government policy of streaming students into schools of "one clear medium," that is, either English-medium secondary schools or Chinese-medium secondary schools (Hong Kong Education Commission Report No. 4, 1990, p. 100).

But the crux of the matter remains concealed or misrepresented: What does bilingual interaction actually look like in the secondary classroom; how, and why, are teachers and students doing what they are doing; and what are the possible consequences of what they are doing (cf. Heap 1990)? The former colonial governor and the post-1997 Hong Kong officials have ducked all these questions by subtly imposing a "theory" about a particular form of educational provision that is not based on any concrete evidence. They have been asserting that teachers and students are speaking a pidginized, unacceptable form of language in the classroom and that this has negative consequences for young people's language development. They have also been saying that this must be stopped by streaming students into two groups: one qualified to be taught solely in English, the other unqualified, to be taught purely in Chinese or the mother tongue (meaning spoken Cantonese and written standard Chinese).

The aim of this chapter is to systematically and empirically address the crux of the issue, that is, the unanswered questions about the medium of instruction in Hong Kong secondary schools. As someone who has gone through the educational system and experienced the linguistic and socioeconomic realities in Hong Kong, I am keenly aware of and very concerned about the barriers that exist for some pupils in our society. I would like to see the provision of equal educational opportunities for all schoolchildren, to develop their potential and to ensure a better socioeconomic future for them. It is with a view to contributing to an openly, empirically verifiable account of the socio-economic, linguistic, and classroom realities in Hong Kong that this chapter has been written.

The following section examines the historical and socioeconomic conditions out of which classroom codeswitching has evolved in Hong Kong schools. The third section presents empirical analyses of actual instances of classroom codeswitching in Hong Kong secondary schools. The social, cultural, and educational functions of classroom codeswitching are discussed here. The fourth section focuses on the theoretical justifications and consequences of the most recent linguistic streaming policy implemented by the government in September 1998. The last section examines the origins of the many painful dilemmas in which the majority of students, teachers, parents, and school principals find themselves. It also discusses trends and changes in post-1997 Hong Kong and their implications. The section concludes by outlining the cost and benefits of the current English-dominated educational system and proposes directions for future work.

THE HISTORICAL AND SOCIOECONOMIC CONTEXT OF CODESWITCHING IN HONG KONG SCHOOLS

Despite its international cosmopolitan appearance, Hong Kong is ethnically rather homogeneous. About 97% of its population is ethnic Chinese, and Cantonese is the mother tongue of the majority. English native speakers account for not more than 3% of the entire population. Until July 1, 1997, when Hong Kong's sovereignty was returned to China and Hong Kong became a Special Administrative Region (SAR) of China, English native speakers constituted the privileged class of the society. Now, the socioeconomically dominant group in Hong Kong is the English-conversant bilingual Chinese middle class. This group also had considerable power and privilege during the colonial era.

English has long been the language of educational and socioeconomic advancement, that is, the dominant symbolic resource in the symbolic market (Bourdieu 1991) in Hong Kong. Since 1997, it has remained a socioeconomically dominant language in Hong Kong society. In the Chief Executive's Policy Address on October 8, 1997, the importance of developing English language skills among students was stressed because English skills are seen as playing a key role in maintaining Hong Kong's status as an international trading and financial center. A 1998 survey on business corporations in Hong Kong also found that the majority of business corporations said they would prefer employees with a good command of English to employees with a good command of Chinese (*Sing Tao Jih Pao*, May 21, 1998). Most important, English remains the medium of instruction in most universities and professional training programs.

It can be seen that the symbolic market is embodied and enacted in the many key situations (e.g., educational and job settings) in which symbolic resources (e.g., certain types of linguistic skills, cultural knowledge, specialized knowledge, and skills) are demanded of social actors if they want to gain access to valuable social, educational, and eventually material resources (Bourdieu 1991). For instance, a Hong Kong student must have adequate English resources to enter and succeed in the English-medium professional training programs and in order to earn the qualifications to enter high-income professions.

However, the symbolic capital of English has long been unevenly distributed across different social groups. Luke and Richards (1982) used the term "societal bilingualism" to describe the Hong Kong sociolinguistic situation in the pre-1997 era, in which two largely mono-lingual communities coexisted without interacting with each other. These two communities were not only linguistically but also culturally, socially, and economically distanced. This led to the need for a class of bilingual "linguistic middlemen" (Luke and Richards 1982), who mediated between the English-speaking ruling class and the Cantonese-speaking majority. This elite bilingual class enjoyed social and economic benefits second only to the small, English-speaking ruling class. Apart from mediating between the ruling class and the mass of the population, this elite class also served as a model for the growing aspirations of the majority. There was a widespread belief—"the Hong Kong dream"—that anyone could enter this elite class; the only condition was that she/he had to attain a good mastery of the English language, the most highly valued resource in the symbolic market.

This dream persists today. However, for the majority of Hong Kong people, the "dream" remains a dream because they and their children hardly have access to the necessary symbolic capital to attain a mastery of English. The recent focus on the importance of the social context of learning has led many second and foreign language learning researchers to conclude that language learning results only from participation in authentic communicative events (Savignon 1991). Sociocultural theories in education also point to the importance of the availability of opportunities for learners to participate in communities of practices in order to learn particular practices (Moll 1990; Lave and Wenger 1991). These opportunities are, however, sociopolitically structured (Peirce 1993, 1995). Unlike the English-speaking children or the children of the bilingual elite, who inhabit lifeworlds where English is readily used in their family and community (e.g., their parents speak English, watch English television, or read English magazines and newspapers), the majority of Chinese children in contemporary Hong Kong live in a lifeworld where it is both impossible and unnatural to use English: their parents cannot speak English, understand English television, or read English newspapers and magazines (Yu and Atkinson 1988; Lin 1996). Individuals who have attained a high level of English proficiency despite their monolingual family and community background are rare and usually have a history of extraordinary personal and family sacrifice and investment. For instance, the parents encouraged their children to watch English television programs although they themselves did not understand a word; they strived to employ a private English tutor to provide English help for their children.

What are the origins of the elite bilingual class in Hong Kong? High-quality English-medium secondary and tertiary education has always been accessible only to the wealthy and a very small number of well-performing students sifted through the public examinations.

Typically the wealthy children enter exclusive English-medium kinder-gartens and primary schools that are feeder schools for a small number of prestigious high-quality English-medium secondary schools in the colony. These secondary schools also admit a small proportion of their students from those scoring high in public examinations. Their gradu-ates make up Hong Kong's bilingual elite.

With the expansion of secondary education in the late 1970s, a large number of non-wealthy and non-elite students went to secondary schools, and their parents all demanded English-medium education for their chil-dren because of the socioeconomic value of English in the society. While the small number of prestigious English-medium schools continue to recruit wealthy students and top-scoring students through the feeder school system and the public examination system respectively, the major-ity of nonprestigious English-medium schools get limited-English-speak-ing students from the majority of the population. Both the students and the teaching staff in many of the latter lack the English resources to learn and teach effectively in English; the only strategy they can adopt in such a dilemma is teaching and memorizing model English answers for the examinations. Even in the English language lessons, apparently devoted to improving students' English proficiency, classroom practices reflect both the teachers'[3] and the students' lack of English. The valuable sym-bolic resources of English remain beyond their reach despite their painful efforts in both teaching and learning (Lin 1996).

Contrary to the claims of some authors, such as Goldstein and Liu (1994, 706), most schools consider English to be an important subject and assign the largest proportion of school time to English. For instance, many secondary schools in Hong Kong assign 10 lessons to English language in a 6-day cycle of 48 lessons, while Chinese language and math receive only seven and six lessons respectively. Students are also keenly aware of the importance and value of English for future studies and jobs, although they often find English difficult to learn, uninterest-ing, and irrelevant to their daily life (Lin 1996). They find themselves forced to learn English and have mixed feelings about English (Pierson et al. 1980; Pierson 1987; Lin 1996). They live in a lifeworld where few have adequate linguistic resources to use English at all; even if they had such resources, they would find it unnatural and pompous to use English (Wong 1984, cited in Fu 1987; Lin 1996). They are thus placed in a frustrating dilemma, in which they universally recognize the im-portance of English for their future but at the same time have little access to the symbolic capital necessary for successfully acquiring it. It is out of this paradoxical context that widespread codeswitching in allegedly English-medium schools has arisen, and it is only in this context that classroom codeswitching can be appropriately understood. To see how the larger social context can pose local dilemmas for teachers and students alike and how they draw creatively on the discursive resources available to them in dealing with their dilemmas, let us turn to the next section.

TAKING A CLOSE LOOK AT CODESWITCHING IN HONG KONG SCHOOLS

Few studies of classroom codeswitching among teachers and students who share the same native language in Hong Kong have described how and when codeswitching actually takes place. They have largely assumed codeswitching to be a more or less homogeneous and objectified phenomenon and have proceeded to correlate codeswitching with other performance variables or theoretically constructed learning variables (e.g., Johnson et al. 1985; Biggs 1990, 1991). Rather little attention has been given to why, when, and how teachers and students coproduce the rather diverse phenomena that have all come to be known as classroom codeswitching.

Very few studies so far have analyzed actual instances of classroom codeswitching: One carried out by Johnson (1983, 1985) focused on teaching and learning in different areas of the curriculum; the other was a study I carried out in the early 1990s in English language lessons (Lin 1990).

Johnson (1983, 1985) fully transcribed five content lessons (geography, history, math, science, social studies) from five different Anglo-Chinese secondary schools. He then analyzed switched utterances in their discourse context. He identified four main factors associated with code choice. English was found to be associated with text-dependent, formal, didactic, and memory-based functions, whereas Cantonese was found to be associated with text-independent, informal, explanatory, and understanding-based functions. While this is an important finding, this classification does not provide a way of capturing the subtle interactional dynamics associated with codeswitching. In the following discussion, I reexamine some of Johnson's data samples (1985) (see Extracts 1–10) and try to refine and deepen his analysis, to gain a closer picture of codeswitching in content lessons.

In M. Johnson's Example 4 (1985, 48), a math teacher is moving round the class checking work, and he finds that two pupils have not done their homework (see Extract 1).

Extract 1

024   How about you?

025   Oh. . . neih meih jouh hou hah? Chahn Gwai-hou . Laahndi-wo. Neih ne? Neih leuhng go jouh matyeh? Hah? Mhgeidak-jo dou

yauh ge me! Hah? Gung fo dou yauh mh geidak jouh ge me? Hah? Neih leuhng go jouh matyeh?
[Oh... You haven't done it eh Chahn Gwai-hou. So lazy. And you? You two why? What? Forgotten? How can that be? Eh? Is there such a thing as forgetting to do homework? What? You two, what do you think you're doing?]

Johnson mentions that English is used typically for formal statements and instructions that are directed to the whole class and relate directly to the conduct of teaching and learning, while the use of Cantonese normally reflects a departure from this situation. However, he also notes that, this general tendency notwithstanding, English may also be used relatively informally with the whole class, as when a teacher says to the whole class, "Keep up your work," or with individual students, as in Extract 1. But Johnson points out that the "tongue-lashing" given to the two students in this example is handed out in Cantonese, and it is doubtful that English would be used in the same way (1985, 47–48).

If English can be used both "formally" and "informally," with the whole class and with individual students, but something like "tongue-lashing" is done only in Cantonese, then Johnson's "formal/informal" classification does not provide us with a very useful description of the possible social meanings that are being implicitly communicated when a teacher codeswitches. Further analysis is needed.

To analyze any social interaction or action, social scientists draw on their linguistic and cultural knowledge as members of the same cultural-linguistic group as the social actors whose interaction or actions they are studying (Winch 1958; Garfinkel 1967). The social scientist is thus a member-analyst drawing on the same interpretive resources that the social interactants themselves depend on to make sense of social and cultural phenomena (Heap 1976). To understand the interaction in Extract 1, what is required of the analyst is an intimate knowledge of the implicit meanings that can be signaled by the use of the different codes among the Cantonese people in Hong Kong. For instance, a Hong Kong Cantonese does not normally speak to another Hong Kong Cantonese in English; if she/he does, she/he will be interpreted as signaling social distance, power and in short **baahn yeh** (meaning: "acting," "putting on airs"). These interpretations may be waived only in special institutional situations where institutional constraints apply, as in a law court or in the classroom, where Cantonese social actors typically suspend their ordinary roles and (or) take on (additional) institutionally defined English-speaking roles.

When we examine Extract 1 again, we notice that the teacher has been speaking English to the first student ("How about you?") when he is about to check his work. He then lets out an exclamation ("Oh"), apparently upon noticing that the student, Chahn Gwai-Hou, has not done his homework. This is followed by a "tongue-lashing" done entirely in Cantonese. It is the discovery of a student's not having done his homework that triggers the teacher's switch from English to Cantonese. As suprasegmental features such as changes in pitch and loudness have not been recorded in the transcription provided by Johnson, we have few clues to other contextualization cues that accompanied the teacher's codeswitch. But his exclamation of "Oh" indicates his surprise in this situation.

It seems that when the teacher switches from English to Cantonese, he is contextualizing a shift in frame (Goffman 1974); he is signaling a suspension of both the definition of the situation as an English-medium math lesson and his institutional role as an English-speaking math-cum-English teacher whose implicit concerns include the teaching and learning of not only mathematical knowledge and skills but also academic English for math and ordinary conversational English. That explains why English is used even when the topic is not related to academic math, that is, when he is about to check the student's homework, he speaks to him in conversational English, "How about you?" However, by switching from English to Cantonese, he is highlighting to his students a different set of concerns that he now demands them to pay attention to: the extremely unacceptable behavior of the two students, who have not fulfilled their responsibilities and obligations as students.

The teacher appears to be appealing to implicit native cultural norms and values to admonish the students for not having done their homework. What is being both appealed to and reaffirmed is the cultural logic that when students have not done their homework, it is culturally appropriate for the teacher to call them lazy and that in Hong Kong society students cannot absolve themselves of their responsibility by saying that they have forgotten to do their homework. The force of the teacher's admonition lies in its appeal to this cultural logic, which is shared by the teacher and students (cf. Heap 1986, on the notion of "cultural logic"). It is culturally acceptable for Cantonese teachers to say, quite harshly and ironically, things like **"Gung fo dou yauh mh geidak jouh ge me**?!" (meaning: "Is there such a thing as forgetting to do homework?!") in situations such as the one depicted. It is likely that the admonition would not have had the same force if it had been made in English rather than Cantonese, the native language of both the teacher and the students. By switching to their shared native tongue, the teacher in Extract 1 is doing a number of things: He is suspending the English pedagogic frame, highlighting a shift in his concerns, starting to talk to the students as "one cultural member to another cultural member," and invoking and reaffirming native cultural norms and values. What is happening here is therefore both a forceful admonition of unacceptable student behavior and attitudes and the reaffirmation and reproduction of the native cultural norms and values regarding the responsibilities and obligations inherent in the role of a student. These could not have been accomplished without the codeswitch to Cantonese.

Switches to Cantonese do not necessarily always involve an appeal to or reaffirmation of native cultural values; sometimes they are used mainly for their effect in highlighting frame shifts and changes in the teacher's concerns. Extract 2 is an example. The teacher begins his lesson in English and then breaks off and switches to Cantonese to deal with latecomers; once they are settled, he switches back to English to continue with the lesson work (Example 1 in Johnson 1985, 47).

Extract 2

008   Close all your text books and class work books....

012   **Yauh di tuhnghohk meih faan laih. Faaidi!**...
        [*There are some classmates not back yet. Be quick!*]

017   Now, any problem about the classwork?

Johnson analyzes the Cantonese utterance as an example of an informal aside made in Cantonese. While agreeing partially with this analysis, I would however note that if the teacher's intention was to mark out a mere topical digression, he could well have done this by means other than codeswitching, such as intonational changes, hand-claps, or pauses to bracket the aside (see examples of these in Lin 1990, 32–36). The use of these contextualization cues (Gumperz 1984) does not involve a violation of the institutional "use-English-only" constraint that teachers in Anglo-Chinese secondary schools are well aware of. I therefore argue that what is being signaled here is not only a topical aside, but also a radical break in the English pedagogic frame and an urgent change in the teacher's concerns. By the switch from English to Cantonese the teacher seems to be relaying to his students this implicit message, "Now I'm so annoyed by these latecomers that I have to put aside *all* kinds of teaching, including that of English teaching, and concentrate on one single task: that of getting you to settle down quickly! And you'd better take my command seriously, as I'm single-minded in enforcing it!" This break in the English pedagogic frame to highlight a different, urgent set of concerns cannot have been achieved without the teacher's switch from English to Cantonese.

The key, therefore, to understanding the implicit meanings signaled by codeswitches lies in a recognition of the sociolinguistic fact that whenever Hong Kong Cantonese have something urgent and earnest to relay to one another, they do so in their shared native language; whenever Hong Kong Cantonese speak to one another in English despite their having a common native language, it is usually because of some institutionally given reasons, such as to teach and learn the English language. When teachers want to establish a less distanced and non-institutionally defined relationship with their students, they will also find it necessary to switch to their shared native language, Cantonese, as in Extract 3. This time the teacher is commending the students' work. Johnson mentions that throughout the first part of this lesson the teacher is returning and commenting favorably in Cantonese upon the students' science projects, and Extract 3 begins with a transcription of the last part of this section (Example 5 in Johnson 1985, 48–49).

Extract 3

094   **Jauh chin keih mh hou jeung keuih yat tek jouh tek jouh lohk go jih ji lo douh, saai jo di sam gei**
          [*but don't kick it into the waste paper basket, a waste of your effort*]

095   **Waahkje neih ho yih jeung tiuh sin cheun hei keuih diu hai neih go fong douh; hou leng ge. Mh hou saai jo keuih; ho yih jih gei lo faan laak**
          [*or you can put a thread through it and hang it up in your room; very beautiful. Don't waste it; you can get it back yourself*]

096   Now you take out your note book, we come back to Mathematics. Turn to Exercise Eleven C. We look at the problems.

Johnson points out that the transition to the main business of the lesson is marked by the switch to English, which then predominates throughout the remainder of the lesson. He describes this lesson as "an extended example of the informal/formal continuum between Cantonese and English" (1985, 49). However, I find that, here again, the terms "formal" and "informal" do not provide the best description of what is happening. English is a language of power and social distance in the wider society, and any Cantonese person, no matter how fluent in English, has to switch to Cantonese if she or he is serious about establishing a genuine and friendly relationship with another Cantonese person in Hong Kong. The teacher could have done his praising of the students' work in English, but the effect would have been different. He would still be seen by the students as distancing himself from them even when praising them if the praise were given in English; the students would still be seeing him as a Cantonese hiding behind the mask of an English-speaking teacher who remained socially distanced from them. A teacher therefore has to switch to Cantonese to talk to students if she or he wants to establish a warm and friendly atmosphere. On the other hand, the teacher can always switch back to English to resume a more distanced stance, for instance, to facilitate a pedagogic task at hand. In other words, codeswitching adds to a teacher's repertoire of communicative resources in the classroom. With creative use of these communicative resources, a teacher can effectively negotiate different role-relationships with the students, as a teacher, a friend, a discipline-enforcer, or a cultural advisor, whenever the need arises (for further examples, see Lin 1990).

Codeswitching can also serve the function of establishing bilingual academic knowledge, as in Extract 4, where a science teacher is talking about a chemical solution (Example 2 in Johnson 1985, 47–48).

Extract 4

017   Do you still remember this? This solution is called potassium permanganate solution.

019   **Fui-mang-yeuhng ge yuhng-yihk laak**
          [*Potassium permanganate solution that is*]

          Batgwo ngohdeih mh haih hou seuiyiu ne gei nidi meng
          [*But we don't much need to remember these names.*]

022   So, question A, what happens to the color when you add in water?

Johnson analyzes the Cantonese utterances as a "direct translation" and an "informal aside" that is yet "related to the teaching and learning situation." The most interesting thing about this example has, however, not been brought out in his analysis.

The teacher's juxtaposition of the English chemical term, "potassium permanganate solution," with its Chinese equivalent is interesting. The origins of the "Chinese" word used here are in the modern Chinese scientific literature, where Western knowledge has been translated and indigenized. The indigenization of modern Western science started as soon as China came into contact with Western knowledge directly or indirectly through Japanese translations in the nineteenth century.

Today, all branches of modern Western knowledge have been fully indigenized and well established with standardized Chinese nomenclatures in China and Taiwan.

This teacher is atypical in his bilingual familiarity with chemical terms. Most Hong Kong teachers, who have largely been trained in the former colony's English-medium schools and higher education institutes, are unfamiliar with the Chinese counterparts of most English scientific terms and have difficulties using Chinese scientific texts (Tung 1990). However, this teacher knows both terms for the chemical solution being discussed and smoothly introduces them side by side, with the English term immediately followed by its Chinese counterpart. The effect of this juxtaposition of English and Chinese scientific terms by the teacher is that the students can know that there exists a corresponding body of scientific knowledge in Chinese, that chemistry exists in both languages, that their teacher is familiar with both systems, and that it is possible for them to know both as well.

However, immediately after the teacher has introduced the equivalent Chinese term, he says, "**batgwo ngohdeih mh haih hou seuiyiu ne gei nidi meng**" (meaning "but we don't much need to remember these names"). Then he switches back to English to ask a question about the properties of the chemical solution. It is as if he has to hurry to make a clarification about the status of the Chinese knowledge that he has just shown himself to be well versed in. He is in effect telling his students that they will not be held accountable for having learned any of these Chinese terms though he may introduce them all the same. In other words, he seems to be conveying to his students the message that this extra Chinese knowledge may be good to have but is not required for the examination. This is also evidenced by his not writing out the Chinese term for his students. In Hong Kong, teachers typically inform their students about which topics of all those covered in class will be required in the examination and which are only supplementary or interesting topics to know about but do not count as "knowledge-required-for-examination." The switch from English to Cantonese serves first to introduce corresponding Chinese knowledge and then to clarify the status of the Chinese knowledge just introduced. It reflects both the teacher's resistance to and compromise with the monolingual English objectives of the curriculum. The result of this teacher's resistance and compromise is what I call "English-dominant academic bilingualism." In Extract 5 (Example 14 in Johnson 1985, 56), a geography teacher uses a similar "English Key Term—Chinese Key Term" discourse format (Heap 1988) to establish bilingual knowledge of a geographic term, but without downgrading the value of the Chinese part of the pair.

Extract 5

045   So that means breaking up the land and then carrying away the
         small pieces of sand into the sea; then we call it erosion

047   **Cham sihk jok yuhng**
         [*erosion*].

049   O.K. Now besides a cliff......

The juxtaposition of the English and Chinese academic terms here
has the effect of establishing academic bilingualism. Moreover, there
are cognitive advantages in introducing the Chinese equivalents of
English terms as well. For instance, the Chinese term, "**cham sihk
jok yuhng**," is rather transparent in its meaning; it is made up of
words that mean "invade-erode-effect." As Johnson remarks (1985,
56), the term is not in common Cantonese usage; however, what he
does not point out is that the components that make up the term are
common Cantonese words from which a Cantonese speaker can easily
infer the meaning of the specialized term. In fact, this is a characteristic
of many Chinese counterparts of English specialized terms. By knowing both the English and Chinese terms, students can not only
understand scientific texts in both languages but also form richer
multiple conceptual connections (Gagni 1993) that facilitate their
understanding and learning of the underlying scientific concepts.
However, the teacher does not write out the Chinese term for the
students, probably reflecting a compromise with the "use-English-
only" institutional constraint. Another interesting regularity I have
noticed in Johnson's classroom data is that even when the teachers
introduce both English and Chinese terms side by side, they invariably
do so in the English-Chinese sequence, reflecting the subsidiary status
of Chinese to English. Besides, English is the medium of all texts and
written work in school. Therefore, despite the teacher's efforts to
introduce English terms along with their Chinese counterparts, the
effect is still one of English-dominant academic bilingualism.

What is much more frequently reflected in the classroom data
however, is what I call "Cantonese-annotated English academic
monolingualism," that is, that the main purpose of using Cantonese (L1) is not to establish knowledge of bilingual academic
terms, but to expediently annotate English (L2) key terms, key
statements, or texts to students who have limited English linguistic resources. In Extract 6 (Example 23 in Johnson 1985, 60),
Cantonese is used to annotate an English key term, "climate,"
and its underlying concept.

Extract 6

546   Climate **jauh haih gong keuih chyuhn nihn pihng-gwan ge tin hei dim yeung yeung**
        [Climate *is to say the average weather condition during the whole year.*]

547   **haih gong pihng-gwan ge,** alright
        [*It's talking about the average,* all right?]

548   **Jik haih gong muih-yat-nihn la, gam jik haih wah?**
        [*That is, during a year; so, in other words ...*]

549   difference between weather and climate is the weather is telling
        us the daily changes, all right? The daily changes...But climate is
        the average weather condition during a year. All right?

After explaining the concept of "climate" in Cantonese, the teacher switches back to English to state the difference between the concepts of "weather" and "climate," using a definition of "climate" that has been annotated in Cantonese in the immediately preceding utterances. What is to count as the official, legitimate knowledge corpus established in the lesson (Heap 1985) seems to be the concluding English part. The preceding Cantonese utterances are merely expedient annotations of what is to be taught and learned: the English knowledge statements about the concepts underlying the English academic terms. In other words, the concern is to establish English academic knowledge with expedient Cantonese annotations. This is reflected in the use of the key term (KT) annotation discourse format: "L2 KT–L1 Annotation," such as "Climate **jauh haih gong**" (meaning: "Climate is to say").

Another typical annotation discourse format that I have recovered from Johnson's data has the following structure: L2 Topic–L1 Annotation. It is exemplified in Extract 7 (Example 9 in Johnson 1985, 52), where the same geography teacher (as in Extracts 6 and 5) uses Cantonese to annotate English knowledge to her students.

Extract 7

056   The sea is here, all right. This is the sea ... the sea

058   Now, can you see this is a big piece of land ...

059   **Yat louh gam san seuhng heui la, hah, hou chih Gauluhng Bundou gamyeung**
        [*It extends right across, like the Kowloon Peninsula.*]

060   O.K, a big piece of land with a part of it going into the sea. **Haih**
        maih yauh yat bouhfahn san jo cheutheui hoi gam ga
        [*Is there a part of it going into the sea?*]

The teacher introduces the topic in English (056-058), and then switches to Cantonese (059) to provide an annotation of the preceding English topic; then she switches back to English (060) to introduce a little more about the topic, and then again immediately switches to Cantonese (060), translating and reformulating the preceding English statement, "a big piece of land with a part of it going into the sea," into a Cantonese rhetorical question, "**Haih maih yauh yat bouhfahn san jo cheutheui hoi gam ga?**" (meaning, "Is there a part of it going into the sea?"). The "L2 Topic–L1 Annotation" discourse format is used twice in a chain in this example: the first time, to provide an illustrative elaboration in L1 for the immediately preceding L2 topic; the second time, both to translate and to draw students' attention to the fact expressed in the immediately preceding L2 utterance by reformulating it as an L1 rhetorical question.

The use of this annotation format has not only the "linguistic brokerage" effect of ensuring students' comprehension of L2 topics, but also the educationally favorable effect of relating the unfamiliar L2 academic topics to the students' familiar lifeworld experiences, which are naturally encoded and expressed in the students' native language. For instance, the teacher in her L1 annotation (059) illustrates the preceding L2 topic with an example from the students' lifeworld: "**hou chih Gauluhng Bundou gamyeung**" (meaning "like the Kowloon Peninsula"). By using the L2-L1 discourse format, the teacher is doing both linguistic brokerage and academic brokerage for her students; she is the important linguistic and academic middleperson who helps to bridge the gap between the unfamiliar L2 academic world of the school and the familiar L1 lifeworld of the students. She makes English-medium education accessible, meaningful, relevant, and thus more bearable and less alienating for students who are in the dilemma of having limited English resources and yet desiring an English-medium education for its socioeconomic value.

While these bilingual classroom practices reflect the teachers' resistance to the "use-English-only" institutional rule in order to make school learning more meaningful and accessible to their students, their practices also reflect their acquiescence to the domination of English academic monolingualism; they accept that the official goal of the curriculum is to establish English academic knowledge and that Chinese academic knowledge does not have legitimate status in the curriculum. The role of Cantonese is only one of annotation. The domination of English academic monolingualism is reflected in the sharp contrast between the frequent instances of "lone" English academic terms (those occurring without their

Chinese counterparts) inserted into Cantonese utterances (as in Extract 8, which is Example 16 in Johnson 1985, 57) and the absence of any instance of "lone" Chinese academic terms inserted into English utterances:

Extract 8

093   **Hai go** headland **ne, hai ni douh yahp bihn ne, ho lahng yih ging yauh go** archway form **jo**
[*In this* headland, *at this place inside, an* archway *has probably already been* formed]

The subsidiary status of the L1 having only an annotation role in the classroom is further reflected in the special structure of the knowledge coproduction format (Heap 1985) that I have recovered from Johnson's data. The typical knowledge coproduction format in monolingual classrooms has the structure of Elicitation-Response-Feedback (E-R-F); however, the recurrent format I have found in the data has the following expanded structure: E (L2-L1) - R (L1) - F (L1-L2). This is exemplified by Extract 9 (Example 11 in Johnson 1985, 53).

Extract 9

012   Now last time we talked about the coast of Hong Kong.

013   Do you remember? What adjective can we use to describe the shape of the coastline of Hong Kong? Hmm?

015   Is it a shape like triangles? Squares? Circle?

016   What kind of shape is it? Hmm?

017   **Pihng mh pihng? Haih maih hou pihng gam ga?**
[*Regular or not? Does it appear to be very regular?*]
Dim yeung yeung? Hoi on sin haih dim ga? Dim yeung yeung?
[*What is it like? What is the coastline like? What is it like?*]

STUDENTS ANSWER [Unfortunately, no transcription of students' answers was provided in Johnson 1985]

019   **Hah? Waan. Hou waan huk. Hou ngaahm chaahm.**
[*Pardon? Very curved. Very jagged.*]
Ngaam mh ngaam a? Haih mh haih?
[*Is that right? Is it or isn't it?*]

020   So we find that the coast of Hong Kong is very ... irregular.

In Johnson's analysis, Extract 9 is a typical example of teachers accepting L1 answers to save time. What is missed in his analysis, however, is that while time may indeed be saved, the more educationally important effect of the use of such an L2-L1 elicitation sequence (012–017) seems to be that of enabling students to contribute to the coproduction of an officially certified corpus of lesson knowledge (Heap 1985). The L2 and L1 parts of the elicitation sequence are parallel in content to each other: the L1 part basically reformulates the L2 part into a question to which the students can respond by drawing on their familiar L1 knowledge and lifeworld experiences. The conversely structured L1-L2 feedback sequence (019–021) following the students' response serves to ratify the students' contribution, first by echoing it (the students have most probably responded in L1, given the teacher's echoing of their answers in L1) and then by translating it and incorporating it into an acceptable English knowledge statement ("So we find the coast of Hong Kong is very ... irregular"), which is to count as part of the official corpus of L2 lesson knowledge coproduced by the teacher and students. The discourse format, E (L2-L1) - R (L1) - F (L1-L2), exemplified in this excerpt reflects the teacher's attempt to elicit and value any contribution from the students in the process of knowledge coconstruction. Since what the students are able to offer are often their most familiar knowledge and lifeworld experiences, encoded and expressed in their L1, the teacher uses this special discourse format to elicit, transform, and incorporate their otherwise illegitimate L1 contribution into the official L2 knowledge corpus. This reflects the teacher's pragmatic response to the dilemma of trying to value and build on all that the students bring with them to the classroom on the one hand and fulfilling the curriculum requirement of building L2 academic knowledge on the other.

The bilingual discourse practices of teachers such as these show that they are pragmatic educational practitioners who both value and build on their students' current knowledge, as most educational theories recommend. Their bilingual practices often reflect their attempt to relate culturally and linguistically distant L2 academic topics to students' familiar lifeworld experiences to make school learning relevant and interesting to them. An example of this is shown in Extract 10 (Example 46 in Johnson 1985, 71), where a history teacher switches from English to Cantonese to make a pun. He has been teaching about Napoleon and the final campaign at Waterloo.

Extract 10

451   Waterloo. **Ngohdeih wan dou Wo-Da-Louh Douh ... da louh dauh.**

[*We find Waterloo Road... hit father*]

The teacher capitalizes on the similarity of the historical place name, "Waterloo" with the name of a road in Hong Kong and with a Cantonese phrase meaning "hit father." In Johnson's analysis, this is an example of a teacher who enjoys making puns. However, it seems to me that the effect created may be more than that of just an enjoyable pun; it may also have the psychological effect of making things that belong to the distant L2 academic world appear as close as those that exist in the students' immediate L1 lifeworld.

By reanalyzing Johnson's data, I have tried to show that bilingual classroom practices such as these represent highly creative uses of communicative resources. Bilingual discourse practices can have the effect of acculturation (e.g., Extract 1), efficient classroom management (e.g., Extract 2), and establishing a closer relationship with students (e.g., Extract 3). They can also have the effect of establishing bilingual academic knowledge (e.g., Extracts 4 and 5). Typical bilingual discourse formats (e.g., Extracts 6–10) reflect the teacher's role as a linguistic and academic broker rendering English-medium education accessible and meaningful to students with limited English resources. While they reflect the teachers' resistance to the "use-English-only" institutional rule, a practice that makes English-medium education more bearable and less alienating for the students, they also contribute to the teachers' acquiescence to the dominance of English academic monolingualism. Bilingual classroom practices such as these are teachers' pragmatic responses to the self-imposition of an English-medium education by students and parents. Many students and parents have come from a social world where there is little access to the English symbolic capital necessary for the development of a competence in English and who see English-medium school education as their only chance for a better socioeconomic future.

The teachers' and students' bilingual classroom practices represent their local, pragmatic solutions to the problems created by the imposition of a foreign language as the medium of instruction despite their having a common native language. These bilingual practices alleviate the painful dilemmas brought about by the symbolic domination of English in the society. For instance, teachers help students to comprehend the English terms and concepts of their English textbooks through the use of Cantonese annotations. They alone, however, cannot solve all the problems created by that domination. For instance, students still have to cope with all the written work and assessment in English. Because of their limited English proficiency, they have to resort to rote-memorization strategies. The bilingual oral teaching strategies observed cannot reduce the wide gap between the students' expressive competence in English and the expressive competence required by their English assignments and examinations.

However, the government's implementation of a policy of streaming primary school leavers into English-immersion schools or Chinese-medium schools in September 1998 has placed the majority of parents, students, teachers, and school principals in another painful dilemma. It is to a discussion of the theoretical justifications for and the educational consequences of linguistic streaming policies that I turn in the next section.

BILINGUALISM OR LINGUISTIC SEGREGATION? THE JUSTIFICATION AND CONSEQUENCES OF THE STREAMING POLICIES

The major theoretical justification for the streaming policies came from a paper by Swain (1986). In that paper, she delineates "the separation approach" and "the threshold hypothesis" as two ingredients to the successful use of English as a medium of instruction in Hong Kong. The separation approach is said to be superior to the bilingual approach (which she calls "the mixing approach") in producing better second-language performance, based on certain studies conducted in the North American setting. The threshold hypothesis, which is based on some studies of French immersion in Canada (Cummins and Swain 1986), states that second-language immersion programs will bring about high attainments in both academic learning and second-language learning only if the students have attained a threshold level in their first-language cognitive academic proficiency and a threshold level in their L2 proficiency. Based on these two hypotheses, she concludes with the following recommendations:

> To conclude, what I am suggesting is that positive intervention needs to occur in the medium of education issue in Hong Kong. The mixing of languages that exists in most Hong Kong secondary schools serves neither the goal of academic achievement nor second language learning to maximum effectiveness. An English medium option can be highly effective in both, and can be justified if it offers both. Thus, in order to provide the necessary conditions for a successful English medium stream, enrollment should be limited to students who have achieved high levels of cognitive academic proficiency in Chinese and who have demonstrated a level of English adequate for being able to profit from instruction in it. (Swain 1986, 6)

Swain's recommendations reflect a straightforward application of theoretical principles in important educational decisions without taking into account the sociocultural, economic, and political context in which educational institutions and practices are situated. The historical and socioeconomic origins of classroom codeswitching in Hong Kong discussed earlier have been completely ignored. The recommendations neglect the fact that given the socioeconomic domination of English in Hong Kong and the uneven distribution of English linguistic capital among different social groups in Hong Kong, the objective effect of linguistic streaming will not be the innocuous division of children into one group that learns English by one method (English immersion) and another group that learns by a less effective method (English as a subject). The objective effect of such a streaming policy in the Hong Kong context will be the segregation of children in terms of social class, learning opportunities, cultural opportunities, and job and further study possibilities. In this respect, the observations made of French immersion regarding one particular region of Canada by Canadian educational researchers (Burns and Olson 1981) are instructive.

> The fact that one group, which is largely middle class, learns French in what is generally judged to be the most effective way functionally possible (Lapkin 1978; Shapson and Kaufman 1978) while the other group, containing most of Northern Ontario's Anglophone working class, learns a more spotty variety of French or none at all, raises profound social policy questions concerning how these groups will relate to each other and to the Francophone community in the next generation. The consequences . . . also raise policy questions concerning equality of opportunity. (Burns and Olson 1981, 33–34)

A similar segregation effect is likely to result from the implementation of linguistic streaming policies in Hong Kong, only with much more disastrous social consequences, given the much greater socioeconomic importance of English in Hong Kong than that of French in Canada. In the early 1990s, warnings were already being given. The Linguistic Society of Hong Kong (1992) described the streaming policy as elitist and socially divisive. Elitism, however, does not seem to be a problem for some, who argue that the streaming policy is the best way to produce a highly fluent English-elite work force for the economy (e.g., Johnson 1994; Goldstein and Liu 1994).

It appears to me that the greatest problem with the streaming policy in Hong Kong is not elitism per se but *elitism without meritocracy*; that is, it is not so much a problem to have an elite in a society if everybody in the society has equal opportunities to enter the elite class, which seems to be what has been assumed by Johnson (1994) and by Goldstein and Liu (1994). However, it is outright social injustice if only the children of the elite can become members of the elite. Those who have supported past and current streaming policies frequently appeal to the economic argument for the importance of English in Hong Kong and usually tacitly assume that all children in Hong Kong have the same degree of access to English linguistic capital, their difference in English ability being solely a function of the amount of individual hard work and motivation (e.g., Goldstein and Liu 1994).

The key to understanding the social injustice underlying the streaming policies lies in understanding the two major features of situations of symbolic domination (Bourdieu 1991): first, the formation of a universally recognized, unified, legitimized symbolic market and second, the perpetuation of the uneven distribution of symbolic capital across different social groups, with the dominated group having the most limited access to symbolic resources. Both conditions exist in postcolonial Hong Kong society. Seen in this context, the Hong Kong government's streaming policies represent a blatant form of social injustice and symbolic domination. The objective effect of such policies has been that of perpetuating the lack of symbolic resources for the majority of children. With the banning of classroom codeswitching, teachers can no longer do linguistic brokerage for students who have limited English resources. Their lack of symbolic capital and consequently lack of social mobility are perpetuated.

Since the former colonial government's announcement of a streaming policy in 1994, difficult dilemmas have been created for many parents, students, teachers, and school principals. A few examples reported in the Hong Kong press follow.

Some schools that have, over the years, gradually and partially shifted to Chinese-medium education in certain subjects and certain grades have had to reverse their efforts because the Education Department now requires all schools to clearly declare their medium of instruction to be either English or Chinese. These schools have to switch back to English-medium instruction, since they do not want to be labeled as second class, as Chinese-medium schools have traditionally been stigmatized given the socioeconomic domination of English in Hong Kong society.

The Education Department has advised the majority of schools to change to Chinese-medium schools; however, most schools (about 60% in 1994, according to the *Wah Kiu Daily*, October 20, 1994) have defied its advice. School principals and teachers in these schools are operating under increasing pressure from the Education Department, which is going to conduct linguistic and academic tests, questionnaire surveys, and classroom observations in these schools to ascertain the effect of using an inappropriate medium of instruction.

Some teachers in a school that is among the 30% of schools advised by the Education Department to declare themselves to be English-immersion schools are reduced to directly reading out from English textbooks in the lessons, because of their limited English proficiency; their students have complained that given the way these teachers teach, they would do better without a teacher (*Ming Pao*, November 28, 1994).

The parents of the children of one school recently marched to protest their school's decision to change their medium of instruction to Chinese (Holland, 1994).

Some teachers of a school that has decided to change into a Chinese-medium school recently expressed a sense of helplessness; they said that personally they wanted to teach in Chinese, but they feared that given the socioeconomic importance of English in the society their graduates would not have bright prospects (*Express News*, May 23, 1994).

Amid and despite many public protests in December 1997, the SAR Hong Kong government reasserted the firm implementation of the streaming policy in September 1998 and issued a list of 100 schools deemed to have the English ability on the part of both their students and their teachers to constitute the select group of English-medium schools. The remaining over-300 schools were forced to switch to Chinese-medium status in September 1998. Parents, students, and school principals of 20 schools protested strongly; finally, in March 1998, the government allowed 14 more schools to remain English-medium. Many of the selected 114 schools are located in rich middle-class residential areas, while in some outlying remote areas there are no English-medium schools at all. This elitist selection policy was lamented by the parents and school principals who were seen as losers in the competition (*South China Morning Post*, March 14, 1998).

WHERE TO FROM HERE? A COST-BENEFIT ANALYSIS

Hong Kong is a place plagued with contradictions and paradoxes: It ranked eighth of the twenty-four "high-income economies" listed in *The World Development Report 1992*, and yet none of the twenty-four economies' highest-earning 20% of households took in more than 50% of the society's total income, with the exception of Hong Kong (Tsang 1994). There is a widening gap between the rich and the poor (Tsang 1994), and educational researchers cannot ignore the role played by educational institutions, policies, and practices in producing and reproducing social stratification based on a mastery of English. The domination of the symbolic market by English and the perpetuation of the uneven distribution of English linguistic capital has continued to construct "social failures" out of the majority of children in Hong Kong. Even if the provision of equal socioeconomic and educational opportunities for all children may not be the concern of the elite, they cannot continue to reap the same benefits in a society that has increasing social inequalities and youth frustration. Such a society cannot maintain its stability and social cohesion.

Some Hong Kong people may attempt to use English to draw a boundary between Hong Kong and China because of their Sinophobia. They stress the role of English in keeping the international status of Hong Kong, a status unique and distinct from that of China (*The Nineties Monthly*, September 1992). They fear the invasion of the job market by Chinese-educated professionals if they change the British- and English-based professional and higher education systems. However, in using a foreign language to draw a boundary between Hong Kong and China, they are actually also drawing a boundary within Hong Kong, a boundary between those who have access to English linguistic capital and the majority of Hong Kong Chinese who do not have such access.

The current low status of the Chinese language in Hong Kong's tertiary and professional education system and, consequently, in all sectors of the schooling system continues to undermine the linguistic and cultural identity of the majority of students and their confidence in the value of learning Chinese. Despite the return of Hong Kong's sovereignty to China in 1997, the majority of students and parents in 1998 still subscribed to the notion that English will continue to be socioeconomically more important than Chinese. The effect of such low confidence in the value of Chinese is poor mastery of the Chinese language among the majority of students. On the other hand, since they live in a social world where there is little access to English linguistic and cultural capital, they do not achieve a mastery of English, either.

It seems that Hong Kong people need to awaken to the fact that Hong Kong's economy has become increasingly dependent on China's economy since the 1980s (Ho 1994). The development of China's international economic standing has also been impressive: At the end of 1994, China's total trade ranked about the tenth largest in the world, and its foreign exchange reserve the fifth largest (Ma 1995). With these rapid economic changes in train, Chinese is likely to become the language of trade and commerce in Asia (Pease 1994). Hong Kong people need to realize that English alone cannot maintain the economic success of Hong Kong, and a balanced bilingual competence in both Chinese (usually meaning spoken Putonghua and written Standard Chinese in Hong Kong) and English is becoming increasingly economically important. The 1998 Asian financial crisis and the economic slowdown in Hong Kong further speak to the increasing economic dependence of Hong Kong on China.

The post-1997 years may be a time for Hong Kong people to reconsider their priorities. Our justification and acceptance of, or acquiescence to, the subordination of all educational goals to the single dominant goal of learning English for its alleged importance to our economy is merely a reflection of a deeper and greater subordination: the total subordination of ourselves to commercialism. The highly examination-oriented schooling system and English-dominated higher education system serve primarily the function of work-force training, screening, and credentialing. Hong Kong people must begin to ask the question that Lee (1994, 218) has asked, "How do issues of the essence of both the Chinese and the western traditions such as *ren* (humanity), life purposes, social justice, ethics, currently being repressed or ignored within educational discourse be returned to the educative process?" We are becoming more and more like the one-dimensional man and woman in advanced industrial society (Marcuse 1964). Hong Kong people have to do a cost-benefit analysis of the current English-dominated education system. We can no longer delude ourselves: We are all playing a part in the creation and perpetuation of the many painful dilemmas that parents, students, teachers, and school principals find themselves in, if we continue to justify, accept, or acquiesce in the subordination of all cultural and educational goals to the single dominant goal of learning English. Nearly thirty years ago, Cheng and associates (1973) asked Hong Kong people who accepted an English-dominated education the question of "At what cost?"; today, we need to ask the additional question of "At *whose* cost?" As shown in this chapter, an English-dominated education system yields benefits for a small elite who have access to English symbolic capital at a high cost for the majority of Hong Kong people who do not have such access.

It seems that Hong Kong people need to put their cultural and educational goals into the front seat and mobilize to change those policies, institutions, and practices that perpetuate the symbolic domination of English in Hong Kong. For instance, we should start to consider the possibility and desirability of having a bilingual rather than a monolingual English-medium higher education system. A bilingual education system can take different forms, such as gradual partial immersion (i.e., some subjects gradually taught in English and some maintained in Chinese) and/or bilingual texts (Lin 1997). While much further research is needed to examine the different effects of the different forms, insisting on a strict system of monolingual medium education creates social injustice with inevitable linguistic segregation effects in the Hong Kong context.

NOTES

1. This chapter is a substantially revised version of a paper that first appeared in *Linguistics and Education, 8 (1)*, 1996. It has been updated to take account of the

political changes in Hong Kong in July 1997. I would like to thank Marilyn Martin-Jones and Monica Heller for their helpful comments and suggestions. The limitations of the article are, however, my own.

2. The term "bilingual code" is used instead of "mixed code" in this chapter, as the latter has too often been exploited by language purists to refer disparagingly to bilingual language use.

3. Nonprestigious secondary schools in Hong Kong often cannot attract English-conversant teachers and often have to employ non–English majors to teach English.

Transcription Conventions

The data presentation format in Extracts 1–10 is that adopted by R. K. Johnson (1985): tape-recorder counter numbers precede utterances. Bold font indicates the original Cantonese utterances. The English translations of Cantonese utterances are all in italics, between square brackets. The English utterances are all in normal format. (The Yale transcription system is employed for the Cantonese utterances.

REFERENCES

Biggs, J. B. (1990). Effects of language medium of instruction on approaches to learning. *Educational Research Journal, 5*, 16–26.

Biggs, J. B. (1991). *Handling change in the language medium of instruction: Effects involving ability, locus of control, and approaches to learning.* Paper presented to the Sixth Institute for Language in Education International Conference, Hong Kong, December 17–19, 1990.

Bourdieu, P. (1991). *Language and symbolic power.* Cambridge, Mass.: Harvard University Press.

Burns, G. E., and Olson, P. (1981). *Implementation and politics in French immersion.* Toronto: Ontario Institute for Studies in Education.

Cheng, N. L., et al. (1973). *At what cost—Instruction through the English medium in Hong Kong schools.* Hong Kong: Shum Shing Printing Co.

Cheung, Y. S. (1984). Conflicts in the uses of English and Chinese teaching in Hong Kong. *Language Learning and Communication, 3(3),* 273–288.

Cummins, J., and Swain, M. (1986). *Bilingualism in education: Aspects of theory, research and practice.* London: Longman.

Express News. (1994, May 23). Sighs over switch to mother-tongue instruction (in Chinese).

Fu, G. S. (1987). The Hong Kong bilingual. In R. Lord and N. L. Cheng (Eds.), *Language education in Hong Kong* (pp. 27–50). Hong Kong: Chinese University Press.

Gagni, E. D. (1993). *The cognitive psychology of school learning.* New York: Harper Collins.

Garfinkel, H. (1967). *Studies in ethnomethodology.* Englewood Cliffs, N.J.: Prentice Hall.

Gibbons, J. P. (1979). U-gay-wa: A linguistic study of the campus language of students at the University of Hong Kong. In R. Lord (Ed.), *Hong Kong Language Papers* (pp. 3–43). Hong Kong: Hong Kong University Press.

Gibbons, J. P. (1987). *Code-mixing and code-choice: A Hong Kong case study.* Clevedon: Multilingual Matters.

Goffman, E. (1974). *Frame analysis.* New York: Harper & Row.

Goldstein, L., and Liu, N. F. (1994). An integrated approach to the design of an immersion program. *TESOL Quarterly, 28(4),* 705–725.

Gumperz, J. (1984). Ethnography in urban communication. In J.C.P. Auer, and A. di Luzio (Eds.) *Interpretive sociolinguistics: Migrants, children, migrant children* (pp. 1–12). Tubingen: Narr.

Hall, R. A. (1944). Chinese Pidgin English: Grammar and texts. *Journal of the American Oriental Society, 64,* 95–113.

Heap, J. L. (1976). What are sense making practices? *Sociological Inquiry, 46(2),* 107–115.

Heap, J. L. (1985). Discourse in the production of classroom knowledge: Reading lessons. *Curriculum Inquiry, 15(3),* 245–279.

Heap, J. L. (1986). Cultural logic and schema theory: A reply to Bereiter. *Curriculum Inquiry, 16(1),* 73–86.

Heap, J. L. (1988). On task in classroom discourse. *Linguistics and Education, 1,* 177–198.

Heap, J. L. (1990). Applied ethnomethodology: Looking for the local rationality of reading activities. *Human Studies, 13,* 39–72.

Ho, H.C.Y. (1994). The state of the economy. In P. K. Choi and L. S. Ho (Eds.), *The other Hong Kong report: 1993* (pp. 75–94). Hong Kong: Chinese University Press.

Holland, F. (1994, April 7). Parents urged to learn "mother-tongue" benefits. *Hong Kong Standard,* p. 6.

Hong Kong Education Commission. (1990). *Education Commission Report No. 4.* Hong Kong: Government Printer.

Johnson, R. K. (1983). Bilingual switching strategies: A study of the modes of teacher-talk in bilingual secondary school classrooms in Hong Kong. *Language Learning and Communication, 2(3),* 267–285.

Johnson, R. K. (1985). *Report of the ELTU study of the oral medium of instruction in Anglo-Chinese secondary school classroom.* Hong Kong: Faculty of Education, University of Hong Kong.

Johnson, R. K. (1994). Language policy and planning in Hong Kong. *Annual Review of Applied Linguistics, 14,* 177–199.

Johnson, R. K., Chan, R.M.L., Lee, L. M., and Ho, J. C. (1985). *An investigation of the effectiveness of various language modes of presentation, spoken and written in Form III in Hong Kong Anglo-Chinese secondary schools.* Hong Kong: Education Department, Hong Kong Government.

Lapkin, S. (1978). Bilingual education in Ontario: Issues and directions. *Interchange, 9(4),* 11–19.

Lave, J., and Wenger, E. (1991). *Situated learning: Legitimate peripheral participation.* Cambridge: Cambridge University Press.

Lee, M. (1999). *Code switching in local magazines: A critical analysis of media texts.* Unpublished M.Phil. thesis, City University of Hong Kong, Hong Kong.

Lee, W. M. (1994). Education. In P. K. Choi and L. S. Ho (Eds.), *The other Hong Kong report: 1993* (pp. 193–220). Hong Kong: Chinese University Press.

Lin, A.M.Y. (1990). *Teaching in two tongues: Language alternation in foreign language classrooms* (Research Report No. 3). Hong Kong: Department of English, City Polytechnic of Hong Kong.

Lin, A.M.Y. (1996). *Doing-English-lessons in secondary schools in Hong Kong: A sociocultural and discourse-analytic study.* Unpublished doctoral dissertation, University of Toronto, Canada.

Lin, A.M.Y. (1997). Bilingual education in Hong Kong. In J. Cummins, and D. Corson (Eds.), *The encyclopedia of language and education: Bilingual education (Vol. 5)* (pp. 279–289). Dordrecht, The Netherlands: Kluwer Academic Publishers.

Linguistic Society of Hong Kong. (1992). A response to commission report No. 4. In K. K. Luke (Ed.), *Issues of language in education in Hong Kong* (pp. 167–178). Hong Kong: Linguistic Society of Hong Kong.

Luke, K. K. (1984). Expedient and orientational language mixing in Hong Kong. *York Papers in Linguistics, 11,* 191–201.

Luke, K. K. (1990, May). Is Chinese-English code-mixing a disaster? (in Chinese). *Hong Kong Linguistic Society Newsletter, 8,* 30–32.

Luke, K. K., and Richards, J. C. (1982). English in Hong Kong: Functions and status. *English World-Wide, 3(1),* 47–64.

Ma, S. Y. (1995). The Renminbi threat to the Hong Kong dollar? *Asian Wall Street Journal,* March 9, 1995.

Marcuse, H. (1964). *One-dimensional man: Studies in the ideology of advanced industrial society.* Boston: Beacon Press.

Martin-Jones, M. and Romaine, S. 1986. Semilingualism: a half-baked theory of communicative competence. *Applied Linguistics, 7(1),* 26–38.

Ming Pao. (1994, November 28). Poor English tarnishes teachers' reputation (in Chinese).

Moll, L. C. (Ed.). (1990). *Vygotsky and education.* Cambridge: Cambridge University Press.

The Nineties Monthly (1992, September). Keeping distanced from Mainland culture: A historical similarity between Hong Kong and Taiwan (in Chinese).

Pease, R. M. (1994, September 19). Mandarin may become Asia's Language of Commerce. *Asian Wall Street Journal Weekly,* p. 12.

Peirce, B. N. (1993). Language learning, social identity and immigrant women. Unpublished doctoral thesis, University of Toronto.

Peirce, B. N. (1995). Social identity, investment, and language learning. *TESOL Quarterly, 29(1),* 9–31.

Pierson, H. D. (1987). Language attitudes and language proficiency: A review of selected research. In R. Lord and N. L. Cheng (Eds.), *Language education in Hong Kong* (pp. 51–82). Hong Kong: Chinese University Press.

Pierson, H. D., Fu, G. S, and Lee, S. Y. (1980). An analysis of the relationship between language attitudes and English attainment of secondary school students in Hong Kong. *Language Learning, 30,* 289–316.

Savignon, S. J. (1991). Communicative language teaching: State of the art. *TESOL Quarterly, 25(2),* 261–277.

Selinker, L. (1972). Interlanguage. *International Review of Applied Linguistics, 10,* 209–231.

Shapson, S., and Kaufman, D. (1978). A study of late immersion French program in secondary school. *Canadian Modern Language Review, 34(2),* 186–193.

Sing Tao Jih Pao (1998, May 21). English important for job promotion: Blow to mother-tongue education [in Chinese].

South China Morning Post (1994, May 13). Teaching medium will not be forced.

South China Morning Post (1998a, March 14). 14 schools to keep English in mother-tongue compromise.

South China Morning Post (1998b, March 14). Winners celebrate with cheers and hugs while losers come to terms with failure.

South China Morning Post (1998c, March 15). Warning against language mixture.

Swain, M. (1986). *Two ingredients to the successful use of a second language as a medium of instruction in Hong Kong. Educational Research Journal, 1,* 1–6.

Tsang, S. K. (1994). Income distribution. In P. K. Choi and L. S. Ho (Eds.), *The other Hong Kong report: 1993* (pp. 361–368). Hong Kong: Chinese University Press.

Tung, P.C.S. (1990). Why changing the medium of instruction in Hong Kong could be difficult. *Journal of Multilingual and Multicultural Development, 11(6),* 523–534.

Wah Kiu Daily (1994, October 20). 60% of schools defy E.D.'s advice on medium of instruction (in Chinese).

Winch, P. (1958). *The idea of a social science.* London: Routledge and Kegan Paul.

Wong, C. (1984). *Sociocultural factors counteract the instructional efforts of teaching through English in Hong Kong.* In manuscript. University of Washington.

Yu, V.W.S., and Atkinson, P. A. (1988). An investigation of the language difficulties experienced by Hong Kong secondary school students in English-medium schools: II. Some causal factors. *Journal of Multilingual and Multicultural Development, 9(4),* 307–322.

II

Coping with Contradiction and Creating Ambiguity

8

"Like You're Living Two Lives in One Go": Negotiating Different Social Conditions for Classroom Learning in a Further Education Context in England[1]

Celia Roberts and Srikant Sarangi

INTRODUCTION

The student who talked of "living two lives in one go" was describing his experience of Further Education (FE) in a London-based college. The tension he felt between his life outside college and that within is one of a number of tensions and contradictions inherent in FE classrooms in inner cities. The students on the relatively low-level vocational courses described here had had disappointing examination results at school and often had a history of feeling failed by the school system. Yet they were presenting themselves for more formal education after their compulsory schooling had finished at sixteen. Students and staff were also working within a broader tension that arose out of the FE vocational curriculum. Despite the official assumption that students were being prepared for the world of work, the great majority of students saw the course they were on as a step toward higher education.

Such classrooms are particularly significant in the life chances of minority ethnic group students, who are overrepresented on such vocational courses (Bash 1989; Eggleston, Dunn, and Anjali 1986; Sarangi 1996). With this in mind, our aim in studying these classrooms is to examine some of the ways in which inclusion and exclusion is worked out interactionally in classroom routines. In this chapter, we will compare the discursive practices of two vocational education tutors, and we will draw attention to the ways in which they manage the contradictions inherent in the positions they assumed.

We revisit here a project on equal opportunities and vocational training that we undertook in the early 1990s (Roberts et al. 1992).[2] Of the four classrooms we studied, two had a 100% intake of minority students. In the other two classrooms that are the focus of the study here, only three students in one class (Liz's class) were white and only one in the other class (Frances's class) was white, whereas both the teachers were white. The majority of students in Liz's class were of South Asian origin. In Frances's class, about one-third were of Afro-Caribbean origin, one-third of South Asian origin, and the remainder from a variety of backgrounds, mainly China and Southeast Asia. Of this latter group, a few did not have English as their dominant language. In total, only 4 out of the 74 students were white. The students were all on the Business and Technician Education Council (BTEC) course,[3] in which they were introduced to various workplace-related topics, including the organizational structure of work settings, spoken and written communication at work, and dealing with finances. They were expected to use role play and to write work-based reports as a means of acting out and reflecting on business practices.

These students are attempting to reestablish their classroom-learner credibility, having "failed" to obtain sufficient qualifications on leaving school. In the words of one of the teachers who participated in our study, "I have a feeling that we can turn many of these people eventually into successes whereas at the moment—they might well regard themselves as failures . . . so, that I think is the challenge in BTEC First Diploma."

Tutors we worked with were committed to trying to create successful learning environments, but they did this in quite different ways and with somewhat different results. This seems a different scenario from the ethnographic study of "counter-school culture" by Paul Willis (1977), where "the lads" were "accomplishing failure" by being actively involved in resisting the dominant educational ideologies. In the classes we studied, there was a greater sense of optimism, shared by students and teachers alike, although this meant living through some of the tensions we have already referred to.

This chapter is rather different from most of the other chapters in this book in that we are not dealing with overt struggles and conflicts over language and educational provision. Indeed, to borrow Hewitt's (1992) term, issues of ethnicity are unstressed (and linked more often to issues of self-presentation) rather than stressed (and linked to political issues and contestation). This is not to say that issues of ethnicity are therefore unimportant—quite the contrary. The fact that these classes were almost entirely filled with ethnic minority students in areas where minorities make up only 20% to 25% of the population suggests strong social stratification along ethnic lines. White students were either encouraged to stay on at school to take more academic courses or did not display the strong commitment to and faith in education of the minority groups (Eggleston et al. 1986). Discrimination in the job market was a further reason that so many minority students opted for FE (Brown 1984).

Such vocational courses thus represented a vital second chance for those minority groups who had already been labeled as academic failures by the school system. The issue was to what extent the social conditions for learning created in the classroom by Frances and Liz challenged the history of being failed by the school system. Of the two classrooms, one teacher (Frances) was relatively more successful than the other in helping students to pass the course and in preventing dropouts. We argue that her approach was a reflexive one. As we will see, reflexive practitioners can mobilize cultural and linguistic resources creatively in working with students to find alternative identities. Before giving an account of the two classrooms, we will outline the theoretical backdrop to our work.

THEORETICAL BACKDROP

The theoretical part of this chapter is grounded in critical social theory and in ethnographic approaches to the fine-grained detail of interaction. In other words, it attempts to combine interactional sociolinguistics with theories of social structure, but not by any simple reading off from interactional data to social structure. Our interest, to put it in Gumperz's (1992a, 41) words, is to find "a way of showing how discursive practices relate to or enter into everyday social action."

Bourdieu and the Myth of Meritocracy

We draw heavily on Bourdieu's theories relating to language and symbolic power (Bourdieu 1991, 1994; Bourdieu and Wacquant 1992) and, specifically, on his notions of symbolic capital and the linguistic market—fitting metaphors for the business-orientated curriculum that the students were experiencing. In his writings, Bourdieu exposes the myth of the meritocracy. He does this through three key notions: symbolic economy, field, and habitus. The notion of the *symbolic economy* is considered just as powerful as the financial one, with its own market and its own forms of capital. Bourdieu distinguishes between three forms of capital and market: economic (material), cultural (knowledge, skills), and symbolic (accumulated prestige, honor).[4] Within the symbolic economy, the linguistic market is one of the most powerful since every interaction has within it the traces of the social structure that it expresses and helps to produce. To quote Bourdieu (cited in Bourdieu and Wacquant 1992, 145), "Every linguistic exchange contains the *potentiality* of an act of power, and all the more so when it involves agents who occupy asymmetric positions in the distribution of the relevant capital."

Bourdieu refers to this phenomenon as the "legitimate language" (or discourse), which, he says, is invested with normalcy and standardness. For instance, in the classroom context, a particular communicative style will acquire legitimacy as students collude in reproducing this style. The legitimate language is one that is not only *understood* but also *listened* to (Bourdieu 1991, 55). In other words, the legitimate language is not only the standard or "correct" language, it also has to be spoken by a legitimate speaker. Taking this further, we would argue that it is not just a matter of dominant groups having been invested with "legitimate language" in a deterministic way, but that certain discourse practices construct and legitimize dominant speaking subjects and consequently come to be recognized in the public domain as having material reality.

Ways of speaking—and, as we see in the data to follow, the term includes ways of interacting—reproduce existing power relations. Certain ways of speaking, or communicative styles, are privileged by particular teachers, depending on their educational ideologies. These become the legitimate discourses in that classroom, and students who "tune in" to them have a better chance of being successful. These discourse practices will vary not only across institutions and levels of education but across different classrooms.

The second notion is that of *field*—a particular form of what Bourdieu calls "social space"—in which there is a hierarchy, depending on the amount of symbolic capital one has. The most obvious and telling of these fields is the educational one. Indeed, Bourdieu suggests that education has the monopoly in reproducing the linguistic market. Educational qualifications, for instance, allow one form of capital to be converted to another. Cultural capital, in the form of qualifications, can buy symbolic and material capital in the form of a prestigious and well-paid job. Similarly, a job interview requires candidates to make use of their cultural resources in order to gain, at least in relative terms, the symbolic and market power of the job on offer. This is particularly relevant to Further Education, where the emphasis is on vocationalization and where students try to translate their work experience into academic outcomes, which will, in turn, put them in a strong position to return to the world of work.

The third notion is that of *habitus*: a set of dispositions that incline us to behave—to act and react—in a certain way. This disposition to move, talk, think, and feel in a certain way is learned from our earliest years, operates below the level of consciousness, stays with us, and is transposable across contexts. It gives us, in Thompson's (1991, 27) words, "a practical sense or 'feel' for the game." According to Bourdieu (cited in Bourdieu and Wacquant 1992, 145),

> Any speech act or any discourse is a conjecture, the product of the encounter between, on the one side, a *linguistic habitus*, that is, a set of socially constituted dispositions that imply a propensity to speak in certain ways . . . and on the other side, a *linguistic market*, i.e., a system of relations of force which impose themselves as a system of specific sanctions by determining the "price" of linguistic products.

In the classroom context, which concerns us in this chapter, the habitus of students will need to coincide with what is regarded as the "legitimate language" or, to extend Thompson's metaphor, with "the rules of the game." Different teachers will attach different sets of "prices" and "sanctions" to the linguistic products in the classroom setting, and through such a differentiation construct "failed" or "successful" learner identities.

The notion of habitus is an important one in trying to understand how the processes of inclusion and exclusion come about. It is primarily about feeling comfortable with who you are. For the dominant class this sense of comfort coincides with a sense of social worth. There is an essentialism built in. You feel pretty much the same, whatever fields you find yourself in. You can be the same *you*, because *the way you are* is rated highly within those groups and through those practices that are constructed as distinctive and powerful. This, of course, has nothing to do with any special talents, but rather with being positioned in a social class where habitus and "circuits of power" coincide (Clegg 1989). To quote Bourdieu (1994, 11):

> The dominant agents appear distinguished only because, being so to speak born into a position that is distinguished positively, their habitus, their socially constituted nature, is immediately adjusted to the immanent demands of the game, and they can thus assert their difference without

needing to want to, that is, with the unselfconsciousness that is the mark of so-called "natural" distinction: *they merely need to be what they are in order to be what they have to be*, that is, naturally distinguished from those who are obliged to strive for distinction. (our emphasis)

The point is that the linguistic capital required to perform well in the institutions of our society coincides with the habitus of the dominant class.[5] They know the rules of the game. This group does well, which is credited to intrinsic merit rather than to the inevitable outcome of such a coincidence. In Bourdieu's terms, habitus and its relationship to institutional fields is mutually reinforcing. It is a vicious circle in which those outside the dominant class are excluded or exclude themselves. Within the dominated classes, there is disruption, discomfort, and resistance once one crosses the boundaries into the powerful institutional fields. Although Bourdieu does not deal with subjectivity and emotion as a major theme, it comes through in his language, as in the ideas of "symbolic violence," "struggle," "labor," "denial," and "belonging."[6]

On (Not) Playing by the Rules of the Game

The key question that concerns us here is: What implications does Bourdieu's theory have for analyzing situated classroom encounters? As a critical writer, Bourdieu does not offer specific solutions, but rather an understanding of how ways of speaking (or modes of talk) sustain our hierarchical society.[7] The difficulty with his notions is that they appear to be overdetermining (see, among others, Bernstein 1990; Giroux 1983; Jenkins 1983; for a counter-critique, see Lash 1993 and Bourdieu's [1994] own "reply to some objections"). There seems little room for understanding how social change might come about within a marketplace culture where "habitus" is presented as something durable. Nor does his work concern itself with the possibility of structuring and restructuring social relationships (see, for instance, Giddens [1976] and Fairclough [1992]) through and within interaction. Finally, issues of race and ethnicity are largely absent from his work, as is the younger generation in an FE setting.

We turn to the notion of the "game" as derived from Bourdieu's concepts of the market and the field. It is a metaphor for everyday ritualized activities within social space. The focus on everyday activities within the market allows an interactional perspective that Bourdieu himself does not pursue. But, we would argue, the idea of the "game" cries out for analysis of the rules and how they are played or challenged. The rules, Bourdieu argues, are in place to maintain the dominant position of a particular class, but the rules themselves are constructions of that class and so have the potential to be changed.

As far as the game metaphor is concerned, it is the rules of the game that divide one group from another. The rules (maintained by the dominant group for its own survival) are safe and in place until they are challenged by the dominated groups. Playing the linguistic markets is a game that both the dominant and the dominated groups must believe in. Even in the act of struggling against the game, as a member of the dominated group, one believes in it or one would not struggle. Bourdieu says the illusion of the game has to be maintained, and he implies that the reality behind the game is masked for the dominated classes. But we would argue that it is the dominant class who believe most completely in the illusion of the game. It has no disjunctures of experience that could bring the game into view. It is the imposition of the (rules of the) game by the dominant group as a natural and inevitable means of social advancement that constructs the dominated groups as having a fixed identity. According to this prevailing view among the dominant class, the single, fixed, marginalized identity of the subordinate groups can be exchanged for a new dominant-class one if individuals from the dominated class have the ability and the motivation to make the exchange.[8]

The kind of social order just outlined leaves the dominated groups in a given society in one of the following four positions. First, the dominated group fails to see the situation as a game, takes it as naturalized ideology, and consequently aspires to "better" ways of talking and acting. Second, the dominated group knows it is a game, which it wants to participate in by adhering to the rules of the game as given, thus shifting its position and contributing to the status quo. Third, the group works with the game, in order to appropriate the rules to its own advantage, and thus takes an active role in changing some of the rules over a period of time. Finally, the dominated group can always resist the dominant ideology by exposing the game itself and unmasking the rules that the dominant group uses to shield itself against any potential rupture. In asymmetrical settings such as FE classrooms, however, the more powerful participants, the teachers, may be willing to expose and challenge the rules themselves and work with students in appropriating aspects of the game. Such teachers may also see themselves as acting out a number of identities in which their class, ethnicity, professional socialization, relationships, and empathy with students will all be reflected.

For students, space, ambiguity, and opportunities to feel comfortable about a new identity while retaining other identities are created where teachers recognize and openly display that it is a game. In other words, both parties involved in the game acknowledge that there is not a single, controlling discourse but a layering of discourses within a particular communicative act—so that it is possible to "live two lives in one go."

And thus the four positions "on playing the game" suggested earlier are not themselves exclusive: People may work within and across a number of them at different times.

Linking the Symbolic Order with the Interactional Order

We turn now to explore the relationship between Bourdieu's account of the symbolic order and recent work within anthropology and socio-linguistics where the focus is on the interactional order. In general respects, the work of John Gumperz (Gumperz 1982a, 1982b and 1992a) provides a bridge between Bourdieu and the fine-grained, detailed analysis of interaction of the Conversation Analytic tradition (Sacks et al. 1974; Schegloff et al. 1977; Schenkein 1978; Sudnow 1972). Gumperz's work connects with Bourdieu in seeing linguistic resources as the cultural capital that contributes to maintaining an ethnically stratified society. Language and, we might say, legitimate language is a dimension of discrimination (Gumperz 1982a, 1982b).

Critics of Gumperz's position have argued that this framework allows little room for individual agency and creativity in redefining social relationships, a criticism also leveled against Bourdieu, as we have indicated. However, the notions of "contextualisation" (Gumperz 1982a) and "rhetorical strategies" (Gumperz 1992b, cited in Roberts and Sarangi 1995) imply the possibility of negotiating an alternative social space. Contextualization cues are the means whereby participants in social encounters have opportunities to come to shared interpretations of meaning. In accordance with Gumperz, Auer (1992, 4) suggests, "Contextualisation therefore comprises all activities by participants which make relevant, maintain, revise, cancel . . . any aspect of context which, in turn, is responsible for the interpretation of an utterance in its particular locus of occurrence."

This reflexive notion of "contextualizing language" (see also Duranti and Goodwin 1992) as indexing a set of assumptions—ways of doing things—ties up with Bourdieu's notion of habitus in a particular field. To this extent, in institutional settings, it can account for the means by which power is sustained, but not for how it is challenged, as Heller (1992) has pointed out.

Nevertheless, if it is allied to the notion of rhetorical strategies, contextualization can be seen as a process whereby relationships and identities are negotiated and renegotiated. "Rhetorical strategies" (Gumperz 1992b, cited in Roberts and Sarangi 1995) are the ways of speaking that develop out of routine interactive experiences. This is parallel to Bourdieu's (1994, 13) insistence that one's habitus has to do with the "generative capacities of dispositions." In ever more complex and multicultural urban environments, these rhetorical strategies become more complex as people explore and affirm multiple identities. The implication for the kind of educational settings illustrated next is that those who are in positions of relative power need to develop and diversify their rhetorical strategies if they are to make judgments about students' performance and offer opportunities that contribute to a more socially just society. In what follows we shall show how the ambiguity surrounding multiple identities is acted out interactionally in two FE classrooms.

STUDYING TWO CONTRASTING CLASSROOMS

In this section, we look at ways in which classroom interaction provides opportunities (or not) for the education game to open up a more fluid social space in which identities can be negotiated and renegotiated. In addition to drawing on Bourdieu's game metaphor, we invoke Gumperz's (1981) notion of the social conditions for classroom learning.

Working toward a possibility of change within the FE setting, we try to approach our classroom study from the point of view of critical ethnography, which aims to be emancipatory and concerned with social change. It is worth bearing in mind that critical ethnography has been criticized, notably by Hammersley (1992, 109), for asserting an oversimplified oppressor/oppression model. However, we would take issue with this conceptualization. It seems possible to work toward social change through ethnography without taking up such a simple model. As we have suggested, the ideological "game" played in education is often hidden from the view of both students and teachers; certainly, there is no straightforward imaging of teachers as oppressors. An ethnography that acknowledges the ambiguous social space of the classroom and works toward unmasking some of the educational "games" played out in it is what we would like to think of as critical ethnography.

The kinds of students we are studying here cannot be subjected to any neat formulation of social identity along class, ethnicity, age, or gender lines. The local young people who enter the FE college bring with them their "youth" identities and some, often contested, sense of racial and ethnic identity, but not a specific class identity in Bourdieu's sense.[9] Among others, Gilroy (1987), Hall (1992), Heller (1999), Hewitt (1992), and Rampton (1995 and this volume) point out that identities and boundaries are much more fluid than traditional studies of race and ethnicity have suggested. Gilroy, for instance, argues that ethnicity is not the fixed, bounded entity it used to be. Similarly, Hewitt (1992) in his work on language, youth, and ethnicity suggests a radical destabilization in which at least two modalities of ethnicity are generated: One is stressed, political, and contesting; and the other is unstressed and realized through the local multi-ethnic vernacular. In other words, in certain contexts, ethnicity becomes the focus for self- and group presentation, while at other times the rhetorical strategies used are those shared by most young people in the shared community.

In our study, where the focus was on teacher-student interaction, there were no examples of the stressed modality of ethnicity. The students used the local London vernacular to talk to teachers, and the issues of exclusion and inclusion depended on the extent to which they tuned in to the specific cultural style of the classroom, as created by the teachers.

Tuning in to the Individual Classrooms

Let us turn our attention to the cultural environments of individual classrooms as a way of finding out not only how each classroom maintains and reproduces its own ethos but also how individual students tune in to a particular classroom culture and consequently become successful. Of the two focal classrooms in this study, the discursive practices of one teacher, Liz, focused on the analytical, on tightly structured tasks and the display of knowledge. Students with developed classroom learning skills did well in this classroom. The other focal classroom in this study, where Frances was the teacher, had a different environment and different underlying values. The focus here was on student experience and informal social relationships. In a number of ethnographic interviews with Liz and Frances, their theories of learning emerged. As they talked about their approaches to teaching/learning, reacted to videos of themselves in the classroom, and discussed individual students, certain recurring metaphor types characterized their discourse. Our account of these theories of learning was triangulated with the classroom practices we observed and videorecorded. Against the theoretical backdrop of Bourdieu, we can see these discourses as the defining features of classroom habitus for certain groups of students.

Liz's Classroom: A Tight Ship. Liz's theory of learning centered around learning as an organized activity, and the metaphors she used were those of control: The course was conceived of in physical terms with metaphors of the body and of building, and it was characterized in terms of the transmission of rational knowledge. Someone had to be the "backbone," so that others could "lay the foundation" and "build on it." In addition, she said, "You have to be a finisher," and that depended to a large extent on "knowing the score," "having the right garb," "adopting the appropriate tone," "knowing when to tread carefully and when not to," and so on. The classroom was like a "tight ship," where continual monitoring of "performance" was an important feature.

The social space was tight: "You've got to respect each other's personal space. Be accessible, do your job . . . but not over-familiar, because that is death." The rules of the game were brought to the open to be followed, and there was little room for ambiguity. Liz also frequently used metalanguage to disambiguate academic tasks and interpersonal relations, although her metalanguage signaled interactional troubles with individual students, as we shall show later on.

Frances's Classroom: A Garden of Geraniums. Let us now turn to the second classroom, where Frances was the teacher. Frances, at one stage, described herself ironically as "a little mother hen," the students as "geraniums that haven't been watered" and her classroom as a natural environment where individuals could "flower." Her theory of learning centered around "interaction" and "social contact," as she drew upon metaphors of ecology/growth and nature (e.g., "a little mother hen," "they're still flowering") as well as metaphors from the "game"—both the idea of a physical game and the idea of board games (e.g., "track," "boundaries," "puzzle," "bouncing things off" the students). Her ideological position was that the authority of vocational education could be challenged. She did not seek authority through the subject. Because of the kinds of social relations she constructed with the students, identities were negotiable and the interpretive frames (triggered by contextualization cues) were open rather than closed. This allowed for interactions to be multiply framed and for participants to use different voices. (We are using the concept of multiple-framing here as it has been used by Maybin 1994.)

A Schematic Representation of the Social Spaces Being Constructed in the Two Classrooms

At the risk of ironing out some of the complexity of classroom interaction in both classes, it is possible to contrast the two as follows:

Frances's Classroom— Relatively more:	Liz's Classroom— Relatively more:
Inductive	*Deductive*
Social equality	*Social hierarchy*
Informal	*Formal*
Loose structure	*Tight structure*
Personal experience and development	*Conceptual development*
Communicative relationships	*Task metaskills*

| *Extended teacher-student interaction* | *Structured student-student interaction* |
| *Individual opinions valued* | *Display of knowledge skills valued* |

There are some parallels here with Bernstein's notions of strong and weak classifications in pedagogic practices (Bernstein 1990). In Liz's classroom, the relationships were explicit and hierarchical and the boundaries clear. Frances's classroom was regulated around more implicit meanings, the boundaries were more permeable, and there was more room for ambiguity. Different educational ideologies, expressed through the teachers' metaphors and worked out in classroom routines, created different linguistic marketplaces, and so a different set of assumptions operated about the socially constituted dispositions of the students.

CONSTRUCTION OF STUDENT SUCCESS AND FAILURE THROUGH TALK

Content and Procedural Talk

As we have shown, the two teachers had strikingly different views about classroom learning. For Liz, it was "knowing the rules," "getting in," "making it explicit," and so on that distinguished successful students from less successful ones. For Frances, however, it was a "nurturing" and "caring" approach that allowed students to determine discourse routines at their own pace.

In both classrooms, talk contributed to the construction of student identities, but did so in different ways. Here, we focus on the talk between the teacher and small groups of students working on business-related tasks. This talk was characterized by many of the features of classroom talk identified in school-based research both in teacher-fronted settings (Sinclair and Coulthard 1975; Mehan 1979; Edwards and Westgate 1987) and in teacher/small-group interaction (Barnes 1976; Green and Wallat 1981; Bloome and Goldman 1982; Biggs and Edwards 1991). The talk is routinely a mix of content talk, such as eliciting and giving explanations, examples, and justifications, and procedural talk in which the task is organized and checked up on and the means of accomplishing it are commented on (see Erickson [1982] on task structure and participation structure). Both types of talk have been the subject of much description and analysis, but they have tended to be studied without fully accounting for the "social conditions for classroom learning" (Gumperz 1981). In other words, they have not accounted either for the metacommunicative messages that position the students in relation to the teacher or for the history of communicative relationships developed in particular classrooms (see Sarangi [1998] on the mediating role of metatalk).

In our study, there was a tendency for relatively problematic students (as perceived by the teachers) to receive and use more procedural talk than content talk, but overriding this pattern was the quality of talk, either procedural or content, and the social relationship that it indexed.

Talk and the Social Conditions for Learning in Liz's Classroom

First, we take some examples from Liz's classroom. Some of the features of metatalk are shown in the interaction presented in Extract 1 between Liz and Ravi, who was a student Liz had doubts about. The lesson occurred toward the end of the first term of the course, and by the end of the term, Ravi had dropped out.

Extract 1[10]
```
01   L:   [moves to a group of three students and has eye contact with Ravi who is
          sitting next to Shiv] Come on we must get this finished by (   )
02   R:   I know
03   L:   Now, what are you looking for?
04   R:   Five, ten, twenty-five
05   L:   No, what's the question? Not what are you looking at, but what are
          you looking for? What does the question say?
06   R:   Complete the following (   )
07   L:   You're looking for (0.5) to find the average output. Ok, how do you
          find the average?
08   R:   You get that and [gestures with hands, looks at Shiv and laughs]
09   L:   Now think about it. What is an average? How do we find an average?
10   R:   (   ) mean (   ) sort of thing [smiles and looks at Shiv]
11   L:   Yeah, OK, then fair enough—so what is the mean? How do we find
          the mean? because this is the type of average I want there
12   R:   [reads and mumbles, shifting gaze to his work]
```

In this example, Liz's attention is focused on Ravi. Liz opens the interaction with a procedural comment, "*Come on, we must get this finished by. . . .*" When she starts to question him, she uses a form of "hyper-questioning," both within a turn (see turn 5) and across turns (turns 9, 11). The term *hyper-questioning* draws on Erickson's (1976) notion of "hyper-explanation" in intercultural communication. "Hyper-explanation" is used by white interactants in powerful positions to produce long and increasingly less abstract statements on the assumption that the client cannot understand them. Here "hyper-questioning" involves two features: repeated questioning within a turn without turn-taking pauses (turns 5, 9, 11) and a high rate of questioning across turns (3–11), in an increasingly less abstract form.

One of the effects of Liz's hyper-questioning is that Ravi avoids eye contact with her (turn 12), which may be an indication of his unwillingness to play the game with Liz. Instead, Ravi colludes with his fellow student Shiv, smiling at him rather than engaging in answering the question. A further source of communicative trouble is Liz's strategy of talking about talk, metatalk, to repair Ravi's apparent error at turn 4.11. Metatalk has the function of arresting the flow of talk in order to attempt a repair of the other's problem. This often occurs in clarificatory side-sequences. It is, of course, a commonplace of much classroom interaction; but in our data, a pattern emerged in which teacher's talk about talk was, on the one hand, a productive strategy with students rated as relatively successful on the course and, on the other hand, a marker of discomfort with those students such as Ravi who were not doing well.

In the previous extract, Liz's use of hyper-questioning and metatalk appears to construct an increasingly disengaged response from Ravi, as can be seen from his minimal response in turn 10. A little later on, Liz returns to Ravi on similar progress-checking business; on this occasion Ravi not only avoids eye contact but leans far back in his chair, away from Liz as if to remove himself from the interaction all together. This pattern of apparent interactional discomfort reflects a difficult social relationship and serves to reproduce it. It also constructs a negative identity for Ravi that is set against Liz's presuppositions about what an appropriate student should be like.

In the next example, in Extract 2, taken from Liz's classroom, which involves another student, Mahmud, there is a shift from content talk to procedural talk:

Extract 2

01   L: [to whole class] Try and think of three or four points that each group can raise.
[to T] It's a good point, very good point. [to M] What sort of ideas have you come up with?

02   M: We've done this so far we've said that |

03   L: | Will you buy a decent pen, a decent biro? because it's it really is very funny isn't it? One there. One there as well. What sort of pens do you use?

04   M: [silence]

05   L: Yeah, anything, present to me ( ) presentation has been improved. Have you actually tabulated that yet and put it into a nice table?

06   M: Yeah

07   L: You have. Have you got that with you?

08   M: [silence]

09   L: Okay [looks at B's work] this looks really nice, doesn't it? The way that is presented ... it's so much easier to read. And that's where you get downgraded, you see, in your design and visual discrimination.

If it's hard for me to follow and hard for me to read then that
obviously is not going to get a distinction in being clear and concise
and informative, okay?

In turn 3, Liz interrupts the content talk—"What sort of ideas have
you come up with?"—with procedural talk—"Will you buy a decent
pen?" This is followed, as in the previous example, by hyper-questioning, both within this turn and across turns (see turns 5 and 7). Liz moves
from a general exhortation to more concrete questions, for example,
about what sort of pens Mahmud uses (turn 3), a request for him to
show her his table (turn 7), and finally, in turn 9, an appeal to gain his
agreement about the importance of presentation skills. Like Ravi in
example 1, Mahmud (M) reverts to a minimal response (turn 6) and
silence (turns 4 and 6), which suggests that something has gone wrong
in the interaction. Turn 9 illustrates clearly how Liz chooses to elaborate
on the procedural aspects of the task (i.e., presentation of content),
rather than the task itself, when she asserts the superior quality of B's
work and thus warns M of the educational consequences of poor presentation—"that obviously is not going to get a distinction." What this
implies is that the rules of the game are fixed and need to be conformed
to, for one to succeed in the educational field. Liz is imposing the rules
while making students like Ravi and Mahmud aware of the consequences of breaking the rules or the damage from not playing the game.
It is not clear whether Ravi and Mahmud are resisting the rules or are
simply ignorant of the rules of the game.

In the two preceding examples, we have suggested that certain
kinds of procedural talk—hyper-questioning, metatalk—both index
and serve to reinforce difficult social relationships. They appear to
disrupt learning, not in any creative way but by contributing to the
formation of social conditions that are a barrier to learning. They also
reflect a tightly structured hierarchical relationship between teacher
and students, which means that students must acquire "a feel for the
game."

Talk and the Social Conditions for Learning in Frances's Classroom

In Frances's classroom somewhat different social conditions prevail
as a result of different discursive practices. Here, procedural talk takes
on a different function, as does the role of questioning. In Extract 3, two
students, Danny and Garth, both of Afro-Caribbean origin, have made
rather slow progress with the task: to write brief notes for a phone call
and then write a letter of complaint. Frances moves over to Danny and
Garth and stands in front of their table:

Extract 3

01 D: How long have we got left? I've just started on this letter
02 F: You've got enough time [*smiling*]
           [*D looks at his watch*]
03 G: As in six minutes
04 F: Well, that was the given time I gave you but er |
05 D: | that was to make
           us panic but nobody seemed to panic
           [*F moves her head from side to side, smiles*]
           [*D laughs*]
06 F: Wouldn't really matter how much time I gave you would it? (1.0) or
           would it?
07 D: [*smiles*] Oh yeah because | [*looks down & picks up task sheet*]
                                  |
08 G: yeah | [*looks up*] If you gave us two minutes
           [*looks half down, raises eyebrows*]
09 F: Would you do it?
10 G: Yeah I'd do it I'd rush it
           [*both D and G put heads down and look at their work*]

This encounter takes one minute to accomplish, but a great deal is going on in this short time. When Danny calls Frances over, he asks how much time they have left to complete the task—in other words, a procedural question. He offers the information that he has only just started on the second and most time-consuming task, presumably to negotiate for an extension of the six minutes left. Frances indirectly accepts the bid for more time but in such a way as to open up the interaction for further negotiation. Danny and Garth, in different ways, ask for confirmation. Garth does this (in turn 3) humorously by stating pedantically how many minutes are left (rather as a teacher might). Danny's response to Frances's "that was the given time" shifts the topic from the practical (they now know she is giving them more time) to a "meta" level, talking about why she gave them that deadline. In effect, Danny has come over to the teacher's side and is talking within her frame of reference. Frances elaborates Danny's topic by implying that the students never seem to have a sense of urgency, but she then focuses on Danny and Garth: "Wouldn't really matter how much time I gave you would it? (1.0) Or would it?," which Danny and Garth read as a request for a display of their keenness or ability to manage time well. (The frame shifts back to the frame at the beginning of the encounter.) They both agree that it would matter how much time there was, and Garth implies that he would take a time limit seriously because he cares about his work and does not want to rush it. Danny and Garth seem to have managed to justify their rather slow progress by showing Frances that her time limit tactic did not work, but at the same time they have demonstrated their personal keenness.

This latter point is subtly accomplished, in the last few lines, in the way that Danny and Garth coordinate their own behavior as a team. Danny agrees with Frances, "Oh yeah," but finishes his sentence nonverbally by picking up his task sheet and showing her that he is getting on. As Danny looks down, Garth looks up and, like Danny, gives only part of his response verbally, using raised eyebrows, smiling, and emphatic intonation to express his concern. On Garth's final "rush it," both students put their heads down as if to signal that the hypothetical case that Frances has proposed has become a reality for them. What we find here is that although the interaction begins with Danny asking a formulaic question, Frances does not answer formulaically and so sets up the space for the whole encounter to become multiply framed, thus illustrating the idea of ambiguity, of a more open social space as suggested earlier. In a sense, Frances invites Danny and Garth to initiate an evaluation and critique of her own regulative behavior.

Interactions between Danny and Garth and Frances were markedly egalitarian. They were typical of the majority of the class, but there were individuals whom Frances felt she could not "bounce things off." They could not tune in to her preferred teaching style. Similarly, there were students who could tune in to Liz's preferred style, which was analytical and task-oriented, as there were others who could not. This tuning in (or not) was part of the process of constructing a certain type of student with a certain habitus.

Social Conditions, the Rules of the Game, and Possible Exclusion

In Liz's class, the game had to be played by the rules, or you were excluded. In Frances's class, the game was brought out into the open, so to speak, for what it was. Within this more active social space, it was OK to role-play the teacher and to use interactional strategies that were not part of, as Bourdieu would say, the "legitimate language" (see Extract 3). In Liz's class you had to acquire the dominant discourse, but you could not take on the role of teacher. The following is what Liz had to say about Mahmud, who was taking a leading role in a group discussion:

> Mahmud is now adopting the role that I was adopting prior to the discussion. I came throwing out ideas, what about this, what about that. . . . Mahmud is adopting the very same technique and the other three are answering him. It's not really a discussion on equal terms. He is really throwing out the questions and making them reply to them.

In her account, Liz constructed Mahmud negatively on the grounds that the latter was appropriating the teacher's voice and thus bringing about a hierarchical pattern of student-student interaction. In Frances's class, however, you could take on the role of the teacher within the game, but you did not have to use the legitimate language all the time. It is quite possible to regard Frances's classroom practice as a form of social control—what Bernstein (1975) would categorize as a shift from ritual to therapeutic control. However, this view fails to account for the ambiguity and complexity of individual teacher-student relationships over time and the genuine empowerment that may occur in particular instances.

In these two classrooms, the allowable discourses (and so the allowable identities) were different. In Liz's classroom, students were positioned into the first of the two categories just outlined; students either succeeded or failed, but the rules of the game could not be changed and the game was never explicitly acknowledged as such. In Frances's classroom, students and teacher worked within a third and fourth position, acknowledging the game and being aware of the possibilities of resistance.

Similarly, metatalk, hyper-questioning, and procedural talk served to disrupt and so reinforce prevailing social conditions in each classroom. In Extract 1, we see that the flow of activity was disrupted in order to construct a discursive identity for Ravi, that is, his voice became the voice of the question as Liz required him to read it out: "What does the question say?" By contrast, Frances's metacommunication, as in Extract 3, contextualized the multiple framing and so, cumulatively, the multiple identities allowable in her classroom. Frances and Danny and Garth together disrupted the routine teacher-student interaction, and in doing so they reinforced the more open, negotiated, ambiguous relationships that characterize her class.

We suggest not that Liz's classroom did not offer opportunities for learning but that it was a more traditional classroom. It was easier for students with a more traditional student identity to tune in. Students succeeded where they were seen to be "on task" within the boundaries of the task-driven classroom that she created. Those who did not, Liz described (herself implying the "tuning in" metaphor) as "off key." More traditional students who accepted this task-driven environment did well.

In Frances's class, the students who did well were those who opened up, had ideas, and negotiated a relatively "equal" status with her. Those who were narrowly task-driven and overanxious about the task tended to do less well but would no doubt have been more successful in Liz's class. Overall, since there were many fewer traditional students in both classes, Frances's group was relatively more successful.

CONCLUSION

In this chapter, we have used Bourdieu's notions of symbolic economy, field, and habitus to suggest, in the cumulative interactions of classrooms, that such notions need not be as determining as Bourdieu's work seems to imply. Where teachers from the dominant social class bring multiple identities and multiple voices to the interactions, and so the possibility of altering or appropriating the rules of the game with participants from dominated groups, then there is the possibility of some, however localized, social change.

We have looked, in particular, at two aspects of discourse—the use of metalanguage and rhetorical strategies—to illuminate the possibilities for challenging the interactional order in Further Education classroom contexts. We have also, in passing, raised the issue of feelings and emotion in making social evaluations and wish to stress this connection between comments on personality and social behavior and how these are interactionally accomplished.

We also raised the issue of reflexive politics. We have used the linguistically and culturally diverse FE context to try to show how teachers from the dominant class can create, interactionally, a more active social space within which those from outside the group can have a feel for the game and still feel comfortable about who they are in a particular field. In order to do this, such professionals need, to use Bourdieu's word, to "labor" at being reflexive so that the entrenched polarity between "them" and "us," between passing and failing, between "getting along" and "getting on" is not such a foregone conclusion, along deeply rutted social lines.

NOTES

1. This chapter is an abridged and substantially revised version of an article that first appeared in *Multilingua (14(4)*, 363–390) under the title " 'But are they one of us?' Managing and evaluating identities in work-related contexts." We are deeply indebted to Marilyn Martin-Jones for her meticulous editorial feedback on an earlier version of this chapter.

2. The project entitled "Quality in Teaching and Learning: Four Multicultural Classrooms in Further Education" was funded by the Training, Education and Enterprise Directorate, Department of Employment (1990–1993).

3. BTEC is the acronym for the Business and Technician Education Council, which was first established in 1983. It has now been superseded by a national awarding body called Ed Excel.

4. Note that these different forms of capital operate within an exchange system in a given society, allowing for transfers between them.

5. We use the notion of "class" in Bourdieu's sense, as sets of agents who occupy similar positions in social space and hence possess similar kinds or similar quantities

of capital, similar life chances, and similar dispositions. This notion is different from the Marxist view of class, which is defined in terms of the ownership and non-ownership of means of production, or the Weberian definition of classes in relation to the distributive sphere (at the level of market interaction).

6. The debates on language in socially and ethnically stratified nation-states have tended to separate off and ignore issues of affect. Besnier (1990) and Lutz and Abu-Lughod (1990) assert the sociocultural nature of emotions and challenge the widely held view that emotions are not seen as amenable to sociocultural analysis. These authors take the Bakhtinian view that language is saturated not just with ideology but with emotion (see also note 8).

7. It is important to note that Bourdieu categorizes himself as a critical writer, in the historical ontological tradition, who is concerned with social change. He resists calling himself a theorist or a structuralist and offers a defense of his work against what he calls "theoreticist" readings (see Calhoun et al. 1993).

8. Many of the students in the study came from non–working class-backgrounds; the two main parental occupations stated were "self-employed" and "skilled."

9. The following broad transcription conventions are used here and in all other extracts:

( )   inaudible speech

[ ]   comments about nonverbal behavior

| overlapping speech

(1.5)   length of pause in seconds.

10. Note that we are using metatalk in a broader sense than Sinclair and Coulthard (1975), who use metastatement to define a comment about a future activity in the lesson to help students understand its structure.

REFERENCES

Auer, P. (1992). Introduction: John Gumperz's approach to contextualization. In Peter Auer and A. Di Luzio (eds.), *The contextualization of language* (pp. 1–37). Amsterdam: John Benjamins.

Barnes, D. (1976). *From communication to curriculum*. Harmondsworth: Penguin.

Bash, L. (1989). Education goes to market. In L. Bash and D. Coulby (Eds.), *The Education Reform Act*. London: Cassell.

Bernstein, B. (1975). *Class, codes and control: Vol. 3. Towards a theory of educational transmissions*. London: Routledge.

Bernstein, B. (1990). *Class, codes and control: Vol. 4. The structuring of pedagogic discourse*. London: Routledge.

Besnier, N. (1990). Language and affect. *Annual Review of Anthropology, 19,* 419–451.

Biggs, A. P., and Edwards, V. (1991). "I treat them all the same": Teacher-pupil talk in multi-ethnic classrooms. *Language and Education, 5(3),* 161–176.

Bloome, D., and Goldman, C. (1982). Literacy learning, classroom processes and race. *Journal of Black Studies, 13(2),* 207–226.

Bourdieu, P. (1991). *Language and symbolic power*. Edited and introduced by John B. Thompson; Translated by G. Raymond and M. Adamson. Cambridge, Mass.: Polity Press.

Bourdieu, P. (1994). *In other words: Essays towards a reflexive sociology*. Cambridge, Mass.: Polity Press.

Bourdieu, P., and Wacquant, L. (1992). *An invitation to reflexive sociology*. Cambridge, Mass.: Polity Press.

Brown, C. (1984). *Black and white Britain*. London: Heinemann.

Calhoun, C., LiPuma, E., and Postone, M. (Eds.). (1993). *Bourdieu: Critical perspectives*. Cambridge, Mass.: Polity Press.

Clegg, S. (1989). *Frameworks of power*. London: Sage.

Duranti, A., and Goodwin, C. (Eds.). (1992). *Rethinking context: Language as an interactive phenomenon*. Cambridge: Cambridge University Press.

Edwards, A. D., and Westgate, D.P.G. (1987). *Investigating classroom talk*. London: Falmer Press.

Eggleston, J., Dunn, D., and Anjali, M. (1986). *Education for some*. Stoke-on-Trent: Trentham Books.

Erickson, F. (1982). Classroom discourse as improvisation: Relationship between academic task structure and social participation structure in lessons. In L. C. Wilkinson (Ed.), *Communicating in the classroom*. New York: Academic Press.

Fairclough, N. (1992). Discourse and social change. Cambridge, Mass.: Polity Press.

Giddens, A. (1976). *New rules of sociological method*. London: Hutchinson.

Gilroy, P. (1987). *There ain't no black in the Union Jack*. London: Hutchinson.

Giroux, H. (1983). Theories of reproduction and resistance in the new sociology of education: A critical analysis. *Harvard Educational Review 52(3)*, 257–293.

Green, J., and Wallat, C. (Eds.). (1981). *Ethnography and language in educational settings*. Norwood, N.J.: Ablex.

Gumperz, J. (1981). Conversational inference and classroom learning. In J. Green and C. Wallat (Eds.), *Ethnography and language in educational settings* (pp. 3–23). Norwood, N.J.: Ablex.

Gumperz, J. (1982a). *Discourse strategies*. Cambridge: Cambridge University Press.

Gumperz, J. (Ed.). (1982b). *Language and social identity*. Cambridge: Cambridge University Press.

Gumperz, J. (1992a). Contextualisation revisited. In P. Auer, and A. Di Luzio (Eds.), *The contextualization of language* (pp. 39–54). Amsterdam: John Benjamins.

Hall, S. (1992). The question of cultural identity. In D. Hall, D. Held, and T. McGrew (Eds.), *Modernity and its futures* (pp. 274–316). Cambridge, Mass.: Polity Press.

Hammersley, M. (1992). *What's wrong with ethnography?* London: Routledge.

Heller, M. (1992). The politics of code switching and language choice. *Journal of Multilingual and Multicultural Development, 13(1&2)*, 123–142.

Heller, M. (1999). *Linguistic minorities and modernity: A sociolinguistic ethnography*. London: Longman.

Hewitt, R. (1992). Language, youth and the destabilization of ethnicity. In C. Palmgren et al. (Eds.), *Ethnicity in youth culture* (pp. 27–41). Stockholm: Stockholm University.

Jenkins, R. (1983). *Lads, citizens and ordinary kids*. London: Routledge.

Lash, S. (1993). Pierre Bourdieu: Cultural economy and social change. In C. Calhoun et al. (Eds.), *Bourdieu: Critical perspectives* (pp. 193–211). Cambridge, Mass.: Polity Press.

Lutz, C., and Abu-Lughod, L. (1990). *Language and the politics of emotion*. Cambridge: Cambridge University Press.

Maybin, J. (1994). Children's voices: Talk, knowledge and identity. In D. Graddol, J. Maybin, and B. Steirer (Eds.), *Researching language and literacy in social context*. Clevedon: Multilingual Matters/Open University.

Mehan, H. (1979). *Learning lessons*. Cambridge, Mass.: Harvard University Press.

Rampton, B. (1995). *Crossing: Language and ethnicity among adolescents*. London: Longman.

Roberts, C., and Sarangi, S. (1995). But are they one of us? Managing and evaluating identities in work-related contexts. *Multilingua, 14(4)*, 363–390.

Roberts, C., Garnett, C., Kapoor, S., and Sarangi, S. (1992). *Quality in teaching and learning: Four multicultural classrooms in further education*. Sheffield: TEED, Department of Employment.

Sacks, H., Schegloff, E., and Jefferson, G. (1974). A simplest systematics for the organization of turn–taking for conversation. *Language, 50(4)*, 696–735.

Sarangi, S. (1996). Vocationally speaking: (Further) educational construction of "workplace identities." *Language and Education 10(2&3)*, 201–220.

Sarangi, S. (1998). "I actually turn my back on [some] students": The metacommunicative role of talk in classroom discourse. *Language Awareness 7(2&3)*, 90–118.

Schegloff, E., Jefferson, G., and Sacks, H. (1977). The preference for self-correction in the organization of repair in conversation. *Language, 53(2)*, 361–382.

Schenkein, J. (Ed.). (1978). *Studies in the organization of conversational interaction*. New York: Academic Press.

Sinclair, J. McH., and Coulthard, M. (1975). *Towards an analysis of discourse: The English used by teachers and pupils*. Oxford: Oxford University Press.

Sudnow, D. (Ed.). (1972). *Studies in social interaction*. New York: Free Press.

Thompson, J. B. (1991). Editor's Introduction. *Language and symbolic power*. Cambridge, Mass.: Polity Press.

Willis, P. (1977). *Learning to labor*. Aldershot: Saxon House.

9

Constructing Hybrid Postcolonial Subjects: Codeswitching in Jaffna Classrooms

Suresh Canagarajah

INTRODUCTION

Postcolonial communities and subjects are characterized by profound linguistic and cultural hybridity, and the language policies imposed by different political agencies fail to take into account the tensions and ambiguities manifest in linguistic practices in these communities. Nationalistic regimes in local contexts and/or transnational agencies from the West contribute to the imposition of monolingual policies that are influenced by long-term material interests and subtler ideological considerations. Such policies fail to relate to the heterogeneous cultural values and language attitudes that exist in local communities and classrooms. It is therefore fascinating to observe linguistic practices at the everyday level in such contexts as a means of understanding the manner in which people cope with the monolingual policies imposed on them.

My own concern has long been with the linguistic conflicts experienced by the Tamil community in Sri Lanka. Language is at the root of the sociopolitical malaise there, a malaise that has been tearing the country asunder for over a decade of ferocious warfare between majority Sinhalese and minority Tamils, costing at least 50,000 lives, by conservative estimates. This chapter focuses on linguistic policies and practices in Jaffna, the northern peninsula of Sri Lanka that has historically been the cultural, religious, and political center of the Tamils. The Tamils in Jaffna speak a distinct Tamil dialect. From 1990 to 1995, the militant nationalist organization LTTE (Liberation Tigers of Tamil Eelam) set up a de facto regime in much of the area in the Jaffna peninsula that it "liberated" from the Sinhala government and provisionally renamed Tamil Eelam. The boundaries of this de facto state have been changing, depending on the power shifts stemming from the ongoing military struggle with the Sri Lankan state. Some of the areas where this data was gathered in the 1990–1994 period have now come under the control of the Sri Lankan army.

In this chapter, I show that, while the LTTE has imposed a Tamil-only policy for communication in public domains in Jaffna, in one specific educational setting, that is, classes where English is taught as a second language (ESL), an equally constraining English-only ideology prevails. This English-only ideology derives from the English Language Teaching (ELT) institutions of the center that influence language educational policy making around the world. This creates a conflict for Tamil teachers and students in ESL classrooms. In their day-to-day classroom conversations, they are compelled to negotiate the tension between the two opposing ideologies. They do this in creative and strategic ways, which frequently give rise to codeswitching between Tamil and English. I will argue that this codeswitching and linguistic negotiation is in keeping with the hybrid cultural ethos long established in this part of South Asia and that it also serves to construct hybrid postcolonial subjectivities in both classroom and community contexts.

THEORETICAL BACKGROUND

I start from the assumption that social institutions are characterized by relative autonomy (see Aronowitz and Giroux 1993). Although the influence of the dominant social groups is always there, most institutions have a measure of freedom to mediate, modify, and resist ideological impositions. However, there is always a conflict between the interests and functioning of local institutions and dominant social groups and their agencies. This state of affairs will explain how it is possible for two conflicting ideologies to be articulated in Jaffna society. While the political dominance of the LTTE regime enables a Tamil-only ideology to persist at the national level, the English-only ideology manifest in the discourse of local ELT practitioners gains its power from transnational center-based institutions. Moreover, individual schools have some autonomy, which enables them to distance themselves from both these ideologies or to form slightly different ideologies, though they cannot totally escape from these influences. What this means is that, at the national level, various institutions (like political institutions, educational institutions, media, industries) can reveal slightly different ideological tendencies, even though LTTE's pronouncements may carry the most weight, at least at face value.

Since the focus of this chapter is on the everyday negotiation of ideologies in classroom discourse, I will be presenting the ideologies of the LTTE and the ELT enterprise in Jaffna in a generalized fashion, which may appear to imply that I see them as unified. However, I must emphasize that I am not assuming that ideologies are always monolithic or consistent. There are internal contradictions within ideologies at the conceptual level. There are also inconsistencies between policy and practice. This explains how the LTTE can profess a Tamil-only ideology but permit the teaching of English as a second language and how, at the same time, they can use English for some political and administrative functions and employ Western political discourse in conducting their nationalistic struggle. These ideological inconsistencies can be exploited by people within institutions like schools for oppositional purposes.

Since language choices and discourse practices reproduce ideologies, observing interpersonal communication at the everyday level is important for understanding macrolevel political processes. The practices observable at the local level can hold considerable significance for the reproduction and transformation of macrolevel institutions. The linguistic strategies that subjects adopt to negotiate dominant ideologies can reveal modes of resistance, and they can also provide insights into the communicative processes involved in the construction of alternative ideologies and subjectivities. Language plays a key role in social processes, such as the affirmation of identities associated with particular interests and ideologies. People take on different identities and, thus, their language practices are fluid and subject to change. It is for these reasons that I see simple acts of classroom codeswitching as possessing significance. Close study of the day-to-day codeswitching practices of students and teachers in classrooms in contexts such as Jaffna can give us insights into ways in which students and teachers negotiate dominant ideologies, while at the same time affirming their own desired identities and values.

MY RESEARCH IN JAFFNA CLASSROOMS

The data considered in this study comes from observations of class-room teaching by 24 teachers. The observations were carried out in selected schools in rural and urban areas in the Jaffna peninsula. The original purpose of the study was to analyze the functions of first-language (L1) use, that is, use of Tamil in ESL classrooms, but the focus was gradually narrowed down to an exploration of the role of codeswitching in classroom talk. Access to these classrooms was facili-tated by the fact that these teachers were enrolled in a diploma course in English language teaching at the University of Jaffna, where I was teaching. As part of their course, the teachers were required to do a two-month-long practicum, which was graded. Each teacher was vis-ited at least three times during the period by two supervisors, including the author. The observation of each class was followed by extensive discussions with the teachers about their classroom practice. The super-visors also discussed the performance of each teacher periodically among themselves. I took extensive ethnographic notes on the context of each teaching situation and, wherever possible, I noted down the statements of teachers and fellow supervisors. The codeswitching data was gathered by means of a combination of audiorecording and on-site manual transcription. In my interpretation and analysis of this class-room data, I have also drawn on ethnographic work carried out over four years in classroom and community settings in Jaffna. This work involved sociolinguistic recording of conversations in a range of sites in the community, such as in urban markets, in villages, and in educa-tional settings, including the University of Jaffna (see Canagarajah 1993, 1995). Some of my reflections on the meanings of the codes and contexts in the data are also based on my own lived experiences as a native member of this community.

THE IDEOLOGICAL CONTEXT

Tamil-Only Ideology

The language politics of the LTTE need to be considered as a response to the status of elite bilingual Tamils as well as to that of Sinhalese speakers within the Sri Lankan state. With the establishment of colonial power by the British in 1815, English became the main form of linguistic capital associated with material and symbolic rewards for local sub-jects. Today, Tamils who are bilingual in English and Tamil are still educationally successful, they monopolize the professions, and they enjoy social status. They are also relatively unenthusiastic about the formation of a separate Tamil state, as they still have interests vested in the Sri Lankan state. Their commitment to the Tamil language is also relatively weak, as they have their sights set on cosmopolitan values. As part of a broader ideological commitment to social change and to the emancipation of the primarily monolingual rural population, the regime in Jaffna has therefore had to insist on a Tamil-only policy. In the new linguistic order in Jaffna, it is now the bilinguals who are disadvantaged, as they often find it difficult to carry out institutional transactions without the use of any English.

The Tamil-only ideology also stems primarily from the language politics of the 1950s, though there are also deeper roots, which I will return to in the latter part of this chapter. In 1956, the Sri Lankan state adopted a Sinhala-only educational policy aimed at mobilizing the Sinhala masses in postcolonial Sri Lanka. Though this policy was largely designed to counter the influence of English-speaking locals and to give a local language a central role in the nation-building project of the postcolonial period, it had the effect of discriminating against the Tamil-speaking people on the island. From that period onward, language became a core value in the construction of a distinct Tamil ethnolinguistic identity, whereas during colonial times it had been the Saiva religion that had been the main emblem of their identity. It is from this background that we can also understand another component of LTTE ideology, namely, their insistence on the use of "pure Tamil." Avoiding borrowings from the different languages imposed on the community at various points in history is considered to be a means of signaling one's "pure" Tamil identity. The languages in question include Portuguese, Dutch, and English as well as Sinhala. "Pure Tamil" therefore has high symbolic value within the community. Today, in Jaffna, avoidance of borrowing or codeswitching has become a way of showing one's solidarity with the cause of Tamil nationhood and one's commitment to cultural autonomy.

Since it heads a de facto regime, the LTTE has not constituted statutory bodies to make language laws. Thus, even the most casual pronouncements of the military leaders pass for law in Jaffna. Military officials publicly insist on the need to use only Tamil for formal and informal purposes in the community. They use the civil institutions and political infrastructure under their control to promote the currency of Tamil and to enforce its sole use. They are able to regulate language use when they turn back petitions or applications tendered in other languages or in mixed Tamil to the police department, at the pass office (for movement outside the liberated zone), in the law courts, and at village councils. I observed one face-to-face verbal interaction between a woman and a police officer in a pass office that was particularly telling. I include it here (Extract 1) to illustrate how the Tamil-only ideology operates in daily discourse.

Extract 1

Officer: **appa koLumpukku een pooriinkaL?**
             'So why are you traveling to Colombo?'

Woman: **makaLinTai** wedding-**ikku pooren.**
             'I am going for my daughter's "wedding"'

Officer: **enna? UnkaLukku tamiL teriyaataa?** England-**ilai iruntaa
             vantaniinkal?** //
             'What? Don't you know Tamil? Have you come here from
             England?'

Officer: **enkai pooriinkaL?**
             'Where are you going?'

Woman: **cari, cari, kaLiyaaNa viiTTukku pooren, makan.**
             'Okay, okay, I am going to a wedding, son'

The petitioner's use of a single English borrowing (i.e., "wedding")
doesn't pass unnoticed. Although it takes some time for her to realize
her blunder, she corrects herself, as her petition can easily be turned
down for such mistakes. In fact, on occasion, military officials go further
than this to periodically warn people of the ideological and cultural
"evils" of using English. These evils include damaging traditional Tamil
culture, hindering the nationalist struggle, providing access to unnec-
essary foreign distractions, and instilling a permissive Western lifestyle.

The endeavors of the regime are indirectly and unwittingly aided by
the Sri Lankan government's economic and fuel blockade and by the
cutting off of power to the "liberated zone." The Tamils in Jaffna are
therefore cut off from channels of information and communication in
English (or in any other language) from outside the region. The regime
itself carries out a censorship of published literature and printed matter
coming into the region. The local television and radio transmissions,
begun on a limited scale by the regime, use only Tamil. The regime thus
attempts to carry out its plan of "purifying" Tamil and enforcing its sole
usage through the mass media.

While Tamil is clearly the official language in both a statutory and a
symbolic sense, it is also catching on as a working language in certain
other domains. Formal meetings in educational and professional institutions are mostly held in Tamil. Ironically, even the Chief Guests'
address in the traditional English Day celebrations in schools is now
being made in Tamil. The meetings of the university statutory bodies
are also held in Tamil (whereas they used to be solely in English).
Minutes are kept in both languages. Even such gatekeeping processes

as interviews and selection tests for jobs are increasingly conducted in Tamil. English does still function as a language of wider communication (in the horizontal sense of enabling interaction across ethnic groups in the island), and it is used for international purposes. That is, spokespersons for the regime communicate with negotiating teams from the Sinhala south and with foreign journalists in English. But the place of English in these situations is not explicitly planned or acknowledged, it is simply the default option.

The ideology of Tamil-only is aided by the emergence of a monolingual elite in this society. The majority of cadres and the highest officials of the regime are now monolingual in Tamil and come from the previously nondominant caste/class groups. Members of the traditionally bilingual elite, in professional and intellectual circles, are now either totally monolingual or L1 dominant. It is important to note, however, that the ideology of the regime is not accepted wholeheartedly by everyone in the community. Aside from those who are still bilingual, many monolingual Tamils feel that the linguistic and cultural agendas of the regime are a bit too extreme. There is no direct resistance to the regime, as it is widely perceived to be exercising its power in totalitarian ways.

An English-Only Ideology

The regime in Jaffna has not introduced definitive language education policies, although it has established a parallel educational system to that of the Sri Lankan government. It has been quite interventionist in the development of curricula in the social sciences and the humanities, at both secondary and tertiary levels. It has insisted on the use of a "purified" Tamil as the medium of instruction for all subjects. In addition, the regime has begun conducting its own examinations for secondary schools according to its revised syllabi. However, paradoxically, it has turned a blind eye to school-level teaching of English, allowing the existing program of the Sri Lankan government to operate here. (Here, I should add that some of the institutions of the Sri Lankan state still function in Jaffna, existing parallel to the separatist regime's own structures.) The regime simply takes the position that nothing should be done to encourage the acquisition of English through the institutions under its control. Propping up the status of Tamil in other public institutions and in other areas of the school curriculum appears to be seen as more important than meddling in school-level acquisition of languages.

How then is ELT constituted in Jaffna schools? From having been the medium of education during colonial times, English has been reduced to a separate subject (ESL), which is taught from year 3 onward in both the Jaffna and the Sri Lankan school systems. Sandwiched between other subjects, which are taught in either Tamil or Sinhala, the English class is now the only part of the curriculum in which some measure of English is used. ESL is a compulsory subject until year 11, although a pass is not necessary at that level to proceed further. ESL is not taught in schools thereafter, and proficiency is not a criterion for university admission. The objective of the ESL program is primarily to build formal competence for instrumental purposes. Academic needs feature large in the curriculum, apart from formal and semiformal uses in institutional contexts. In a largely skills-based program, the emphasis falls heavily on reading and writing, with a written final test (and no assessment of listening or spoken skills). The English targeted is closer to "standard" British or American English, even though the teachers themselves generally use an educated Jaffna English in the classrooms. Though British and American textbooks have been widely used and though the British Council and the Asia Foundation still continue to make generous donations, the Ministry of Education in Sri Lanka is increasingly publishing its own texts, drawing on the expertise of foreign scholars. These books are also used in Jaffna. While they may contain local characters and situations, they still eschew local discourse conventions and local varieties of English. Needless to say, scholars see a need for systematic and comprehensive planning of formal language learning for all levels of education in Jaffna and Sri Lanka (see Fernando 1994; Goonetilleke 1983; Hanson-Smith 1984).

Although English teachers and education officers are all locals, the policies and prescriptions on English language teaching from the Anglo-American center still influence periphery countries (see Phillipson 1992). In fact, most of the ESL educational administrators who come from the middle-class bilingual circles share the values and perspectives of the center. Furthermore, the educational institutions are dependent on the center for research/pedagogical publications, expertise, and sometimes funding (through cultural agencies like the British Council and the Asia Foundation). Periodically, consultants are invited by the Sri Lankan Ministry of Education to provide in-service training and curricular advice. They also collaborate in developing textbooks and testing instruments. It is not surprising therefore to find that local teachers' perspectives on ELT are influenced by the dominant notions, methods, and pedagogical fashions of the center. Teachers who have been to state-run training schools are familiar with the different versions of the communicative approach to language teaching and learning and profess the virtues of other recent methods. The carefully graded and integrated textbooks, designed centrally by the Ministry with the help of Western experts, are generally task-oriented and communicative. ELT orthodoxies still predominate. Thus, in informal interviews, local teachers expressed to me the following types of views: that English should be the sole medium of the ESL courses; that the more English is taught, the better; that the earlier English teaching is begun, the higher the proficiency of students will be; that the language acquired should be "standard" American or "standard" British English. During my tenure as a teacher and administrator at the University of Jaffna, my attempts to encourage the use of Jaffna English (the local nativized variant) in the teaching of spoken English and accommodation to the use of L1 in ESL classes to facilitate L2 acquisition were vigorously resisted by the teachers. Phillipson (1992) describes such views and pedagogical practices as "the monolingual fallacy" and associates them with the hegemonic functions of the center.

For a variety of reasons, such as the professional background of local teachers, unsystematic planning of ESL by local educational institutions, the fact that the Sri Lankan government's institutional arrangements for the teaching of English are still in place within the de facto Tamil state, the inconsistencies in the ideological agendas of the LTTE, and the devaluing of the importance of language education planning by the Tamil regime, ELT policies in Jaffna are still heavily influenced by external agencies in the center. The situation in Jaffna is not unlike other third-world contexts where center-based ELT institutions have a considerable influence on language education planning and teaching practice, despite the nationalistic aspirations of local governments. In Jaffna, as elsewhere, there is considerable tension between planning agencies concerned with the status of Tamil across different public sector domains and those involved in the planning and development of English language education in Jaffna. The Tamil-only policy of the local political regime and the English-only policy adopted in ELT circles do not sit well together. The wider political agendas that motivate these language policies are quite different: while English-only policies in small postcolonial communities contribute to the integration of English teachers and their students into global ELT networks dominated by Anglo-American agencies and thereby ultimately contribute to the imposition of center hegemony, local language-only policies are calculated to achieve cultural and political autonomy from the forces of globalization, especially those from the West.

BILINGUAL DISCOURSE PRACTICES OF TEACHERS AND LEARNERS

How are these conflicting ideologies and agendas negotiated in the classrooms in Jaffna and in the everyday interactions between teachers and students? The teachers in my study insisted in interviews with me that they used or permitted only English. They were predisposed to an English-only ideology by their training, by the wider educational policy, by the teaching material they used, and by the teaching methods they had adopted. However, when I observed and audiorecorded their classes, I was struck by the preponderance of codeswitching in two kinds of classroom interactions: teacher/student and student/student interactions. In many cases, the teachers indicated that they had only become aware of their use of L1 after I had drawn their attention to the instances in my recordings. Though the views of the teachers about language use in the classroom were center-influenced, their actual pedagogical practices and the frequent codeswitching were clearly responses to local conditions and were due to conflicting social and cultural tendencies.

Let us consider some of the linguistic interactions in these classrooms to understand the ways in which conflicting values, roles, and statuses were negotiated. I found, for example, that teachers used a considerable amount of Tamil for pre-activity directions, while the pedagogical activity proper was in English. In Extract 2, taken from a year 7 class, the teacher was setting up an oral exercise. To do this, she had to get the class to assume that the student standing in front represented the persona depicted in the card she was holding. The question-and-answer exchange read out from the textbook by the students was typical of the unnatural ways in which conversations were depicted in this textbook.

Extract 2

Teacher: We will practice question forms next. *(to Student 1)*
             niinkal vaankoo.
             'You come'

             (Student 1 comes forward and Teacher gives her a picture to hold)

             (To class) **cari, iva inta paTattu aal enTu yosiyunkoo.**
             'Okay, imagine that she is the person depicted in the picture'

             (To Student 2) **ini niir ummuTaya keeLvikalay vaasiyum.**
             'Now you read your questions'

Student 2:   Who are you?

Student 1:   I am a policeman.

This and numerous other scripted interactions from the textbook were conducted in English, with an implicit acknowledgment that English was the official code of the classroom. Tamil emerged as the marked code for this context. It was used for interactions that were not considered overtly pedagogical. The use of Tamil personalized the institutional relations between teachers and students. It served to build a rapport between teachers and students by evoking the values and ethos of the community outside the classroom. However, this was done in such a way that Tamil did not conflict with the status of English as the dominant/established code for the classroom.

In this and other classes, the teachers also resorted to Tamil in order to make commands or give admonitions in the classroom. Tamil was also used for encouragement and compliments. In situations where teachers faced hesitant or nervous students, they switched to Tamil. This had the effect of putting students at ease, conveying the teacher's sympathy and, in general, creating a less threatening atmosphere. Extract 3 is taken from a year 8 class:

Extract 3

Teacher: What is the past tense form of "swim"? // Come on. // **enna piLLayal, itu**
                                                        'What,   children,
            you don't
            teriyaataa? poona vakuppilai connaniinkal.
            know this? You told me in the last class'

Student 1: swimmed=

Student 2: =swam

While the students did not respond initially (note the pauses after the teacher's opening utterances), the switch to Tamil ushered in a range of answers. Furthermore, the "come on" in English that preceded the switch was not as successful in eliciting a response as the Tamil utterance was (note the second pause). Although the Tamil words used by the teacher were, by themselves, not too endearing, the switch to the learners' L1 carried the affective connotations. The status of Tamil as the marked code for the context made it possible to achieve this change in footing. The teachers were tapping into the affective potential of using the vernacular.

Since Tamil signified in-group solidarity for the students, they frequently used it when pleading with the teacher for excuses or special favors. Take, for example, the following exchange from another year 8 class shown in Extract 4.

Extract 4

Teacher: What did I give for homework yesterday?

Student 1: Page forty.

Teacher: Okay, take them out, I want to correct your work first. *(Goes toward Student 2)*

Student 2: **naan ceiya marantuTTan**, Miss.
            'I forgot to do it'

In switching to Tamil to explain to the teacher that she had forgotten to bring her homework, this student was asking the teacher to step out of her institutional role (and the power it brings with it) and to employ the values of in-group solidarity. The teacher continued to use English, thereby conveying that she was unwilling to abandon her institutional persona and that she preferred to uphold institutional norms. The codeswitch by the student was clearly a strategic gamble, as she was attempting to redefine the context and the classroom relationships to her advantage.

In interactions I observed outside the strict demands of the lessons, teachers and students generally used Tamil. Teachers also switched to Tamil when they wanted to discuss extrapedagogical matters, like events in the town or personal matters. Such asides were kept distinct from strict instructional activities. In these asides, teachers and students switched to Tamil and, in doing so, evoked identities that were different from the institutional teacher/student identities symbolized by their use of English. Since Tamil was the code associated with interpersonal interactions outside the classroom, the use of L1 in these contexts evoked identities from lifeworlds beyond the classroom and defined the interactions as nonpedagogical.

While the preceding extracts show how codeswitching functioned in the process of classroom management, the following extracts reveal how codeswitching contributed to the negotiation of content during pedagogical activities. Teachers switched to Tamil when they wanted to discuss culturally relevant anecdotes, when they wanted to give explanations, or when they wanted to provide illustrations to clarify the lesson content. Sometimes, the teachers made asides in Tamil during the course of long monologues in English. This often occurred when they were referring to the world beyond the classroom. In Extract 5, taken from another year 7 class, this function is interactively achieved by teachers and students. Through this process, teachers also related the lesson content to knowledge gained outside the classroom, thus bridging the gap between school and home.

Extract 5

Teacher: Today we are going to study about fruits. What fruits do you usually eat? //
inraikku niinkal viiTTilai enna palankaL caappiTTa niinkaL? cila peer
'What fruits did you eat this morning at home? Don't some **kaalamai caappaaTTikku paLankaL caappiTiravai ello?** people eat fruits for breakfast?'

Student 1:   **naan maampaLam caappiTTanaan**, Miss.
'I ate mangoes'

Teacher: Good, mangoes, eh? **maampalam enRaal** mangoes.
'Maampalam means mangoes'

Student 2:   **vaaLappaLam caappitta naan,** Miss.
'I ate bananas'

Teacher: Okay, bananas.

The students did not respond to the general question posed in English (note the initial pause), but there was a torrent of response when the teacher reframed the question more specifically in Tamil and related it to their home context. Thereafter, the teacher proceeded to subtly introduce the English vocabulary items related to the lesson by translating into Tamil the fruits the students mentioned.

So far, I have focused on the teacher/student interactions. I now turn to the student/student interactions that took place away from the eyes and ears of the teacher, as part of what I have called elsewhere the "classroom underlife" (Canagarajah 1997). In moments such as these, student discussions in Tamil helped them to explore aspects of the lesson content in additional depth. Subtle, secretive exchanges took place between students while the teacher was talking or otherwise occupied. Students prompted each other with correct answers, they translated sentences or phrases in the textbook, and they clarified the content for themselves in Tamil. These practices appeared to be contributing to their learning. Take, for instance, the exchange shown in Extract 6, between students in a third year 8 class:

Extract 6

Teacher: *(Reading aloud)* . . . it is our duty to look after trees and replace them through reforestation. *(To class)* Reforestation means replanting trees and vegetation *(Continues reading aloud)*....

Student 1:   Reforestation **enRaal ennappaa?**
              'What does "reforestation" mean?'

Student 2:   **kaaTaakkam. umakku teriyaataa?** Social science-**ilai paTiccam.**
              'Don't you know reforestation? We studied about that in social science'

Student 1:   **enna? kaTukalai aLikkiratoo?**
              'What? Destroying forests?'

Student 2:   **illai appaa. marankalai tirumpa naTukiratu.**
              'No, man. Replanting trees'

The second student's explanation served to relate the teacher's utterance to knowledge that the students had gained from other subjects taught through the medium of Tamil. Student/student interactions such as this provided safe spaces for reflecting on the lesson content.

Sometimes the students used only Tamil in these safe spaces as they undertook the prescribed lesson activity. English was the marked code, and it was primarily used for rhetorical effect. In one of the activities I observed, in a year 9 class, students had been divided into small groups and asked to arrange strips of utterances into a coherent dialogue. The students conversed among themselves in Tamil as they rearranged the dialogue and prepared to read it out in English to the teacher. As their conversation in Tamil unfolded, they translated the dialogue strips into Tamil, they made judgments on the appropriateness of their attempted sequences, they guessed at the probable purpose and direction of the dialogue, and they sought help from their peers on difficult words in the strips. Whenever such activities were assigned, inevitably, students used Tamil to interact with each other while working on the task.

THE WIDER IMPLICATIONS OF THESE BILINGUAL DISCOURSE PRACTICES

As we can see, the teachers and students in my study were doing more than just carrying out the lesson activities. They were also constantly engaging in code alternation, which had significant implications for the construction of identity and the negotiation of group membership. The English teachers not only belonged to a bilingual cosmopolitan, anglicized community of practitioners but also participated in wider social networks where Tamil was used. Similarly, the students not only were learners of English who were aspiring to membership of an imagined cosmopolitan/bilingual community but also participated in networks where vernacular forms of Tamil were used. The codeswitching revealed how the teachers and the learners took on, affirmed, and negotiated different identities, from one context to another. In situations clearly framed as pedagogical, the teachers had to play the role of English teachers and the students had to take on the role of English students. At other moments, they were ill at ease in these roles. In such situations, they shifted to Tamil to symbolize solidarity. Furthermore, through codeswitching, teachers and students managed the power differences behind their institutional roles. The teachers assumed more or less authority by moving in and out of English and Tamil. Through these codeswitching practices, the contexts of interaction were continually being defined and redefined. The participants in different classroom conversations were either maintaining the norms relevant to the institutional context or shifting to extrapedagogical (community-based) norms. These ESL classes were thus sites for the skillful management of identities, roles, values, and group membership through codeswitching. The codeswitching also enabled participants to deal with conflicting communicative norms and ideologies.

What are the implications of these classroom discourse practices for the students' acquisition of English as a second language? As I have shown, there was considerable use of Tamil, Tamilized English, and extensive codeswitching, although the teachers professed to be using only "standard" British or American English. Moreover, there was little use of English as a language of active communication. English was reserved largely for reading aloud from the textbook and for oral exercises. The broad pattern of language use in these classrooms can be characterized in this way: Monolingual communication through the medium of English was accomplished with conscious effort in highly routinized classroom exchanges, while more spontaneous use of language was characterized by frequent codeswitching. This perhaps reflects the conditions in which the learning of English was taking place: The acquisition of "standard" English and the ability to speak monolingually were prerequisites for school success and for gaining access to knowledge and opportunities beyond the boundaries of Jaffna, while, on the other hand, a facility with codeswitching was needed for negotiating everyday interactions. Above all, codeswitching is what the learners got most exposure to and practice in during their English classes, although this was never explicitly addressed in discus-

sions about the English curriculum. The classroom discourse practices
I observed and audiorecorded ran counter to the explicit policies and
orthodoxies associated with ELT in different parts of the world.

Codeswitching plays a significant part in communicative life in Jaffna
society. In other work on the linguistic practices of Tamil speakers in
this context, I have shown that codeswitching (involving different
codes: Tamil and Tamilized English) is a pervasive feature of social life.
I have argued that this is becoming the chief means by which bilingualism persists in Jaffna society (see Canagarajah 1995). Codeswitching is
thus an established norm outside the classroom, and it is increasingly
common inside the classroom. In the classroom context, teachers and
students draw on their experiences of codeswitching in other domains
of their lives. They bring values, identities, and attitudes developed in
their lifeworlds outside school into their classroom discourse. By the
same token, the code alternation inside the classroom lends legitimacy
to codeswitching outside. Codeswitching is clearly a communicative
resource of considerable social value in the Jaffna context, and the
learners who develop this form of communicative competence accrue
particular advantages in their lives inside and outside school.

What we find then is that the everyday language use in classrooms
in Jaffna diverges from the monolingual policies of both periphery and
center agencies, both the Tamil-only policy and the English-only policy.
In developing their policies, neither center nor periphery agencies have
taken adequate note of the cultural realities of the local communities
and schools. The interests of ordinary people are different from those
pursued by the regime, and they dictate different sociolinguistic practices. Many ordinary people in Jaffna still see a need for English as a
language of wider communication and for gaining access to certain
material and symbolic rewards in their own community, rewards that
derive from the global hegemony of English. The regime's Tamil-only
policy is thus rarely observed in practice. At the same time, the English-
only policy imposed upon teachers and learners in Jaffna schools by
those who adhere to narrow ELT orthodoxies is often disregarded.
Teachers and students use Tamil to convey solidarity, and they also use
it because they have the same broad nationalist sentiments as the
regime. Teachers and students do make some efforts to conform to the
English-only policy of the educational institutions, but they are also
continually finding spaces for the subtle use of Tamil and Tamilized
English.

The codeswitching practices of these classrooms constitute a subtle
mode of resistance to the agendas of those who control policy in both
political and educational domains. The Tamil-only policy of the local
regime is perceived by many to be simplistic, rigid, unrealistic, and
impractical in that it ignores the international currency of English and

takes no account of the sociolinguistic norms already established within Jaffna society. Through their codeswitching in local community contexts and through the use of hybrid language forms, local people distance themselves from this homogenizing tendency. They opt instead for the linguistic and cultural pluralism that is still rooted in Tamil social life. At the same time, they are also resistant to the hegemony of British and American varieties of English. They use English on their own terms, with the character and forms that they themselves provide, to meet their own needs, values, and purposes. They infuse the language with their own linguistic conventions, resisting its hegemonic discourses and the values associated with standardized forms.

Paradoxically, it is in a period when Tamil nationalism is at its most militant and politically successful that the local community is most internationalist in its orientation. During my ethnographic work in this local community, I was particularly struck by the fact that local Tamil speakers are now aware of, linked with, and influenced by the West as perhaps never before in history. This is partly because the nationalist struggle has had to be internationalized to maximize its successes. There are, for example, Tamil lobbying groups in Western capitals whose aims are to put pressure on governments to stop supplying arms and aid to Sri Lanka and to seek recognition for Eelam. Tamil information centers in the West operate hotlines, electronic networks, and news groups to keep the world informed about day-to-day military and political developments in Jaffna. Furthermore, the need for arms for the military struggle against the Sri Lankan army and for specialized training requires liaison with foreign military and other external agencies. In addition, as a side effect of the war, thousands of Tamils have sought economic and political refuge in European cities. New urban communities of Tamil speakers have become established, and these local communities keep in touch across the diaspora. People in Jaffna itself are able to survive in this war-torn area only through cash and gifts sent by their acquaintances abroad. Many individuals still expect to go abroad for political or economic reasons and thus are aware of the need for an international language. The local polity is linked to international communities far more than the regime recognizes.

It must be further noted that ever since the colonial era, there has been ideological tension in Jaffna that has given rise to different attitudes toward the use of English. On the one hand, there was the Saiva-Tamil philosophy, which was first articulated by the revivalist Arumuga Navalar in the late nineteenth century (Navalar 1872, reprinted 1951). Navalar promoted a religio-linguistic chauvinism and called for a return to "traditional" cultural practices. On the other hand, there was a long-established liberal-democratic tradition inculcated by the educational institutions of the missionaries and epitomized in the Youth

Congress of Ceylon in 1936. Within this latter tradition, openness to other "cultures" and enlightened contemporary philosophies was encouraged (see Sivatamby 1990). While the former strand of thought was associated with opposition to English, the latter was favorable to it. The presence of these conflicting ideologies and value systems in the Tamil cultural heritage points to the complexity of the cultural politics being played out in Jaffna today. It also accounts for the hybrid subjectivities assumed by local Tamil speakers. In a sense, then, there is an ongoing struggle to define the cultural character of the local community. While the Jaffna regime seeks to define the "authentic" Tamil culture in terms of "traditional" linguistic and cultural practices, local people feel part of a hybrid tradition that has been shaped by the diverse cultural influences that have been felt in this part of South Asia over time.

The bilingual discourse practices I observed in ESL classrooms in Jaffna need to be understood in the light of the broader trends discussed in this chapter: the contradictions in the sociopolitical domain where the nationalistic struggle still needs global links; the contradictions in the history and traditions of the community, where hybrid values have been nurtured and also eschewed (in indigenous religiopolitical movements); and the contradictions facing students who, at one and the same time, feel the pressures of the international market forces associated with English and espouse nationalistic sentiments, while feeling that their identities are rooted in Jaffna.

CONCLUSION

Rather than viewing the Tamil speakers of Jaffna as victims of symbolic violence, caught up in power structures and processes of social reproduction beyond their control (as would be implied by Bourdieu and Passeron's 1977 model of education), I would argue that they should be seen as active and creative agents who, through their day-to-day communicative practices, respond in diverse and complex ways to the unique political and symbolic order of contemporary Jaffna. I see them as having sufficient agency to rise above these limiting ideological influences to construct their own alternative subjectivities in strategic ways. Building on the recent radical literature on postcolonial subjectivity (see, for example, Said 1993; Bhabha 1991; hooks 1990), I hold that hybrid subjectivity is a position of strength, as it is able to withstand the totalizing (and essentializing) tendencies of both center and periphery agencies. The detachment that the subjects of my study have from monolingual and culturally essentialist discursive positions (from whatever quarter) enables them to resist policies that contribute to symbolic domination. The everyday linguistic practices of the students and teachers in Jaffna classrooms and of people in local community contexts provide evidence of the subtle ways in which they are still able to define their own subjectivity, even in a context where hegemonic agendas are imposed.

TRANSCRIPTION CONVENTIONS

//	pause of 0.5 seconds or more
=	latched utterances
[ ]	overlapping utterances
?	rising intonation
.	falling intonation
italics	additional notes (e.g., nonverbal communication)
bold	Tamil utterances
' '	translation in English

Note

I use the term "Tamilized English" to refer to a mixed-language variety that is becoming an increasingly common communicative mode in this community. I explain its sociolinguistic significance elsewhere (see Canagarajah 1995).

REFERENCES

Aronowitz, S., and Henry, G. (1993). *Education still under siege: The conservative, liberal and radical debate over schooling*. South Hadley: Bergin Garvey.

Bhabha, H. K. (1991). The post-colonial critic. *Arena, 96*, 61–63.

Bourdieu, P., and J. P. Passeron. (1977). *Reproduction in education, society and culture*. London: Sage.

Canagarajah, A. S. (1993). Critical ethnography of a Sri Lankan classroom: Ambiguities in opposition to reproduction through ESOL. *TESOL Quarterly, 27(4)*, 601–626.

Canagarajah, A. S. (1995). The political-economy of code choice in a revolutionary society: Tamil/English bilingualism in Jaffna. *Language in Society, 24(2)*, 187–212.

Canagarajah, A. S. (1997). Safe houses in the contact zone: coping strategies of African American students in the academy. *College Composition and Communication, 48(2)*, 173–196.

Fernando, S. (1994). Taking stock of university ELT and planning for the nineties. In M. Gunasekera et al. (Eds.), *Compendium of University ELT Papers: 1987–1991* (pp. 1–25). Colombo: ELT units of Sri Lankan universities.

Goonetilleke, D.C.R.A. (1983). Language planning in Sri Lanka. *Navasilu, 5*, 13–18.

Hanson-Smith, E. (1984). A plan for the improvement of English instruction in Sri Lanka. *Navasilu, 6,* 26–30.

hooks, b. (1990). Choosing the margin as a space for radical openness. In *Yearning: Race, gender and cultural politics* (pp. 145–154). Boston: South End.

Navalar, A. (1872). *Yaalpaana samaya nilai [Religion in Jaffna].* (Reprinted, Jaffna: Navalar Sabai, 1951.)

Phillipson, R. (1992). *Linguistic imperialism.* Oxford: Oxford University Press.

Said, E. W. (1993). *Culture and imperialism.* New York: Alfred Knopf.

Sivatamby, K. (1990). The ideology of Saiva-Tamil integrality: Its socio-historical significance in the study of Yalppanam Tamil society. *Lanka, 5,* 176–182.

10

Language Values and Identities: Codeswitching in Secondary Classrooms in Malta

Antoinette Camilleri Grima

INTRODUCTION

Secondary education in Malta is imparted through two languages: Maltese and English. Both languages are taught as subjects in all schools in Malta, and they are also used to varying degrees and in varying ways as media of instruction across the curriculum. Codeswitching between Maltese and English is a common feature of communication between teachers and learners in secondary classrooms. In this chapter, I will be arguing that we need to look closely at these codeswitching practices and place them against the historical and social background of the islands in order to arrive at a fuller understanding of how language choice and codeswitching reinforce the different values associated with each language within the linguistic economy of Maltese society.

The role of language in education in Malta has not been given serious consideration until very recently. It has been a non-issue and has not generally been discussed. As Corson (1990, 1) says, "Language policies across the curriculum are viewed by a growing number of educationists as an integral and necessary part of the administrative and curriculum practices of modern schools, *yet relatively few schools anywhere have seriously tackled the problem of introducing them"* (my emphasis). In Malta, to date, no official language policy has been drawn up for schools.

I have myself gone through the state education system, and I have taught at various levels: primary, secondary, and tertiary. In the past, it never occurred to me, either as a student or as a teacher, to question the use of language/s in education. Echoing my own experience, teachers I interviewed in 1992 confirmed that I was asking them to think and express their ideas about the matter for the first time in their lives.

I started doing research into code switching in the classroom in 1990. My original plan was to work on the teaching of Maltese as a mother tongue, but I soon realized that it was going to be necessary to give due consideration to the bilingual discourse so prevalent in secondary class-rooms. I knew it would be useful for future language planning in education to gain insights into the dynamics of the bilingual medium in Maltese classrooms. The research was timely, since the Ministry of Education set up a Maltese language board in 1995 with a brief that included formulating recommendations about language education pol-icies. They also noted the need to develop an extensive study of the situation.

LANGUAGE IN SOCIAL AND POLITICAL INSTITUTIONS IN MALTA

Maltese has been spoken for centuries on the islands of Malta. It originates from Arabic. Malta was under Arab rule from A.D. 870 to 1090. But since then, Maltese has undergone various processes of linguistic change as a result of contact with speakers of Sicilian, Italian, and English (see Cremona 1990; Mifsud 1992).The Maltese language and the patterns of linguistic diversity on the islands are contemporary prod-ucts of Malta's geographical position, close to Europe and to Africa (see map).

English was originally introduced in Malta by the British colonial powers (1800–1964). It took almost a whole century before English was first taught, and eventually used as medium, in local education. In 1879, Keenan, who headed a commission of inquiry into the position of the English language in Malta, reported that, because of commercial condi-tions, English was in growing demand, but it was given little or no attention in primary schools. Its use was forbidden in thirteen out of fourteen classes of the Lyceum (the only secondary school) and in seventeen out of eighteen classes in the university. Keenan therefore

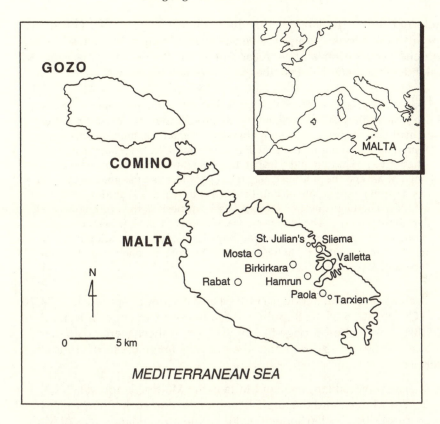

proposed changes so that English might find a place in the Maltese education system. For instance, a policy was implemented whereby persons knowing English were given preference in government posts. It was only in the 1934 constitution that English was given official status alongside Maltese.

Nineteenth-century Malta was very pro-Italian. It was a staunchly Catholic country, and it still is (about 75% of the population goes to church regularly). It had strong religious and cultural ties with Italy. Italian had been for several centuries the cultural and political language of the Maltese intelligentsia. Dobie (1967, 13) says that there was an undercurrent of hostility to the English language, which was regarded by Catholic priests as a threat to their religion. Some priests ranked among the most prominent Maltese political figures of the time. They publicized their devotion to Italian as a safeguard of their faith. In addition, the members of the legal profession and the propertied classes generally regarded the use of Italian as a means of showing their superiority to the lower classes (see Dobie 1967, 34). The people's own tongue was looked down upon, underrated, and neglected; it was referred to as "the language of the kitchen." As Aquilina (1964, 181) points out, it took a long time before either English or Maltese gained official recognition and were accepted by the upper classes of the islands. Frendo (1975) describes the situation as follows:

> Nineteenth-century Maltese society is probably a unique example of a case in which trilingualism became a battle-ground in the successful quest for a national identity. Maltese nationalism rotated in time on this triple paradox: the championing of Italian as a non-Maltese national language; the active promotion of the British Imperial power as a means of expunging Italian; and the gradual emergence of Maltese as a national tongue and as a prime expression of anti-British sentiments. . . . Paradoxically, the Maltese language question emerged as a synthesis of the pro-English and pro-Italian rivalry. The Maltese vernacular served as a social and emotive bond and became a natural unifier. Both Anglophiles and Italophiles thus contributed unwittingly to the success of Maltese nationalism and nationhood. (p. 22)

Malta gained independence in 1964 and became a republic in 1974. In the Constitution of the Republic of Malta (Department of Information, Malta 1974, Section 5, page 2), English and Maltese were given official status. Maltese was designated the national language in the following terms:

1. The national language of Malta is the Maltese language.
2. The Maltese and the English languages, and such others as may be prescribed by Parliament, shall be the official languages of Malta and the administration may for all official purposes use any such language.
3. The language of the Courts shall be the Maltese language.
4. Save as otherwise provided by Parliament, every law shall be enacted in both Maltese and English and if there is any conflict between the Maltese and English texts of any law, the Maltese text shall prevail.

Maltese is officially used nowadays in a range of institutional contexts. Parliamentary debates are carried out in Maltese, and records are only kept in Maltese. Maltese is also used in the law courts and in all activities related to local politics. Maltese became the language of the church in Malta following Vatican Council II (1964), which decreed the use of peoples' languages in church instead of Latin, which had until then been the only official church language. A number of private and state-owned radio and television stations broadcast in Maltese. On television, however, films, documentaries, and foreign news reports are transmitted daily in English without dubbing. The Maltese also have access to a large number of Italian television stations, which are very popular in Malta. Political and religious publications are almost all in Maltese. Newspapers, books, and magazines are published in both Maltese and English.

Despite the constitutional guarantees just cited, English has been steadily gaining importance in the last few decades. It is an indispensable language of communication in tourism, Malta's largest industry. Malta currently receives over a million tourists annually (Malta's own population is 350,000). Tourists come largely from the United Kingdom—about half a million a year—and other European and English-speaking countries.

Also, in the civil service almost all written work is carried out in English. This practice carries over from the British colonial administration, despite the fact that the Prime Minister's Secretary requested the use of Maltese in two consecutive letters in 1987. Civil servants who graduate from the University of Malta and who undergo all their training through English find it difficult to suddenly switch to Maltese as a written medium. There is, as yet, no language planning body in Malta that can engage in terminology development and offer the relevant linguistic guidelines. Spoken communication largely takes place in Maltese.

A working knowledge of English has become an increasingly desirable goal. English is important in Malta not only for education purposes but also as a language of international communication in Malta itself, because of the impact of tourism. This, as we shall see, has given rise to the use of English as the first language of socialization for some families and in other social milieux. At the same time, however, Maltese has been increasingly gaining importance in a number of social domains, as described earlier.

THE SHAPING OF LANGUAGE REPERTOIRES AT HOME AND AT SCHOOL

In Malta, two broad social groups can be identified: one group with a primary orientation to English and the other with a primary orientation to Maltese. They exhibit different patterns of language use within the family; for the children in each group, the language ecology of the home is very different. This has consequences for their education and for the way they define their identity as Maltese citizens. I discuss these groups in the two following sections.

English at Home and at School in Malta

The most influential social group is the small but increasing number of people who prefer to use English as a first language with their children (see Borg et al. 1992). Originally this was a very exclusive group who, having acquired a taste for the prestige associated with English, chose it as their major means of communication. Nowadays, among members of this group, English is spoken in the home by one or both parents and is acquired as a first language by their children. In a few cases, Maltese is only acquired through formal teaching at school and through contact with speakers of Maltese outside the home. In most cases, both Maltese and English are used interchangeably by parents and children at home. This group of Maltese speakers of English is mostly concentrated in the high-class, tourist areas of Sliema and St. Julians, on the outskirts of Valletta (refer to map). Many British people lived in these seaside resorts during the colonial era and probably served as models for local families aspiring to upward social mobility.

Schooling until the age of sixteen became mandatory in Malta in the early 1970s. As more students stayed on in secondary school, English became a more highly valued commodity. This coincided with rapid urbanization and a massive increase in tourism. An increasing number of parents sought to expose their children to as much English as possible. They began to emulate the social and linguistic habits of the higher classes.

This change in language practices and values was also related to developments within the private education sector. During the period of British colonial rule, some Catholic religious orders came to Malta from Britain. They opened their own private schools where English was the only medium allowed. In fact, pupils were punished if they were caught using Maltese (Navarro and Grech 1984). Upper-class parents tended to send their children to these private schools, thereby reinforcing the value of English.

However, in the early 1980s, as part of the sociopolitical movement of the time, the exclusive character of private schools was eventually challenged. They came under enormous pressure to abolish their school fees and accept children from all social backgrounds. After a change of government in 1987, church schools were obliged to choose their pupils by ballot and government subsidies were introduced. As the availability of private English-medium education increased, more and more parents sought to pass English on to their children in preparation for an English-medium schooling. Indeed, simply possessing a knowledge of English came to be equated with possessing an education (see Camilleri 1987, Ellul 1978). This is similar to what Phillipson (1988, 1992) has described as *linguicism*, with particular reference to postcolonial situations. Zammit Mangion (1992) describes current parental attitudes towards English in Maltese schools as follows: "Very often the standard of a school is measured by the amount of English used by the teachers and the pupils in the lessons and by the amount of English that is taught to the pupils" (1992, 386).

However, as more children from varied social backgrounds started to attend the private church schools, the use of Maltese in the classroom was inevitable. The English-speaking elite reacted by opening other private schools that enforced the use of English. In this way, they held onto power over their own preferred form of educational provision. Today, they continue to serve their own ends through these elitist schools, maintaining educational provision in the form to which they are accustomed.

Maltese at Home in Different Regions of Malta

Maltese is acquired as a first language by the vast majority of children in Malta (over 90% of the population, according to Borg et al. 1992). It is the first language of most parents and is spoken in almost all local neighborhoods. However, it is important to note that there is considerable sociolinguistic diversity in Malta. There are a number of regional varieties of Maltese as well as a standardized form of the language.

Dialects of Maltese are still widespread in both rural and urban areas. In areas like the island of Gozo, several small towns and villages on the main island of Malta and some larger towns like Mosta and Birkirkara (refer to map), a distinct dialect of Maltese is spoken. In many homes, the primary language of socialization for the children is the local dialect. Standard Maltese is a superposed variety. It is explicitly taught by parents or other family members, and it is learned formally at school alongside English (see Camilleri 1987). The standard is based on the regional variety spoken in urbanized areas like Hamrun, Paola, and Tarxien (refer to map), so the Maltese that is acquired as a first language by children at home in these areas is close to the standard. English is learned at school.

Social Differentiation, Maltese Language Loyalty, and Changing Language Values

The boundaries between the two broad social groups in Maltese society described above are clearly drawn, and the values of each group are echoed in the ways in which they represent the "other." Maltese people who prefer to speak English are labeled "snobs" or, in Maltese, **tal-pepè**. Speakers of Maltese dialects are often stigmatized as "uneducated" and "unsophisticated." People who insist on using standard Maltese are called "language purists."

Nevertheless, different varieties of Maltese serve as powerful emblems of regional and national identity and command considerable language loyalty. Two recent case studies carried out in specific local areas of Malta provide revealing glimpses into contemporary attitudes about language in Malta and the ways in which processes of social differentiation currently operate. I will refer to each study in turn.

Attard (1995) conducted a study of the language attitudes and preferences of eight-year-old children from Rabat, a semirural town in the west of Malta, who were speakers of the local regional dialect. The children all said that they preferred to use Maltese. The following example gives their own words (Attard, 1995: 22):

Child 1:
L-Ingliz tuzah meta jigu l-Inglizi.

Child 1:
English should be used with English people.

Child 2:
Jien nuza l-Malti ghax jien Maltija.

Child 2:
I use Maltese because I am Maltese.

Child 3:
Kieku nuza l-Ingliz kieku shabi joqoghdu jghadduni biz-zmien.

Child 3:
If I were to use English I would be ridiculed by my friends.

Child 4:
L-Ingliz nuzah mal-barranin.

Child 4:
I use English with foreigners.

Child 5:
Mela jien tal-pepè!

Child 5:
As if I'm a snob!

The children's responses show that they were already keenly aware of the processes of social differentiation at work in Maltese society and reveal that they felt strong social pressures to conform to local conventions of language use.

Spiteri (1994) conducted a qualitative study of the contemporary language practices of one extended family in Malta and also built a picture of changes in patterns of language use taking place over time in this family. He showed that the use of English, especially with young children, was a transient phenomenon. As the children grew older, the family used more and more Maltese.

He conducted interviews with four sisters in the family and found that they grew up with the idea that English was for children, while Maltese was for adults. When they eventually reached adulthood and married, they made divergent language choices although all four married Maltese-speaking men. However, as their children grew older, they all reverted to using primarily Maltese.

Maltese has for many years commanded language loyalty within the domain of the home for the majority of Maltese people, while English has gained ground in public institutional life. However, there are now signs that language attitudes are changing within the wider society. Influential Maltese people are beginning to redefine the value of their own language. Recently, an elite movement for the promotion of the Maltese language has been gaining ground. It is led by prominent poets, authors, and professional people. It poses a challenge to the symbolic dominance of English and asserts the rights of speakers of Maltese.

LANGUAGE USE IN SCHOOLS IN MALTA

Schools in Malta are obliged to teach Maltese as a subject in order to obtain a license to operate, but apart from this, there is no official language education policy. In the National Minimum Curriculum Regulations for secondary level, the language medium is not mentioned. As far as primary education is concerned, it is vaguely stated that:

> Maltese will be the first language used in teaching but the teacher should also seek to speak English so as to accustom children to understand and speak the language. Those children who speak English at home should be trained to a more correct use of the language, in addition to their being taught Maltese. (Department of Information, Malta 1989, Schedule B6)

Attard (1995) conducted classroom observation sessions in a year 4 primary classroom with eight-year-old children to study the use of Maltese and English. In examining the print environment of the classroom, she noted that all the charts hanging on the classroom walls were in English, except for the social studies chart—a subject studied through the medium of Maltese. Many notices unrelated to a particular subject, such as rules of behavior, safety regulations, and a sign urging children to put all their efforts into their work, were written in English. One notice, called "Rules of the Classroom," was written in English (Attard 1995, 11) as follows:

1. You must not talk in class.
2. You must not eat in class.
3. You must put up your finger when you need to ask something.
4. Do not go out of your place without the teacher's permission.

Evidence from such studies indicates how widespread the use of English, especially written English, is in the children's learning environment, even at primary level.

In addition, informal use of language by teachers and school administration staff is often characterized by the use of codeswitching between Maltese and English. The examples were recorded by Attard (1995, 17).

Assistant head of school to a teacher:

Miss **ghandek tfal li fallew iktar minn** three times?	Miss **are there any children in your class who have been absent more than** three times?
Miss at ten o'clock **se nitilqu ghall-quddies.**	Miss **we depart for mass** at ten o'clock.

Year 4 teacher to researcher:

ghax jghidulek li jkunu fehmu then you call them to work a sum **u ma jkunux jafu kif jahdmuha**	Well, [the children] **tell you that they have understood** [the sums] and then you call them to work out a sum [on the blackboard] **and they wouldn't know how to work it out.**

In the absence of national policy guidelines within the state education system, the onus of the choice with regard to language medium falls on the schools, and more specifically on the individual teacher. A teacher's use of language in the classroom depends on factors like the type of school (e.g., private or state), the teacher's age and training, and his or her own school experience and family language background. As already mentioned, private schools in Malta generally favor the use of English as a spoken medium inside and outside the classroom. A considerable number of foreign students are enrolled in private schools; these schools have a deliberate policy of placing these students in different classes, which makes it necessary for all teachers and learners to interact in English.

State schools in Malta do not have explicit language policies. However, the individual heads of schools can exert an influence on the choice of language, as by demanding that all learners address them in English or, conversely, by using Maltese at all morning assemblies or on school prize days or by writing in Maltese in school circulars or in letters to parents.

In the classroom, the teachers' own experiences at home or as students at school are reflected in their own use of language. Teachers who come from English-speaking families are more likely to use English as a spoken medium in class. Teachers who attended English-medium

schools, especially private schools, are more likely to use English themselves in the classroom.

The training that teachers have received is also likely to have shaped
their views about language use in the classroom. Until the mid-1970s,
teacher training in Malta was run by British religious orders (see
Zammit Mangion 1992). Teachers trained before the mid-1970s are more
likely to use English as a medium of instruction than younger teachers
who have been trained since then at the University of Malta by Maltese
staff (Camilleri 1993, 1995).

As part of my wider study of bilingualism in education in Malta, I
interviewed a number of teachers (Camilleri 1993). They indicated that
English was their preferred medium with learners from high-ability
groups, while Maltese was the only possible medium with "weaker"
learners. This view also carries over into extracurricular activities. For
instance, in Attard's recent study, we see that during the Christmas
festivities in one school, students from lower-ability groups were given
parts in Maltese to play, while the students from higher-ability groups
were given parts in English (Attard 1995, 23). Practices such as these
reinforce the perception that Maltese is the language of those who are
less well educated in Maltese society and English is the language of
those who are highly educated. The year 4 teacher in Attard's study
(1995, 23) had the following to say in Maltese and English, about the
way she deals with the language medium issue:

Minhabba li jien nibghat lit-tfal tieghi fi private school ikolli nkellimhom bl-Ingliz biex ikunu kapaci jikkomunikaw mal-friends taghhom u jifhmu dak li tkun qed tghid it-teacher.	As I send my own children to a private school I have to speak to them in English so that they will be able to communicate with their friends and to understand what the teacher is saying.
Allura minhabba li d-dar sirt nikellem hafna bl-Ingliz, meta niĺi l-iskola, qed nispicca nkellem lit-tfal tal-klassi tieghi bl-Ingliz ukoll. Minhabba f'hekk qed nispicca kemm-il darba naghmel translation ta' dak li nkun qed nghid ghax hemm xi whud li huma low ability u ghalhekk nibza' li ma jkunux qed jifhmu.	Since I speak in English at home, when I come to school I end up talking to the children in my class in English as well. As a re-sult I often end up translating what I'm saying because there are some low ability [children] and I'm afraid that they do not understand me otherwise.

Some secondary school teachers and some lecturers at university
level argue that Maltese is a better means of spoken communication
with all students. They have observed that the use of English in the
secondary classroom and in the lecture theater creates a barrier between

the teachers and the lecturers and the students. In contrast, the use of Maltese permits more learner participation, as the majority of students feel more confident to speak Maltese than English.

The use of spoken English in every classroom stems from the fact that English is the language adopted for written purposes in any subject. The only subject examined only in Maltese is Maltese language and literature. The examinations for some other subjects can be answered in either Maltese or English. These are religious knowledge, Maltese history, social studies, and systems of knowledge. ("Systems of knowledge" is a group of subjects that includes history of the Mediterranean, philosophy, man and science, and art and communication.) Each foreign language is examined through the medium of that language. All other subjects are examined in English. This is a carryover from the long tradition of administering British examinations in Malta. Students are now examined locally within the framework of the Maltese examination system, but the language of most of the examinations continues to be English. Moreover, almost all textbooks used in schools are in English. Some of the textbooks used in those subject areas that are optionally examined in Maltese are available only in English. As a result, almost all reading and writing activities in Maltese classrooms are carried out in English.

Given the strong position of English worldwide, most Maltese people believe that Malta is in a privileged position. Having had English-medium education for many years, they are reluctant to do away with English altogether. The weight given to English across the curriculum in Malta thus far has enabled members of the Maltese elite and the professional classes to further their education in English-speaking countries. English is a highly valued commodity within the global marketplace. As I mentioned earlier, it is also the language that dominates the tourist industry on which so many people depend.

Some members of the professional classes and those who aspire to upward social mobility argue against a more widespread use of Maltese in education. They fear that if Maltese gains more importance it will replace English. As a result, they feel, Maltese students will suffer a loss of English-language proficiency, and consequently Malta as a nation will experience isolation from the rest of the world. This argument prevails despite the fact that Malta has applied for membership in the European Union.

Those who are in favor of promoting bilingual education believe that Maltese can be given parity with English without a concomitant decline in students' English proficiency. Their arguments are framed with reference to democratic principles, social justice, and pedagogical theory. They claim that the provision of bilingual education is the only viable option for children in Malta.

RESEARCHING LANGUAGE IN MALTESE CLASSROOMS

The rest of this chapter draws directly on the extended research project I carried out from 1990 to 1993 (Camilleri 1993). The project involved micro-ethnographic observation in classrooms, transcription of audiorecorded and videorecorded lessons, and informal interviews with teachers. The purpose of the interviews with teachers was to discuss and to check their own understanding of patterns of language use in the lessons.

The focus of the study was on sixteen lessons in eleven different subject areas from form 1 to form 5, in five different secondary schools: three Junior Lyceums for girls (these were students from higher-ability groups), one Junior Lyceum for boys, and one private school for boys. All the teachers in the sample had agreed to be involved in the project. The sample of lessons was across the curriculum range, and the teachers had different ages and training profiles. The teachers' ages ranged from 23 to 50. Only three male teachers participated. They were ages 27, 35, and 50 respectively.

The research was of an ethnographic/interpretive nature. My aim was to investigate how teachers and learners accomplished lessons bilingually in the absence of any official policy on the medium of instruction. I wanted to identify and describe the structure of the bilingual classroom talk and to examine, in particular, the ways in which teachers drew on the codes available to them to negotiate meanings with the learners. I found this approach to my data particularly useful. It helped me to understand some of the reasons why codeswitching is used as it is by teachers in Maltese classrooms.

CODESWITCHING IN DIFFERENT TEACHING/LEARNING EVENTS

An important component of communication in the classroom is the way in which teachers and learners talk about texts in their interactions with each other. Written texts are considered to be the basic points of reference and are constantly being reiterated, paraphrased, and reinterpreted by teacher and learners. As Lemke (1989) has pointed out:

> The problem of learning through texts is . . . fundamentally a problem of translating the patterns of written language into those of spoken language. Spoken language is the medium through which we reason to ourselves and talk our way through problems to answers. . . . When we approach written text, we need to be able to do more than just decode letters to sounds. . . . To comprehend it, we need to be able to paraphrase it, restate it in our own

words, and translate its meanings into the more comfortable patterns of spoken language. (136)

Lemke was referring to the situation in monolingual classrooms. In bilingual classrooms, such as those in Malta, an extra dimension of "translation" is involved: Written texts in English are "translated" into spoken texts in Maltese. In the lessons I observed in secondary classrooms in Malta, both Maltese and English were used, and most of the bilingual discourse focused on texts written in English. In different areas of the curriculum, the use of English technical terms and phrases within stretches of Maltese speech was a common occurrence. This accounted for almost 80% of codeswitching in the corpus I recorded.

Extract 1, taken from a mathematics lesson in a form 4 class, serves as an illustration. Most of the time the teacher used Maltese. The details of the problems that were read out in English from the textbook were discussed in Maltese.

Extract 1. A mathematics lesson

L: (*reading from textbook in English*) A square room has a square carpet placed in it . this leaves an uncovered area of nine meters square . the area of the whole room is twenty-five meters square . find the length of one side of the carpet

T: **issa . di tixbah . lil din t'hawn hux veru** (*points to the blackboard*) . **imma** l-area **tahielna mahduma di d-darba . sewwa . issa** .. area **illi ghandha** a square room **x'ghandha** a square room

Ls: **kollox indaqs**

Ls: four sides equal

T: **kollox indaqs** four sides equal **orrajt** (*points to the drawing on the blackboard*) square root **immarkajniha . issa** has a square carpet symmetrically placed in it . il-carpet **ikbar jew izghar mill-kamra**

L: (*reading from textbook in English*) A square room has a square carpet placed in it . this leaves an uncovered area of nine meters square . the area of the whole room is twenty-five meters square . find the length of one side of the carpet

T: **now . this is similar . to this one here isn't it** (*points to the blackboard*) . **but the** area **is given to us already this time . correct . now** .. **the** area **of a** square room **what does** a square room **have**

Ls: **everything equal**

Ls: four sides equal

T: **everything equal** four sides equal **alright** (*points to the drawing on the blackboard*) square root **we have marked it . now** has a square carpet symmetrically placed in it . **is the** carpet **smaller or bigger than the room**

Ls: **izghar**

Ls: **smaller**

T: **izghar Marica suppost qeghdin attenti u ma niktbux . orrajt din ukoll hija** square **qed nimmarka is-**sides **jiena** (*marks the figure on the blackboard*) . **halli ma nitgerixx ghandna . ee** this leaves the area uncovered of nine meters square **mela ghandi l-bicca t'hawnhekk** uncovered (*points to the drawing on the blackboard*) . . **taqblu mieghi**

T: **smaller Marica you ought to be paying attention and not writing away . alright this is also a** square **I am marking the** sides (*marks the figure on the blackboard*) . **so that I do not get confused we have . eh** this leaves an uncovered area of nine meters square **so I have this part** . uncovered (*points to the drawing on the blackboard*) . **do you agree with me**

The teacher explained the text in Maltese by gradually eliciting from the learners the meaning of the problem that was read in English. For example, the teacher wanted to check whether the learners had understood the concept "square" by eliciting responses from them in Maltese. The learners replied, some in Maltese, "**kollox indaqs**," and some in English, "four sides equal." The teacher gave feedback on both contributions by codeswitching "**kollox indaqs** four sides equal."

This particular teacher came from a Maltese-speaking background but was trained in the British colleges in the early 1970s. As I indicated earlier, English is preferred as a spoken medium of instruction by older teachers. However, codeswitching from English to Maltese does occur in predominantly English-medium classes when teachers accommodate to the learners' language choices. In this particular class of "weak" learners (as the teacher herself described them), textbook English was supplemented by explanations in Maltese. The teacher interacted with the learners in Maltese to ensure understanding.

This is how some of the teachers I interviewed explained the need for this kind of codeswitching:

The home economics teacher (see later reference to her lesson):

meta nuza l-Ingliz mhux kollox jinftiehem

when I use English not everything is understood

The mathematics teacher:

ma kontx inhossni nikkomunika maghhom bl-Ingliz

I did not feel I could communicate with them through English

Another teacher (male, university trained, who worked in a girls' Junior Lyceum):

ma tistax taffordja tkellimhom bl-Ingliz il-hin kollu ghax jintilfu	one can't afford to speak to them in English all the time because they feel lost

In most of the classes I observed, teachers switched from English to Maltese at various points during the lesson in order to elicit a response from the learners. Let me take as an example a biology lesson at form 3 level in a private school (Extract 2). The lesson was largely conducted through the medium of English. The teacher came from an English-speaking family and was trained in a British college. She was reviewing the structure of leaves.

Extract 2. A biology lesson

T: they are surrounded by the kidney-shaped cells they are called guard cells . what else . I told you there is something in particular about them I told you that these guard cells . have something in particular the epidermis cells don't have it . what do they have ... **x'ghandhom ghidna** s-cells **l-ohrajn bhall**-palisade cells **u** s-cells **ta'** l-**i**spongy layer . **kellhom** il-chloroplasts **biex jaghmlu** l-photosynthesis . **orrajt** . **imbaghad ghidna** fl-epidermis **irid ikun trasparenti bhal** . **issa dawn** il-guard cells . **li jaghmlu** l-istomata . **orrajt** . **x'ghidna li fihom** .. **dawna fihom** il-chloroplasts . **ukoll** . now let me explain to you why they have the chloroplasts . ok

T: they are surrounded by the kidney-shaped cells they are called guard cells . what else . I told you there is something in particular about them I told you that these guard cells . have something in particular the epidermis cells don't have it . **what do they have we said that the other** cells **like the** palisade cells **and the** cells **of the** spongy layer . **they had the** chloroplasts **to make the** photosynthesis . **alright** . **then we said that the** epidermis **must be transparent like** . **now these** guard cells . **that make the** stomata . **alright** . **what did we say they have** .. **they have the** chloroplasts . **as well** . now let me explain to you why they have the chloroplasts . ok

(some time later)
T: did you understand it . **orrajt mela tghidli** Kenneth .. tell me in your own words **kif taghmel** l-istomata **biex tinfetah u biex tinghalaq**

(some time later)
T: did you understand it . **alright so can you tell me** Kenneth .. tell me in your own words **how does the** stomata **open and close**

L: **waqt** il-**í̇urnata bis**-sunlight **taghmel** il-glucose **u** . **eem bil**-glucose **din tistreccja**

L: **during the day it uses** sunlight **to make glucose and** . **with the** glucose **it stretches**

T: tistreccja ghax tiehu . l-ilma

L: l-ilma

T: ok

T: it stretches because it takes .
water

L: water

T: ok

Notice that in Extract 2, the teacher poses the same question twice. She first asks a question about the guard cells in English. She says, "What do they have?" She then repeats it in Maltese and amplifies a little bit on her question. She does not wait for the learners to reply, but a little later she elicits a response from one particular learner. She says, "tell me in your own words **kif taghmel l-**istomata **biex tinfetah u biex tinghalaq"** (tell me in your own words **how does the** stomata **open and close**). This time the learner answers in Maltese, demonstrating that he had understood the processes involved in the opening and closing of the stomata. In this way, the teacher opened an opportunity for the pupil to make a contribution to the review session in a medium that was more comprehensible to all the learners.

Extract 3 is taken from a home economics lesson in a form 5 class in a girls' Junior Lyceum. The teacher was college trained. On this particular occasion, she was working out a family budget with the learners.

Extract 3. A home economics lesson

T: how much

L: three

T: three children **u** how much do you pay

L: twenty

T: twenty . **iva ejja nghidu**

Ls: **imma dawk** flat **ghandhom**

T: **ahna** we are talking about a flat

L: **ija ahna dar ghandna**

T: how much

L: three

T: three children **and** how much do you pay

T: twenty

T: twenty . **well let us say**

Ls: **but they live in a** flat

T: **we** we are talking about a flat

L: **yes we live in a house**

T: orrajt mela ejja naghmluha twenty-five **halli ma niſſieldux sewwa** . twenty-five . every four months . **mel'ejja nghidu** twenty-four . **ha niſu aktar**

T: **alright then let us say** twenty-five **so that we won't quarrel alright** . twenty-five . every four months . **so let us say** twenty-four . **this will be more**

L: **ahjar hekk ghax tiſi** four pounds

L: **this is better because it works out at** four pounds

Ls: (*laughter*)

Ls: (*laughter*)

The lesson was predominantly in English. In Extract 3, the teacher switched to Maltese, signaling that she was ceding a point to the learners. Eventually one learner agreed with the teacher's decision on practical grounds: "**ahjar hekk ghax tiſi** four pounds" (that is better because it works out at four pounds). At this point, there was laughter from the learners. The disagreement in this exchange had been resolved.

Although this home economics lesson was conducted largely through the medium of English, the teacher made frequent use of Maltese discourse markers. Take, for example, her use of "**issa**" (now), "**mela**" (so), and "**orrajt**" (alright) in Extracts 4 and 5.

Extract 4

T: **issa** when we talk about money . what is important for us . to do . let's say the money that comes into the family . to the home .. **mela** budgeting . it is important that we will be able . to manage . our money properly . **issa** and how can we . manage . how can we budget our money

Extract 5

T: it should be well . distributed . **mela** . let me tell you what we are going to do . first of all we are going to see . what money . **orrajt** . can come . into the family . **issa** we are going to consider let's take an average kind of family

On several occasions, in a number of different lessons, a teacher's language switch co-occurred with a change in the nature of the ongoing classroom activity. Codeswitches co-occurred with an aside or with a change in topic or served to distinguish different kinds of talk at different stages in the interaction. In Extract 6, the teacher was dictating notes in English in an economics lesson with a form 3 class. At one point she switched to Maltese to say: "**hekk tinkiteb**" (this is how you write it). Then she switched back to Maltese, "**harsu ftit 'il fuq qabel ma** tiktbu n-notes," to ask the students to stop taking notes and look up and listen to the explanation. Here the code contrast between English and Maltese served as a means of distinguishing her classroom management utterance from the talk about the main teaching/learning activity of dictation.

Extract 6. An economics lesson

T: is called . a post-dated cheque . **hekk tinkiteb** (*writes on blackboard*) a post-dated cheque . point number nine . **harsu ftit 'il fuq qabel ma tiktbu n-**notes

T: is called . a post-dated cheque . **this is how you write** (*writes on blackboard*) a post-dated cheque . point number nine . **look up before you write down the** notes

In Extract 7, an example from an integrated science lesson with a form 1 class in a boys' state school, the teacher switched back and forth between English and Maltese as she tried to get the attention of the learners at the start of the lesson.

Extract 7. An integrated science lesson

T: right can I have silence now (*learners quieten down*) **irridkom toqoghdu attenti hafna . ghal-les**son ok **ghaliex hija . sa nibdew** unit **Ídid . xi ftit mill-affarijiet li . sa naghmlu . f'dan il-unit sa jkollkom zgur fl-ezami allura tridu toqoghdu attenti iktar**

T: right can I have silence now (*learners quieten down*) **I want you to give your full attention to** the lesson ok **because it is . we are going to start a new** unit **. some of the things that . we are going to do . in this unit are definitely going to come out in the exam and therefore you must pay more attention**

CONCLUSION

In this chapter, I present examples of the language practices I observed and recorded in a small sample of secondary schools in Malta. In all the classes I observed, the teachers used codeswitching as a communicative resource for discourse management purposes: in providing explanations, in introducing new topics, or in making asides. They also used codeswitching to distinguish between talk about lesson content and talk related to the negotiation of the social relations of the classroom, like building a rapport with students or asserting the teacher's authority. Codeswitching provided a crucial means of accomplishing lessons across the curriculum and managing the problem of working with texts that are mostly written in English. However, it also reflected the sociolinguistic conditions beyond these schools and classrooms and, I would argue, ultimately served to reproduce the dominance of English in the daily cycles of life in these classrooms.

In their classroom conversations, the teachers and learners appeared to be continually attending to the symbolic values associated with Maltese and English. English was associated with formal, written discourse: It was a means of establishing distance between speakers, readers, and writers; the use of English as a teaching medium discouraged participation by learners. In contrast, the use of Maltese created an informal atmosphere, established warmth and closeness between the participants and encouraged participation, and discussion on the part of the learners.

Another significant issue was the preference for English as a spoken medium of instruction among older teachers (primarily those over 35 years), and the preference for Maltese, often mixed with English, among younger teachers. This pattern of linguistic preferences reflected the changing nature of language values and communicative practices in post-independence Malta. British institutional structures and British forms of educational provision and assessment have been replaced by Maltese ones, which has been accompanied by an increase in the use of Maltese. However, rather than replacing English entirely, Maltese is increasingly mixed with it, to the extent that Borg (1988) prefers to speak in terms of the emergence of a mixed Maltese-English variety. Borg argues that this type of codeswitched discourse is common in several domains, including education and administration. Few institutional contexts in Malta are characterized by monolingual communication in Maltese (or English); however, the ability to work with texts in English is a crucial resource for access to positions of power and influence in Maltese society.

Many people in Malta value the Maltese language and generally endeavor to promote it. At the same time, they view English as a language of power and influence within a global economy. Few people want to cut themselves off from their Maltese heritage and use only English. At the same time, few people are willing to observe a Maltese-only principle in their conversational interactions. By codeswitching, one avoids being associated with "Maltese purists," on the one hand, and with "snobbish English speakers," on the other hand. By codeswitching, one can appear to know enough English to be considered an educated person while espousing a Maltese identity. This extends to the ways in which teachers use language to construct their professional identities within the school context. Their codeswitching can be seen as a way of managing more than one identity and of avoiding being seen as too purist or too snobbish. At the same time, codeswitching is a crucial communicative resource for managing the dilemmas imposed by the lack of a clear language policy.

TRANSCRIPTION CONVENTIONS

In the examples and extracts in this chapter, the following conventions are followed:

All the transcribed data (from audiorecordings of interviews and of bilingual classroom talk) is presented in columns. The left-hand column shows the transcribed extract and the right-hand column shows the English translation. Maltese is highlighted in bold throughout. The English translation of the Maltese is also shown in bold in the right-hand column to reflect the code contrasts in the left-hand column, while the original English utterances remain in normal font.

No punctuation marks are used.

The dots represent pause length.

T   Teacher

L   Learner

Ls   Learners

REFERENCES

Aquilina, J. (1964). The English language in Malta. *Journal of the Faculty of Arts, Royal University of Malta, 3*, 181–198.

Attard, D. (1995). *L-Użu tal-Malti u l-Ingliz fil-klassi tar-raba' sena*. Undergraduate project, University of Malta.

Borg, A. (1988). The maintenance of Maltese as a language: What chances? *European Workshop on Multicultural Studies in Higher Education*. Strasbourg: Council of Europe, 89–106.

Borg, A., Mifsud, M., and Schiriha, L. (1992). The position of Maltese in Malta. Paper presented at a Meeting for Experts on Language Planning. Council of Europe, Valletta, Malta. Unpublished manuscript.

Camilleri, A. (1987). *Language, education and socialization in Mgarr*. B.Ed. (Hons.) dissertation, University of Malta.

Camilleri, A. (1993). *Bilingual teacher talk in Maltese secondary classrooms*. Unpublished Ph.D. thesis, University of Edinburgh.

Camilleri, A. (1995). *Bilingualism in education: The Maltese experience*. Heidelberg: Julius Groos Verlag.

Corson, D. (1990). *Language across the curriculum*. Clevedon: Multilingual Matters.

Cremona, J. (1990). The romance element in Maltese: A review of the problems. *Transactions of the Philological Society, 88(2)*, 163–199.

Department of Information, Malta. (1975). *Constitution of the Republic of Malta*. Government of the Republic of Malta: Malta.

Department of Information, Malta. (1989). *National minimum curriculum regulations*. Government of the Republic of Malta: Malta.

Dobie, E. (1967). *Malta's road to independence*. Norman: University of Oklahoma Press.

Ellul, S. (1978). *A case-study in bilingualism: Code switching between parents and their pre-school children in Malta*. Cambridge: Huntington Publishers Ltd.

Frendo, H. (1975). Language and nationality in an island colony: Malta. *Canadian Review of Studies in Nationalism, 3*, 22–33.

Keenan, P. J. (1879). *An inquiry into the system of education in Malta*. London: Charles Thom.

Lemke, J. L. (1989). Making text talk. *Theory into Practice, 28(2)*, 136–141.

Mifsud, M. (1992). *The non-semitic element in Maltese verbal morphology: A descriptive and comparative study of loan words in Maltese*. Ph.D. thesis, University of Malta.

Navarro, J. A., and Grech, M. (1984). *A study of select linguistic features of Maltese-English*. Paper presented in partial fulfillment for the award of Diploma in Language Studies, University of Malta.

Phillipson, R. (1988). Linguicism: Structures and ideologies in linguistic imperialism. In T. Skutnabb-Kangas and J. Cummins (Eds.), *Minority education: From shame to struggle* (pp. 339–358). Clevedon: Multilingual Matters.

Phillipson, R. (1992). *Linguistic imperialism*. Oxford: Oxford University Press.

Spiteri, S. (1994). *Bir-razza u bir-radika: Sociolinguistic aspects of the language behavior of a Maltese middle-class family*. Postgraduate project, University of Malta.

Zammit Mangion, J. (1992). *Education in Malta*. Malta: Studia Editions.

11

Classroom Interaction and the Bilingual Resources of Migrant Students in Switzerland[1]

Lorenza Mondada and Laurent Gajo

The presence of migrants in the classroom represents a significant challenge, from a theoretical as well as a practical point of view, given that schools are responsible for socialization and learning. This chapter will focus on situations that enable us to capture some types of conversational interactions that occur in classrooms where migrant children are present. It draws on a study that was conducted in reception classes (*classes d'accueil*) especially designed for the children of migrants who have recently arrived in French-speaking Switzerland. We will focus in particular on the way in which the bilingual resources of these students are taken into consideration in the daily life of the school. We will also consider the conditions under which the multilingualism of migrant children can contribute to their integration and academic success and to the development of their ability to integrate new linguistic resources into their repertoires. We then conclude with a brief reflection on the extent to which schools recognize and value the potential inherent in such multilingualism.

IMMIGRATION AND EDUCATION: SOME THEORETICAL AND EMPIRICAL CHALLENGES

The presence of migrant children in the school system presents a complex challenge: Their presence at school, a central location for the reproduction of social structures and networks, raises the fundamental issue of whether a pluralist society is actually possible or how it may be realized (cf. de Certeau 1987). Migrant children introduce new cross-cultural and multi-ethnic elements to the "host" society, but they are also frequently associated with problems such as academic failure, discrimination, difficult socioeconomic conditions, and tensions between ethnolinguistic groups (Heller 1999). This leads us to investigate the conditions in which the sociocultural and linguistic potential of migrants can be realized, both for the benefit of the migrants themselves and for that of the "host" society.

Migrants at School: A Social Laboratory

A class with a large number of immigrants may be regarded as a social laboratory, which prompts us to ask the following questions: How are integration and dialogue, rather than exclusion and discrimination, accomplished in multicultural situations? What makes a school multilingual in its outlook? What makes schools acknowledge the diversity of languages, practices, skills, and lived experiences with language represented among their students? Or, on the other hand, what makes a school impose a normative vision of language as an object of study within a fixed curriculum? What makes a school define its mission in a homogenizing manner with monolingual terms of reference? The classroom provides us with an opportunity to investigate the possibilities for a collective project, for experiences that have been jointly constructed, for identities that are negotiated rather than defined in an essentialist and rigid manner.

The notion of *l'étranger* ("other" or "stranger") has played an important theoretical and methodological role in the history of sociology. It offers an alternative way of formulating a view of a society: one that questions facts, deconstructs certainties, and relativizes values (Harman 1986; Tabboni 1988). The concept is emically constructed on both a local and a general level, since every social group is confronted with its own *étranger*, as a sort of duplicate of itself (Derrida 1997). The notion has been applied in the study of different social phenomena, ranging from legal provisions to administrative procedures, from socioeconomic positions that are accessible and actually occupied to different types of face-to-face relationships. This can lead to configurations that are primarily defined by their own boundaries, with people focusing on themselves and on their demands for a recognition of their own identities. Or it can lead to configurations that are defined by an opening-up, characterized by dialogue and exchange. It can also lead to situations of crossing and mixing (Rampton 1995) or to the realities of exclusion and discrimination (Roberts 1992).

These extremely diverse and often ambiguous images of l'étranger highlight the initial theoretical challenge posed by the presence of migrants: How are migrants actually categorized? What are we to make of the public discourse that refers to migrants as if they constituted a uniform, homogeneous, and unambiguously defined category when there exists a multitude of definitions? Indeed, migrants can be defined according to a number of different characteristics: historical (early or later waves of immigration; first-, second- or third-generation migrants), cultural (familiar, closely related cultures compared to "exotic" cultures, which are difficult for the "host" society to understand), administrative (status as migrant, immigrant, or refugee; different types of work permits), and individual (different types of migration and integration objectives). How do schools actually categorize children of migrant or refugee origin when they open special classes, decide whether to keep newly arrived migrants in separate classes or to place them together with second-generation children who are struggling at school, or decide how to help refugees who have fled wars or how to place children of diplomats or international corporate executives?

The problem of categorization of migrants can be understood in ways that go beyond questions of public visibility. Migration has overt but also hidden dimensions, many of which remain invisible to observers as well to the migrants themselves. In the public sphere, migrants are often categorized in ways that are reduced to differences in physical features or customs; however, we often fail to see that these phenomena are part of a broad process of social construction through which they become "other," "different," or "strangers" (Mondada 1999, 2000).

Practices that configure, respect, or reject the various categories of migrants are themselves part of a contradictory intellectual and sociopolitical realm. This issue is closely related to a whole series of studies and standpoints that recognize, describe, and attribute value to hybrid processes of identity formation in which we see a bricolage of identities due to the presence and mingling of multiple cultural resources. This is especially evident in recent work on the phenomenon of "crossing" (Rampton 1995), a type of linguistic innovation that occurs mainly in urban environments. Similar phenomena have been documented in work in the areas of postcolonial and gender studies, which focus on the reconfiguration of identities that traditionally have been suppressed or marginalized by colonial or patriarchal structures (Bhabha

1994; Butler 1990). What unites all these studies is that they challenge an essentialist and reifying approach toward categories and share an interest in pursuing new and blended forms of categorization. Given these current trends, however, we also ought to ask what will become of the school as it is traditionally conceived, based on monolingual and native-speaker norms and considered as the site of maintenance and reproduction of such norms (Rampton 1990; Leung, Harris, and Rampton 1997).

The phenomenon of "crossing" and other means of rearranging identities by means of linguistic resources seem to occur mostly in liminal and interstitial spaces where norms and customary social constraints are suspended (Rampton 1995, 234–235). We may well ask ourselves if such spaces and practices are not diametrically opposed to those of school. However, as Heller (1994) has shown, a close look at any school reveals that its social and temporal spaces are not uniform. This heterogeneity arises in the contexts of everyday classroom events, in situated tasks in which students are categorized and managed in terms of their linguistic behavior, in moments when specific points in a lesson are being negotiated, in a conversation, in a discussion, or during a game in the school yard. By describing these activities, we shall try to understand some of the different ways in which schools acknowledge yet simultaneously reject the rich and diverse cultural and linguistic resources of their migrant students.

Migrants at School in French-Speaking Switzerland: The Case of Portuguese Children

The data presented here come from a study conducted in French-speaking Switzerland, more specifically in the canton of Neuchâtel.[2] In this region, the school system has implemented a program designed to provide an initial orientation for children who have recently arrived in the canton and who do not speak the local language. The objective of this specific program, and of the *classes d'accueil*, is to provide migrant children who speak languages other than French with the opportunity to acquire the linguistic skills necessary to join the mainstream classes within a period of six months to a year (language is therefore identified as one of the basic visible markers of "otherness"). In these classes, the focus is on basic skills in the three subjects that are considered to be the most important in the school system: French, mathematics, and German as a second language.

These *classes d'accueil* are like other transitional structures (cf. Martin-Jones and Saxena 1995, 1996, reprinted in this volume) that form the basis of provision for the education of migrant children and prepare them for transfer to the mostly monolingual majority system. Such transitional structures are characterized by contradictory objectives. They reflect the tensions present in the school's handling of diversity: The actual classes are multicultural meeting points, and yet, given the broader school aims and the definition of the students for whom the classes are intended, day-to-day practices in such classrooms may often serve to promote homogeneity. In fact, while the wider program brings together children from many different cultural backgrounds, it actually serves to silence the diverse voices of the children, as only one norm is referred to and one target pursued: instruction in the official language of the school. The diverse resources of the students are treated in a homogenizing fashion, within a monolithic language order. Students are categorized as: "speakers of other languages," "foreigners," or "migrants." Such categories, however, only serve to give the appearance of uniformity to what are actually highly diverse migrant trajectories.

The teachers working with the classes we have observed and audiorecorded are also affected by the paradoxical nature of the program. Few of them have been trained to work in a multicultural environment, and some of them became involved not so much because of a positive choice but because of their need to find employment. Also, there is very little specific teaching material available (but see Perregaux 1994, 1998; Magnin Hottelier et al. 1994).

The cultural diversity in these *classes d'accueil* is therefore paradoxical. It is extremely visible, and yet its existence is denied by categorizing students in a way that does not take account of their multiple identities. In the classes we worked in, the students were between twelve and sixteen years old. They included a large number of Portuguese and Spanish children whose parents worked in poorly paid jobs. They also included children of businesspeople who worked in high-tech industries, children of Turkish and Kurdish migrants and refugees, children of refugees from Kosovo, Albania, and Bosnia, and children of some refugees of South Asian origin, particularly Tamils.

The students in these heterogeneous classes were accorded different degrees and types of visibility. The Portuguese children, who made up the largest group and who are the focus of this study, were generally seen by the teachers as part of a "problem-free community." The teachers often favorably compared these students to those who had fled war zones and who were frequently expected to have serious psychological problems. The Portuguese students were also favorably compared with those whose culture was seen as being more distant and whose behavior was difficult for teachers to understand and interpret. The Portuguese children were perceived as being relatively problem free, in spite of the fact that their unusually high rate of academic failure was a matter of great concern for the Portuguese authorities and associations in Switzerland and meant that these children were more likely to end up occupying low positions in the labor market. Portuguese children were therefore experiencing the problems typically associated with migration while ostensibly belonging to an unproblematic group (Oriol 1984).

As they belonged to a large group of migrant students, Portuguese children were involved in extremely variable majority-minority relationships in the classroom, which were frequently difficult to determine. They often managed these situations by drawing on flexible communicative resources that adjusted easily to different classroom activities and that sometimes involved adopting French as a *lingua franca* and as the official language of the school. These communicative resources enabled the youngsters to feel at ease in their *classe d'accueil* and to negotiate as best they could the different interactive contexts of their daily lives. They frequently encountered different types of discontinuities between school (with its linguistic norm based on standard French) and other domains of their lives, where other codes predominated. These other domains, networks, and interlocutors included friends who spoke French and networks where French was used as a *lingua franca*; peer groups distinguished by the use of a vernacular French; their parents and their community of origin, where Portuguese was used and where French was only used for exchanges with outsiders. However, the scope of these communicative repertoires was not recognized explicitly by teachers, who were all too quick to evaluate them in terms of other, more conventional, academic and decontextualized language skills.

In addition, these Portuguese children had considerable academic difficulties once they switched to the mainstream classes. Their problems were often associated by the teachers with a lack of writing skills and with difficulties in learning German, the first foreign language encountered in the school system in this part of Switzerland and a decisive factor in the evaluation of the students' performance.

The skills of these migrant students, including the ability to put together the pieces of their experiences, to improvise, and to adapt to new situations, as well as their skill in speaking different language varieties, most of which were unfamiliar to their teachers, constituted a potential wealth of resources that the school did not seem to know how to exploit. While the linguistic and cultural diversity present in the *classes d'accueil* could very well have been acknowledged in the discourse of the teachers, in practice it was dealt with as a difference that had to be overcome rather than as a resource that could be cultivated (Bhatt and Martin-Jones 1992). We found evidence of this in the surprisingly monolingual management of classroom activities, where only French was valued and where many switches to the students' mother tongues were disregarded (cf. Gajo 1998).

These different ways of dealing practically and locally with the linguistic and cultural diversity that existed in these *classes d'accueil* raise key issues related to the links between interactions experienced at school, the acquisition of language in both formal and informal settings, and the potential of bilingualism and multilingualism, both unrecognized and recognized as a resource for learning. The coming together of these various issues is increasingly taken up in Swiss work on migrants at school, and they are currently at the forefront of recommendations addressed to politicians and educators (cf. Frischherz 1997; Müller 1997).

An Interactionist Approach

The issues outlined here can be examined in many different ways. These include approaches based on statistics about migration or about school failure rates, on surveys focusing on the linguistic representations and attitudes of various actors, or on test results that identify a range of relevant skills. We propose to take an interactionist approach. Such an approach lends itself to investigating the complexity of the issues we are interested in here: learning processes, different types of academic integration, and the management of a multilingual environment. We will connect these issues to activities as they are embedded in the school context (Gajo, Koch, and Mondada 1996; Gajo and Mondada 1998).

Considering interactions in context allows us to understand the specific ways in which three central dimensions of the problems we are concerned with gradually develop in the practices and contexts of school. The three dimensions are processes of schooling and socialization, processes of categorization, and learning processes.

Processes of Schooling and Socialization. Schools are social spaces with complex networks of various social actors. Daily activities such as teaching, evaluation, administration, and supervision and the ways in which these are organized result in the valuing or devaluing of the characteristics, resources, and achievements of students. By deciding what counts and what does not count as academic success, the school is actively engaged in constructing school failure and success, on the basis of its construction of categories that are considered to be educationally relevant. These processes occur via streaming and/or the provision of special education (cf. Cicourel 1974; Mehan 1986).

Processes of Categorization. Schools are places where countless modes of description, classification, and streaming of students are used. These processes of categorization focus, in particular, on students' identities, linguistic abilities, and sociolinguistic competences. During activities in class, teachers identify salient characteristics of the students, which they then use to categorize them in different ways (Mondada and Py 1995; Mondada 2000). Analyzing communicative practices as elements of processes of categorization allows us to consider them in terms of how they are practically accomplished and not in terms of their objective qualities (cf. Moerman 1974; Wieder and Pratt 1990).

Learning Processes. An interactionist approach allows one to consider the abilities of students not with reference to some universal, abstract, and individualistic type of cognition but as cognition that is built into the very practices of an interactional and intersubjective context (cf. Lave 1993). Linguistic knowledge, in particular, is acquired in a situated manner, through interaction inside and outside the classroom (cf. Vasseur 1993; Krafft and Dausendschön-Gay 1994; Véronique 1997) and in diverse ways depending on the type of activity and the context (cf. Gajo and Mondada 1998). Furthermore, it is configured in and through use and distributed among various actors in the classroom, who co-construct knowledge during their collaborative interactions (Rogoff 1995).

BILINGUALISM AS A POTENTIAL RESOURCE

There is an ongoing debate in the research literature, in education (Baker 1995), and in daily life about the advantages and disadvantages of bilingualism. Two different points of view tend to be expressed: On the one hand, there are those who are concerned with bilinguals and with the diversity of language histories that they can have; and, on the other hand, there are those who are primarily concerned with monolinguals and the choices available to them for second-language learning. Depending on one's standpoint and one's points of reference, learners are either individual bilinguals who command considerable prestige or disadvantaged groups of minorities. The judgments that people make also vary greatly. Furthermore, a number of factors that ought to be clearly distinguished have become blurred: the paths taken toward bilingualism, the conditions of access to it, and the purposes and complex outcomes of bilingualism and language education. One of the major problems with this debate is the fact that it often takes monolingualism as its starting point, that is, bilinguals are being judged on the basis of criteria developed for and by monolinguals. Even the terminology used to write about bilingualism is evidence of this (cf. Cook 1997).

In order to adopt critical distance from the issue of advantages and disadvantages, we approach the issue as a matter for empirical research. Uncritical arguments for or against bilingualism are rejected. We will begin by underlining the very specific and entirely different nature of bilingual competence (cf. Grosjean 1989, 1994; Romaine 1989; Cook 1997). We will therefore first attempt to describe the specific nature of bilingualism. This requires us to consider both discursive and cognitive evidence. Second, we will show, by means of socio-discursive evidence, the conditions under which bilingual competence is likely to constitute a resource and an asset.

The Competence of the Bilingual

A bilingual person's competence can be understood to exist at two distinct levels: at the level of the actual communicative repertoire and at the level of strategies used in interaction and in language acquisition. The communicative repertoire clearly consists of two linguistic codes, which allow the bilingual to access a wider field of communication. However, this repertoire is not merely the sum of two languages (one language plus one language) but rather their combination (via their interaction). As a result, we find particular discursive occurrences, such as codeswitching or cross-linguistic markers (cf. Lüdi and Py 1986; Heller 1988). Unfortunately, however, these particularities are often not recognized for what they are, but instead are seen as signs of linguistic deficiency that must be overcome, as linguistic oddities, or as impurities (cf. Cadiot 1987).

In this chapter, however, we will focus on the strategies and resources available to bilinguals. There is no dearth of psycholinguistic literature on the subject. There is ample writing on the topic of communicative strategies and language learning even though the connection between the two is not often very clear. There is also a substantial body of research on bilingualism in general. Increasingly, there is a certain overlap between the two areas that attributes a heightened importance to metalinguistic or metacognitive processes. Bilingualism entails an increased metalinguistic capacity (cf. Titone 1993). Heightened metalinguistic awareness at the level of phonology and syntax, a keener perception of the arbitrariness of linguistic signs, and a greater cognitive flexibility are some of the more specific consequences of bilingualism (cf. Cook 1997, for a comprehensive overview). Greater creativity, better skills of analysis and abstraction, and a more refined communicative sensitivity are some further advantages (cf. Lüdi 1998).

A number of researchers hypothesize that bilinguals have greater ease and resilience when it comes to overcoming communicative problems or breakdowns. In an attempt to explain this trait, the notion of strategic competence has been developed (Canale and Swain 1980; Tarone 1984; Little 1996; Berthoud 1995).

Studies in this area clearly suggest that learning through problem solving is situated at the highest level of cognitive operations, since it creates "obligations" for learning in moving from activities in the area of what is known to activities in the area of what is unknown (cf. Hainaut 1983). Bange (1992) shows the effectiveness of such strategies for addressing problems by pointing out the link between communication and learning. He refers to the acceptance of uncertain knowledge as an example of such a strategy.

It appears then that bilingual advantage can be identified in the richness and complexity of metalinguistic abilities. These can be seen at two levels: in the perception and handling of linguistic utterances themselves and in the management of communicative activities and language learning. With reference to the taxonomy suggested by Oxford (1990), one might say that the bilingual disposes of particular resources both for direct strategies (cognitive strategies, to use the terminology of O'Malley and Chamot 1990) and for indirect strategies (metacognitive and social strategies, again O'Malley and Chamot 1990), even if it is only the latter that appear to be metalinguistic in the strict sense.

These different studies give us sufficient grounds not only to assume that bilingual competence does exist but also that, in some sense, it exceeds the competence of monolinguals. Still, a number of questions remain unanswered, particularly the following question: Is it bilingualism that gives rise to certain cognitive competencies, or is it rather these competencies that allow bilingualism to develop (cf. Cook 1997)? In any event, it appears that the concept of bilingual advantage needs to be modified to take account of socio-discursive and contextual factors.

Bilingual Competence: Its Activation and Its Visibility

Taking the interactionist approach, for which we are arguing here, not only means considering interaction as a tool that enables one to manage communicative activities but also means considering interaction as the very locus where such activities are constituted. Language competences are therefore seen as bound up with situated practices. As a result, not only do we have to take the social parameters of the communication situation into consideration, but we must also see them through the role they play in discourse. It is within the more or less negotiated construction of an interaction that bilingual competence will or will not be called into play.

An integral part of any interaction is, of course, the representation that each participant has about the other(s): how the identities and skills of the other(s) are perceived. These representations are constructed *in situ*. This has been clearly shown in studies of attitudes and motivations of people involved in educational programs (cf. Candelier 1993), as well as in studies of the sociopolitical and educational status of the languages involved. Yet this is still not sufficient for an understanding of how bilingualism and a bilingual's resources are constructed with regard to a range of social and situational parameters (cf. Hamers and Blanc 1983).

The issue becomes even more complicated as the link between bilingualism and the acquisition of new languages becomes clear. The hypothesis concerning the advantages of bilingualism involves postulating that the acquisition of any new and additional communicative skill is facilitated by bilingual procedures that have already been developed through prior experience. However, some substantial evidence needs to be provided. This comes, on the one hand, from accounts of communicative behavior that, while being very efficient for solving communicative difficulties, does not necessarily lead to successful language acquisition (Vasseur 1991; Dausendschön-Gay and Krafft 1997). On the other hand, there are accounts of difficult contact situations that are marked by exclusion and the stigmatization of migrants by members of the "host" society. Here, the ability of migrants to learn the "host" society's language is constrained, and second-language abilities are often rapidly fossilized in such situations.

In our study, we hoped to be able to observe the emergence of bilingual advantage especially in the learning of the third language: German. We anticipated that the strategies that were worked out and tested when the second language, French, was learned, would be used once again. But, again, situational parameters got in the way. The resources that had been called upon and developed in the learning of French had been based as much on interactions outside the classroom as inside. However, any contact with German was restricted entirely to the classroom. Furthermore, French-Portuguese bilingualism was supported by the proximity of the two languages (cf. Gajo 1996), which was not the case for German.

All of the preceding led us to expect that bilingual competence would be configured in a variety of ways. Only within the context created through the interactions themselves could we assess bilingual competence. It was also through the interactions that we could identify ways in which bilingualism was serving as a resource, which depended for its activation on local conditions. This runs counter to a number of studies where it is merely assumed that bilingualism is an asset (cf. Baetens Beardsmore 1986; Lüdi 1998).

MULTILINGUALISM AT SCHOOL: ITS LIMITS AND ITS POTENTIAL

Researching the various manifestations of multilingualism in a school means confronting oneself with a situation that is highly complex and characterized by a multitude of possible observations and a number of contradictions. With regard to what can be observed, one can concentrate on a range of discourses: statements made by school authorities, the curricula, the discourse of teachers, and the demands made by parents and associations. But one can also concentrate on a variety of practices: interactions in class; different means of evaluating student performance, either immediately in the classroom or later during staff meetings; recreational activities during recess; and chatter, games, and talk between students during class. The multitude of observable situations involve different players, types of activity, heterogeneous contexts, and divergent perspectives. Whether and how multilingualism becomes an issue at school very much depends on whether the issue is raised by a teacher faced with a committed member of a multicultural association, by a parent who is complaining about his/her child's academic difficulties, by other teachers meeting to address issues related to children from different ethnic groups attending the same school; or by students during a task in the classroom.

What is important, then, is to locate these different positions, that is, to examine them in the proper context in which they arise or are constructed in and through practice. Any stance taken with regard to a particular issue is always locally situated. In fact, an issue acquires a certain relevance (or not) through the practical activities within which it arises. It needs to be seen in terms of its place within a whole structure or within the unfolding of a series of events and in terms of the purpose of the activity itself. All these elements play a role in the way the issue is expressed, what it is directed toward, and how it is being argued. The issue of multilingualism at school should, we believe, be accounted for in terms of how it can be observed and recognized within the various practices in which it arises.

We focus on everyday activities in the classroom, not because we wish to reduce school to these activities but because they are central to the school context (Mondada 1995). The questions we ask concern the extent to which multilingualism is either recognized or rejected, how it is used as an available resource not only for addressing difficulties but also in order to accomplish the task of learning, and how it is disregarded as a potential resource for activities in the classroom. Multilingualism will therefore be considered in terms of how it takes shape in all the multifaceted organizational activities in class and not in terms of how it is presented, announced, and called for in more public discourses in other contexts. In order to accomplish this, we do, however, need to consider the methods, in the ethnomethodological sense of this term, that teachers use to categorize their students and their linguistic output. We also need to recast the question concerning bilingual advantage in terms of how it is either integrated or becomes stigmatized through the practices of both teachers and students, how it is used by all social actors involved as something that is either valuable and efficient or inadequate and inefficient. In order to accomplish the task, we shall analyze a few extracts from classroom interactions that depict a continuum of situations ranging from rejection to explicitly calling upon the students' multilingual abilities. Between these two poles, we find situations of ambiguity in which the multilingual resources in the classroom are not openly acknowledged and need to be interpreted by the participants.

Ambiguities

The situations that we have called ambiguous are interesting primarily because they show that the traces of multilingualism identifiable in interaction are not evident for the participants and may even cause problems of identification and interpretation with regard to the status and role of the participants in the communicative event. In these instances, however, the ability to categorize both speakers and their utterances, as displayed by students and by teachers, is of crucial importance. In Extract 1, we therefore examine how the use of the first language, in this case, Portuguese, by some of the students was dealt with in practical terms, in the local context of a classroom activity. Transcription conventions are presented at the end of the chapter.

The following examples are taken from two classroom settings. Extracts 1, 2, 4, and 6 come from the first classroom. There were about 15 students in the class (the total number varied throughout the year). The students were between 13 and 16 years old, with the majority being 14. Most of the students were Portuguese. There were also some Albanian, Turkish, Spanish, and English students. Extracts 3 and 5 come from the second setting. This was a special *classe d'appui* (support class) organized for just one student,[3] aged 11, so all interactions were dyadic in nature. The student was Portuguese, and the teacher was Spanish-speaking. The teacher in this second setting had an interest in Spanish culture.

Extract 1. *"Say it in French."*

1   Te   qu'est-ce que tu en as pensé d'cette cassette
            what did you think of the tape

(7 sec)

2   M   j'sais pas
         I don't know

3   Te   tu sais pas
         you don't know

4   M   non
         no

5   Te   tu n'en penses rien
         you don't think anything about it.

6   M   moi j'ai déjà pensé mais: . j'sais pas comme:
         I did think of something but: . I don't know how:

7   Te   t'as d'la peine à l'exprimer\ . essaie .. ça fait rien si tu
         you're having trouble expressing it\ . try .. it doesn't matter if you

8   t'trompes ... on va essayer d'comprendre/
         make a mistake ... we'll try to understand

(5 sec)

9   *(whispering in Portuguese; laughter from B)*

10   Te   qu'est-ce que ça t'a fait comme effet quand tu vois ça\ .
         how do you feel when you see that\ .

11   ça fait plaisir/
         does it feel good

12   *(whispering in Portuguese)*

13   Te   ça te plaît/ .. tu trouves qu'c'est bien/
         do you like it/ .. [do] you think it's good

14   M   non
         no

15   T   **o Benfica**
         Benfica

16   Te   (c'est?) pas bien/
         (it's?) not good/

17   D   **mas a Benfica xxx tanta xxx violência assim às (claras)**
         but Benfica xxx so much xxx violence so (clear)

18   T   **xxxxxxxxxxx**

19   S   **o Benfica é um corno . eu matava-o**
         Benfica is piece of shit {lit: horn} . I'd kill it

20   P   **olha . olha . olha**
         look . look . look

21   B   **acaba a conversa**
         shut up {lit: end the conversation/talk}

22   S   **uma pessoa acá matava-o**
         someone here would kill it

23   P   **o Bruno**
         Bruno

24	S	não [mas era assim
		no but it was like this
25	P	[BRUNO [Bruno . chama lá esse::
		BRUNO Bruno . can you call this one
26	Te	[essayez d'le dire en français
		try to say it in French
27	P	o Benfica é um corno [fala aí nesse relato que o Benfica é um corno
		Benfica is a piece of shit . say there in this report that Benfica is a piece of shit
28	Te	[Simon Simon
		Simon Simon
29	M	e o Porto é um
		and Porto is a
30	B	o Benfica é um cor-
		Benfica is a piece of sh-
31	P	a granda Porto
		the great Porto
32	Te	vous le dites en français
		say it in French
33	M	mas não ganharam mais
		but they didn't win any more
34	P	sabes que o:
		do you know that
35	Te	ouh ouh/
		hey hey
36	B	non ça va madame
		no it's OK ma'am
(3 sec)		
37	M	le film de hier c'est un p'tit peu triste
		the film yesterday is a little bit sad
38	Te	c'est ^un peu triste/ . oui
		it's a bit sad/ . yes
39	B	ouais ouais madame\ . c'est un peu triste
		yeah yeah miss\ . it's a bit sad

The discussion in Extract 1 concerns a film about violence at school that the class had seen in the previous lesson. The discussion did not proceed smoothly and led to problems of turn taking; the students were not very forthcoming and did not participate. With her questions (1–5), the teacher selected a specific student, M, who, however, did not reply. M's reticence was gradually accounted for by difficulties of expression (6–7) rather than a reluctance to participate (2–5).

In this situation, the teacher attempted to encourage communication by reducing the normative pressure on the students to speak good French and by relaxing her control of classroom discipline; she asked the student to express himself in any way he could (7–8), and she allowed the others to whisper in Portuguese and even laugh, without reprimanding them. While she continued with her questions (13, 16), the students began to talk about two football teams: Sports Lisboa e Benfica (Benfica) and Futebol Clube do Porto (Porto). They talked about each team's chances of winning, the relative quality of the two clubs, and violence in football. The teacher did not intervene initially (15–25). She was unable to judge either the content or the value of these exchanges, and she did not make any direct reference to them; she could have seen them either as a valuable period of dialogue and collaboration related to the lesson, or she could have interpreted them as mere chatter and could thus have put a stop to them. The fact that the exchanges were conducted in Portuguese could have been interpreted by the teacher as an attempt on the part of the students to find a way of completing the task and thus producing the expected response or, on the contrary, as a way of undermining the (mono)lingual norm of the school and therefore as something that had to be checked.

The teacher was faced with the difficult task of interpreting the use of Portuguese as a "contextualisation cue" (Gumperz 1992) indexing an activity that was or was not related to the classroom activity at hand. This problem was not immediately resolved by the teacher, who let the exchange continue in Portuguese. When she did intervene in 26 and 32, she reacted to a turn in the conversation that was in Portuguese: Her reaction displayed her interpretation of the previous turn. Her intervention and interpretation were, however, ambiguous: she used anaphora ("say it in French"), thus leaving it up to the participants to interpret her remark. Her anaphoric reference could have referred to what was said in the previous turn, or it could have referred to the response she expected to her question.

The students were working together to develop a discussion topic in Portuguese, centered on football, but they were also aware of the somewhat defiant nature of their behavior. This was demonstrated by the call for order made by B (21), who did not respond to P's calls (23, 25) and who concluded the move into Portuguese by going back to French and to the activity (36). In this turn, B responded to a call from the teacher in 35, which was followed by a silence from the other students. The discussion activity then continued in French, and the initial question (in line 1) received an answer in French.

The teacher's intervention therefore achieved its objective: While she tolerated and even supported an exchange in Portuguese and possibly assumed that the exchange was directed at the task in hand, something (either the nonsequential turn taking, the multiple floors, or the Portuguese) seemed "out of order" to her. She reestablished "order" (28, 36) and asked the students to switch back to French (using a modalized request in the first instance and then an imperative). The use of Portuguese had been neither clearly approved nor disapproved, although her sense of order and the use of French were clearly linked for her. Although the participants' verbal behavior was oriented toward the fact that a language other than that of the class was used, they played with the fact that it was difficult to determine what type of contextualization cue Portuguese actually represented here. It is interesting to note that the meanings of switches to the students' L1 can apparently be left loosely defined in some cases; the ambiguity can be maintained for all practical purposes. It is probably one way of dealing with recurrent and necessary switching between languages when not all speakers involved have the same multilingual skills but wish, nonetheless, to avoid any breakdown in communication (Mondada 1998).

Rejection of Bilingualism

Other examples from our classroom data were, however, less ambiguous and demonstrated that bilingual resources could be ignored and even rejected by the teacher, even if they could help in accomplishing the classroom task. They appeared to be seen as a transgression or an error and not as a sign of collaboration. Extract 2 is an example.

Extract 2. *"Simon, you'll be sent out."*

1 Te Marie/ . nous t'écoutons\
       Marie/ . we're listening
2 P   ouais Marie/
       yeah Marie/
3 Ma [moi::
       [I::
4 P   [tu peux commencer\
       [you can start
5 P   **ah tu disseste que tinhas um truc p'ra . interessante p'ra contar**
       oh you said that you had something to . interesting to tell
6 Ma qu'est-ce que j'dis/
       what do I say/
7 S   c'était une fois/
       there was once
8 P   comment est le film de:::
       what's the film like
9 S   tu contes ton histoire/
       you tell your story/

10	Te	tu parles de quelque chose qui t'a intéressé
		talk about something that interested you
11	S	ouais ouais / tu contes une histoire [à la classe
		yeah yeah / tell a story [to the class
12	Te	[Simon/ tu parleras quand
		[Simon/ you can speak when
13		ce sera ton tour
		when it's your turn
14	M	xxxxxxxxxxxx
15	Te	Martin aussi
		Martin too/
16	M	**vão se encontrar**
		they are going to meet

(3 sec)

17	S	**conta que andaste com uma pessoa e depois deixaste-a e depois**
		say that you went out with this person and then you left him/her and then
18		**com outra e depois [xxxxx**
		with another and after that [xxxxx
19	Te	[Simon/ on va te mettre à la porte ou bien/
		[Simon/ you'll be sent out unless

(6 sec)

20	Ma	je sais pas:/
		I don't know: /

(2 sec)

21	Te	est-ce que tu as vu un film/ est-ce que tu as lu un livre/ .
		have you seen a film/ have you read a book/ .
22		est-ce que tu as VU quelque chose d'intéressant/
		have you SEEN something interesting/
23	Ma	moi j'ai lu un livre\
		I read a book
24	P	moi aussi / c'est un film
		me too / it's a film
25	S	**xxxxxx ó filha/ para te acompanhares** (bas)
		xxxxxxxx hey love / to go out with you (in a low voice)
26	Te	Simon/
		Simon/
27	M	parle en français/
		speak French
28	Te	tu vas à la porte hein/
		you'll be sent out OK?
29	P	tu vas à la porte/ (rit)
		you'll be sent out (laughs)

In Extract 2, there is an apparent difficulty in selecting the next student to carry out the task, which consists of telling a story or describing an event of the student's choice. The teacher has asked Marie[4] to tell her story. The other students participate in the task, though in an unexpected manner.

They confirm and support the request of the teacher (cf. P in 2 and 4, who reinforces the request of Te when MA hesitates in 3). This type of collaboration is a kind of mockery, as seen in the turn of M (27), who anticipates the substance of the warning initiated by Te in (26) and completed in (28). The mockery is also seen in the turn taken by P, who repeats and revoices the warning made by the teacher in (28). In both cases, M and P take the "voice" of Te and adopt her declarative stance.

The students suggest, in French, a framework for the story, seemingly trying to help the student who has been selected to fulfill the task (in 7, 8, 9, 11). This occurs with the help offered by Te in 10. This prompts a rebuke from the teacher (in 12), who regards these comments as being in violation of the turn distribution controlled by the teacher and not as a means of helping the student who has been asked to speak.

They suggest, in Portuguese, a content for the story (5, 16, 17, 18). The use of Portuguese here serves both as a potential contribution to the task at hand and as a contextualization strategy (cf. preceding discussion). This momentarily transforms the classroom activity into one that is remote from the task. It transforms it in two ways: First, the parody of collaborative classroom conduct is reinforced; second, a mocking version of a stereotypical feminine story is attributed to Marie by the guys in the class. In this instance, the use of the L1 is taken by the teacher as having a subversive effect, and it is contained (19). This containment could be interpreted as a dual reaction: on the one hand, to the transgression of the classroom "order" and, on the other hand, to the positioning of the female student by the male students. However, it is not clear whether the teacher is taking into account here the gendering of the interaction, since the talk is in Portuguese.

The disapproval shown for the use of the bilingual skills of the students occurs here as part of classroom management. This type of classroom management intervention not only structures how knowledge is presented and learned or how classroom activities are conducted in general, but it also contributes to the maintenance of the interaction order of the classroom. The use of the L1 is not merely an alternative means of expression here; it affects the very structuring of activities in the classroom. The teacher demonstrates quite clearly here that the issue for her is not the choice of the language that enables one to communicate a message as clearly as possible, but the procedures that ensure or threaten order in the classroom. In this way, Portuguese is being categorized as a language of transgression and subversion, not only of the linguistic norm in the class but more generally of the norms of the school.

Recognition of Bilingualism

The ways in which the languages of the students are categorized, that is, the contextual values that they are given during an activity, are developed *in situ* during the course of an activity itself, rather than being based on a general principle or criterion. For this reason, they can reveal the way in which the person who categorizes accounts for, interprets, and gives meaning to the events in which she or he is involved.

Thus, in contrast to Extract 2, we sometimes came across other situations in the same classes, where the use of the L1 was not only tolerated but encouraged, as in Extract 3.

Extract 3. *"You can say it in Portugese."*

1	Te	quand est-ce que tu es venu à l'école à Boudry / quand est-ce
		when did you come to the school in Boudry/ when did
2		que tu as commencé /
		you start/
3	J	euhm de- (sigh)
		um of
4	Te	à peu près: tu as pas besoin de dire la date exacte/ . quel mois
		more or less: you don't have to give the exact date/. Which month
5	J	euh . . j'ai des deux . . deux de : . de euh .. ah:: . euh
		um .. I have from two .. two of: . . of um .. uh:: . um
6	Te	tu peux le dire en portugais hein si tu:
		you can say it in Portuguese alright if you:
7	J	**agosto**
		August
8	Te	deux août / le deux août/ [t'es venu ic[i /
		second of August / the second of August /[you came he[re/
9	J	[oui [oui
		[yes [yes

This extract is taken from the special class where the teacher could speak Spanish and where she was working with just one student. The activity focuses on learning how to introduce oneself and talking about oneself. The teacher's question included various reformulations of the question in order to facilitate the task (1). Given the difficulties that the student was having, the teacher eventually simplified her question in French (4) and then invited the student to use Portuguese to communicate (6). Up to this point, the student's utterances had been very hesitant

(3, 5), but now he responded immediately and even spoke before Te finished speaking (6). The reply, **agosto** (7), was translated by the teacher, and J just confirmed this by using the affirmative and not repeating. The communicative objective here was clearly given more importance than any potential learning to be achieved.

Other factors may also prompt the use of the L1, as demonstrated in Extract 4.

Extract 4. "How do you say 'canapé' in Spanish?"

1	Te	comment est-ce qu'on dit canapé en espagnol Nadia
		how do you say 'canapé' (couch) in Spanish Nadia
2	Ma	[sofa
		sofa
3	N	[sidio
		couch
4	Te	comment/
		how/
5	N	sidio
		couch
6	Ma	pero yo digo sofa
		but I say sofa
7	T	ah ah
8	Z	xxxx
9	Te	oui le sofa / .. le mot le sofa se dit aussi en français Nadia
		yes the sofa/ .. the word sofa is also used in French Nadia
10		exactement le même hein/ . [xxx
		exactly the same right/ . [xxx
11	A	[y en portugais aussi
		[and in Portuguese too
12	B	[en portugais aussi
		[in Portuguese too
13	C	[xxx
14	Te	canapé aussi en por- en esp- en turc/
		couch also in Por- in Spa- in Turkish
15	H	oui
		yes
16	Te	en portugais
		in Portuguese
17	A	ouais
		yes

Extract 4 is taken from the larger class, which included students with different language backgrounds, including speakers of Spanish,

Portuguese, and Turkish. During a vocabulary exercise, the teacher started with the French word *canapé* and built a first bridge toward other languages by asking Nadia, a Spanish student, for the Spanish translation. When two options were offered, she built a second bridge through choosing the option that allowed her to make another link between Spanish and French (this time *canapé* was equated with the word "sofa"). This then set off a general searching for equivalents in other languages. (The teacher's hesitations and repairs in naming the languages in 14 suggests that she was distracted by students drawing her attention to the different languages that used the same word).

It is interesting to note how these links between languages delimit common spaces and allow words to be produced by analogy and generalization between languages. These cross-linguistic links can be both accepted and rejected in school activities. Categorizing such forms as "potentially belonging in-between-two-languages" can be accomplished in order to respond to the need for lexical production or to facilitate cross-linguistic comprehension, or to make a connection with the country of origin. However, such categorical links are rejected when the purpose is to impose a monolingual norm that establishes boundaries and separates distinct cultural spheres.

Limits to the Utility of Bilingualism

A teacher's positive inclination towards an L1 can be a source of comfort for the student and create an atmosphere of mutual cooperation. It is, however, not a guarantee of communicative success, as shown by Extract 5.

Extract 5. *"I was at a 'rancho'"*
(Te is the teacher, J is the student, and Re is the researcher)

1	J	[ouais / et après moi jou:er::/ comme ça:/ . après moi:: une
		[yeah / and after me play::/ like that: / . after me:: a
2		plaxxx de Genève et s'appelait des: .. (sigh) des des
		plaxxx from Geneva and was called + plural indefinite article, uttered twice)
3	Te	tu dis un petit mot en portugais xxxx
		say a little something in Portuguese xxxx
4	J	**rancho**
5	Te	t'as été [dans un
		you were [at a
6	J	[des choses qui: se qui chantent/ après fait des choses/ qui
		[things that: that sing/ after doing things/ that

7		c'est très joli / comme ça:
		is very pretty / like that
8	Te	xxx
9	J	comme ça/ . hum
		like that/ . mm
10	Te	de la danse/
		dancing/
11	J	ouais mais:
		yes but:
12	Te	t'as été dans une disco/
		you were at a disco/
13	J	non pas: [
		no, not: [
14	Te	[xxx
15	J	pas hum disco / danse euh / a beaucoup de (ton; temps) . de . ta
		not uh disco / dance uh / have (there are?) many (tone; times) . (has
16		ta déjà venu \ .. mhm .. les groupes
		has ?) already come \ uhm these groups
17	Te	oui::/
		yes::/
18	J	des ronches / comme ça:
		of 'ronches' / like that:
19	Te	mhm mhm [pis c'est
		uhum uhum [so that's
20	Re	[c'est des danses portugaises/
		they're Portuguese dances
21	J	ouais
		yeah
22	Te	c'était de la musique portugaise / c'était une fête portugaise /
		it was Portuguese music / it was a Portuguese festival
23		[y avait une fête portugaise à Genève / c'est pour ça que tu es allé /
		[there was a Portuguese festival in Geneva / that's why you went
24	J	ouais
		yeah
25	Te	[ouais,
		[yeah
26	Re	ils avaient des habits / . des habits euh traditionnels
		they had costumes / . traditional uh costumes
27	J	ouais
		yeah
28	Te	c'est des danses folkloriques je pense
		they're folk dances I think
29	J	c'est ÇA
		that's IT

Extract 5 is taken from the beginning of one of the special lessons (with the teacher and just one student) while the researcher was present. The teacher was asking J about what he had done over the weekend. This prompted an account, which was then hindered by a lexical problem. Given the difficulties encountered by the student (1–2), the teacher suggested that he should use his L1 (3). This, however, failed, as the expected mutual intelligibility between L1 and L2 did not materialize and the word *rancho* did not help the teacher or the researcher to understand.

This sequence is nonetheless interesting, as it shows the activation of various resources to solve the problem. After having supplied *rancho* in Portuguese (4), in response to the teacher's request, J approximated the word to the French *"ronches"* (18) in the hope or expectation that some proximity existed between the L1 and L2. Given the failure of this L1 usage, other means (such as gestures, synonyms, paraphrasing, and corrected reformulation of the interlocutor's descriptions) were increasingly employed by the teacher as well as by J. In other words, the sequence introduced a certain symmetry of knowledge-building between the teacher and the student through the emergence of a problem for both sides. It was the beginning of a truly collaborative effort for both, facilitated by the dyadic nature of the interaction. It may then be assumed that even though the use of the L1 was unsuccessful, for the teacher this strategy offered the benefit of showing that she valued knowledge that only the student possessed and that she tried to reconstruct in collaboration with the student.

Making Use of the L1 and L2 in Learning an L3

Up until now we have concentrated on classroom interactions that demonstrate what happens when the language of origin of migrant students and the official language of the school come into contact. We addressed this issue by identifying a variety of possible sequential contexts in which the relationship between the two languages played itself out. Another issue, however, and one that the Swiss educational system raises, is the effect of adding yet another language to the school context. This is the case with German, which is the first foreign language taught in francophone Swiss schools.

Extract 6. *"Introducing yourself."*

1   Te   also ich heisse Christa . ich komme aus der Schweiz aus Luzern
              OK my name is Christa . I am from Switzerland from Lucerne
2   ich wohne in Neuchâtel . ich bin 26 jahre alt
              I live in Neuchâtel . I am 26 years old

3 E comment dit êtes-vous mariée /
how do you say are you married /
4 Te sind sie verheiratet /
are you married /
5 E sind sie vi:[
are you mi:[
6 Te [verheiratet
[*married*
7 E verhei:[
mar:[
8 Te [ratet
[*ried*
9 E [ratet
[*ried*
10 S [ratet
[*ried*
11 B [ratet
ried
12 Te nein
no
13 E nein
no
14 Te nein ich bin nicht verheiratet
no I am not married
15 E je n'sais pas . c'est difficile pour moi
I don't know . it's hard for me
16 S oui est difficile pour tous je crois je n'ai pas compris ce
yes it's hard for everyone I think I haven't understood what
17 qu'elle a dit
she said
18 Te mhm das stimmt gar nicht . ich habe zwei zwei Schwestern versteht
uhm that's not true . I have two two sisters . do you understand
19 ihr das das / und einen Bruder . ok
that that / and one brother . OK
20 S einen Bruder
one brother
21 Te OK jetzt bist du dran . tell dich vor
OK now it's your turn . introduce yourself
22 S **começa**
begin
23 B c'est moi qui commence / parler de quoi /
it's me who starts / to talk about what /
24 E **[apresenta-te**
[*introduce yourself*

25	S	[apresenta-te
		[introduce yourself
26	Te	ja dich vorstellen
		yes introduce yourself
27	B	ich heiss Bernardo euh[
		my name is Bernardo uh [
28	Te	[ja
		[yes
29	B	ich komms aus Portugal . ich wohnen in Boudry euh
		I am from Portugal . I live in Boudry uh

The classroom activity shown in Extract 6 focused on introducing oneself in German: The teacher began by introducing herself (1–20). One student, B, was then nominated to do the same (21). In this sequence, which was primarily aimed at eliciting the use of German (L3), the students relied both on French (L2) and on Portuguese (L1). Metalinguistic questions (3), comments (15–16), requests for clarification and verification in French (23), and instructions in Portuguese (22, 24–25) can all be observed here. The students only used German to produce the kinds of utterances expected of them, but not to organize the activity. There was a clear distribution between the communicative activities accomplished in the L1 and L2 and those in the L3. While German was constructed as the target form to be produced, French was the language that allowed the activity to be organized and guaranteed mutual comprehension and intelligibility for the task. Portuguese, for its part, was less frequently used than French, since it had a restricted number of users: It was employed by the young migrants as a tool with classmates when difficulties arose, but to the exclusion of the teacher and other students and not as a general comment addressed to everyone.

In this context, it could be said that this exercise in using German established French as the linguistic departure point for learning the foreign language. It constructed French as the language of the classroom, both in the interactions between students and in the interactions between students and the teacher. The German spoken by the students was simply too basic to maintain communication, and Portuguese was not shared by a sufficient number of participants.

The German class therefore presented itself almost automatically as a multilingual space that attributed specific functions to the languages that were present. The fact that French was "tolerated" and that the teacher did not insist on sole use of the target language immediately opened doors to varied languages of origin, even though the roles of L1, L2, and L3 thus became specialized. The well-structured and purposeful way in which the various available languages were called upon clearly shows that bilingualism was being recognized as a resource.

Nonetheless, this resource was above all a communicative one and defined in terms of a repertoire rather than in terms of a strategy (at least as far as the teacher was concerned). The students' limited repertoire in German was therefore compensated for by the repertoires in the other available languages, primarily French. This was the language common to all participants, and it was also the language of the school. Strategic competence (as discussed earlier) was therefore absent in this classroom context, where bilingualism and the functional distribution of languages had the effect of lessening the stakes involved in taking turns at speaking German. The bilingual advantage that had already accrued to these migrant children on the basis of having learned French as an L2 was unlikely to be utilized in situations such as the one previously examined, and thus the children were unable to make evident the very specific competencies that they had developed.

In order to take this explanation further, we can broadly outline the following differences between French and German classes. The French classes set up the language both as a vehicle and as a subject of learning. French was the language of the class and of the world beyond the classroom. It was the language of the institution and the language of the wider society. Apart from French, other languages were treated as possible means of expression but were not shared and therefore ran the risk of causing the teacher communicative problems.

The German classes set up the language primarily as a subject of learning, while French, with the help of the languages of origin, ensured that communicative problems were overcome and that communication in general took place. Thus reference seemed to be made to German, but it was never really used. All languages were treated as potential communicative resources, while French was the language most needed since it was the most widely shared.

Asymmetrical relationships, which typically emerge in any context that involves a linguistic out-group, were clearly present in the French class. This was considerably less pronounced in the German class. In the German class, the learning context was even more asymmetrical since an advantage that had accrued to the migrant learners from the French class could not be exploited in the German class.

DRAWING ON THE POTENTIAL OF MULTILINGUAL REPERTOIRES IN THE CLASSROOM

The stretches of classroom interaction that we have analyzed here point to a typology of situations that may be further elaborated. The diverse ways in which bilingual resources are used in the classroom clearly demonstrate not only that the recognition of multilingualism at school should be addressed in general terms, but the locally situated unfolding of activities must also be carefully considered. What transpires when considering these activities is that the appearance or disappearance of the students' L1 is not random but very much depends on the ways in which classroom activities are handled both by teachers and by students.

The L1 is most often integrated when the management of classroom interaction follows a more communicative approach, as opposed to one that focuses on formal and normative elements of learning. The L1 is treated as a resource for removing obstacles in a communicative exchange. Its appearance is therefore quite brief ("say a little something in Portuguese," as in Extract 5), very local, and, given the closeness of the two languages, does not further topicalize the particular characteristics of the L1. But this does not nearly exhaust all possibilities. We also have an example where the L1 is being used and referred to as part of the learning context, where it helps to expand the set of available linguistic forms and makes possible a reflection on the similarities and differences between the languages involved (Extract 4). This allows different languages to become a part of the very subject of the lesson and assigns value to them, as well as having the advantage of being based on the collaborative initiative of the students themselves.

In contrast to these two cases, where the recourse to a student's language is demanded and accepted, in other cases relying on that language is seen as noncollaborative and even unacceptable. In such situations, the very language that is called upon to maintain order in the classroom and is used to structure student behavior in the classroom also happens to be the linguistic norm of the school, the official language, and the language of the wider social order. These situations arise most often in larger classes (as opposed to special classes for individuals or small groups), in classes where the teacher is less confident with the students' languages of origin (as contrasted to a teacher familiar with one or more of them), or in classes where the teacher is less didactically prepared to deal with cultural and linguistic difference. The *classes d'accueil* are transitional places where no rules or programs are imposed. They can be furnished by teachers and students with a monolingual frame of reference as well as a multilingual one, depending on the contingencies and on the practical purposes of ordinary life in each classroom.

What we can see behind these possible responses are potentially different educational models. Out of the practical activities of teachers and students can arise models that are not formulated in any official statement. These models are developed through the everyday management of classroom activities that can be seen as local opportunities.

However, such models can also turn into rigid patterns as a result of stereotypical ways of responding to multilingual classroom realities. Multilingualism can express itself in interstitial spaces that are not explicitly devoted to it but do serve to tolerate and foster it; at the same time, categorization processes, which recur over and over again, can lead to the sedimentation of normative frames, some of which might be stigmatizing in effect.

As far as teachers are concerned, all this depends on how the constant work of interpreting situations, activities, and exchanges is accomplished. It involves categorizing linguistic forms used by the students (such as "French" / "not French," "something intelligible" / "something totally opaque," "a possible solution" / "a possible diversion") as well as categorizing the students themselves (as "good/bad student" or as "speaker of another language" or as "bilingual"). Such categorizations play an important role; they allow a situation to become intelligible to its participants as well as defining a student's profile and providing a means of assessing his or her performance (cf. Mondada 1999, 2000).

Migrant students are, however, also involved in the task of interpretation and categorization. This enables them to act in what they consider to be appropriate ways. These students are faced with a heterogeneous linguistic environment that necessitates a tremendous effort in terms of judging the value, utility, and efficiency of each linguistic variety used, while simultaneously remembering that value, utility, and efficiency are varied and change from one context to another and from one social environment to another (from the classroom to activities outside school, from the local school to the heritage language and cultural center). These efforts are likely to be essential for the bilingual competence of the migrant and define what we have elsewhere called the "categorization competence" of the learner (Mondada 2000).

The importance of one language over another, the recognition or rejection of the L1, and the valuing or stigmatizing of multiple and diverse abilities are not determined by general rules established by the school, although they can reinforce the norms presupposed by the institution. They can be observed as emerging aspects of interactions between various social actors who define them in a dynamic fashion, reinforcing them and giving them official recognition or subverting and changing them. Across these contexts, bilingualism or the bilingual advantage very rarely enters the game explicitly; it is woven into the very accomplishments that define the context. It is the very process of definition that itself builds the context and renders visible or invisible the advantages, the potentials, and the opportunities for multilingualism.

TRANSCRIPTION CONVENTIONS

Unless otherwise indicated, *Te* always refers to the teacher; all others are students.

(2, 3, 4 sec)	pauses with length in number of seconds
MANger	emphasis
. .. ...	pauses of smaller or greater length
(manger?)	word(s) not clear
:	lengthening of a syllable
xxx	impossible to understand
/	rising intonation
\	falling intonation
^	liaison
un-	interruption
[	overlap
(laughter)	nonverbal cues, such as laughter

Fonts

Palatino	French
Helvetica	German
Palatino boldface	Portuguese
Courier	Spanish
Italics	English translation

NOTES

1. We wish to extend warm thanks to Marilyn Martin-Jones and Monica Heller for their work on the English version of this text and for their stimulating comments. We would also like to thank Alexandra Schorah for translating our original French version into English and Maria Clara Keating for checking the English translation of the Portuguese data.

2. Project FNRS-PNR33 no. 4033-35777 entitled "Apprentissage du français et de l'allemand en Suisse romande par des élèves alloglottes: mobilisation et construction des compétences linguistiques, discursives et socio-culturelles en situation scolaire et non scolaire" (The learning of French and German in French-speaking Switzerland by students who are speakers of other languages: activation and structuring of linguistic, discursive and socio-cultural skills in an academic and non-academic setting), conducted at the Centre de Linguistique Appliquée at the University of Neuchâtel between September 1993 and September 1995. During the project, ethnographic fieldwork was carried out in ten special classes in different areas of the

Canton of Neuchâtel, especially in and around Neuchâtel itself and La Chaux-de-Fonds.

3. The *classes d'appui* (support classes) are offered in schools where there are no *classes d'accueil* (reception classes). They run throughout the whole school year. They are organized according to need and can be provided for individual students and/or for small groups.

4. In this class, the students' original names were regularly translated into French by the teacher.

REFERENCES

Baetens Beardmore, H. (1986). *Bilingualism: Basic principles*. Clevedon: Multilingual Matters.

Baker, C. (1995). *A parents' and teachers' guide to bilingualism*. Clevedon: Multilingual Matters.

Bange, P. (1992). À propos de la communication et de l'apprentissage en L2, notamment dans ses formes institutionnelles. *AILE, 1,* 53–85.

Berthoud, A. C. (1995). *Être migrant: Un atout pour l'acquisition des langues? Actes du colloque transfrontalier communication et circulation des informations, des idées et des personnes*. Lausanne: Université de Lausanne.

Bhabha, H. K. (1994). *The location of culture*. London: Routledge.

Bhatt, A., and Martin-Jones, M. (1992). Whose resource? Minority languages, bilingual learners, and language awareness. In N. Fairclough (Ed.), *Critical language awareness* (pp. 285–301). London: Longman.

Butler, J. (1990). *Gender trouble: Feminism and the subversion of identity*. London: Routledge.

Cadiot, P. (1987). Les mélanges de langue. In G. Vermes and J. Boutet (Eds.), *France, pays multilingue. Vol. 2: Pratiques des langues en France* (pp. 50–61). Paris: L'Harmattan.

Canale, M., and Swain, M. (1980). Theoretical bases of communicative approaches to second language teaching and testing. *Applied Linguistics, 1(1),* 1–47.

Candelier, M. (1993). *Entre le choix et l'abandon: les langues étrangères à l'école, vues d'Allemagne et de France*. Paris-St-Cloud: Didier-Crédif.

Cicourel, A.V. (Ed.). (1974). *Language use and school performance*. New York: Academic Press.

Cook, V. (1997). The consequences of bilingualism for cognitive processing. In A.M.B. de Groot and J. F. Kroll (Eds.), *Tutorials in bilingualism* (pp. 279–299). Mahwah, N.J.: Lawrence Erlbaum Associates.

Dausendschön-Gay, U. (1997). Bilan provisoire du SLASS et perspectives de recherche. *Cahiers d'acquisition et de pathologie du langage, 15,* 25–32.

de Certeau, M. (1987). *Économies ethniques: pour une école de la diversité*. In *L'Éducation multiculturelle* (pp. 170–196). Paris: OCDE.

Derrida, J. (1997). *De l'hospitalité*. Paris: Calmann-Lévy.

Frischherz, B. (1997). Lernen, um zu sprechen—sprechen, um zu lernen. Diskursanalytische untersuchungen zum zweitspracherwerb türkischer und kurdischer asylbewerber in der deutschschweiz. *Germanistica friburgensia* 16. Universitätsverlag Freiburg.

Gajo, L. (1996). Le bilingue romanophone face à une nouvelle langue romane: un atout bilingue doublé d'un atout roman? *Etudes de linguistique appliquée 104,* 431–440.

Gajo, L. (1998). Minorisation, identité bilingue et acquisition d'une nouvelle langue en situation de migration. *Grenzgänge, 9*, 38–54.

Gajo, L., and Mondada, L. (1998). Contexte, activité discursive et processus d'acquisition: quels rapports? In M. Souchon (Ed.), *Pratiques discursives et acquisition des langues étrangères. Actes du Xe colloque international "Acquisition d'une langue étrangère"* (pp. 91–102). Besançon, 19–21 September 1996. Besançon: Centre de Linguistique Appliquée.

Gajo, L., Koch, P., and Mondada, L. (1996). La pluralité des contextes et des langues: Une approche interactionnelle de l'acquisition. *Bulletin suisse de linguistique appliquée, 64*, 61–86.

Grosjean, F. (1989). Neurolinguists, beware! The bilingual is not two monolinguals in one person. *Brain and Language 36*, 3–15.

Grosjean, F. (1994). Individual bilingualism. *The encyclopaedia of language and linguistics* (pp. 1656–1660). Oxford, U.K.: Pergamon.

Gumperz, J. J. (1992). Contextualization revisited. In P. Auer and A. di Luzio (Eds.), *The contextualization of language* (pp. 39–53). Amsterdam: Benjamins.

Hainaut, L. d' (1983). *Des fins aux objectifs*. Paris: Nathan.

Hamers, J. F., and Blanc, M. (1989). *Bilinguality and bilingualism*. Cambridge: Cambridge University Press.

Hamers, J. F. (1994). Rôle des réseaux sociaux dans le maintien de la langue maternelle, dans le développement bilingue et dans le développement de la littéracie. *Bulletin VALS-ASLA 59*, 85–102.

Harman, L. D. (1988). *The modern stranger: On language and membership*. Berlin: Mouton de Gruyter.

Heller, M. (1994). *Crosswords: Language, education and ethnicity in French Ontario*. Berlin: Mouton de Gruyter.

Heller, M. (1999). *Linguistic minorities and modernity*. London: Longman.

Heller, M. (ed.) (1988). *Codeswitching: Anthropological and sociolinguistic perspectives*. Berlin: Mouton de Gruyter.

Krafft, U., and Dausendschön-Gay, U. (1994). Analyse conversationnelle et recherche sur l'acquisition. *Bulletin Suisse de Linguistique Appliquée, 59*, 127–158.

Lave, J. (1993). The practice of learning. In S. Chaiklin and J. Lave (Eds.), *Understanding practice: Perspectives on activity and context* (3–34). Cambridge: Cambridge University Press.

Leung, C., Harris, R., and Rampton, B. (1997). The idealized native-speaker, reified ethnicities and classroom realities: Contemporary issues in TESOL *Occasional Papers in Language and Urban Culture, 2*. Centre for Applied Linguistic Research, Thames Valley University, London.

Little, D. (1996). La compétence stratégique examinée par rapport à la maîtrise stratégique du processus d'apprentissage des langues. In H. Holec, D. Little, and R. Richterich (Eds.) Stratégies dans l'apprentissage et l'usage des langues: vers un cadre européen commun de référence pour l'enseignement et l'apprentissage des langues vivantes (études préparatoires). Strasbourg: Editions du Conseil d'Europe, pp. 9–40.

Lüdi, G. (1998, October). L'enfant bilingue: Chance ou surcharge? *Acta Romanica Basiliensia, 8*, 13–30.

Lüdi, G., and Py, B. (1986). *Être bilingue*. Berne: Peter Lang.

Magnin Hottelier, S., et al. (1994). *Kaléido: Inventaire sélectif de supports didactiques*. Neuchâtel: Commission Romande des Moyens d'Enseiguement (COROME) & Institut Romand de Recherches et de Documentation Pedagogique (IRDP).

Martin-Jones, M., and Saxena, M. (1995). Supporting or containing bilingualism? Policies, power asymmetries, and pedagogic practices in mainstream primary classrooms. In J. W. Tollefson (Ed.), *Power and inequality in language education* (pp. 73–90). Cambridge: Cambridge University Press.

Martin-Jones, M., and Saxena, M. (1996). Turn-taking, power asymmetries, and the positioning of bilingual participants in classroom discourse. *Linguistics and Education, 8(1)*, 105–123.

Mehan, H., Hertweck, A., and Meihls, J. L. (1986). *Handicapping the handicapped: Decision making in students' careers.* Stanford: Stanford University Press.

Moerman, M. (1974). Accomplishing ethnicity. In R. Turner (Ed.), *Ethnomethodology* (54–68). Harmondsworth: Penguin.

Mondada, L. (1995). Analyser les interactions en classe: Quelques enjeux théoriques et repères méthodologiques. *Actes du 3ème Colloque d'Orthophonie/Logopédie "Interventions en groupe et interactions"* (pp. 22, 55–89). Université de Neuchâtel, 29–30 September 1994. Neuchâtel, Switzerland: Travaux Neuchâtelois de Linguistique (TRANEL).

Mondada, L. (1996). La construction discursive de l'altérité: Effets linguistiques. Traverse. *Revue d'histoire (Bâle), 1*, 51–62.

Mondada, L. (1999). L'accomplissement de 'l'étrangéité' dans et par l'interaction: Procédures de catégorisation des locuteurs. *Langages* (special edition, J. Arditty and M. T. Vasseur (Eds.), Interaction en langue étrangère), 20–34.

Mondada, L. (2000). La compétence de catégorisation: Procédés situés de catégorisation des ressources linguistiques. In P. Martinez and S. Pekarek (Eds.), *Actes de la Journée d'Etude "Notions en questions: Les contacts de langues en didactique,"* Paris: ENS Editions & Didier Erudition, 81–102.

Mondada, L., and Py, B. (1994). Vers une redéfinition interactionnelle de la notion d'apprenant. In *Actes du 9e Colloque Acquisition des Langues: Perspectives et Recherches, St.-Etienne, 13–15.5.1993* (pp. 381–396). St.-Etienne: Université de Saint-Etienne, 381–396.

Müller, R. (1997). *Sozialpsychologische grundlagen des schulischen zweitspracherwerbs bei migrantenschüler innen.* Aarau - Frankfurt am Main - Salzburg: Verlag Sauerländer, SPL Band 21.

O'Malley, J., and Chamot, A. (1990). *Learning strategies in second language acquisition.* Cambridge: Cambridge University Press.

Oriol, M. (1984). L'émigré portugais ou l'homme multi-dimensionnel. *Revue suisse de sociologie, 10(2)*, 541–562.

Oxford, R. (1990). *Language learning strategies: What every teacher should know.* Rowley, Mass.: Newbury House.

Perregaux, C. (1994). *Odyssea: Accueils et approches interculturelles.* Neuchâtel: COROME.

Perregaux, C. (1998). Avec les approches d'éveil au langage, l'interculturel est au centre de l'apprentissage scolaire. *Bulletin VALS-ASLA, 67.*

Rampton, B. (1990). Displacing the "native speaker": Expertise, affiliation and inheritance. *ELT Journal, 44(2)*, 97–10.

Rampton, B. (1995). *Crossing: Language and ethnicity among adolescents.* London: Longman.

Roberts, C. (1992). *Language and discrimination: A study of communication in multi-ethnic workplaces.* London: Longman.

Rogoff, B. (1995). Observing sociocultural activity on three planes: Participatory appropriation, guided participation, and apprenticeship. In J. V. Wertsch, P. del Rio, and A. Alvarez (Eds.), *Sociocultural studies of mind.* Cambridge: Cambridge University Press.

Romaine, S. (1989). *Bilingualism*. Oxford, U.K.: Blackwell.

Tabboni, S. (Ed.). (1986). *Vicinanza e lontananza: Modelli e figure dello straniero come categoria sociologica*. Milano: Franco Angeli.

Tarone, E. (1984). Teaching strategic competence in the foreign language classroom. In J. Savignon, and M. S. Berns (Eds.), *Initiatives in communicative language teaching*. Reading, Mass.: Addison Wesley.

Titone, R. (1993). Apprendimento precoce di una L2, bilinguismo e sviluppo metalinguistico. *Rassegna italiana di linguistica applicata, 25(3)*, 137–147.

Vasseur, M.-T. (1991). Solliciter n'est pas apprendre: Initiative, sollicitation et acquisition d'une langue étrangère. In C. Russier, H. Stoffel, and D. Véronique (Eds.), *Interactions en langue étrangère* (pp. 49–59). Aix-en-Provence: Université de Provence.

Vasseur, M. T. (1993). Gestion de l'interaction, activités métalangagières et apprentissage en langue étrangère. *AILE, 2*, 25–59.

Véronique, D. (1997). Remarques sur les activités communicatives en L2 et les activités cognitives d'appropriation linguistique. *CALAP. Processus d'acquisition en dialogue, 15*, 9–24.

Wieder, D. L., and Pratt, S. (1990). On being a recognizable Indian among Indians. In D. Carbaugh (Eds.), *Cultural communication and intercultural contact* (pp. 45–75). Hillsdale, N.J.: Erlbaum.

12

Authority and Authenticity: Corsican Discourse on Bilingual Education

Alexandra Jaffe

INTRODUCTION

On Corsica, the power of educational institutions to define and rank identities and to legitimize dominant language and culture has been a critical part of the island's collective experience. Since the beginning of the twentieth century, the school has been a key agent of change in a process of language shift from Corsican to French that accelerated after World War I. For many older Corsicans alive today, the school was where they had their first intensive introduction to the French language. French educational documents and popular schooling narratives alike attest to the nature of the language ideologies that were so explicitly voiced in the French classroom. French education not only established French as a language of power but also defined it as the sole legitimate language. Corsican was denigrated as a *patois* that merely served as an obstacle to children's mastery of the French language, the chief vehicle of French culture and citizenship.

It is no surprise, then, that the school has been a central site for the linguistic revitalization movement that began in the early 1970s. Teaching Corsican in the schools has long been advocated by Corsican language planners as a practical means for transmitting the language and as a symbol of the legitimacy of Corsican language and culture. For Corsican nationalists, this legitimation of Corsican is tied to claims on national identity and rights to political self-determination.

The first major act of the Corsican language revitalization movement concerned education. In 1973, the Corsican language association *Scola Corsa* campaigned hard, successfully, and with considerable public support for the inclusion of Corsican under the provisions of the 1951 Deixonne law, which permitted "regional languages of France" to be taught up to three hours a week in the public schools. Corsican language education has remained a central pursuit of Corsican language planners, and in many ways they have been extremely successful. Corsican is now taught at every educational level and is available for more than three hours a week at certain levels (notably middle school) and in urban school sites. At the university level, students can receive degrees all the way through to the doctorate in Corsican and can compete for a specialized national teaching status as professors of Corsican by taking a competitive exam.

With all these institutional gains, it would be logical to assume that Corsican was a mandatory school subject. Yet, this is not the case. In fact, proposed language legislation making Corsican an "official" or "co-official" language (with French) and making bilingual education obligatory has failed to pass (or be implemented by) the Corsican Regional Assembly on three separate occasions. It would be oversimplifying to say that all the political resistance to these language planning measures had to do with ideologies of language. In the 1980s, strong Corsican nationalist sponsorship of any motions promoting the use of Corsican led some conservative politicians to cast a negative vote in order to distance themselves from the nationalist movement. Yet the Assembly is a representative body, and as the following interview data (and my subsequent monitoring of the topic) shows, public support for mandatory Corsican education has never been overwhelming.

In this chapter, I examine the debate over compulsory Corsican education, drawing on data from the Assembly deliberations and from a corpus of survey and interview data collected in 1988–1989. At the heart of this debate are competing ideas about (a) the bases for Corsican's legitimacy and value as a language of identity and (b) relations of power and authority in the Corsican cultural and linguistic context. I use this debate to address the question of how discourse about schooling both reproduces dominant language ideologies and social hierarchies and contests the legitimacy of the school's symbolic order. The data illustrates the constraints imposed on social actors by dominant structures and processes. I argue that the overall shape of the public debate over mandatory bilingual education is heavily circumscribed by dominant ideologies of language and identity.

First of all, the desire to teach Corsican in the schools is itself one of several language planning strategies whose goal is to legitimize the minority language in dominant terms. Dominant ideologies also structure popular resistance to language planning in that the terms of the debate are organized around opposing value sets attached to Corsican and French. This relationship is a diglossic one: a product of language domination. At the same time, some of those who oppose mandatory Corsican language education contest the very foundation of hegemonic practice in the school, namely, the naturalization of power relations in ideologies of language and education. In opposing the imposition of Corsican, they lay bare the ideological and coercive nature of the school. In doing so, they both affirm the power of the school to set values and influence ideas and articulate a certain amount of "role distance" from the school setting and its construction of their identities as students and citizens.

EXPERIENCES WITH DOMINATION: LANGUAGE AND SCHOOLING IN CORSICA

The ideologies of language, identity, and citizenship promulgated in French schools beginning in the late nineteenth century reflect a long European political and intellectual heritage, in which a monolingual norm is the foundation of national identity. As Hobsbawm (1991) and Higonnet (1980) have pointed out, shared linguistic/cultural unity has dominated European definitions of nationhood ever since the "linguistic terror" following the French Revolution. In their analysis of contemporary European popular discourse about language and nationalism, Blommaert and Verschueren show that the logic of "One Language, One Nation" continues to have enormous power. They observe, for example, that in European coverage of international events, "the absence of the feature 'distinct language' tends to cast doubt on the legitimacy of claims to nationhood" (1992, 357). As Gal (1992, 448–449) writes, when cultural identity is the precondition for political legitimacy, "language is understood as an expression of communal spirit and the uniformity of language is important not for efficient communication and broad participation, but as proof that the speaking subject is an authentic member of the nation, linking speaker and language to the past and its (invented) traditions." In short, what we see is an "essentialist" view of the relationship of language to cultural identity and of the link between cultural identity and political legitimacy.

There is, however, a central paradox in the way this essentialist view was deployed in France. The "ineffable" and primordial cultural and linguistic unity that served as the foundation of national unity was directly contradicted by actual practice. Many Frenchmen did not speak French, and rather than simply existing, Frenchmen (to borrow a phrase from Eugene Weber) had to be "made."

The school was one of those formative institutions. Schoolteachers who went out into the provinces at the turn of the century were viewed as frontline troops in the government's campaign to create France and French people through language. The guiding light of this mission was the link between language and rationality, civilization, culture, virtue, and citizenship. An 1880 Army report made the connection between literacy and social/moral status explicit: "The young Bretons who do not know how to read, write or speak French . . . are promptly civilized; they lose the prejudices of their 'pays,' abandon native suspicions, and when they return to the village, they are sufficiently frenchified to frenchify their friends by their influence"(Weber 1976, 299).

Xavier Culioli's account of the way his grandfather, a schoolteacher in Corsica around 1911, represented the value of French to his pupils reflects many of the same themes:

> Dominique apprenait les richesses du français à une vingtaine d'enfants qui s'acharnaient . . . à ne pas employer leur langue maternelle . . . "le français, mes enfants," leur expliquait Dominique, "vous servira à se débrouiller dans la vie. Plus de quinze mille des nôtres sont dans l'armée. Comment l'auraient-ils pu s'ils n'avaient pas appris la langue de notre pays, la France? Je vous demande, donc, de ne pas parler le patois . . . si l'un d'entre vous était surpris à parler le corse, il serait puni. Non par méchanceté, mais parce que vous devez vous astreindre à une certaine discipline. Plus tard, vous remercierez l'école de la République pour ses bienfaits . . . Bande de bourricots! Faites donc un effort . . . vous voulez pousser la charrue toute votre vie?

> Dominique taught the richness of French to about twenty children who struggled painfully not to use their mother tongue. "French, my children," he explained to them, "will help you to make your way in life. There are more than 15,000 of our men in the Army. How could they have done this if they had not spoken French, the language of our country, France? I ask you, then, not to speak patois. If you are caught speaking Corsican, you will be punished; not out of spite, but because you must submit yourselves to a certain discipline. Later, you will thank the school of the Republic for its gifts. . . You herd of donkeys! Make a little effort! Do you want to push a plow all your lives?" (Culioli 1986, 172).

In the interviews I conducted with them about early school experiences, middle-aged and older Corsicans made comments that showed how Corsican, like other regional languages, was both devalued as a lowly peasant language in school and perceived as an obstacle to the acquisition of correct French and the social rewards it conferred. Some people even remembered the forms of punishment that were meted out to children for speaking Corsican at school. Jean-Marie, born in 1950, said, "In school, all the kids whispered and played in Corsican. It was: *'Oui, Madame'* to the teacher, then back to our whispers . . . we were punished for it, made to feel like peasants for speaking Corsican. It was a handicap for learning French." The practices and attitudes of teachers in Corsican schools with regard to children's use of spoken Corsican varied. Although some Corsican teachers used to give a child an object (*symbole*) to hold in shame until it could be passed on to the next transgressor (a practice reported in Brittany, Occitanie, Scotland, Wales, and elsewhere), there were also Corsican teachers who were relatively tolerant of the use of the language in the classroom. There was, however, considerable intolerance of any "interference" from Corsican in students' written French. Octave, born in 1911, said, "I remember getting my papers back at school, with *corsisme* 'corsicanism' written all over them in red pencil" (my translations of interviews). It was Octave's generation that was described by Biron, a school inspector, who wrote in 1928:

Le dialecte est ici la seule langue vivante. Naturellement, les enfants jouent ou se disputent en corse. Quel entrain leurs débats! Et quelle volubilité dans leurs discussions! En classe, le tableau change. C'est le français qui crée l'atmosphère, mais un français imposé et pour tout dire une langue étrangère . . . les petits se renferment dans une sorte de timidité sauvage . . . Quant aux grands, ils jettent mécaniquement leurs réponses dans le moule fourni par les questions. Chez tous, les facultés semblent paralysées.

The dialect here is the only living language. Naturally, the children play and quarrel in Corsican . . . what spirit in their debates, what volubility in their discussions! In class, the picture changes. It is French that creates the atmosphere, but an imposed French; really, a foreign language . . . The little ones take refuge in a sort of primitive timidity . . . As for the older students, they form their responses mechanically in the mold offered by the questions. In all of them, their faculties seem paralyzed. (in Marchetti 1989, 124, my translation)

These brief sketches of the school experience for Corsicans draw attention to a number of important issues. The school was a place where students were alienated from their mother tongue. Moreover, teachers and parents collaborated in the view that this alienation was an appropriate price for the success offered by French language competency. This competency was a prerequisite for active citizenship. Not only were Corsican and French language and identity represented in polar terms, but it was also clear that acquiring a French identity involved relinquishing other forms of linguistic and cultural attachment. The school thus contributed in a significant way to a diglossic division of linguistic use and value in Corsican society.

RESPONDING TO DOMINATION: LANGUAGE ACTIVISM

Language Revitalization and Ethnic Nationalism

When Culioli's grandfather taught school in the first quarter of the twentieth century, French was the second language of most Corsicans. By the 1960s, however, there were significant numbers of young Corsicans who did not speak Corsican and whose first language was French. A huge socioeconomic shift had already taken place: The students taught by Culioli's grandfather and others had resolutely opted not to "push a plow" all their lives and had emigrated in large numbers to the French continent and colonies, often to work in the civil service. Language shift was an accepted part of this scenario. It was only in the late 1960s that the decline in the use of Corsican became a significant cultural and political issue and the Corsican language revitalization movement was born.

The history of Corsican language revitalization is tied up with the Corsican nationalist movement. Many early language activists were also political activists, connected to autonomist groups like the UPC (**Unione di u Populu Corsu** 'The Union of the Corsican People'). They were, by and large, young and highly educated; and their political consciousness was raised in the late 1960s, during the tumultuous years of student riots and social change that took place in the French universities they attended. This social and political climate focused their attention on the institutional perpetuation of social inequalities and encouraged resistance. The end of the Algerian war and Algerian independence also focused attention on the inequalities perpetuated by colonialism. At the same time, these young Corsican intellectuals became aware of other ethno-nationalist movements in France (the Basque country, Brittany, Occitanie) and elsewhere in Western Europe. Authors of these movements, in particular the outspoken and prolific Robert Lafont, provided a new ideological framework, in which Corsica was an "internal colony" whose culture and people had been exploited and repressed.

What I want to underscore is that the Corsican ethno-regionalist movement and the notion of "internal colonialism" that it adopted did not contest the fundamental categories and assumptions of the nationalist model of language and political identity. Rather, Corsican militants sought to redefine their position, from one of weakness to one of strength within the dominant model. Corsican nationalists appropriated a discourse that naturalized the link between language and nationhood in order to support their political claims that Corsica was a repressed, colonized, dominated nation with "natural" rights to self-determination. The slogan **Morta a lingua, mortu u populu** [The death of a language is the death of a people] appeared in nationalist literature (and can still be seen in contemporary graffiti).

At the same time, the decline in the use of the Corsican language also symbolized the crisis of Corsican culture brought on by French oppression. In *Main Basse Sur Une Ile*, the 1971 nationalist manifesto (Front régionalististe corse 1971), the authors cited severe losses in the speaking population of the language, writing that a Corsican child under eighteen "makes sure not to pronounce a single word in the language of the adults . . . to address a young woman in Corsican would be considered crude. Asking a Corsican child for directions . . . reaps a response in French" (1971, 65).[1] These examples were used in the manifesto as evidence of the way that French domination had led "Corsicans [to] become the agents of their own alienation" (1971, 63, my translation). Also cited as evidence of this alienation was the social evaluation of mixed forms of language: "*on ne manquera pas de brocarder . . . le moindre corsisme [en français] mais . . . il va de soi que le gallicisme en parlant corse n'est, en revanche, aucunement ridicule*" [The smallest Corsican interference in French invites mockery, but it goes without saying that gallicisms in Corsican are not perceived as ridiculous at all. (1971, 65)

Though the French state was identified as the villain in the historical picture painted by Corsican nationalists, the decline of the language was also seen as threatening the very foundation of the nationalist platform, which amounted to a claim on an ineffable, immutable cultural identity. The nationalists became aware, as Balibar puts it, that the People must be produced (1991, 93). In other words, asserting the link between language and identity partially reflected an existing state of affairs—many Corsicans believed in this connection, and considerable numbers still spoke Corsican—and partially reflected a hope in an unrealized ideal of Corsican unity since not all Corsicans were corsophones.

While this is the very same paradox seen in the production of the French people, we will see that it becomes far more problematic in a minority language context. In the following section, I describe the goals and outcomes of language legislation between 1973 and 1985. This is followed by a discussion of public and political discourse on both sides of the mandatory education issue as it had been framed up until the time of my research. The final section analyzes the text and the outcomes of a 1989 motion on linguistic "co-officiality" that took place after my survey. My analysis was conducted in the light of the themes that emerged from the survey data.

Bilingual Education 1975–1985: Pragmatic and Symbolic Value

From the outset, then, Corsican language planners sought to make both practical and symbolic gains with Corsican language education. They were counting on the schools to create the Corsican speakers who were crucial to the definition of Corsican cultural identity and political autonomy. The school was to take up Corsican language socialization of children where parents had failed (and were still failing). At the same time, Corsican language education was a form of status planning; the implantation of Corsican into official, public domains and institutions previously occupied only by French was intended to raise the status of the language. This was assumed to have an indirect, positive influence on language attitudes and through them, language practices.

The successful inclusion of Corsican in the school curriculum as a result of the 1973 Deixonne law campaign had considerable symbolic impact, but rather limited practical consequences: Not only was the amount of allowed instruction small, but it was also optional for both the teachers and the students. Corsican was not taught with any consistency from one school to another. While adult "re-acquisition" classes flourished during the 1970s (particularly among Corsicans living on the continent in places like Paris, Toulon, and Marseilles), there was no groundswell of parental support for private Corsican language schools. Where parents in the Basque country, Brittany, and Wales had banded together to support minority language nursery schools outside the state system, only one such school had been started in Corsica,[2] and Corsican parents had been lukewarm, at best, in their support of the three hours of optional Corsican education allowed by the state.

The election of the first Regional Assembly in 1982 provided a new political venue for the pursuit of official recognition of Corsican and concrete policies for implementing bilingual education and bilingualism in public life. Although the Assembly had not supplanted the existing departmental structures, which retained primary control over government resources, it was the first elected body to represent the island as a whole. Corsican language activists looked to the Assembly to play an active role in championing Corsican language rights.

Beginning with the first Assembly, language activists pushed for officialization of Corsican. In 1983, language legislation was introduced. The following is a brief extract that pertains to the different public contexts in which Corsican was to be officially used:

> *Pris acte du caractère fondamental de la langue comme ciment de la culture, et de l'urgence de mettre en oeuvre une réelle politique de réappropriation culturelle qui traduise la volonté de l'Assemblée de rendre sa langue à son peuple . . . a décidé de s'engager dans une politique de bilinguisme dans le cadre d'un plan triannal qui sera élaboré en concertation avec l'Etat . . . d'ores et déjà, parallèlement, l'usage de la langue corse sera généralisé dans le cadre de la toponymie des lieux, des villages, des villes, dans le cadre de l'information et de la formation audio-visuelles, ainsi que pour certains actes de la vie publique.*

Officially recognizing the fundamental role of the Corsican language as the cement of culture, and the urgency of putting into practice a concrete policy of cultural reappropriation which translates the desire of the Assembly to give the people its language back . . . [the Assembly] has decided to commit itself to a policy of bilingualism, to be implemented in a triennial plan to be elaborated in collaboration with the State. . . . In parallel, from now on, the use of the Corsican language will be generalized in the names of places, villages, towns, in the context of news and audiovisual training, as well as in certain public documents. (cited in Marchetti 1989, 209)

While this is a strong statement of support for bilingualism, it is not a mandate for Corsican language education. In assembly debate preceding this motion, it was clear that the chief proponents of the resolution were in favor of making bilingual education mandatory, but were forced by majority opinion to compromise by backing down from this position. The battle cry of the 1980s, "mandatory bilingualism," was an attempt to turn the official recognition of the Deixonne law into a concrete commitment of resources, to make it work. It was also a response to the fact that, in a general way, the actual use of the language had lagged behind advances in its status in the political arena. This was even true within the nationalist fold; with rare exceptions, militant public demands for recognition and promotion of Corsican language and culture were in French. This was true of nationalist manifestos such as *Main Basse Sur Une Ile*, and later, the "little green book" of a more radical separatist group. French also predominated in their weekly newspapers and, for the most part, in their meetings. In 1985, at an annual congress, the nationalist coalition party found it necessary to reaffirm its commitment to the use of Corsican within the ranks, "*pour éviter de se retrouver . . . confronté à l'énorme contradiction de revendiquer une langue que l'on est soi-même incapable d'employer*" [to avoid finding ourselves confronted with the enormous contradiction of campaigning for a language that we ourselves are incapable of using] (*U Ribombu* no. 203, 7).

To summarize, promoting Corsican in school was intended to (a) claim the same unchallenged linguistic and cultural authority and legitimacy accorded to French (to the state and to Corsicans); (b) raise the status of Corsican among Corsicans and indirectly contribute to its maintenance through extrascholastic (family) transmission; (c) be a practical tool of language transmission and prevent language death by stepping in where families were not supporting language maintenance; and (d) symbolize cultural identity and unity (with various goals, including political autonomist ones).

These goals have both persuasive and coercive elements, which are linked to the tension between the image of Corsican as a primordial heritage (reflected in the possessive in the phrase "giving the people their language back") and the problem of decline in Corsican language practice and competence. The phrase "giving the people their language back" also places agency squarely in the hands of language planners; they are not talking about officially sanctioning existing minority language practices and language values, but rather about creating new social fields of value by allowing and requiring the practice of the minority language. In other words, the text of the 1983 motion reveals the militants of the 1980s trying to work the attitudes-practice relationship in reverse by tapping into the power of (imposed) practice to influence attitudes. In doing so, they attempted to harness not only the symbolic power of dominant models of language but also the material power of the process of domination itself. The enforced practice of French, just as much as ideas, had led to the devaluation of Corsican. The institutions of French public life had forced French on them; now they would use those same institutions to force Corsican on themselves.

The 1983 motion was immediately rejected by then French Prime Minister Mauroy, who stated that given the pressing needs to educate French schoolchildren in ever-expanding domains of knowledge (presumably technical and scientific), it was not possible for the government to impose instruction in Corsican language and culture on those who did not wish to take it. The Assembly, plagued by other political problems that led to its dissolution (and the election of a new body of representatives) that same year, did not respond.

The next move came in 1985, when Castellani, an autonomist representative to the Assembly, brought a new motion on bilingualism to the floor. The Castellani motion was based on the results of a 1984 roundtable on bilingualism organized by the *Conseil de la culture, enseignement et cadre de vie* [Council of Culture, Education and Social Environment] (CCECV) to which political leaders from all parties had been invited. The motion called for Corsican language teaching to be made obligatory for the state while remaining optional for the student, which had been the consensus opinion to emerge from the roundtable.[3] Despite the wide political representation at the roundtable, its consensus dissolved in the Assembly. The lengthy debate on this motion resulted in an impasse. Since members were unable to agree on either the principle or its execution, the Assembly effectively tabled the matter by voting to convene another ad hoc committee to study the question.

POPULAR AND POLITICAL DISCOURSE ON MANDATORY BILINGUALISM

Between 1988 and 1989, I did ethnographic and sociolinguistic field-work on Corsica. Part of my data collection on language attitudes involved questioning people about their support for mandatory Corsican language education. My written survey included the question, "Should the teaching of Corsican be mandatory?" Respondents were asked to write short rationales for their answers (which were explored in interviews). I also asked respondents to characterize the quality and quantity of current Corsican language education and to say whether or not they thought it was sufficient. The sample size for the written survey was 160, and I followed this up with interviews conducted with 60 of those people.

Before going into the results, I should note that the sample was not as representative of the general population as I had hoped it would be. With 43% men and 57% women, there was an 8% overrepresentation of women. There were 13% fewer "inactive" (non-employed) respondents in the survey than in the general population, and the "inactive" portion of my sample was overrepresentative of students. My sample also un-derrepresented (by 20%) the number of people over 45 in Corsica, a category that is disproportionately swelled (in relation to the national average) by the large number of Corsican retirees. White- or blue-collar semiskilled workers were also underrepresented by about 13%, and man-agers and academics were overrepresented by 7%. The sample was also biased in another way. Approximately 20 questionnaires were returned by mail from members of Corsican associations (*amicales*) on the French continent. These self-selected respondents were often ideologically predis-posed to support Corsican language and culture. Overall, the data collec-tion process was biased in this direction, since those who made themselves accessible to me were more likely than not to be pro-Corsican.

The statistical results can be summarized as follows: 50% of the sample were for mandatory teaching of Corsican, 33% were against, and 3% were undecided. I should also note that 16% of the respondents did not respond at all to the question, which is an indicator that the question was a sensitive one. Given the built-in bias of my sample, I am inclined to see these results as exaggerating the extent of public support for mandatory bilingualism in 1989, an interpretation that is supported by the political fate of mandatory education bills.

It is also interesting to see how responses to this question correlated with responses to a survey question that asked people to comment on the quality and quantity of language teaching in the schools at the time. Of those who thought that Corsican was not taught enough in the schools, 22% were either against making that teaching mandatory or had a null response to the question. To put it another way, 44% of those who were against mandatory Corsican education were, in principle, in favor of increasing the amount of Corsican taught in the schools. This shows the extent to which it is the mandatory nature of the instruction and not the instruction itself that is at issue.

The Argument in Favor of Mandatory Education: The Symbolism of Pragmatic Concerns

Some of those who were for mandatory Corsican reflected many of the arguments outlined by Castellani (and held by many language planners). Like Castellani, they made explicit reference to past and current failures of Corsican speakers to transmit the language to their children. They advocated mandatory bilingualism as a way to improve the current uneven quality of Corsican language teaching with state resources and policy. The schools were, in effect, a way to sidestep the problem of unsupportive/apathetic parents. One subset of these respondents (and, I should say, of language planners) viewed Corsican language education as a viable way of actually creating new Corsican speakers. Some were skeptical about the level of fluency and practice likely to be achieved by school instruction but were committed to providing some sort of stopgap in the face of failures of parental transmission.

Others saw Corsican language education as being of value because it was likely to have a more indirect effect on practice. They evoked the link between status and attitude, saying that official, mandatory status for Corsican would convince parents and students that the language was being taken seriously and prompt them to take it seriously as well. As one of the respondents wrote, "*Le choix des sujets optionnels est fait le plus souvent pour des raisons utilitaires. Si le corse reste optionnel, il continuera à être peu choisi et disparaîtra*" [The choice of optional subjects is most often made for utilitarian reasons. If Corsican remains optional, it will continue to not be chosen [since its value is not utilitarian] and it will disappear.] The continued salience of this utilitarian focus can be seen in the comments one teacher made at a roundtable on Corsican language teaching in 1993. "**Quand'è vo dumandate à un parente chì hà cinque figlioli,**" he said, "**Cuuficialità, chì ne pensate? Bislinguismu, chì ne pensate?**" dice "**Chì i mo cinque figlioli dumane**

appiinu u stentapane!" [When you ask a parent with five children, "What do you think of co-officiality? What do you think of bilingualism?" he/she says, "I think that I want my five children to learn how to earn a living in the future."] (*Arritti* 1993).

The school curriculum emerges in this discourse as providing both symbolic and pragmatic incentives for people to speak Corsican. First, the school is an institution that both prepares students for the job market and constitutes, in itself, a significant marketplace for the conferral of rewards (grades) that have economic repercussions. A subject that is treated seriously by the school acquires utilitarian value. At the same time, parents and students read the content and implementation of the curriculum as a symbolic indicator of the social status of a particular subject. This emerges in the comments of student and parents. Students told me that the fact that Corsican classes were scheduled late in the evening or early on Saturday morning and the lack of seriousness or rigor (on the part of students and teachers) in some Corsican classes were clear signs that the subject was undervalued by the school. Some parents reported to me that their children had dropped Corsican as a result of these kinds of experiences and observations. It was also clear that exams have played a significant role in shaping both parental and student attitudes. Some parents reminded me that at the Collège (junior high) level, optional subjects had no exams, which was a sufficient reason in and of itself for students to dismiss them as unimportant. The impact of exams on parents' attitudes and behaviors was confirmed for me by a discussion with a woman who taught Corsican classes in an after-school program at a youth center. She had seen her enrollments rise dramatically when parents realized that their children were going to be tested in Corsican at school.

Some other brief examples provide insights into the ways in which the insertion of Corsican into the taken-for-granted authoritative practices and routines of the school served to socially legitimate the language among people who were not actively involved in ideological debates over Corsican language education. Having gotten to know two mothers of primary school children through a Parents' Association, I went with them to sit in on some Corsican lessons. The two women took part with great enthusiasm in a very basic Corsican spelling test their 7-year-old children were taking and sang along with the class when the teacher led them in Corsican songs. The mothers did not do very well on the spelling test, even though they said they had learned a little from their children's homework. Both said they would like to go to the classes at the school more often, but did not want to disrupt the class. Neither woman spoke Corsican often; neither one would have been likely to make the effort to drive 20 miles to the closest major city to take adult evening courses in Corsican that were offered there, but insofar as this instruction concerned their children, they had become involved. In the village where I lived during my fieldwork, I also saw the way that children's Corsican homework engaged children in talking in (or at least about) the language with their elders. One of my neighbors was quite proud of how she had helped two high school girls to prepare for the optional exams in Corsican they took as part of their baccalaureate (school-leaving) exams.[4]

The Primordial Link: Language, Nation, and Identity

In his arguments before the Assembly, Castellani represented Corsican education as an ethnic birthright, a kind of claim put forth by some of the survey respondents who approved of mandatory Corsican teaching. Several respondents (with autonomist political leanings) were very explicit about the link between language, culture, and political identity:

"Étant la langue de la Nation Corse, elle devrait avoir la même importance que le français dans la vie courante en France."

Being the language of the Corsican nation, Corsican should have the same importance as French in contemporary French life.

"S'il reste optionnel, il souffrira un coup mortel en peu de temps. Il est absolument nécessaire qu'il soit une langue à part entière, c'est-à-dire, co-officielle avec le français. Comment peut-il avoir un Peuple Corse sans l'affirmation et l'expression de sa langue? Comment parler de la culture corse sans parler de la langue corse?"

If it remains optional, it will soon suffer a mortal blow. It is absolutely necessary for it to be an independent language, that is, co-official with French. How can you have a Corsican People without the affirmation and expression of its language? How can you speak of Corsican culture without speaking about the Corsican language?

"Du moment qu'une langue est le véhicule—et de la vie intellectuelle et du quotidien—d'un peuple ou d'une ethnie, elle devrait être obligatoire".

From the moment that a language is the vehicle—of both everyday and intellectual life—of a people or an ethnic group, it ought to be mandatory.

In reference to the question of political parity, two respondents evoked Resolution 192 of the European Council, which affirms the rights of linguistic minorities. This resolution was aimed at establishing aggressive programs for the promotion of regional/minority languages and culture by member states. France had signed the resolution but had made few changes in its linguistic policies at the time of the poll.

There were quite a few respondents who emphasized "pure" cultural value rather than the cultural basis of political rights. They were in favor of mandatory Corsican because:

"Sur le territoire corse, il serait normal [de l'enseigner] . . . en tout cas, cette instruction ne pourrait pas être nocive. Les allergiques peuvent toujours s'installer ailleurs."

On Corsican territory, it should be normal [to teach it] . . . in any case, teaching it could not do any harm. Those who are allergic [to this] can always go and live somewhere else.

"Il est important pour toutes les régions de retenir leurs identités, leurs traditions, tout ce qui leur rend différentes, afin de ne pas tout fondre dans l'anonymat."

It is important for all regions to retain their identities, their traditions, everything that makes them different, in order to avoid melting into anonymity.

"Raisons! Parce que c'est notre vie, notre culture, nos racines . . . bien que je me reconnaisse autant dans la culture française. Mais ce que nous avons, nous devons garder."

Reasons! Because it is our life, our culture, our roots . . . even though I identify myself equally with French culture. But what we have, we need to hold on to.

One respondent wrote simply, *"Parce qu'il est parlé"* [Because it is spoken].

In the last two responses in particular, Corsican is represented as something that Corsicans individually and collectively have; its good health is not questioned. Yet many of the respondents who argued for the cultural value of Corsican acknowledged the social frailty of the practice of Corsican and the lack of mobilization around the cause of education. This acknowledgment was clearly difficult to reconcile with the image of the language as a "natural" foundation of Corsican cultural identity. Some responded to this difficulty by talking about Corsican language education as a way of "sensitizing" people to the value of the language. In doing so, they implicitly separated identity (which remained constant and authentic) from sensibility or consciousness (which fluctuated in response to historical/social conditions). Others adhered to a more Whorfian view that speaking a heritage language could re-create a lost cultural unity. For these people, mandatory Corsican classes were a last resort in the face of a lack of collective will—they offered the possibility of convincing a handful of individuals, who might be the vectors of a greater collective linguistic conscience in the future.

The Arguments Against Mandatory Corsican: Oppositional Values

Those who opposed mandatory Corsican disagreed with the use of any form of coercion. The most frequently cited reason for opposing mandatory bilingualism was an objection to any limits on freedom of choice. Survey respondents came to this position from a variety of philosophical perspectives. As the numerical survey results suggest, there were those who were for Corsican language instruction, but against the idea of it being imposed. *"Liberté de choix,"* one person wrote, *"mais les structures pédagogiques ont besoin d'être beaucoup plus développés qu'elles ne sont"* [Freedom of choice, but pedagogical structures need to be much better developed than they are now.]

Some respondents articulated the argument for freedom of choice with reference to universal principles of democracy and human rights:

"Nous ne sommes pas un état totalitaire . . . lisez l'Article 10 de la Déclaration des Droits de l'Homme."

We aren't a totalitarian state . . . read Article 10 of the Declaration of the Rights of Man.

"Imposer le corse serait une atteinte grave à la démocratie et aux droits de l'homme . . . les jeunes sont usités de leurs travaux à l'école, où ils apprennent l'indispensable pour survivre; est-il raisonnable, pour soi-disant raisons culturelles, leur imposer encore un sujet?"

To impose Corsican would be a serious threat to democracy and to human rights . . . young people are worn out by their schoolwork, where they are taught what they need to know to survive; is it reasonable, for so-called cultural reasons, to impose yet another subject on them?

I would argue that the use of this human rights discourse with regard to a school subject is rhetorical hyperbole, but this does not mean that it exaggerates Corsican cultural resistance to that which is imposed. If we explore this resistance, we find that it has several facets and origins. In the last quotation, for example, the rhetoric of "freedom of choice" is clearly related to the undervaluation of Corsican. Comments like the last one echo French prime minister Mauroy's rationale for rejecting the 1983 language bill. In the 1985 debate, several members of the Corsican Assembly voiced objections on the same order ("How can we fit this into students' busy schedules?"). Just below the surface of this discourse is language hierarchy. While there is no reason to make the effort to "fit in" or "impose" a subject that is not "important" or "necessary for survival," there are no objections raised to the imposition of "im-

portant" subjects. French language and culture are important and necessary, Corsican language and culture are not.

Some respondents in the survey who opposed mandatory Corsican
made this practical and symbolic language hierarchy even more explicit, saying that Corsican should not be taught because it was a
"dialect." In the 1985 Assembly debate, several Assembly members
evoked the "dialect" status indirectly by citing Corsican dialectal diversity as an insurmountable pedagogical obstacle ("But which Corsican
shall we teach?" they asked). Others labeled it a language but said it
was disqualified as a school subject because it was "neither official nor
a vehicle of everyday communication," or "without power or utility."
One person wrote, "*À quoi bon ça sert ailleurs? Le français est la langue des
relations internationales*" [What is it good for elsewhere? French is the
language of international relations]. A student at the University commented, "*Les gens du village me disaient,* **Amparate prima u francese,
dopu pudete amparà u corsu**" [People in the village said to me, learn
French first, then you can learn Corsican].[5] He also told me that even
though his parents and other villagers liked the fact that he studied
Corsican at college and that he spoke it to them, they continued to reject
the idea of mandatory Corsican education.

Oppositional Essentialism. The attitude of these villagers was not
uncommon and is reflected in other arguments given by survey respondents in which they insisted on the intrinsic value of Corsican language
and culture, but located that value in the individual's voluntary choice
to speak the language. This sentiment is a logical outcome of the
experience of diglossia; as we have seen, few corsophones have learned
Corsican outside the voluntary, affective domain, and Corsican is important to them because it is not imposed like French (see McDonald
1989, 154). Here, we see a familiar pattern, in which Corsican identity
is asserted on the basis of maximal distance from things French. This
makes sense of the Corsican politician's assertion in the 1985 debate on
the Castellani bill that he had the impression that he was contributing
to the death of his mother tongue.

This essentialization of oppositional identity can also be seen in
public and political reactions to another proposal for the officialization
of Corsican in place names. Up until the mid-1990s, the official
spellings of place names on signs and other public documents were
an irregular mixture of gallicizations ("*Ile Rousse*" for "**Isula Rossa**")
and tuscanizations ("Porto Vecchio" for "**Porti Vechju**"). In protest,
a fair number of existing signs have been "corrected" with spray
paint, usually when it is a matter of changing a vowel ("Vero" to
"**Veru**"). A photo used on a poster of the nationalist teachers' union
(the SCI) promoting bilingual education shows a group of small

children making one of these corrections with their hands rather than the spray paint nozzle: They reach up on a sign and cover the horizontal lines of the final letter of *"Corté,"* so it will read **"Corti,"** as it is pronounced and spelled in Corsican. However, neither the text adopted in the 1983 motion for bilingualism nor the Assembly's expressed intentions in the 1985 motion calling for signs in Corsican and French to be phased in over a two-year period had had any results by 1987, when the National Institute of Geography conducted a survey of all the municipalities.

In explaining why he did not advocate written Corsican place names, one of my neighbors brought up the name of a neighboring village. If "Venaco" (current spelling) were written "Venacu" (which more closely captures the Corsican pronunciation [benaku]), continental French visitors would deform it by pronouncing the final [u] as [ü]. In this argument, which I later heard publicly aired by the mayor of Venaco (and president of the *Conseil Général* of the department), the French grapheme served as a sort of prophylactic between strangers and the local code of intimacy.[6] The fact that mispronunciation of a place name by strangers is seen as polluting indicates the extent to which Corsicans view Corsican linguistic space as private.

As a consequence of these attitudes, learning Corsican in school was viewed by some people as a contaminating, deauthenticating act. One person wrote that anyone who wanted to learn Corsican was not really Corsican, because *"un Corse serait trop fier, mettre son enfant dans un cours de corse"* [a Corsican would be too proud to put his/her child in a Corsican language class].

This last remark returns us to the theme of familial transmission of the language and paints a picture of social change brought about by years of linguistic and cultural activism. That is, it is only in a context in which speaking Corsican is positively valued and in which maintenance of cultural identity is cast in terms of individual (civic) responsibility) that the failure to speak or transmit the language would be a face-threatening act. The comment also implicitly acknowledges that these "failures" of transmission have taken place.

Other respondents, however, explicitly denied widespread change in the sociolinguistic landscape. Like some of their opponents on the issue of mandatory Corsican teaching, they painted a portrait of the language in good health in comments such as:

> *"Dans chaque maison, il y en a qui parlent corse. Il ne faut pas qu'il soit obligatoire. Peut-être qu'il continuera à être parlé spontanément."*

In every home, there are people who speak Corsican. It is not necessary for it to be mandatory. Maybe it will continue to be spoken spontaneously.

"Le corse s'apprend en famille. Il faut le parler."

Corsican is learned in the family. It has to be spoken.

"Habitant en Corse, tout le monde finit par le parler et le comprendre."

Living in Corsica, everyone ends up speaking and understanding it.

This type of comment was fairly common, both among politicians and among ordinary people. How do we explain such assessments in the context of widespread and seemingly obvious significant language shift? One kind of explanation has to do with the range of personal experiences afforded by a situation of language shift plus diglossia. The diglossic exclusion or reduction of Corsican from many public and institutional domains has, first of all, never prevented (and has possibly intensified the meaningfulness of) interactions in Corsican in the private sphere of intimate and family relations. The habitual Corsican speaker does indeed "choose" to speak Corsican in many situations, and does not feel particularly constrained by the presence of French in official life. These frequent speakers were more likely to be over 45, but there were also some young people who grew up in contexts where Corsican was widely spoken. One young man enrolled in the law school at the University of Corsica told me that his desire to learn to read and write Corsican stemmed from his early astonishment, as a child entering school, that French, which he heard spoken around him, was taught but that Corsican, which he had also always heard, was not. Most importantly, the diglossic compartmentalization of language practices means that people cannot always infer with total confidence private language choice or language preference from public sphere practice. In effect, diglossia in contexts of language domination helps to mask the effects of language domination and the extent of language shift, since people who hear French being used can always imagine its users in another, Corsican language context.

An alternate, and I think equally compelling way of reading these statements in the context of negative attitudes about mandatory Corsican teaching is to view them as a metalinguistic discourse that reflects the image that these Corsicans are prepared to accept of the state of the language. In the same way that having to learn Corsican (or having one's child have to learn Corsican) could be individually deauthenticating, the requirement to teach it could be seen as collectively deauthenticating.

Oppositional Romanticism. In addition to the views expressed in opposition to language intervention, there was also the question of the consequences of doing so. A number of respondents felt that imposing Corsican would have a negative cultural effect, by provoking student rejection:

"Toute imposition est la source de résistance."

Every imposition is the source of resistance.

"La langue ne devrait pas faire partie d'un système contraignant comme l'enseignement obligatoire. Le corse doit rester une langue que l'on aime parler, et parle volontiers . . . les aspects pénibles de l'apprentissage d'une langue, comme la grammaire, pourrait le faire perdre son charme; il y aurait aussi le risque que cet enseignement ferait parler mal le corse, parce que les cours de langue mettent l'accent toujours sur l'écrit, et pas l'orale. Le corse doit être parlé spontanément, comme il l'a toujours été jusqu'au présent."

The language should not be part of a restrictive system like mandatory education. Corsican should remain a language that one likes to speak, and speaks willingly . . . troublesome aspects of language learning, like grammar, could make it lose its charm; there would also be the risk that this instruction would lead to poor oral Corsican, since language courses always emphasize the written over the oral. Corsican should be spoken spontaneously, as it has always been up until now.

"Non. Ce qui est imposé est souvent rejeté et la mauvaise santé du corse ne permet pas ce risque d'echec . . . l'idéal serait que le corse soit choisi spontanément."

No. That which is imposed is often rejected, and the ill-health of Corsican does not permit this risk of failure . . . the ideal would be that Corsican would be chosen spontaneously.

We can note that the last two comments differ in their assessment of how well the process of spontaneous choice is working for the language. What they share is a perspective on the relationship between Corsican language and culture that is romantic, but not essentialist. That is, they do not identify the use of the Corsican language itself (either in the abstract or as spoken practice) as being critical to Corsican identity. Rather, they view the importance of Corsican for Corsican identity as based on the quality of the attachment of its speakers to the language. The love of the language is what counts, and this cannot be taught. The imposition of language courses is not so much deauthenticating as it is not meaningful. As one respondent put it:

"L'apprendre à l'école est mécanique, pas maternel. Il est enseigné comme s'il était l'anglais. Le corse doit être ressenti comme une partie de l'esprit, de la vie."

Learning it in school is mechanical, not maternal. It is taught as if it were English. Corsican should be felt to be a part of the spirit, a part of life.

This sentiment was shared by Petru Mari, a bilingual journalist, who remarked in a 1993 roundtable on language teaching that not many Corsicans seemed convinced that their children should learn Corsican in school. He went on to say that:

"Eppò puru s'elli a fessinu, in casa ùn ci n'hè unu annant'à deci chì parla u corsu naturalemente. Face chì puru s'elli puntessinu à fà chì i figlioli scelganu u corsu, seria una materia cum'è l'altra, inutile cum'elli a piglianu diciaremu l'istruzzione civica."

Even if they were, only about one in ten speak Corsican naturally. This means that even if they were to make a point of encouraging their children to choose Corsican as a subject, it would just be a subject like any other one, as useless as those who take "civics" say that course is." (*Arritti* 1993).

Both the definition of the school as the polar opposite of the domain in which the value of Corsican is located, and personal experiences of the French school system undoubtedly contributed to these respondents' skepticism that anything to do with local culture or deep emotional value could be transmitted in the schools. The potential for a minority language to suffer from its institutionalization is also reported by McDonald, who writes that enrollments in Breton language classes at the *collège* (junior high) level dropped after these classes were made part of the regular curriculum. "Breton was now a subject to be treated like any other subject," she writes, and students were dismayed that it was "no longer fun" and carried the risk of academic failure (1989, 65–66).

As Wald (1986, 115) writes, when a minority language is standardized, "*il perd par le même mouvement ce qui pourrait le rendre 'maternel': son indifférenciation et son antériorité à toute catégorisation*" [it loses in this very movement that which could make it "maternal": its lack of differentiation and its historical resistance to all forms of categorization]. Heller describes a similar reaction among Franco-Ontarian parents, who feared that anglophone access to their schools "would change the nature of the linguistic resource distributed, taking what had been a symbolic emblem of ethnic identity and turning it into a mere technical means of communication" (1994, 110).

The allusion to the "maternal language" is also part of a discourse in which the social and economic determinants of language choices are minimized. Often, this is done by linking the mother tongue literally and exclusively with the language practices of mothers. This is quite explicit in a recent report on the bilingual nursery school that was opened in Corti. In it, the author wrote that a fundamental problem had to be faced: "*Si toutes les mères corses parlaient corse à leurs enfants dès la naissance, pouvait-il y avoir une seule force extérieure capable de porter atteinte à notre langue, qu'il s'agisse d'un État, de l'argent, ou de je ne sais quoi?*" [If all Corsican mothers spoke Corsican to their children from the moment of their birth, could there possibly be any single outside force capable of damaging our language, be it a State, money, or I don't know what?] (Piroddi 1994, 14). This perspective is reflected in a poster that has been widely distributed by the Corti chapter of **Scola Corsa** and is often displayed in public places and in the press as a general call for support of Corsican. Elsewhere I argue that this discourse is a form of scapegoating of the least powerful (women), which serves to distance more powerful members of the society (men) and the society in general from feelings of powerlessness and victimization (Jaffe 1991). The discourse of the mother tongue thus essentializes and compartmentalizes the value of Corsican and deflects attention from the politics of language.

Co-officiality: An Effort to Defuse the Problems of "Mandatory Bilingualism"

In 1989, the CCECV launched the concept of "co-officiality" as a replacement for "mandatory bilingualism." The CCECV, it should be noted, is a consultative council to the Assembly, and its proposal represented a philosophical position designed to shape Assembly legislation, not a formal motion. The CCECV acted as both a cultural think tank and public outreach on issues of culture. The booklet it published on the concept of "co-officiality" was intended to persuade Corsican politicians in the Assembly and to sensitize the general public. In the following, I reproduce some excerpts from that booklet, followed by the eventual official motion brought before the Assembly. The first part of this bilingual document was in French. It opened with the following statement: "*La présence des deux langues, français et corse, est une réalité sur le territoire insulaire*" [The presence of the two languages, French and Corsican, is a reality on the island's territory]. The goal, it continued, was to give those two languages equal legal status. This was followed by a statement invoking the ideal of freedom of choice that figures so largely in popular objections to mandatory schooling. "*Le principe introduit donc une notion de liberté, chacun pouvant désormais utiliser oralement ou par écrit la langue de son choix au cours des relations et des actes publics et non officiels*" [The principle [of co-officiality] thus introduces a notion of freedom, henceforth everyone will be able to use the language of his/her choice in speech or writing in both public and unofficial interactions and documents]. The next section is in Corsican. It reads as follows:

Oghji, si sô calmati i passioni, cresci a cuscenza di l'identità è veni a lingua—u bisognu di a lingua—ad appuntillà issa cuscenza. Si cheri una lingua à paru, micca par minui l'altra, micca pè strappà li pezzu. Nô! piuttostu pà arrichiscia. Arrichi un populu chî si appughjarà à dui lingui. Chî oghji, populi d'Auropa parlendu una lingua sola, ùn asistarà più. Allora, eccu a parolla: cuufficialità. Parolla nova, parolla paura, parolla portatimori. Pà oghji basta à lascià andà, avanzà issa idea. U so essa si farà pedipedi, un passu dopu à l'altru, ch'ellu ùn avissi nimu à pianta si par istrada chî i più belli avanzati sô quilli ch'ellu faci un populu incù tutti i soi.

Today, passions have calmed down, a sense of identity is growing, and the language—the need for the language—is coming to the aid of that growth of understanding. The call is for an equal language, not one in order to diminish the other, not to eke out a living. No! Rather, a language to enrich—a people which can rely on two languages is enriched, in that today, European peoples speaking only one language will no longer exist. So, here is the word: co-officiality. New word, word of fear, word of noise. For today, it is enough to just let the idea go forward. Its essence will emerge little by little, one step at a time, so that no one will have to stop along the way since the most beautiful steps forward are the ones made by every member of a People.

The resolution on "co-officiality" brought before the Assembly contained the following specific assertions: (a) that the French language was the official language shared by all the regions; (b) that the Corsican language was also "official on its own territory, the island of Corsica;" (c) that each citizen could choose to use either Corsican or French in all domains of life; and (d) that public authorities were obliged to create all the necessary conditions for the exercise of that free choice and genuine co-officiality.

The booklet and the motion on co-officiality represented some significant changes in philosophy compared to the two previous motions on bilingualism. First, and most obvious, they gave French an equal, legitimate place in the life of the island. This strategy contrasted with the previous two motions, which had, at least symbolically, proposed a Corsican monolingual norm as a counterforce to the French monolingual norm. "Co-officiality" also departed from the implicit position of the previous motions (as well as how they were clearly read by the public), which was that Corsican is the only true expression of Corsicanness. The co-officiality document asserted both the cultural parity of Corsican and French and the quality of Corsicans' attachment to

Corsican as components of Corsican identity. Nor is the cultural status and authenticity of the Corsican language dependent on the number of people who speak it. Rather, it is linked to Corsicans' participation in the wider European community, where the authors state that monolingualism will be an exception and a handicap. There is an overt effort to depoliticize the language question: "passions have calmed," states the document. It insists that co-officiality means equal, noncompetitive relations between the two languages.

In a preface to the co-officiality text, the chair of the committee that drafted the motion stated explicitly that the idea of co-officiality was an attempt to keep the public eye on the issue of legal parity and to move away from thinking about individual bilingualism (Bassani 1991, 12). We can see the reason for this: A focus on individual experiences may lead Corsicans to underestimate the need for linguistic intervention.

No explicit mention was made of schooling, and the document foregrounded individual freedom to choose a language in all domains of life. In fact, the (boldfaced) section in Corsican almost implied a complete lack of concrete policy, proposing instead to let the idea percolate until it has gained public acceptance. The end of this passage ("the most beautiful steps") spoke to the voluntarist view of culture and the value of language.

However, in the three prefatory texts printed in the booklet on co-officiality distributed by the CCECV, the justification of co-official status for Corsican was made on familiar, "primordial" cultural grounds: "*La langue est un des sanctuaires de l'identité, elle est moyen de se reconnâitre, de se savoir d'un lieu . . . elle est, surtout, une manière de penser*" [Language is one of the sanctuaries of identity, it is how we know who we are, where we come from . . . it is, above all, a way of thinking] (Bassani 1991, 13). Bassani also used the "old" term, claiming that Corsican is the "mother tongue" of Corsican children because it is the language that is linked to their culture. In his preface to the document, the political scientist Olivesi characterized the language as the "*vecteur fondamental*" [fundamental vector] of a strong Corsican cultural identity being threatened by France (Olivesi 1991, 24). These supplementary texts also spelled out some of the ways in which the process of implementation of co-officiality would take shape (such as the right to have Corsican represented in the schools, media, place names, and public acts), and they did not propose waiting for popular consensus to begin the process. In the end, the Assembly voted down the motion. The text of the decision read:

La langue corse est un des principaux éléments constitutifs de notre culture. Vouloir l'imposer, la rendre officielle irait à l'encontre du but recherché qui est de faire naturellement retrouver un idiome qui s'est un peu perdu et appauvri. Pour *le Corse, son usage doit représenter un plaisir et un privilège de pouvoir communiquer dans la langue de ses ancêtres.*

The Corsican language is one of the principal elements constituting our culture. To set about imposing it, making it official, would run counter to the desired goal which is for an idiom which has become slightly lost and impoverished to find itself again naturally. For Corsicans, speaking it should be a pleasure and a privilege to be able to communicate in the language of their ancestors. (cited in *Kyrn*, 1990).

The text of the decision remains anchored to the essentialist view of language and cultural identity, so much so that the authors refuse to acknowledge anything more than a minor crisis for the Corsican language (it is "slightly lost"). We read echoes of public reactions to the idea of mandatory bilingualism: the opposition of "natural" and "imposed" (since Corsican is learned "naturally" and is the "natural" language of culture, to impose it is to deform its essence). The focus in this part of the booklet is still on individual bilingualism, rather than on the issue of legal parity.

We can see that all the efforts made by the CCECV to defuse some of the objections that had stood as obstacles to previous motions fell on deaf ears. "Co-officiality" was simply read as "imposition and officialization," and rejected out of hand on the same bases as opponents had rejected mandatory bilingualism. This represents a refusal in the political class to "hear" the message of "co-officiality." It may also reflect the fact that Assembly members had in fact "heard" the continuing echoes of the essentialist position in the CCECV documentation. As a consequence, they may have reacted on the basis of their own traditional notions of "primordial" identity rather than being prompted to revise their categories of value and identity.

As we have already seen in the survey responses on mandatory bilingualism, this perspective can just as easily be translated into opposition as support for minority language legislation. In the attempt to reconcile "old" and "new" models of language and identity, both the CCECV document and the prefaces in the publicly distributed booklet hesitated between those models. In effect, the dual nature of the document may have muffled its potentially radical message.

Assembly members may also have responded to the policy implications of the motion on co-officiality, which were absent in the motion but which were quite clear in the rest of the text. In fact, the concrete implications of the motion were almost as far-reaching as any of the previous ones, given the striking lack of politico-legal status for the Corsican language.

CONCLUSIONS

A close reading of the debate over language education in Corsica shows the pervasive influences of dominant ideologies that posit an essential link between language and identity and establish a diglossic (polarized) value hierarchy between Corsican and French. The influence of these ideologies can be seen in the philosophies and strategies of language planners, as well as in the comments of both those who supported and those who opposed making Corsican a mandatory school subject. At the same time, the debate shows how the internal contradictions of dominant language ideologies can be exposed, even as they are reproduced. By internal contradictions, I refer to the tension between the essentialist assertion of linguistic identity and a far more pragmatic, social constructionist view and strategy in which language is used as a tool to forge a people. In the former, shared identity is assumed; it prefigures its own linguistic expression. In the latter (Whorfian) view, it is the use of the same language that creates shared identity. This contradiction is masked, in many contexts, by the operations of dominant institutions. In schools, this is done in part by focusing on evaluation of individual achievement (Martin-Jones and Heller 1996, 129) and thereby shifting attention away from the connection between language and the coercive power of so many economic and social structures and institutions. The school is represented as an ideologically neutral proving ground for self-evident values and shared orientations. The legitimacy of school language—and its connection to legitimate identities—is similarly taken for granted.

In one respect, the voluntaristic discourse on the value of the Corsican language invoked by some opponents of mandatory bilingualism contests an essentialized view of language and identity by shifting the location of language value from language as an abstract and formal system to the motives and purposes behind language as social practice. This discourse also refuses the masking of coercion, the anonymity of power, the veneer of consensus. Formed by their experiences as minorities in dominant schools, opponents of mandatory Corsican classes distance themselves and the value of speaking a minority language from the values and practices of dominant institutions like the school.

This distancing is not full and unconditional, and the resistance it represents is only partial. As I have suggested, the mother tongue rhetoric associated with some of the voluntaristic discourse masks the impact of large-scale socioeconomic processes on language choice. My research also suggests that the school still plays a large role in legitimating the subjects and practices it tests and rewards. My sense is that in those schools and programs where doing well in Corsican counts in school success, even those parents who do not philosophically support making Corsican mandatory encourage their children to study Corsican and do well on their exams.

In closing, I would like to touch on two general issues related to minority language, identity and schooling that are raised by this educational debate in Corsica. First, it underscores the fact that the experience of being a minority language speaker is a complicated and multilayered one that engenders multiple and sometimes even contradictory sensibilities. In turn, these sensibilities give rise to both accommodation and resistance to dominant practices and ideologies. Second, the debate shows that there is a significant difference between minority and dominant language markets. Dominant language markets are embedded in much larger and pervasive structures of domination; minority language markets are not. The masking of ideological contradictions in the dominant market is accomplished through the extensive reach and coercive power of a host of social, political, and economic structures. In the absence of such widespread pragmatic clout, bids for power by proponents of minority languages like Corsican are not accepted as authoritative, but rather are evaluated as authoritarian.

NOTES

1. The original French version of this part of the text was as follows "*se garde de prononcer un seul mot dans la langue des adultes . . . s'adresser en Corse à une jeune fille serait considéré comme une grossièreté. Demander son chemin à un enfant corse . . . c'est s'attirer une réponse en français.*"

2. This school was largely the product of the energy of one person, J.-B. Stromboni, a retired electrician who devoted all his time to the support of Corsican.

3. It is worth noting that for the primary grades, obliging the state to provide Corsican language education would make taking Corsican classes the default choice, since parents would have to go out of their way to pull their children out of a part of the curriculum. I asked a wide range of teachers and administrators in charge of Corsican language education how many parents had exercised their existing right to decline Corsican language teaching for their children. Only one case was ever reported to me, in which the child in question was put in the back of the room with drawing materials during a Corsican lesson, which he obviously overheard.

4. The points acquired in these exams amounted to "extra credit": They counted toward the student's score, but poor performance did not count against the student. This makes these exams ambiguous in regard to "seriousness": They confer serious rewards, but no penalties.

5. See McDonald 1989, 94, for a similar reaction to the first Breton to pass the baccalaureate in that language.

6. There is an interesting parallel with the Roma case described by Matras and Reershemius (1991, 108), who write that "many Romani communities fear language standardization as it might facilitate access to the community on the part of non-Roma."

ORTHOGRAPHIC CONVENTIONS ADOPTED IN THIS CHAPTER

Original texts in French appear in *italics*.

Original texts in Corsican are in **bold face**.

All English translations are in regular typeface.

REFERENCES

Arritti (1993). *U Corsu in Scola: Spechju di u corsu in sucietà. Compte-rende des débats sur la langue du 5.11.93.* [Corsican in school: A reflection of Corsican in society. An account of debates about the language]. 138: pp. 8–10.

Balibar., E. (1991). The Nation Form: History and Ideology. In I. Wallerstein and E. Balibar (Eds.), *Race, Nation, Class: Ambiguous Identities* (pp. 86–106). New York: Routledge, Chapman and Hall.

Bassani, L. (1991). La coofficialité: Pourquoi? In *Concept de coofficialité /l'edea di a cuufficialità* (pp. 11–16). Bastia, France: Edizione Scola Corsa.

Blommaert, J., and Verschueren, J. (1992). The role of language in European nationalist ideologies. *Pragmatics, 2(3)*, 355–376.

Conseil de la Culture, de l'Education et du Cadre de Vie. (1989). *Coofficialité/Cuufficialità.* Ajaccio, France: Imprimerie Nouvelle Color.

Culioli, X. (1986). *La terre des seigneurs.* Paris: Lieu Commun.

Front Regionaliste Corse. (1971). *Main basse sur une île.* Corbara: Accademia di i Vagabondi.

Gal, S. (1992). Multiplicity and contention among ideologies: A commentary. *Pragmatics, 2(3)*, 445–450.

Heller, M. (1994). *Crosswords.* New York: Mouton de Gruyter.

Higonnet, P. (1980). The politics of linguistic terrorism and grammatical hegemony during the French Revolution. *Social History, 5(1)*, 41–69.

Hobsbawm, E. J. (1991). *Nations and Nationalism since 1780.* New York: Cambridge University Press.

Jaffe, A. (1991). La femme, le mot et le pouvoir en Corse. *Meridies, 13/14*, 131–146.

Kyrn 1990 May 18, page 13 (monthly periodical, published in Ajaccio).

Marchetti, P. (1989). *La corsophonie.* Paris: Editions Albatros.

Martin-Jones, M., and Heller, M. (1996). Introduction to the special issue on education in multilingual settings: Discourse, identities and power. Part II: Contesting legitimacies. *Linguistics and Education, 8*, 127–137.

Matras, Y., and Reershemius, G. (1991). Standardization beyond the state: The cases of Yiddish, Kurdish and Romani. In U. Von Gleich, and E. Wolff, (Eds.), *Standardization of national languages* (pp. 103–123). Hamburg, Germany: UNESCO Institute for Education.

McDonald, M. (1989). *We Are Not French.* New York: Cambridge University Press.

Olivesi, C. (1991). Concept de coofficialité. In *Concept de coofficialité /l'edea di a cuufficialità* (pp. 23–30). Bastia, France: Edizione Scola Corsa.

Piroddi, J. (1994, May 4). Lingua corsa, lingua materna. *Arritti*, 14.

U Ribombu 1985 203 (7) (weekly newspaper, published in Bastia).

Wald, P. (1986). Diglossia applied: Vernacular mixing and functional switching. In J. Fishman, A. Tabouret-Keller, M. Clyne, Bh. Krishnamurti, and M. Abdulaziz (Eds.), *The Fergusonian Impact* (pp. 417–429). New York: Mouton de Gruyter.

Weber, E. (1976). *Peasants into Frenchmen.* Stanford: Stanford University Press.

13

Languages of State and Social Categorization in an Arctic Québec Community[1]

Donna Patrick

Sociolinguistically speaking, language learning for Inuit in Arctic Québec is a complex process. This complexity is the result of a variety of factors, including the role of Inuktitut as the language of family and community, the historical domination of English, and the recent ascent of French as a language of business and state, that have put immense pressure on schools to provide instruction and resources in all three languages. Since 1975, schools in Arctic Québec have responded to these pressures by providing Inuktitut-language instruction for the first three years of school and offering parents the choice of French- or English-language instruction for their children in the following years.

What seems to be a simple choice between two non-Native languages is, as it happens, an exceedingly difficult one for many parents. In this chapter, I explore what is at stake in this language choice. To this end, I examine the large-scale historical, political, and economic processes as well as the everyday community practices and social conditions that shape parents' concerns and responses to this linguistically complex situation. In this context, it is important to recognize the status of English as the lingua franca of northern Québec—the language that (as a result of English colonial structures and schooling) is used in intercultural communication involving members of Inuit, Cree, Anglo-Canadian, and Québecois groups—as well as the dominant language in North America and internationally. Significantly, though, there has been an increasing awareness among Québec Inuit of the importance of French in the province. The question that naturally arises is how Inuit gain access to these valued symbolic resources and acquire the linguistic skills and literacy practices necessary for the local job market or for higher education. In other words, how are these linguistic resources distributed in local communities and institutions so as to enable Inuit to compete in the dominant linguistic market of Arctic Québec?

While English and French have considerable political and economic power in Arctic Québec and Canada and have been in competition for some time, Inuktitut has rapidly been gaining power and legitimacy within northern political and social institutions since the 1970s. This has been the consequence of Inuit political mobilization in Nunavik (the Inuit name for Arctic Québec), which was itself a direct response to the unilateral decision of Southern-based government and business interests to develop a hydroelectric project on land that the Inuit and Cree had never ceded. After a period of legal battles, the signing of the James Bay and Northern Québec Agreement, a landmark land claims settlement, in 1975, led to the creation of Inuit-run organizations to oversee economic and regional development, health and social services, and education. With Inuit participation in these administrative processes, Inuktitut has increased its status as a language of state bureaucracy; and standardized Inuktitut has become a legitimate state language in Arctic Québec. In other words, Inuktitut is now in competition with French and English in the dominant linguistic market, competing for control in the political, social, and economic spheres in the region.

Inuktitut, as a minority indigenous language, has survived particularly well in Arctic Québec, despite centuries of colonial contact (e.g., see Taylor et al. 1993; Dorais 1997; Patrick 1998). Inuktitut is the language of choice in almost all Inuit homes and in linguistic exchanges between Inuit in the settlement and "on the land"—that is, the areas outside the settlement that have been the sites of traditional harvesting practices. However, as in many minority languages situations, the global power of English (and to a lesser extent French) and the dominant cultural and economic forms associated with it have meant that the maintenance of Inuktitut has become a pressing cause. One of the key strategies in Inuktitut language maintenance has been to "modernize" the language through standardization and to increase its use in social institutions such as schools. Yet, there is a tension between modernization and similar institutional processes, on the one hand, and local cultural and linguistic practices, on the other, given that the latter constitute forms of resistance to the assimilation of Inuit culture by Euro–North American culture. While the use of Inuktitut is strongly linked to social identity (Dorais 1997) and has become socially accepted in politics, social services, and schools in Arctic Québec, there is a paradox inherent in the attempt by Inuit to preserve their culture by "modern" means. That is, the increased modernization of Inuit through participation in Western-based political, economic, and institutional structures also means an increased threat of assimilation into the dominant North American culture.

While large-scale historical, political, and economic processes have come to define the languages of state, power, and resistance, it is also important in investigating the educational choices that parents make regarding Inuktitut, English, and French to consider the role of everyday community practices and the social conditions surrounding the acquisition and use of these languages. Inuktitut and English are both highly valued languages, acquired and used in a variety of social contexts inside and outside school. In contrast, French use is constrained by community practices. Moreover, acquisition of the language is limited largely to the classroom and subject to processes of social selection in the school—despite the importance of French in the political economy of Arctic Québec and the requirement of fluency in the language for many jobs in the region. Constraints on language use have significant effects on Inuit access to valued symbolic resources in the community and on potential Inuit participation in the region's job market.

In what follows, I describe the contexts, processes, and consequences of language learning in Arctic Québec. I first provide some historical background on the political, economic, and social forces at play in Arctic Québec. I then present some ethnographic data from a community in which two aboriginal languages, Inuktitut and Cree, are spoken alongside French and English. In this discussion, I focus on the role of French in the community, since it is the language of power with the most social and cultural constraints on its acquisition and use and thus the language least likely to be spoken by Inuit in everyday community contexts. I provide both interview and observational data (collected during the course of fieldwork in 1993–1994), which reveal the importance of French linguistic resources, both inside and outside the community, and the role of the school as a key site in the distribution of these resources. This latter point will be supported by examples from my fieldwork of how language choice in face-to-face interaction constrains access to French in the community by limiting its use and practice.

HISTORICAL BACKGROUND

> I think it's the main force behind the Inuktitut language, for it to continue to
> be on the face of the earth, for Nunavik. There's so much, I just don't know
> how to put it in words. . . . I suppose one of the important principles of the
> Kativik School Board is that I think it's going to be the main instrument for
> preparing children to [govern] themselves in the future. . . . I'm not a politician,
> but if what they have in mind is an all-Inuit government, and everything is in
> Inuktitut, then um, then the Kativik School Board, and the teacher training in
> particular, are important because the teachers will have to make some changes
> for self-government. . . . I think it's something to do with values. I can't think
> of any other way that there will be changes except through the school and
> children. Maybe there is another way. . . . I like to think that the school is
> important. (Inuk educator, F)[2]

Given the complex history of northern Québec, the development of
dominant and minority language education needs to be examined in
the context of colonial history and the rise of Québec nationalism in the
1960s and of Inuit political mobilization in the early 1970s. The history
of the region can be described in terms of a series of political economic
shifts, beginning with the early "explorers," who were seeking resources that could be profitably exploited by England (Patrick 1994).
This resulted in the founding of the Hudson's Bay Company in 1670
and the establishment of trading posts throughout the region. It also led
to conflict between France and England over control of this region and
finally to the emergence of a sovereign Dominion of Canada, loyal to
the British Crown, which brought aboriginal and French-speaking peoples under its authority. Processes of economic co-optation of the Inuit
hunting economy into the world capitalist system coincided with processes of Canadian nation-building, which continued into the late twentieth century. In the 1950s, wage labor was introduced, contributing to
a new phase of political economic co-optation. This was followed by
another shift in political economic arrangements, as French-speaking
Québecois mobilized to form their own sovereign nation. Arctic Québec
was allotted to Québec in 1912 in a federal-provincial agreement (and
referred to as Nouveau-Québec in the province). Both Canadian and
Québec efforts to legitimize their "sovereignty" have produced interests in this region. The late twentieth century also witnessed a movement for aboriginal nationhood and sovereignty within Canada, and a
claim for Inuit control of Nunavik.

The Emergence of Inuktitut as a Language of Instruction

Up until the 1960s, English was the language of traders and missionaries, and later of federal government agents and schooling. Although

missionaries in the region originally taught in Inuktitut (in particular, teaching children and adults how to read and write using a system of syllabics that earlier missionaries had developed), residential schools run by the Anglican and Roman Catholic churches used English. English was also taught in the federal day schools that were introduced in the late 1950s, since it was the language considered essential for acquiring the resources and skills necessary to enter the modern world.

The introduction of federal day schools coincided with the introduction of a cash economy in those Inuit communities where local people were hired to construct and maintain military or government buildings. In the community to be discussed in this chapter, an army base was constructed in 1955 as part of the DEW (Distant Early Warning radar system). This was an American-sponsored military infrastructure built during the Cold War period across the Canadian Arctic. Prior to the mid-1950s and the introduction of wage labor, exchange at the trading post had been the norm (Patrick 1998); employees at the Hudson's Bay Company usually spoke some Inuktitut or made use of an interpreter, generally an Inuk who worked the post occasionally and spoke some English. Thus, before the shift to a wage economy, Inuit hunters and trappers encountered very few occasions that required them to use English.

In the 1960s, the Inuit of Arctic Québec faced further changes, arising from the 1960 election as premier of Québec of Jean Lesage, the reform-oriented and nationalist leader of the provincial Liberal Party. Previously, as Minister of Northern Affairs and National Resources in the federal Liberal government, he had pushed for an increased government presence in the North. Now, with the goal of promoting economic development, Lesage was eager to assert Québec's presence in its northern region. To this end, the Direction Général du Nouveau-Québec (DGNQ) was established in April 1963, as part of the Ministry of Natural Resources (see Patrick and Shearwood 1999).

With the rise of Québec nationalism in the 1960s, federal government agencies were transferred to the province and administered in French. And with an increased interest in the north, businesses sprang up, administered by French-speaking entrepreneurs. The Inuit thus became increasingly aware that they were living in a French province, albeit in a predominantly English-speaking country. Soon afterwards, the DGNQ took responsibility for education, in cooperation with the provincial Ministry of Education. As noted earlier, English had been the language of instruction in the schools serving the Inuit of northern Québec; and as the DGNQ moved quickly to establish provincially administered schools in northern Québec, the language of instruction inevitably became an issue.

By 1964, the new provincial schools had developed a policy of using English as the language of instruction and of teaching French as a second language in classrooms. However, this policy was challenged that same year by an Inuk at a community meeting held in Kuujjuaq, a major Arctic Québec settlement. Representatives of the federal and provincial governments who had authored the policy were forced to reconsider the issue of the language of instruction, as revealed in the following account, given by a non-Native teacher present at this meeting:

> Mr. Jacob Gordon, who had several school-age children, stood up and asked on behalf of the community if the proposed new provincial school would teach his children in Inuktitut. We waited while the two officials at the head table discussed the question between themselves, *sotto voce*. It was clear they had not thought of this before. It took them a full two or three minutes to formulate their answer: yes, the provincial schools would provide instruction in Inuktitut for the children. They would also employ local people for this purpose. For most of us teachers, this was a new and somehow disturbing idea which contested our own educational aims and mission. (Diveky 1992, 92).

The proposal put forth by the Canadian and Québec governments appeared, then, to have legitimized the use of English and French; and the Inuit had, in effect, been asked to accommodate themselves to a new language of power in Québec. But this situation suggested to at least one Inuk at the time that if French could be promoted as a legitimate school language, in order to ensure its status, so too could Inuktitut. Despite the meager political power enjoyed by Inuit in the early 1960s, government attitudes toward minority language status and maintenance in Québec at that time appeared to be sympathetic. Thus, while French vied with English as a language of power and influence in Arctic Québec, the seeds were planted for the legitimization and standardization of Inuktitut within state-run institutions. The incorporation of Inuktitut language and literacy instruction and the training of Inuit teachers to carry out this task became a concern of school boards in northern Québec in the 1970s; and these school boards would continue as one of the chief arenas for promoting, preserving, and legitimizing this language.

Inuit Politicization and Language Policy

Another key development in the history of Arctic Québec, and of education in this region, was the rise of Inuit political mobilization in the 1970s. This process was sparked when the Québec government and its state-owned corporation, Hydro-Québec, began plans to construct a massive hydroelectric project on Cree and Inuit land that had never been ceded in treaties. The Cree and Inuit response to this was to insist on negotiating a land claims settlement. The James Bay and Northern Québec Agreement (JBNQA) (Government of Québec 1976) was finally signed by the federal and provincial governments, Cree, and the Inuit. What is noteworthy about this agreement as regards Inuktitut language and education is that it gave the Inuit the right to run their own school board and to teach in the languages of their choice. The policy for language of instruction that they chose was as follows: compulsory Inuktitut for the first three years of a child's schooling—that is, grades K, 1, and 2, for ages five to eight—and a choice of French or English for the following years, with Inuktitut then taught as a subject. What this suggests is that the new Inuit administration perceived the need for the development of a trilingual language policy, one that not only affirmed their own language but also included French. This is also reflected in the adoption by Inuit leaders of a policy of "francizing" Inuit institutions in Arctic Québec, that is, granting quasi-official status to French alongside Inuktitut and English, a move that involved the translation into French of official documents such as the Constitution of Nunavik and Task Force reports on education and the justice system.

SOCIAL ASPECTS OF LANGUAGE IN THIS MULTILINGUAL COMMUNITY

Since the rise of French in the administrative and business spheres of Québec, the desire of Inuit to learn this language and the perceived necessity of doing so have increased. The ethnographic analysis that I outline here demonstrates (1) the ways that Inuit have responded to the rise of French in Arctic Québec since the 1970s, (2) the sociolinguistic effects of face-to-face interaction in intercultural communication, and (3) the role that this plays in Inuit access to French language resources in the community.

Before I present this analysis, a word about microlevel processes is in order. An examination of the development of language policy in relation to macrolevel historical, political, and economic processes is important. However, an examination of everyday linguistic practices at the community level is equally important, since the consequences of particular policies can be most clearly seen in day-to-day linguistic interaction and in the social constraints conditioning this interaction. In what follows, I provide examples of ethnographic and linguistic data that I collected during a 14-month period of fieldwork in a multilingual settlement in Arctic Québec, and which I analyzed with a view to characterizing the current linguistic and social practices of this settlement.

Linguistically, this settlement is unique in Québec in that two aboriginal languages, Inuktitut and Cree, are spoken alongside French and English, the two dominant languages of business, state, and education. This, combined with its relatively southerly location and large proportion of Euro-Canadian residents (approximately 100 out of a total population of 1,100), sets this community apart from other ones further north. Despite these differences, however, the shared political economy and history of the region and the institutionalized uses of Inuktitut, French, and English allow for generalizability of research findings to other Arctic Québec settlements.

The data to be presented show how language choice is used strategically to negotiate relations of power and solidarity and how language practices construct social boundaries and can serve to define, include, and exclude social players of different ethnic groups. In other words, social groups, including Cree, French, English-Canadian, and Inuit, are fluid social categories that are constructed, in part, by language practices—either between members of the same group or between members of different social or ethnic groups. In these institutions, the language chosen for communication becomes crucial and can have consequences for the acquisition of second and third languages by community members.

Three examples will serve to illustrate the kinds of situations in which established patterns and expectations of English language use constrain the use of French, despite the fact that Inuit involved in the interaction may be studying in French at school. One of these situations is that in which French language teachers outside the classroom use English with children with whom they are not familiar. Another demonstrates restrictions on the use of French that come from the students of French themselves, who sometimes refuse to use the language, as an expression of solidarity and inclusiveness toward non-French interlocutors or bystanders. A third demonstrates routine language patterns in provincially run institutional settings, such as the health clinic, where because of the unique circumstances of this multilingual community, English is used as the language of intercultural communication, despite the ability of interlocutors to communicate in French.

Social Constraints on Language Choice Between Inuit and Francophones

As noted, language choice in a given social setting may be constrained by various factors, and it may result in particular patterns of behavior with particular consequences. This is illustrated in the following excerpt from an interview with Maryse, a francophone woman who had been living in the Inuit community of this settlement for over five years. When I asked her whether Inuit high school students used French in the community, she responded, *"Non, jamais"* (No, never). The interview continued as given in Extract 1.

Extract 1

D: Est-ce qu'ils parlent français avec toi?

Do they speak French with you?

M: Pas beaucoup. Mais, moi quand je sais qu'ils étudient en français, je vais leur parler en français. Et c'est drôle que tu dis ça, parce que la fille à Maggie, elle étudie en français et mardi passé j'ai joué à badminton avec, et je sais qu'elle et Eva étudient en français, puis à un moment on jouait et elle m'a posé des questions en anglais. Elle sait que moi je parle français, elle sait que je sais qu'elle étudie en français . . . mais mois je dis que c'est correct ça. Il faut leur laisser leur temps, mais moi j'ai répondu en français. Mais si elle n'est pas confortable, même si je pousse, mais je pense que c'est developper une bonne relation quand elle sera plus géniale avec moi, peut-être elle va parler français avec moi.

Not a lot. But, when I know that they are studying in French, I talk to them in French. It's funny that you mention that, because Maggie's daughter, she's studying in French and last Tuesday I was playing badminton with her, and I know that she and Eva are studying in French, and then, while we were playing, she asked me some questions in English. She knows that I speak French, she knows that I know that she is studying in French . . . but I say, well, that's alright. You have to give them time, but I answered in French. But if she isn't comfortable, even when I push and push, but I think that a good relationship with her has to be developed and when she is more friendly with me, then perhaps she'll speak French with me. (Interview with Maryse, a francophone resident)

Maryse then described how she continued to speak French with Maggie's daughter. She noted how other francophones often used English with Inuit who they did not realize were studying in French. Maryse, however, made an effort to use French and continued to describe her approach to interacting with Maggie's daughter (Extract 2).

Extract 2

Mais quelque fois comme quand j'étais avec elle, elle me posait des questions en anglais. Je vais répondre en français et des fois je vais dire les choses et elle ne comprenait pas, quand elle ne comprenait pas, j'utilisais quelques mots en anglais, puis là, je revenais en français. Mais elle, elle ne me parlait pas en français. Mais je dis c'est correct si elle ne le fait pas tout de suite.

But sometimes when I was with her, she asked me questions in English. I respond in French, and sometimes I say things that she didn't understand. When she didn't understand, I used some English words, and then, I switched back to French. But she doesn't speak to me in French. But I say to myself, it's okay if she doesn't do it right away.

Maryse had developed a pattern of using French with people who were just beginning to learn French or who were second-language speakers like myself. I had witnessed her speaking French slowly and clearly, waiting patiently for responses, and continuing conversations with adult Inuit and Cree who were taking beginning language courses. But, as she remarked, she was one of the few francophones who insisted on using French in public places with Inuit French-language students, even though they often replied to her in English.

The use of English in the situations described by Maryse seems to be justified by the following considerations: (1) in the feeling of many people in the settlement, both Inuit and non-Inuit, that Inuit are shy, so that Inuit students of French will use the language only if they feel comfortable speaking it and know their interlocutors; (2) an apparent unawareness of some in the settlement of the importance of French in the economy; and (3) the lack of acceptance of French as a language of intercultural communication in the settlement. It is arguably just a question of time, then, until French is more generally accepted and used as an informal community language.

While there may be some truth to the view that most young people are shy about using a language that they have not mastered and that the Inuit community is not yet prepared to embrace a third language for daily interaction, there are other reasons for young people to choose English over French in community situations. This choice is dependent on the language in which the interaction is initiated, the participants in the interaction, and the patterns of language use that have developed for particular speakers under particular social conditions.

These factors are reflected in the language choices involved in another exchange, which occurred one night in the gymnasium, just as a small group of non-Native players and some older Inuit adolescents were preparing to leave. Three Inuit youth were conversing in Inuktitut as they gathered up their belongings. I recognized two of them from school: one from the French senior high school class, and one from the English class. A francophone teacher in the next badminton court greeted the student who studied in French, "*Salut Anna! Comment ça va?*", to which Anna replied, "*Bien.*" Anna then quickly started speaking in Inuktitut to her friends and did not continue the conversation in French. The francophone teacher who addressed Anna was not her teacher; perhaps Anna did not have a close enough relationship with her to continue the conversation or was simply too shy to use French in a public place. An even more significant factor in Anna's language choice, however, was the high social cost that she would have paid for continuing a French conversation in front of her friends; she would have been speaking a language that her friends did not understand and, in doing so, forming an allegiance with a teacher and a francophone at the expense of her allegiance to her friends.

Underlying these choices in these examples is the continued dominance of English in Nunavik, as a language not only of popular culture, to which young people especially might be drawn, but also of intercultural communication established over decades of contact. In the latter capacity, English appears to have a solidarity function similar to that of Inuktitut, that is, it marks solidarity between Inuit speakers when they are interacting with non-Native French-speaking interlocutors, in situations where the use of French or Inuktitut would risk excluding one of the participants in the interaction.

My final example of language choice involves an interaction between an Inuk boy, William, who studied in French, and a francophone nurse at the nursing station. Although William was in the French stream at school, the nurse had no way of knowing this. (As it happens, it is impossible for nursing staff to know whether a child is studying in French or English unless they have obtained this information elsewhere. My own observations suggested that even a child studying in French will not always say so when asked directly in French and that even schoolteachers sometimes have difficulty keeping track of which children are in the English or the French stream.) Although the Inuit interpreters greeted William and engaged him in a brief conversation in Inuktitut, he was treated by the nurses in English without the benefit of Inuktitut translation, which is reserved for older Inuit. It was unclear, however, how much he really understood about taking the medicine prescribed for him when he was addressed directly in English by the nurse (although his ability to comprehend was admittedly not crucial, given his young age and his caregiver's role in insuring that he took his medicine at the prescribed times).

It was clear in this situation at the clinic that English was the language of interaction with the nurse there—that it was English, rather than Inuktitut or French, that health-care providers used when dealing with Inuit, even when both the health-care provider and the client actually spoke French. This demonstrated the existence of institutionalized patterns of English-language use between non-Natives and younger Inuit (that is, those educated in schools), even in settings where one might expect French to be used by second-language learners.

The use of English instead of French with Inuit is well-intentioned: Francophones are seeking to include Inuit students, patients, clients, and others and to avoid negative reactions, such as being seen as rude or secretive, by using English. It is also perhaps a tacit recognition on the part of some francophones that the position of French in the communicative hierarchy is still unstable in this particular aboriginal settlement, where English is so prevalent. These assumptions are based, in part, on the recognition of francophones in the settlement that English is the second language of most Inuit and the consequent expectation of these francophones that younger Inuit, in particular, will be able to understand English whether they are studying in English or not. Unfortunately, such patterns of language use may also have serious repercussions for students of French who want to master the language, whether for employment or for higher education, since they severely restrict the opportunities that young language learners have for using French outside of the classroom.

These patterns of institutional language use—of francophones using English with Inuit youth, often not knowing whether they are studying in French or English—serve to reproduce the ethnic boundaries that define this community. English, as already noted, is the language of intercultural communication and is used in settings where one might reasonably expect French to be used and practiced by second-language learners. Given the shifting political economy of Nunavik and the importance of French in this process, this situation is of increasing concern to many members of the Inuit community, as we shall see.

Linguistic Strategies and Educational Choices in Arctic Québec

Because of the presence of two dominant European languages in Nunavik, Inuit have faced the prospect of having to become trilingual or of having to find some other effective response to competition between English, French, and Inuktitut in the dominant market. The strategies that Inuit have adopted have reflected the political and linguistic realities of Nunavik. Most have recognized that knowledge of the dominant languages and of Inuktitut is a necessary part of political and economic survival for Inuit, while knowledge of Inuktitut is necessary for both local identity and cultural survival. As one Inuktitut-English bilingual put it:

Extract 3

We are in a situation where we are in Québec, and French is the language of the majority of the province, and being Inuk, trying to maintain our culture and our language, and we're having to deal with three languages, everybody tends to turn to English. But there is a reason for that though, because when we first started in the federal day school it was the only language taught, up until 1975 or 76, so it is the most common language you find here. (Interview with Inuit Municipal Council employee, M.)

The interviews that I conducted during my fieldwork in one Nunavik settlement—37 interviews in all, 25 with Inuit and 12 with non-Inuit—suggest that many Inuit who already know some English are reluctant to learn a second European language. This is especially true given that English is already the dominant second language of this region and that most francophones with whom Inuit are likely to have contact would have at least some knowledge of English; any communications in French could always be translated. These interviews also suggest that in the 1990s more Inuit perceived a need to learn French, even though very few of those educated in English were actively engaged in learning French, seeing knowledge of the language as ultimately necessary, though not currently a priority. In other words, many of the latter recognize the location of Nunavik in a larger French-speaking province and are thus aware of the symbolic domination of French in institutional practices and acknowledge its dominance in state-supported agencies. In practical terms, they know that French is needed to obtain services, among them social and health services and provincial government information (including forms dealing with pensions, welfare, and driver's licenses) in the province as a whole. While it is true that these services can be obtained in English, the limited bilingual competence of staff in government offices in smaller francophone communities may make doing so a significantly more time-consuming process. (The prevalence of French in these domains was noted by both the Inuit and anglophone residents whom I interviewed).

Many Inuit also acknowledge that French is often used in the workplace, especially in positions that involve dealing with provincial departments and agencies or with personnel from southern Québec. Though not all such personnel speak French, almost everyone I interviewed could recall occasions when they had had to deal with a unilingual French speaker or when some aspect of their jobs involved written French. Such a situation is described in the following extract.

Extract 4

D: Did you ever learn French, or want to learn French?

M: I never learned French. It was important in my working areas, because I had to speak to people who only knew French sometimes for the telephone. . . . Even now they ask me "*parlez-vous français*" and I have to say no. Even though I understand that, but . . . I don't know French. (Interview with Inuk Municipal Council Employee, F)

Despite these acknowledgments of the importance of French, those interviewed offered many reasons why they did not make learning the language a priority. One was the limited time that some of them, especially single mothers and others with families, felt able to invest in French. For others, there was also the issue of identity associated with speaking English, which was linked to colonial history—in particular, the dominant relationship between English language practices (of traders, church, and school) and the Inuit cultural and economic practices that characterized this period of contact. One Inuk woman, cited here, identified speaking English as a second language with being Inuk.

Extract 5

[S]ince I'm Inuk, English is my second language. . . . The English came here and they wanted us to learn how to speak English. It is my second language and I really don't know to answer that. I really want to understand very much in English. . . . I'd rather learn English than French. (Interview with Inuk resident, F)

Another reason among those who had already studied English was that they already had access to two of the languages operating in the dominant language market. Moreover, despite the importance of French, English was not only the community's lingua franca but also the dominant language in North America and in international, globalized markets.

What emerged as a real concern for many Inuit who did not speak French was that French language skills might become a prerequisite for employment, so that their ability to obtain employment without these skills could soon be jeopardized. As one Inuk leader explained, living in a French province meant increased exposure to French and possibly demands for French in the workplace. Although French was not yet a requirement, it was certainly already an asset. As many other people interviewed in the community noted, the demand for French in the workplace would only increase, and those who could speak French would have better employment opportunities. The following excerpts demonstrate the concerns that people had regarding the interplay of the three dominant languages and the increasing importance of French in the workplace:

Extract 6

D: Do you think those kids learning French have a chance at getting jobs?

P: Yes, I believe so. Some students I know take French as a second language, at secondary level, but they have to really get used to it. So, sometime, once they feel older and more self-confident, I guess they'll use it more. We don't see that too much here. . . . It would increase our level of confidence, if only we could speak Inuktitut, English and French. (Interview with Inuk Municipal Council employee, M)

Extract 7

this job that I have is nothing but French, with some translation and stuff, I'm able to do this. My co-workers here don't speak French . . . they all . . . they can do the job. You get a little training, you get the hang of it and you can do the job. . . . I've been trying hard to learn French. I even took a six-week immersion course this year, but it's not enough. Like I already have two languages, putting in a third one, you know it's kind of hard. (Interview with Inuk Québec Government employee, M)

Such work-related reasons, coupled with a recognition of the overall importance of French, have motivated some individuals to begin learning the language. However, most Inuit who voiced these concerns opted for a considerably different, longer-term strategy for coping with the trilingual language market in Arctic Québec. This was to place their children in the French stream at school, which (as noted earlier) begins in grade 3. This brings us back to the problem posed at the beginning of this chapter: How do parents decide whether to educate their children in French or English? As we have seen, children studying in English in this settlement receive crucial practice outside of school, since English serves as the settlement's lingua franca, and is preferred in cross-cultural communication. French, on the other hand, is often avoided in communication between French-speaking Inuit and francophones, given social constraints related to solidarity and inclusion. This results in a language-learning context that favors the acquisition of English and allows those students who are studying in English to really master a second language. Parents educated in English are further aware of their inability to help their children with French, whereas they may be able to help their children with English schoolwork. Thus, the choice of one language of instruction over the other is not an easy one, as one mother noted:

Extract 8

I think I made a mistake putting my son in English. Because we are in the province of Québec, it's going to be required that you speak French more than it will be required to speak English in the future if you want to get into the job market. But I can help him more in English, because I know English, but I can't help my daughter who is in French. You know what I mean. (Interview with Inuk Municipal Council employee, F)

Other potential problems that students face with French in school are described in the following excerpt from an interview with an Inuk court worker:

There have been students who have gone to French classes, and we've lost them. They're not speaking in English and they're not speaking in French. Their Inuktitut is okay. My cousin, he went to French school here and he does not speak in French, 'cause he doesn't use it, they don't use it when they're at home, either they speak in English or Inuktitut, so they don't speak in French in the house. So they lose that after they leave the school, they lose French, and they don't speak English very well either. And they can't read. I also have a nephew who can't sign his own name, he's seventeen years old. As I said, there is no discipline in school today, so he didn't learn. He was always doing something else in the classroom and he dropped out and he doesn't even know how to sign his name. He has to look at his name and write it and look at it like that. It's very sad. And there's a lot of people like that now. (Inuk Government employee, F.)

The lack of French practice outside of school, as noted in this interview, and more general worries about education and the possibility that many children are being failed by the system have led some parents to enroll their children in English if they are potentially slow learners. The English stream is assumed to be the easier one, since children can receive more second-language support outside the school than they would if they studied in French. Thus, processes of social selection appear to be operating in the distribution of French linguistic resources. Some students succeed despite the obstacles; for example, during the year when I conducted this research, three French-educated students graduated from high school and were on their way to attend French-language colleges in Montreal. However, many more do not acquire the language levels necessary for further and higher education.

Although there is a recognition of the current importance of French, it is based on a widely held belief that its value will increase even more in the future. As people's proficiency in French as a second language increases, so do their chances of gaining access to French linguistic resources and employment. Children enrolled in French now are thus a parental investment in that future; if they are too shy to speak French in face-to-face interaction in the community, this is not a real worry, since self-confidence and language ability will come with time. This has parallels with the situation of English among Inuit in the 1950s, where in many cases language learners appeared to be making minimal progress, but eventually achieved considerable proficiency (see Macpherson and Macpherson 1991).[3] The strategy of deferring the need to use French but placing a high value on language learning for future use appears to have a dual purpose, namely, to affirm the value of French while at the same time justifying the lack of enthusiasm among adults for learning the language and its minimal use by young people currently being educated in it.

As it happens, the structure of schooling that the Inuit have chosen for themselves highlights the Inuit strategy of educating young Inuit for the linguistic realities of the present and future, while still maintaining a balance between languages at local and regional administrative levels. The first three years of schooling, in which Inuktitut is the sole language of instruction, serve to promote fluency and literacy in Inuktitut, while the later years, in which the school offers a choice between English- and French-medium instruction and assigns Inuktitut a minor pedagogical role, promote fluency and literacy in one of the dominant languages.

CONCLUSION

This chapter has examined the issue of language choice as it pertains to the sociolinguistically complex situation of the Inuit of Arctic Québec. It has demonstrated how, in this instance, language policy and language practice are related and how they are embedded in a specific historical, social, and political economic context. Policy can facilitate processes of language maintenance and language learning, but these are ultimately subject to social constraints on the use of particular languages in particular contexts.

The sociolinguistic data presented here suggest that institutional and social constraints on language use among the Inuit of Arctic Québec pose significant challenges for Inuit students studying in French. While it is attractive for parents to choose French-language education for their children as a means of providing access to valuable symbolic resources, the acquisition and use of this language is to a large extent limited to the classroom and thus to interaction with French-language teachers who are familiar with students. In addition, processes of social selection operating in the school mean that a limited number of students are given access to the symbolic resources necessary to pursue French-language postsecondary studies, which (just like most English-language postsecondary studies) can at the moment be obtained only in Montreal, 2000 km to the south. Students experiencing difficulties in French-language classrooms as well as those who have opted for English-language education have limited access to French elsewhere. The socioeconomic consequences of this situation for the community are significant, since many of the positions now held by non-Native workers require a relatively high level of French language skills, and many of the students possessing such skills are meanwhile being attracted to higher education and job opportunities in the south.

The trilingual language market and the resulting trilingual language policy in schools in Arctic Québec have placed significant pressure on residents as they try to decide what the best education for their children is. In this chapter, I have demonstrated what is at stake at the macro- and micro-levels of communication and of language politics and the forces at play in everyday interaction.

NOTES

1. This chapter is based on Patrick 1998. I wish to thank people of the settlement of Nunavik, which was the site of my research, for sharing their insight about Inuit language, culture, and schooling with me; the Kativik School Board, for their support, financial and other; and the Social Sciences and Humanities Research Council (SSHRC) of Canada for the doctoral fellowship that made this research possible. I also wish to thank Monica Heller, Marilyn Martin-Jones, and Ben Shaer for their editorial suggestions.

2. Excerpts from interviews conducted for this paper indicate the general social position and the gender (M(ale) or F(emale)) of the speaker.

3. A. F. Applewhite, who taught in Inukjuak from 1954 to 1957, had this to say about his former students' knowledge and use of English:

> The pupils were quite accustomed to being in school. They didn't speak much English—actually refused—although most of them understood English. They could read quite well. They could read words, but I never really knew if they could understand what they read. There seemed to be an underlying feeling that they didn't really want to learn English. However, they really did quite well in mathematical skills and language skills. Speaking English wasn't one of the things that they could do, or wanted to do (Macpherson and Macpherson 1991, 76).

REFERENCES

Diveky, G. (1992). The thirty-year turnaround: A teacher's view of changing educational and language policies in N.W.T. In N. Graburn and R. Iutzi-Michell (Eds.), *Proceedings of the Conference: Language and Educational Policy in the North* (pp. 87–101). Berkeley, Calif.

Dorais, L. J. (1997). *Quaqtaq: Modernity and identity in an Inuit community*. Toronto: University of Toronto Press.

Government of Québec. (1976). *The James Bay and Northern Québec Agreement*. Québec: Editeur official du Québec.

Macpherson, N. J. and Macpherson, R. D. (1991). *Dreams and visions: Education in the Northwest Territories from early days to 1984*. Yellowknife: Government of the Northwest Territories, Department of Education.

Patrick, D. (1994). Minority language and social context. *Etudes/Inuit/Studies, 18(1–2)*, 183–199.

Patrick, D. (1998). *Language, power and ethnicity in an Arctic Québec Community*. Unpublished doctoral dissertation, University of Toronto, Toronto, Ontario.

Patrick, D., and Shearwood, P. (1999). The roots of Inuktitut bilingual education in Arctic Québec. *The Canadian Journal of Native Studies, 19(2)*: 249–662.

Taylor, D. M., Wright, S. C., Ruggiero, K. M. and Aitchison, M. C. (1993). Language perceptions among the Inuit of Arctic Québec: The future role of the heritage language. *Journal of Language and Social Psychology, 12(3)*, 195–206.

Contestation and Struggle

Collusion, Resistance, and Reflexivity: Indigenous Teacher Education in Brazil[1]

Marilda C. Cavalcanti

In this chapter, I draw on an exploratory study based on an indigenous teacher education course for a group of young Guarani speakers in a village in the state of São Paulo in southern Brazil. The teacher education course was set up at the request of the community leaders in the village. They approached the university. My colleagues and I undertook to run the course as an action research project that would allow us to reflect on our own practice as teacher educators. As the course unfolded, we became aware that we were experiencing some difficulties in our face-to-face interactions with the Guarani teachers and in coordinating our work with them. This led to a refocusing of the research dimension of the project on these areas of interactional difficulty. One telling episode in this new phase of the project drew our attention to the fact that the Guarani teachers had quite a different agenda from ours. From this point onward, we recast our analyses of the "cross-cultural interactions" in the classroom so as to take account of these diverging interests and the wider political context of the oppression of indigenous people in Brazil.

Our project began with research objectives associated with consensus and collaboration, but we then shifted to a research enterprise premised on the view that participants in such teaching/learning projects have different interests and that the investigation of face-to-face interaction, inside and outside the classroom, needs to take account of the wider power relations that shape these interests. We also came to understand that reflexivity should be a central feature of research encounters of the kind we were engaging in.

This chapter is structured as follows: First, I provide a brief sketch of indigenous education in Brazil and outline some of the issues stemming from research in this context. I then go on to give a brief history of education for Guarani speakers in Brazil. In the later sections, I recount the development of our project, from its initial phase as an action research project on teacher education to the phase where we began to focus our attention on critical analysis of the "cross-cultural interactions" and began to reflect on the asymmetrical relations of power underpinning the project. In the final section of the chapter, I consider the implications of our experience in this project for other teacher educators and for researchers in Brazil.

INDIGENOUS EDUCATION IN BRAZIL IN THE 1990s

Brazil's new constitution, dated 1988, acknowledges that its indigenous population is entitled to bilingual education. However, indigenous education and indigenous teacher education have remained outside the official educational system. There are some exceptions, for example, in the states of Acre (in the north of the country), Paraná (in the south), and Mato Grosso and Tocantins (in the Midwest), where educational projects carried out by nongovernmental organizations (NGOs) and/or university research groups have been successful in placing not only indigenous education but also the indigenous teachers within the educational system. In other words, despite the force of law, in fact very little has been done officially by the government, be it regionally or nationally. Only in 1991 was indigenous education introduced in the new constitution as being the government's responsibility; eventually, in 1994, written directions for a specific policy for indigenous education were produced by the Ministry of Education. A national committee made up of people elected every three years was then formed to discuss aims in this educational area for the next ten years.

This committee has the academic support of university staff from various universities around the country.

RESEARCHERS AND INDIGENOUS PEOPLES

As for research, it should be pointed out that indigenous education per se has not received much attention until recently either. However, the indigenous context has been the focus of intense research interest. The majority of the research projects carried out so far have aimed at the linguistic description of indigenous languages, mainly at the phonological and morphosyntactic levels. (See, however, the study of discourse practices in some indigenous languages developed by Orlandi 1990.) What one sees nowadays is a general insistence by indigenous peoples that any ongoing or new research project should contemplate education in some way or another. This position has been made very clear; if it is not taken into account in a research proposal, its absence may even prevent the development of a project.

Research on indigenous (teacher) education is thus beginning at a very promising and challenging time, when indigenous peoples show a realistic concern for education not only for its pragmatic value but also for the symbolic power it may have. While they are afraid that it may represent a potential threat to their cultural survival, indigenous peoples are attracted to education, because it may mean access to other things: It can be a way of entering into a working relationship with the donors of funds, and it can be a way of opening up new avenues or opportunities. What should be mentioned here is that indigenous peoples have suffered so much oppression over the years that they have developed complex strategies of resistance. They have, for example, learned how to say "no" by saying "yes"; that is, doing things in accordance with the expectations of non-indigenous people while serving their own ends.

One of the questions posed in this chapter is, In whose interest is indigenous education currently being developed? Researchers, universities, NGOs, and educationists may get prestige for doing research and for running educational projects. The same happens to indigenous peoples who show they know what they want regarding education to the donors of funds. At the same time, education and access to literacy (in Portuguese or in the indigenous languages) may be a means for indigenous peoples to claim their cultural and territorial rights.

GUARANI SPEAKERS IN BRAZIL

There are about 3,000 Guarani in the south and southwest of Brazil.[2] There is a much larger population of Guarani speakers in neighboring countries such as Paraguay and Argentina. The Brazilian Guarani have been in contact with the non-indigenous population since the sixteenth century, when the Portuguese colonization of Brazil was officially started. The Guarani people are well known for their strong language loyalty. This surfaces in language and culture maintenance and in resistance strategies. According to Schaden (1962) and also Meliá (1979), this loyalty stems from the belief that religion and language are seen as one and the same, with Guarani being the only real language. As Silva (1994, 39) points out, the term ñe'ë in Guarani means at the same time "language" and "part of the divine human soul." For some Guarani people, all the other languages are seen as "invented" and, therefore, whatever is said in any language but Guarani is to be disregarded. It is not important, relevant, or necessarily true.

In relation to schooling, the Guarani first had contact with the Jesuit missionaries, who were the first religious people to work in Brazil. This contact dates back to the sixteenth century, that is, to the years that followed the first contact with the Portuguese colonizers. The history of the relationship between the Jesuits and the Guarani peoples is a long and complex one. From the beginning, even before the colony acknowledged its indigenous population, Jesuit education was seen as the means to "civilize the wild by conversion to Catholicism." Gomes (1988, 164) points out that the Catholic Church, mainly represented by the Jesuits until 1759, "played an exceptional role in defining the notions of defense and protection in Brazilian discourse about indigenous people." However, at certain times, the missionaries were allies of other forces pitted against the indigenous people. According to Ribeiro (1970), only in the beginning of the twentieth century was there any awareness in the general population of Brazil of the indigenous question. Two opposing views then arose: one that favored the continuation of the efforts to convert the indigenous people to Catholicism and another that argued in rather patronizing terms that lay people should *protect* the indigenous population. The main argument was that they should be assured of their freedom to profess their own religions. One way or another, schooling was always imposed (see Ribeiro 1970).

For Gomes (1988), the three forces that shaped the fortunes of indigenous peoples in Brazil from the outset were the Portuguese colonizers, the state, and the Catholic Church. Historically speaking, these three forces alternated in prestige and in power. Until the eighteenth century, the colonizers and the church had broadly the same views about the indigenous people. As missionary activity diversified in Brazil with the establishment of Protestant missions, different views of indigenous education and of the indigenous people began to emerge.

Today, NGOs play a key role in defining the nature and purpose of indigenous education and in building images of indigenous people. The first NGOs started in the late 1970s. Some of the NGOs have religious links and others do not. (It should be kept in mind that before the NGOs became popular, individual anthropologists, journalists, and lawyers had made their mark in defense of indigenous people.) Parallel to the NGOs, and sometimes under their influence, indigenous associations were started some 20 years ago. The emergence of these associations represents a change in the relationship with the non-indigenous people, that is, in the past, non-indigenous people acted as advocates for indigenous people. Nowadays indigenous communities are represented by their leaders. The emergence of indigenous associations also represents a change in the relationships among different indigenous peoples. The indigenous population of Brazil is characterized by enormous diversity. Different groups have different histories of contact with the colonizers as well as different languages and cultural traditions. They cannot be seen as a monolithic block. They nevertheless share an indigenous identity within a country of continental dimensions.

The Guarani are not alone today in showing overt suspicion regarding educational programs (see Kahn 1994 on the Waiápi; and Silva 1994 on the Guarani Mbyá and on the Pakaanova). When they exist, educational programs do not usually last long. There are many beginnings, but little follow-up. In the words of a Guarani leader recorded by Silva (1983, 147): "The school here within the community, we have our meetings, we always have our meetings . . . and we only speak Guarani. . . . Many times, many white people have come to the community to start a school, to teach the young and the adults. So we decided that, for us, the school has no value because . . . for us it is not important to speak Portuguese." This is illustrative of the degree of resistance among Guarani people to the dominant language and culture.

A TEACHER EDUCATION PROJECT IN A
GUARANI COMMUNITY

The project described in this chapter focused on a Guarani community of about 200 people, located in the state of São Paulo in the south of Brazil. This village is an important religious and political center for the Guarani, and there is considerable movement of Guarani people in and out of the village. The people in this local community gain their livelihood from agriculture and handicrafts.

The leaders of the community took the initiative in setting up the teacher education project in the village. They approached us in our capacity as language teacher educators at one of the universities in the region. We were asked to present a proposal for an indigenous teacher education project. The proposal we developed was an action research project. This was submitted to the indigenous community council for approval. Several meetings took place between the two parties to work out the terms of the agreement. One of the points that was agreed upon was that as a research group, we would not only deal with teacher education but also carry out research of the type that would enable us to reflect on the practice of teacher education. Another point we agreed upon was that the work was to be done in the community. The other immediately relevant point was that we undertook to search for funds to carry out the project. We warned them that we might encounter difficulty in getting scholarships for the Guarani teachers for their involvement in the collaborative, reflexive part of the project, since we knew that this way of organizing research was still not favored by funding bodies in Brazil.

The action research project had as participants six young Guarani men chosen by the community and six members of our research group. Our group included both established researchers and student researchers. Five members of our research team were females. The six young Guarani men, whose ages ranged between 18 and 22, were fluent speakers of a local variety of Portuguese in addition to Guarani. On the whole their oral proficiency in the local variety was stronger than their aural, reading, and writing capabilities in standard Portuguese. Out of the six Guarani, one stood out as the most proficient in standard Portuguese and one as the least proficient. The others appeared to have an intermediate proficiency level.

Portuguese was chosen as the medium of communication. It was a second language for the young Guarani men and our first language. No other option was available, as we did not speak Guarani. However, Portuguese is the language of the dominant society, and we knew that it carried connotations of power and authority. We did however express a strong interest in learning Guarani.

The aim of the action research project was to document and analyze the way in which the teacher education course with six Guarani students unfolded. Our aims were to develop the indigenous teachers' classroom experience and to enable them to strengthen their abilities in spoken and written Portuguese and, at a later phase, to provide discussion and support for syllabus design. According to Cohen and Manion (1980), the two main characteristics of action research are continuous evaluation, leading to the immediate incorporation of partial results, and flexibility, leading to a constant revision of the teaching/learning practices and the aims and design of educational programs. In our case, the evaluation procedure was carried out through constant monitoring in research staff meetings, in meetings with the Guarani participants, and in meetings with the community leaders. The action research elements of the project were recorded ethnographically by individual researchers using research diaries and observational notes. In this chapter, I draw on these ethnographic accounts.

The data was gathered with individuals and/or small groups during the math and Portuguese-as-a-second-language classes held in the community, during the meetings at the university and in the community, and during informal conversations. The fieldwork also involved the use of audiorecordings and informal interviews. Most of the fieldwork was done in the community context, approximately 100 km away from the university base. Only twice did the indigenous group spend a week at the university where our research group was based. The visits were made at their request.

"CROSS-CULTURAL" MISUNDERSTANDINGS?

At first, the work with the six Guarani participants and the six members of our research team appeared to be going smoothly. It should be pointed out that, as a group, we were already well acquainted with research carried out in other Guarani communities, and we were aware that the Guarani are known for the strong stance they adopt in defense of their culture. We looked at the task ahead of us as a challenge. Our aim was to act in a "culturally sensitive way" (Erickson 1987). However, after about two months of work in the community, we found that, when coming back from the fieldwork visits, we often felt frustrated. The frustration was manifested in our conversational exchanges about the development of the work. Fragments from our conversations, such as those quoted in the following, were recorded in the entries in my research diary. (The four researchers involved in these conversations are indicated by the letter "R" followed by a number.)

Making Plans and Carrying Them Out

On one of our field trips, one member of our team, R4, expressed her frustration about the fact that what we had planned was not always implemented.

R4: (on the way to the community): *Será que vamos conseguir dar aula hoje/ pode bem acontecer que tenhamos que voltar para casa sem ter tido a oportunidade de vê-los/*

R4: (on the way to the community) Are we going to be able to give classes today? We might come back without having the opportunity to see them [the indigenous teachers].

On former occasions, when we had gone to the community, the young Guarani men had not been there or had had too many community commitments to be able to have classes. On the day when my diary entry was made, they *were* there and a lesson was given, but as can be seen from the conversational fragment that follows, just giving a class had not been enough to satisfy my co-researcher. She expected more. There was also no guarantee that things would work out on the next field trip.

R4: (returning to the community): *Ah/ não sei se quero continuar/ sinto que a gente nunca consegue fazer o que planejou, e a gente passa tantas horas planejando/*	R4: (returning to the community) Oh, I don't know whether I'd like to go on [with the work]. I feel we never get to accomplish what we plan, and we spend so many hours planning.

Keeping Appointments

We also felt frustrated about the schedules, which always had to be rearranged, resulting in lack of time to carry out planned activities. On the way back from another field trip, R2, another member of our team, said:

R2: *Eu sei que o conceito deles de tempo é diferente/ mas será que não dava para respeitar a hora e o dia marcado de vez em quando/*	R2: I know their concept of time is different from ours, but couldn't they stick to the arranged time and day at least sometimes?

In this same conversation, R2 was complaining about what she saw as a mismatch in commitment. She felt that we had to show respect for their culture and that this respect was not reciprocated. Our feelings of frustration were aired at one of our research meetings. The explanation we came up with was that non-reciprocation could well be a form of resistance strategy to the dominant society, represented by us.

Differing Views about the Content of the Classes

Some anxiety was also expressed by R3, another member of our team, in a conversation with R2 about the indigenous participants' apparent indifference and/or ambivalence toward some of the classes. They seemed to be very involved in the reading and math activities proposed. (All the reading here was in Portuguese.) In fact, the Guarani teachers had said to us they liked the reading and math classes. However, they showed considerable resistance when we wanted to introduce discussion of the initial stages of first-language literacy.

Eye Gaze Direction

The same member of our team, R3, made the following comment in a conversation with R4, but she was quickly reassured by R4:

R3: *Puxa, mas eles não olham para a gente/ Me sinto tão mal/ Acho que eles não gostam das nossas aulas/*

R3: Oh dear, they don't look at you [their heads were always down], I feel so uncomfortable. Perhaps they don't like the classes we give.

R4: *Mas eles estão sempre tão envolvidos com a atividades que a gente leva para a aldeia/*

R4: But they are always so engrossed in the activities we take to the village.

However, the problem of interpreting the significance of eye gaze direction came up on a number of occasions. A note also needs to be made regarding R3's comment about eye gaze direction here: Sustaining eye contact with one's interlocutor carries strong connotations in mainstream Brazilian culture. Avoiding eye contact in conversation can be taken as indifference.

Our Reactions to Their Silence

Long moments of silence characterized the interactions with the Guarani teachers (see Cavalcanti 1991). The silence of the young men in classroom interactions began to be construed by the members of our research team as "indifference." What seemed to be surfacing were "cross-cultural" misunderstandings, but they were never brought up for discussion with the Guarani educators. Our reaction as researchers to the different patterns of silence in the interaction between us and the indigenous teachers was like the tip of an iceberg. All the comments we made when we talked about them stemmed directly or indirectly from our reaction to their silence.

As I have shown elsewhere (see Cavalcanti 1991), we seemed to be filling in with talk every possible space in the interactions (as if silence were not part of interaction). The inter-turn and within-turn silences in the conversational contributions of the Guarani speakers ranged from 5 seconds to 25 seconds. In the first audiorecordings the only voices to be heard were our voices. Later, because we were concerned about cultural sensitivity, we learned to wait for them to break their silence. Then we faced what we perceived to be long intervals with no talk. For us, this learning experience was fraught with a mixture of anxiety and understanding; we learned to teach at a slower pace in a manner that at first was very unfamiliar to us. Besides this, we constantly had in mind the fact that the time taken by students to reply was not going to be immediate. The more aware we were of this interactional problem, the more anxious we became. Their silences were of a different order from those of second-language users of Portuguese, who need planning time in interaction with native speakers. Their level of oral proficiency in the local variety of Portuguese was quite high.

Topic Development and Misunderstanding

Mendes (1994), a member of our team, focused on her own practice in the role of teacher in one math lesson. A number of misunderstandings occurred in this lesson. The silences of the student teachers sometimes made it difficult for her to interpret their turn-taking cues. She sometimes found herself interrupting their turns and changing topics, thinking that the previous topic had been exhausted. The transcript that follows, for example, shows a teacher/student exchange in which a previous topic is brought back into the conversation by the Guarani speaker. However, this surprises the teacher, who does not recognize the relevance of what is being said. The teacher seems to ignore these attempts to introduce a new topic. But the topic seen as new by the teacher is in fact a previously established topic being concluded.

R3 had asked the Guarani educators to list the types of handicraft they make. They listed five types. She then understood that the step of constructing the list was over and started asking about the cost of each one of the types listed. That was the topic planned for her math class. The conversation about cost went on for a while until they started comparing prices and discussing whether the price was adequate to the amount of work put in and the material needed to produce each piece. All of a sudden, one of the Guarani speakers brought in an apparently new topic about the sizes of arrows (Extract 1).

Extract 1

R3: *[quanto] tempo você gastou pra fazê/ o material que você usou pra fazê/né/ tudo isso daí é o que vai contar pra você dar o preço/ então nós vamos fazê assim/ cada coisa do artesanato que você/*

R3: how long it took you to make [it], what type of material you used, right? all this will be relevant to working out the price . then let's do it this way . every type of handicraft that you make

G1: *tem já a flecha/ tem vários tamanhos/ tem mais pequena/ tem mais grande/ tem original/*

G1: there's the arrow already . it's in many sizes, there are smaller ones, there are bigger ones, there are original size ones

R3: *ah..* [the teacher sounds surprised]

R3: oh ... [the teacher sounds surprised]

G1: *original/ tudo/*

G1: all original size

R3: *tem original/*

R3: are there any of the original size?

G1: [inaudible]

G1: [inaudible]

R3: *certo/*

R3: right

G1: *original já é mais caro/*

G1: the original size is more expensive

R3: *qual que é mais caro?*

R3: which is more expensive?

G1: *original/*

G1: the original size

What one sees then are extended turns with no concrete closing. The Guarani usually signal verbally, saying, for example, "I have finished," when they conclude a topic, but no room was being provided for the closing to materialize. It is as if the teacher is asking, "What is going on?" and the Guarani young man is saying, "Look, I haven't finished yet but I am following you." In Extract 1, however, the Guarani speaker combines the topic already concluded by the teacher, "the types of handicraft," with the topic being discussed, "their cost." The teacher did not follow his reasoning. It is only toward the end of the exchange that she seems to gain control again.

In Extract 2, this time in a meeting (see also Cavalcanti and Maher 1993), instead of ignoring the new topic being introduced (i.e., organization), the teacher educators only mention it briefly and do not follow it up. The exchange was part of a conversation about a previous lesson when the teacher educator in charge had set the young Guarani men the task of observing children in the community while they were playing:

Extract 2

R2: *vocês ahn / tiveram tempo de observar as crianças [na aldeia] / como elas brincam / do que elas gostam/*

R2: you um / you've had some time to observe the children [in the community] / how they play/ what they like

G1: *uhn, uhn/*

G1: aha

R2: *ontem a gente falou que os professores às vezes não prestam atenção/ não/*

R2: yesterday we talked about the fact that teachers usually do not pay attention/ do not

G1: *lembram/*

G1: remember?

R2: *quando a gente pára a gente diz pra gente/ é assim mesmo/ nunca tinha prestado atenção/ uma das coisas que a gente tem que aprender/ ah/*

R2: when we stop we say to ourselves: "Is that the way it is"? I had never paid attention to it . one of the things we have to learn, yeah?

G1: *sobre a organização/*

G1: about organization?

R2: *esta ... sobre a organização/ vamos falar um pouco sobre o mundo das crianças/ como é que a criança/ como é que a criança Guarani brinca/ não estou perguntando por curiosidade mas porque este conhecimento vai ser importante na sala de aula/*

R2: This ...about organization? . let's talk a little about the children's world . how is it that the child ...how do Guarani children play? I ask this, not out of curiosity, but because this knowledge will be important [for you] in the classroom.

What was behind these anxieties and frustrations? It appears that they could be traced to a feeling of uneasiness regarding "losing control" over the main strings. As there was this overlap of roles as researchers and teacher educators, the feeling may have been stronger. It is not usual for researchers to simultaneously get involved with teaching and with doing research. Researchers are usually in the more comfortable position of observing a classroom at a distance. They are able to take a detached look at classroom practices, while the teacher in charge has the responsibility of ensuring that the show goes on. The researcher is thus protected, whereas the teacher gets the spotlight. The uneasiness felt by the researchers in our team stemmed from being both researcher *and* researched at the same time. This was also a response to the double threat to knowledge-based power. There were observable cultural differences that we could describe and explain. Since we were playing this double role, we seemed to be operating with the implicit assumption that our culture should speak louder. In other words, we were reacting in an ethnocentric way to the experience of carrying out the action research project. These cultural reflexes may have been the source of the tensions that sometimes emerged after a day of fieldwork. They revealed the contradictions in which we sometimes caught ourselves: We wanted one thing and sometimes did another in seeking a culturally responsive mode of teaching. We complained about their attitudes but at the same time found excuses to justify them, and these excuses were centered on cultural differences. This only became clear to us in the discussions we had in our research meetings.

Again, it is important to stress that there was no tension among us researchers. In our conversations, we usually expressed mild optimism (or perhaps controlled disappointment), but an ambivalence was ever present. There was also no apparent tension between us as teacher educators and the indigenous teachers. Misunderstandings and frustrations were, however, recorded again and again in my diary. These frustrations were also a perennial theme for discussion and reflection in our research meetings back at the university. We acknowledged this as ethnocentrism to be worked on. Back in the field, there was no guarantee that what we had acknowledged could automatically be overcome.

CONFLICTING AGENDAS AND A REFOCUSING OF THE PROJECT

There was, however, a deeper problem, which we did not identify right away: The members of this Guarani community were not interested in teacher education per se but in what this type of education might represent in terms of the development of their young leaders. These young people would at some point have to speak on behalf of the community when dealing with simple red-tape matters or with more complex issues. These problems would have to be dealt with in the world beyond the community. They wanted to develop communicative resources within the community to deal with institutional encounters of various sorts.

The initial agreement that we made with them was to run a teacher education course. When we realized that they were not particularly interested in talking about basic pedagogic issues, the idea that the indigenous teachers might have another agenda began to materialize. This gradual process of realization is quite well illustrated in an exchange recorded in my diary between R1 and R2 (Extract 3). The conversation took place when we first guessed that the Guarani speakers were not interested in teacher education:

Extract 3

R1: *não gosto de me sentir 'usada'/*

R1: I don't like to feel 'used.'

R2: *mas eles devem ter se sentido assim tantas vezes que aprenderam a 'usar'o branco/ é a vez deles agora/ na verdade/ eu não me sinto usada/ por que não consideramos isto de um outro ponto de vista/*

R2: They [Guarani people] must have felt this way so many times that they have learned to 'use' white people. It's their turn now. Actually, I don't feel I am being used. Can't we look at this from another point of view?

Looking back we can now see that the articulation of this hidden agenda was an integral part of the resistance and cultural maintenance strategies deployed by the Guarani educators. We had initially missed a number of clues in the early stages of the development of the project. The first clue came when we expressed interest in doing an action research project in the context of the course. They seized upon this opportunity and appeared to express interest.

It certainly took us sometime to realize what was going on. Our first insight came during a conversation concerning the Guarani educators' tendency to avoid discussion about what underpinned the classroom activities we had proposed for them. This conversation took place after one of the teaching/learning sessions. One of them said: *A gente quer falar como vocês.* (We want to learn to speak like you [i.e., to speak standard Portuguese]). *A gente não quer falar sobre as crianças.* (We don't want to talk about children [about the way they learn to read and write]). They tended to avoid discussions about pedagogic principles, although as teacher educators we kept stressing that the points raised in these discussions should be of interest to them as teachers-to-be. However, on this occasion, as the other young Guarani men agreed to what had been said, at last we seemed to have a clear indication of what their focus of attention and interest was: They wanted to invest in their own education as potential leaders. However, when we brought this back to discuss in a meeting with them, the young Guarani men were evasive. They said they might become teachers one day and cut the discussion short. Then we decided we should focus on developing their proficiency in standard Portuguese and leave aside the teacher education project. Looking back it is now clear that the community had invested in their education (by freeing them from other commitments). One or two of them might end up being teachers, but this role would be seen as secondary to the role played by leaders who could establish links with the dominant society.

Action research is supposed to be a dynamic process, and at this point, it was clear that there was a need for change in the focus of the project. Instead of looking at the processes involved in the joint construction of teacher education by teacher educators and indigenous teachers, we decided to redirect the focus and started looking more closely at the "cross-cultural" misunderstandings and interpret these with reference to the wider power relations that we were caught up in.

CONCLUDING REMARKS

This study has direct implications for indigenous teacher education in Brazil, since this inevitably involves cross-cultural interaction between non-indigenous teacher educators and indigenous teachers. The first implication is that reflexivity is an essential element of this kind of work. The second implication is that it is important to take account of what happens outside of the classroom when teaching/learning events are over. In this study, the frustrations that emerged in the conversations between researchers and the issues that came out in meetings between us and the Guarani participants outside the class threw light on the whole context under investigation and eventually redirected the focus of our research.

There are also clear implications for research methodology. To carry out an action research project, one has to look at oneself as both researcher and researched. As researchers, we are not usually very open to the opinions of the researched when the researched is the *other*. When we begin to scrutinize our own practices, we are likely to detect contradictions between what we say and what we do, and these are quite illuminating. Research can be a tool for exploring what it means to listen to the *other*. In my view, researchers should look at themselves as researched at least once in a lifetime. Because of this experience of being both researcher and researched, I find I am now more acutely aware of the way researchers talk about the researched when reporting results and how they position the researched in the written texts they produce.

TRANSCRIPTION CONVENTIONS

Portuguese is written in *italics* throughout.

English translations are in normal typeface.

Additional notes are included in square brackets.

/   marks pauses.

R   Researcher

G   Guarani educator

NOTES

1. I would like to acknowledge funding from FAPESP (the São Paulo State Foundation for Research Support/Brazil) for the project entitled *Interacão e Aprendizagem de Língua* (Interaction and Language Learning).

2. Out of 140,000,000 inhabitants, there are about 230,000 indigenous people in Brazil. Although this figure represents only 0.17% of the country's population, one should take into account that this small figure represents as many as 170 indigenous languages and 220 ethnic groups. These languages are usually classified into five main families, five small families, and some isolated languages. The contemporary situation is dramatically different from that in the period before the colonization of Brazil. It is estimated that in the 1500s, there was a much larger indigenous

population in Brazil, in the region of 5,000,000 people. It should be added, however, that the indigenous population is nowadays showing some sign of growth.

> [The indigenous peoples have] specific cultural traditions and went through different historical processes. Each of these peoples is unique with its own identity based on its own language, on the land inhabited, on beliefs, habits, history and social organization. At the same time, the indigenous groups share a set of basic elements which are common to all of them and which differentiate them from the non-indigenous society. Thus the indigenous peoples have their own forms of land occupation and exploitation: of community life; their own forms of teaching and learning based upon the transmission of collective and individual oral knowledge." (*Ministério da Educação e do Desporto* 1994, 10)

Besides the indigenous population, the country has a large number of immigrant communities mainly in the south and southeastern regions. However, throughout the years, the Brazilian government has helped to cultivate the myth of monolingualism, promoting (standard) Portuguese as the only language spoken in this country of continental dimensions (8 million km^2). The rural and the urbanized rural dialects of the standard language (cf. Bortoni-Ricardo 1984) are seen as "low-status" Portuguese. Then, besides erasing the local varieties of Portuguese and the people who speak it, the country has erased the various indigenous languages and the various national languages of the immigrant communities and their speakers.

REFERENCES

Bortoni-Ricardo, S. B. (1984). Problemas de comunicação interdialetal. *Revista Tempo Brasileiro, 78/79*, 9–32.

Cavalcanti, M. C. (1991). Interação Guarani/não Guarani: etnocentrismo naturalizado na questão do silêncio inter-turnos. *Trabalhos em Lingüística Aplicada, 18*, 101–110.

Cavalcanti, M. C., and Maher, T. M. (1993). Interação transcultural na formação do professor índio. In L. Seki (Ed.), *Lingüística Indígena e a Educação na América Latina* (pp. 217–230). Campinas, SP: Editora da UNICAMP.

Cohen, L., and Manion, L. (1980). *Research Methods in Education*. London: Croom Helm.

Erickson, F. (1987). Transformation and school success: The politics and culture of educational achievement. *Anthropology and Education Quarterly, 23(4)*, 11–24.

Gomes, M. P. (1988). *Os Indios e o Brasil*. Petrópolis, RJ: Vozes.

Kahn, M. (1994). Educação indígena versus educação para índios. *Em Aberto, 63*, 137–144.

Meliá, B. (1979). *Educação Indígena e Alfabetização*. São Paulo: Edições Loyola.

Mendes, J. R. (1994). *Descompassos na interação professor-aluno na aula de matemática em contexto indígena*. MSc. Dissertation, State University of Campinas/Brazil.

Ministério da Educação e do Desporto (1994). *Diretrizes para a política nacional de educação escolar indígena*. Brasília, DF: Ministério da Educação e do Desporto.

Orlandi, E. P. (1990). *Terra à Vista—Discurso do Confronto: Velho e Novo Mundo*. São Paulo: Cortez e Campinas: Editora da UNICAMP.

Ribeiro, D. (1970). *Os Indios e a Civilização*. São Paulo: Civilização Brasileira.

Schaden, E. (1962). *Aspectos Fundamentais da Cultura Guarani*. São Paulo: Divisão Européia do Livro.

Silva, M. F. (1983). Educação e linguagem segundo os Guarani-Mbyá. *Cadernos de Estudos Lingüísticos*. Campinas, SP: Setor de Publicações/IEL.

Silva, M. F. (1994). A conquista da escola: educação escolar e movimento dos professores indígenas no Brasil. *Em Aberto, 63*, 38–53.

15

Telling What Is Real: Competing Views in Assessing ESL Development in Australia[1]

Helen Moore

> The power of suggestion which is exerted through things and persons and which, instead of telling the child what he must do, tells him what he is, and thus leads him to become durably what he has to be, is the condition for the effectiveness of all kinds of symbolic power that will subsequently be able to operate on a habitus predisposed to respond to them. (Bourdieu 1991, 52)

INTRODUCTION: THE GLOBAL CONTEXT OF EDUCATIONAL ASSESSMENT

In the past 20 years or so, a profound dis-ease with "what people are" has escalated in the discourses of the state, at least in the industrialized world. This dis-ease is a symptom of the complexities faced by modern governments. These complexities include large-scale immigration; issues of race, ethnicity, and language; ongoing mass unemployment; changes in technology and ways of working; and the destabilizing effects of the global economy on trade, debt, national sovereignty, and the ability to make policy.

One manifestation of this dis-ease has been the call for reform in education, a key site in which the individual discovers what, as Bourdieu (1991) says, he or she is and has to be. Hargreaves (1989) using Habermas (1976) describes the postwar "capital accumulation crisis" as reverberating throughout the different parts of the state, "not least within education policy, which experiences its own particular crises."

> These take the form of a succession of critical points where a significant gap is perceived between educational policy and practice on the one hand and society's needs on the other; where existing solutions are seen to be exhausted or have failed, or where new needs have emerged. It is under such conditions that support grows for new styles of state management, different patterns of initiatives; for a new overall strategy which promises to produce a closer match between schooling and society's needs. (p. 103)

The call for new educational strategies in times of uncertainty and change is itself not new. For example, at the height of the Cold War, the Sputnik launch was followed in the United States by interventions in schooling (Apple 1986; Harp 1993). Since the late 1970s, continuing economic instability has, as Apple (1993) says, been exported into education (p. 5). Schools are accused of producing graduates who are not what they need to be to make economies competitive in global markets and in preparation for the twenty-first century. These accusations reflect increasingly instrumentalist and vocationalist goals attributed to schooling.

The current discourses of crisis emphasize the need for "excellence" and improved standards (Apple 1986; Smith and Smith 1990; Lingard, Knight, and Porter 1993). This emphasis carries with it claims that the time has come to turn from the needs of special groups, such as "the disadvantaged," to the needs of all (Block, Cloward, Ehrenreich, and Fox Piven 1987; see also Broadfoot 1986b, 207; Apple 1993, 4; Silver 1990). It reflects the preoccupations of a different alliance from that which previously directed attention to the aspirations of the poor or minority groups (Apple 1993, 4). This new alliance—commonly referred to as the New Right—has initiated a major shift in public policy-making away from creating a "welfare state" and toward instituting "the competitive state" (Cerny 1990, as cited in Knight, Lingard, and Porter 1993).

However, it is important to recognize that "there is no monolithic New Right" (Knight et al. 1993, 9; see also Ball 1990; Dale and Ozga 1993). Rather, New Right politics in different contexts have varied in their focus and contradictions. In Britain and the United States, although the so-called conservative side of politics orchestrated educational re-structuring (for example, the 1988 Education Reform Act in Britain and the 1991 Bush administration's America 2000 national education legislation), the agenda has been carried forward by both conservative and supposedly more progressive political forces. In Australia—the context to be examined in this chapter—educational reform was initiated and implemented by a Labor government whose view of "social justice" generated particular twists in contesting discourses and practices that I shall later describe.

Nevertheless, despite the variations in different national contexts, the effects have been remarkably similar. A striking commonality has been an increased emphasis on assessment. As the bridge between education and the outside public domain, assessment is an obvious focus for political and public attention. Assessment is "one of the most direct links between schooling and society (particularly the labor market)" (Lingard 1990, 171). "Assessment-led" reform has been commonly seen as the solution to the problem of matching schooling to the supposed needs of society (Hargreaves 1989, 99; see also Broadfoot 1996). This is because assessment practices operationalize and formalize what, in Bourdieu's (1991) terms, the child *must do* for his or her schooling to be acknowledged by others. They constitute school experience in explicit terms, regulate it, and translate it into a form that can be communicated to the rest of the school and to parents, employers, and outside educational and credentialing institutions. Because of this power, assessment practices necessarily reflect and affect curriculum, school organization and routines, and what students and teachers do in and beyond the classroom.

In this chapter, I discuss developments during the early 1990s in school assessment practices with particular reference to speakers of English as a second language (henceforth ESL) in immigrant settings in Australia. Unless otherwise indicated, "assessment" is a cover term that includes testing, examinations, and alternatives to these. Linguistic and cultural diversity is now a feature of many industrialized countries and is one of the complexities referred to in my opening paragraph. However, to my knowledge, the Australian school system is the only one, within the current reforms, to have developed tools specifically for assessing ESL development.

What is particularly interesting is that several ESL assessment tools were produced. The differences between them show how options exist in the construction of what learners must do and have to be. My central purpose in this chapter is to argue that these options are significant, in this case for those using English as a second or other language. I will argue that, although Bourdieu's (1991) analysis provides useful cautions, a preoccupation with the inevitable processes of symbolic domination diverts attention from how these processes embody differences that can crucially affect access to social and material benefits by speakers of nondominant languages.

A second aim in this chapter is to explore some of the connections between the political/policy and the curriculum/assessment sites in which the "power of suggestion" operates. My intention here is not to separate policy and pedagogy as "macro/micro" or "policy/implementation" dichotomies. Rather, in discussing how these assessment tools came into being, I hope to illustrate what Nespor (1997) calls "flows rather than states, focusing on networks and the layered connections that knot them together" (p. xiv).

The remainder of this chapter is organized into three major sections. First, I describe the approaches to assessment that gained prominence in the educational reforms of the late 1980s and 1990s and the claims made for them. I argue that these approaches put powerful processes in place that Bourdieu's (1991) perspective allows us to scrutinize. I then consider the specific political and policy context for two examples of ESL assessment developed in Australia that utilize these new approaches. Finally, I attempt to show how differences between these examples have significant implications for what, to adapt Bourdieu's (1991) words, speakers of languages other than English durably might be.

DEVELOPMENTS IN ASSESSMENT

Alternatives to Standardized Tests

In the wake of calls for improved educational standards, many educators expressed fears that testing and examinations would increase. A growing number argued the merits of alternatives in assessing students and subsequently worked to put these alternatives in place (for example, Darling-Hammond 1994; Gipps 1994; Wolf, Bixby, Glenn, and Gardiner 1991).

Typical of their arguments is Wolf and associates' (1991) strategic alignment of their proposals with the America 2000 reforms:

> There is growing, if far from universal, impatience with student assessment that addresses chiefly facts and basic skills, leaving thoughtfulness, imagination, and pursuit untapped. . . . At present we have a national curriculum—a course of study that yields low-level basic skills for a large and diverse population of students (Smith, 1990). But we simply cannot afford schools that train only a very few students in more than decoding level reading, calculation arithmetic, or the kind of writing required for filling out employment forms. (pp. 31, 33)

These authors argued that the "culture of testing" captures only these low-level skills. It also supports a "will-o'-the-wisp chase for all students and schools to clamber above the normal" and "the hegemony of normal curve and two-dimensional statistics" (p. 55). The authors advocated a new "culture of assessment" that documents actual student performance and accomplishment, using "longitudinal and criterion-referenced measures of more than age and level" (p. 55).[2]

> Key to this change is a move from norm-referenced to criterion-referenced evaluations of student learning in which what students can and cannot do is clearly stated. These descriptions have to be anchored at one end in the capacities most children bring to school and at the other end in the capacities all high school students should possess. The point of these developmental sequences is that a student's *real, rather than relative, skills* can be assessed both for the adequacy and the fullness of his or her learning. (p. 52, italics added)

The enthusiasm of Wolf and associates (1991) for alternatives to testing and examinations has been widely endorsed by educators, including ESL professionals. For example, Fred Genesee (1994), the 1994 president of Teaching English to Speakers of Other Languages (TESOL), recommended to members that "portfolios, interactive diaries, student conferences, and anecdotal classroom observations" should complement and reduce the role of standardized tests because they give more and better information and can be intertwined with teaching (p. 3). Teacher-student interaction and collaboration in assessment can "encourage student ownership of assessment and responsibility and enthusiasm for learning," thus making students "active agents of assessment, not merely passive objects" (p. 3).

There is now widespread and varied use of such techniques as portfolios, learner self-assessment, longitudinal classroom-based recordkeeping (also known as profiling), and criterion-referenced (curriculum-embedded) performance-based assessment. Wolf and associates (1991) documented examples that "form the basis of national assessments in countries as large and diverse as New Zealand and Great Britain and states as diverse as California and Connecticut (Baron 1990; California Assessment Program 1990a, 1990b)." Leaving aside the somewhat dubious claim for diversity, to this list can be added various countries in Europe, for example, Sweden and France (Masters 1990; Broadfoot 1984, 1996) and Australia, as this chapter will elaborate.

In their concluding remarks, Wolf and associates (1991) cautioned against assuming that these alternatives do not also contain problems. "Whereas there is considerable criticism of the approaches taken by standardized tests, as yet we have no such critical tradition for new modes of assessment. And we cannot be without one" (p. 60).

This "critical tradition" is now firmly in evidence, and I will draw upon it in the next section. My interest is not directly in implementational or technical issues. Rather I wish to explore how these alternative forms of assessment relate to the wider policy context described in my introduction. The coincidence of their widespread use with the push for "standards" suggests that, far from there being antagonism between the two as educators may have feared, each may be part of the same phenomenon, a possibility I will now explore.

A Struggle, But What's the Game?

While advocates of nontraditional forms of assessment may see themselves as engaged in a struggle that sets educational concerns against New Right agendas, they would do well to note Bourdieu's (1991) statement:

> It is one of the generic properties of fields that the struggle for specific stakes masks the objective collusion concerning the principles underlying the game. More precisely, the struggle tends constantly to produce and reproduce the game and its stakes by reproducing, primarily in those who are directly involved, but not in them alone, the practical commitment to the value of the game and its stakes which defines the recognition of legitimacy. (p. 58)

Broadfoot's (1996) rich, landmark analysis offers considerable insight into the "game" of which *any* educational assessment is part. She proposes that assessment plays three key "mediating" roles between education and society (p. 61).

First, assessment attests an individual's competence in society:

> Whether education consists simply of passing on of the unified body of skills necessary for survival, or is transmitted through the highly bureaucratized, elaborate and costly systems which complex industrialized societies have typically evolved to provide for the wide range of specialist skills they require, some kind of assessment of competence will be necessary, not least because the willingness of individuals to submit to such evaluation reflects and reinforces their commitment to joining that particular society. (pp. 26–27)

Second, assessment is typically associated with the certification that selects people into higher levels of education and employment. It thereby regulates competition between individuals for positions in society that are not open to all. Those regarded as fair and independent experts carry out this certification, a process that contrasts with the allocation of positions on the basis of birth, wealth, land ownership, power, patronage, or chance. Broadfoot (1991) describes this certification process as "the epitome of the apparently meritocratic basis of contemporary society, since in theory it allows free competition based on academic ability and industry and thus is regarded as the fairest basis for the allocation of opportunities for high status or remunerative careers" (p. 32).

Third, assessment is a means of controlling both individuals and systems. It motivates individuals to participate in the socialization processes of formal education, explaining and legitimating their successes and failures in terms of their personal ability and effort (pp. 33–37). Assessment is also used to monitor the performance of educational institutions and systems.

In regard to the second function of educational assessment, Broadfoot (1996) points out that, despite considerable evidence that the certification and selection process is not neutral, "there is still no obvious alternative which seems likely to be more fair" (p. 33). This point can be extended. It is difficult to imagine complex societies functioning in recognizably more just or efficient ways if any of assessment's three roles were abolished or reallocated to some other social mechanism. In this sense, no one can avoid or change the assessment "game" and its stakes. We all rely on myriad forms of attested competence in others. As experts centrally engaged in certification and legitimation processes, educators have a particular practical commitment to this game. Denying or disguising this reality is a romantic illusion that carries the twin dangers of subverting assessment's socially desirable effects and increasing its unpalatable ones. Educators need to recognize the roles of assessment and, on this basis, monitor its effects and what indeed is at stake, as the game is produced and reproduced at different historical points and in different ways. This understanding can provide a basis for reflexive action in attempting to control how these roles are played out and limiting their undesirable effects.

Broadfoot (1996) explains the "changing assessment culture" in terms of political, economic, and social changes in industrialized and postindustrialized societies (pp. 40–65). Fundamental to the sense of crisis I described earlier is what she describes as a widespread loss of the "surprisingly uniform belief in the power of education to liberate the individual while at the same time helping to provide a nation of committed and skilled workers, from among whose number selected individuals could be rationally chosen for positions of power and privilege" (p. 61). Her summary of the "complex concatenation of factors" that have generated this sense of crisis includes the complexities outlined in my opening paragraph (p. 61). These complexities have imposed new requirements on assessment's three roles of attesting individual competence, regulating competition and controlling individuals and systems, and have created new tensions and contradictions in these roles.

For example, rapid technological change necessitates an adaptable, more highly skilled work force and relegates those without such skills to the margins (Broadfoot 1996, 44). Building this work force has meant deferring crucial selection and competition to later in the educational process. But the new work culture has also intensified competition for employment. This competition escalates demands for higher levels and types of certification and also for more detailed judgments about individuals, including their personal qualities, long-term performance, and the nature and quality of their specific educational experiences (pp. 42–57).

Similarly, the deferment of selection and the demand for details strengthens the teacher's role as both mentor and assessor (Broadfoot 1996, 63). Teachers thus have greater scope for "individualized assessment dialogue" with their students, "which increasingly characterizes active learning strategies" and more democratic schooling processes (p. 63). However, Broadfoot (1996) believes it is but "a short step" from assessment as a "pedagogic strategy" to its use as a means of individual and system control (p. 233; see also Auerbach 1986; Tollefson 1986; Smith and Smith 1990). Paradoxically, alternative forms of assessments seen as promoting greater autonomy for educators and more democratic, liberatory approaches to education also offer solutions to the "unforeseen problems of system control" that politicians and others have accused this autonomy of creating (Broadfoot 1996, 58). The wider scope of assessment helps resolve the tensions between "the economically-inspired demands to do more for less and the simultaneous demand for tighter control," since it allows educational goals to expand but makes them a school and teacher responsibility (Lingard 1990, 180). The discourse of standards and the tools of assessment promise state authorities "steering capacity" over schools, while seeming to reduce the need for the expensive personalized hierarchical controls that have governed smaller and less complex education systems (Pusey 1982, 1983, cited in Lingard 1990, 180; Broadfoot 1996, 236; Jones and Moore 1993; Moore 1996a).

I am not proposing that the search for system control is itself undesirable; an education system out of control is in few people's interests. Rather, problems lie in the processes by which steering capacity is currently being achieved and the content it is imposing. According to Broadfoot (1996), these processes and content stem from bureaucratic modes of organization and positivist science that are colonizing the "non-bureaucratic, potentially contradictory languages of professionalism and democratic participation" and extending the "concept of scientific quantitative evaluation into the structuring of the education system itself" (pp. 239–40):

> From the evaluation of systemic performance to the evaluation of individual schools, teachers and pupils there is a common pressure on both producers (teachers and pupils) and consumers (parents and employers) to assume that value can be quantified and expressed in a variety of "performance indicators." (OECD 1992, 240)

This pressure either makes "the relative values of personal choice, culture or belief" seem trivial and marginal when set against "the impersonal, objective canons of scientific logic," or it allows the boundaries between the two to collapse:

> Those judgments which lie at the heart of any assessment procedure are transformed from being evaluations of an individual's qualities or achievements made against a more or less personal, value-laden set of chosen criteria into evaluations in which the criteria are apparently the absolute diktats of scientific efficiency. (p. 22)

This colonization process has two interrelated dimensions germane to my account of how ESL assessment tools were developed in Australia. First, as Lingard (1990) theorizes, "rationalizing science" destroys a crucial basis of classroom practice "by threatening 'natural language' and 'experience,' its two essential ingredients" (p. 181; see also Jones and Moore 1993, 388):

> As soon as the constructed and technical languages are institutionalized and achieve formal legitimacy in the administrative structure, they begin to displace practice by blocking off the very thing that gives it breath, substance and stability, namely, unconstrained reference in ordinary speech to lived experience. (Pusey 1981, 99, cited in Lingard 1990, 181).

Second, the covert nature of the process disempowers both teachers and learners, since it is difficult to contest and, at a deeper level, its content goes unrecognized:

> As assessment is increasingly oriented to explicit norms of performance, to centrally, or perhaps regionally, generated criteria of the individual assessor, the social power which the imposition of those norms represents becomes increasingly invisible, hidden in the guise of a bland neutral technology in just the same way that "corporate planning" disguises value judgments as scientific, rational, objective solutions to problems. (Broadfoot 1996, 233)

What teachers have indubitably recognized is that their attention has been diverted from teaching and their workloads have increased, both serious problems (Hargreaves 1989, 139; Nuttall and Stobart 1994). More subtle but profoundly disempowering effects lie in what Broadfoot (1996) describes as the "normative re-educative strategies" used to bring educational practice within the steering control of state authorities (p. 38). A common strategy is the claim that the performance descriptors in assessment frameworks have their basis in transparently obvious learning outcomes documented in consensual processes between interested parties (Jones and Moore 1993, 388). As my account will indicate, the processes that determine these descriptors may be far from consensual, as managerial interests subvert and outweigh educational ones. Moreover, the assumption that skills and outcomes are "transparent" or real, "out there," and simply waiting to be described, preempts and overrules debate and the disciplinary traditions of knowledge and "critical scholarship" in which educators have been socialized and on which their expertise rests (Jones and Moore 1993, 395). Because scrutiny challenges realities in which people have strong intellectual and emotional investments, conflict (and attempts to suppress it) may be even more vicious, damaging, and disempowering than anything educators have previously experienced in critiquing tests and examinations. This has certainly been the experience in the Australian ESL context.

Bourdieu's (1991) argument, cited in my introduction, is that "the power of suggestion" is a more effective condition for symbolic domination than "telling the child what he must do." In Broadfoot's (1996) words, "the real source of power" lies in "the normative assumptions" on which educators' interactions are based, "albeit unremarked and unopposed" (p. 225). These assumptions "carry the power to determine selectively the way in which issues are discussed and solutions proposed" (p. 225). Those who uncritically argue for broadening the scope of assessment obscure the stakes that relate to the content and process in *any* assessment, namely, the information it produces and suppresses, how this information is generated and suppressed, its purposes and effects, and the exercise of power that inevitably resides in it.

Precisely to the extent that any assessment overcomes the problems of narrowness embodied in exams or standardized tests, it also constructs the diversity it incorporates. Alternative approaches to assessment document what is real about learning no more or less than do standardized tests. Both produce selected views of students and their achievements and contain norms by which to judge students. What students know and do (or don't know and don't do) is not transparently available for description. Rather, what students know and do and how they are judged is constructed by particular assumptions, goals, and processes. The dangerous illusion that alternative forms of assessment can faithfully reflect what is real about learners makes this assessment equally if not more disempowering for students than tests/exams could ever be. As I will demonstrate, very different realities can be created. Part of the struggle is to deconstruct what they are.

In this struggle, the dividing lines are not straightforward. Lingard (1990), using Pusey (1983) and Habermas (1976), argues that development of the new controls on schooling relies heavily on "the expertise of social scientists," including educational experts (p. 180). Positivistic methodologies, "whose constitutive interest is control," are commonly employed to develop criterion-referenced tools for use in classrooms, such as profiles, comment banks, and performance indicators. Their research and development methodologies are not antagonistic to bureaucratic notions of control, but rather feed state authorities' expectations "that even the fine grain of educational practice can and should be more closely structured" (Pusey 1983, 405, cited in Lingard 1990, 181).

Lingard's analysis proposes a divide, not between educators and state authorities, but between positivistic methodologies and what was cited earlier as "unconstrained reference in ordinary speech to lived experience" (Pusey 1981, 99). But the crucial issues of content and process I have just outlined are exactly those expressed through the positivist, technical notions of validity, reliability, and washback, on which assessment experts have worked extensively, albeit often ignoring the wider, value-laden meanings of these terms. Some members of the language-testing profession have moved to address these wider issues (Davies 1997; Hamp-Lyons 1997; McNamara 1997a, 1997b; Norton 1997; Shohamy 1994). As the technical literature has long recognized, the information yielded by any assessment approach is the result of how it *constructs* the capacities children bring to school and what they then achieve. To dismiss either the narrow or broader relevance of these concepts and to turn our backs on what is known about these things in the technical literature is to naturalize assessment and thereby to let loose the worst effects of the romantic illusion I described earlier.

In fact, it is largely the technical experts in assessment who are themselves developing the "critical tradition" for which Wolf and associates (1991) called. A sizable literature, including that in language education, exists on what is often described as the "promise" and the "challenges" in the diverse alternatives to standardized tests and examinations (for example, Boycoff Baron and Palmer Wolf 1996; Brindley 1995; Broadfoot 1986a; Birenbaum and Dochy 1996; Darling-Hammond and Ancess 1996; Derewianka 1997; Gipps 1994; Hamayan 1995; Kane and Mitchell 1996; Linn and Baker 1996; Nuttall 1986; Shavelson, Baxter, and Pine 1992; Torrance 1994). Generally, the critiques do not contest that these alternatives have potential—and now a proven track record—in increasing the scope of assessment and curriculum to include valued knowledge and skills and more of what students can do and that they are more interactive and involving of students and teachers. Further, the problems identified in this critical tradition are not used to argue for a return to the culture of testing, but rather are identified as problems on which assessment experts are variously working to make more desirable alternatives viable and credible (e.g., Griffin 1997; Lynch and Davidson 1994).

Brindley (1998) summarizes the concerns raised in this literature as follows: lack of evidence for construct and content validity; poor consistency in rater judgments; limited generalizability across tasks; problems in ensuring comparability between different practitioners in different contexts; administrative complexity and high costs; and the difficulty of setting cutoff points in deciding achievement levels (p. 53). His terminology reflects the technical concerns of those whose expertise was gained within the culture of testing, but he raises serious issues in regard to the fairness of alternative assessments, especially in high-stakes assessment contexts, for example, university entry and certification for employment (Brindley 1998; Davies 1995; McNamara 1997a, 1997b).

At the classroom level, similar issues have surfaced. Broadfoot (1986b) argues that the combination of traditional curriculum and examinations with classroom-based assessment can actually "reinforce a divisive and inegalitarian educational experience" (p. 209). Records of achievement, institutionalized on a large scale, rely on "the delicate balance of teacher-pupil dialogue—so alien to the essentially authoritarian relationship normally prevailing between the two—will become weighted in terms of the teacher's values" (p. 214). Added to examination results, these records can further disadvantage students whose class and/or cultures do not accord with teacher values and traditional schooling, making "the individual powerless to resist the end product of a continuous and benign surveillance" (p. 214; see also Derewianka 1997, 49–51).

Similarly, Hargreaves (1989) warns against the collapse between summative and formative assessment. He points out that records of achievement for employment purposes document what students do quite differently from those used to gain a developmental perspective and differently again from the student's own perspective (see also Broadfoot 1996, 193). Grid profiles and comment banks, devised to provide reports with some structure and commonality and to solve the problem of teacher time, reduce these diverse perspectives and fit students to descriptions, rather than the other way round. Students who do not conform to the norms described in these profiles disappear from view or are in danger of being seen as aberrant (McGaw 1997, cited in Derewianka 1997, 47). Continuous assessment may also increase the alienation of nonachieving students and, as powerfully as tests if not more so, serve as a means of adjusting students' expectations to their "diminishing prospects" in the competition for further education and fulfilling employment (Hargreaves 1989, 113).

In more deeply penetrating classroom life, alternative approaches to assessment can powerfully shape both students and teachers on a day-to-day basis. As Broadfoot (1996) says, "The responsibility to give an account or to be accountable acts in itself as an important force of control" (p. 39). The new approaches can radically realize Foucault's (1977) notion of panopticism, whereby a person, knowing that he or she is under surveillance but not knowing exactly when, disciplines himself or herself constantly as he or she believes is required (Hargreaves 1989, 136–137). The penetration of assessment into interactions between teacher and student, even into "the child's personal and emotional being," can become "an indefinite discipline; an interrogation without end . . . the constitution of a file that was never closed" (Foucault 1977, 227, cited in Hargreaves 1989, 137). Assessment without boundaries, intent on recording what is real about students and their development, can colonize the minute-by-minute life of the classroom in ways that, in practice, is impossible for standardized tests and exams, no matter how much they dominate the curriculum. Its power is intensified by collaboration processes aiming to make students, as Genesee (1994a) says, "active agents of assessment" (p. 3).

The professed aim of broadening the scope of curriculum through more wide-ranging assessments (known technically as "washback," Wall 1997) is also not assured. Although the new approaches can extend teachers' understandings of teaching and their students, they also report that the constraining pressures on curriculum associated with testing remain and are often intensified (Auerbach 1986; Bamforth and Grieve 1996).

A key stake in current struggles over assessment is maintaining boundaries between the everyday life of the classroom, on the one hand, and, on the other, assessment with its technical requirements for validity and fairness and its inevitable links to system control. The reforms of the 1990s have made it almost impossible for policymakers, educators, students, and their parents to even understand the difference between *learning* and what one must do for one's *learning to be recognized*, that is, what it means to create and maintain productive spaces for teaching and learning that are not assessment driven. Most learners require support and a genuine assurance of judgments that do not have ongoing consequences, as well as confidence in their teachers' expertise in their field and in teaching it. Both learners and teachers must feel free to experiment and to attempt to make what was described earlier as "unconstrained reference in ordinary speech to lived experience" (Pusey 1981, 99). The colonization of this space by assessment *by definition* extinguishes these possibilities.

This discussion suggests that the struggle against the culture of testing may, as Bourdieu (1991) says, mask some of the important principles underlying the game of educational assessment. Those who attack statistics or positivistic science may relieve their frustrations at its practitioners' tendency to tunnel vision. But these attacks ignore the contribution of this field to lessening unfairness and arbitrariness in teacher judgments and large-scale/high-stakes assessments. This expertise is indispensable to the search for new ways to attest valued aspects of learners' knowledge and skills. Similarly, those who propose to eradicate the narrowing effects of tests and examinations by giving greater scope to alternative assessments may find that these changes aggravate different forms of narrowness and injustice. A more fundamental task may be monitoring and constraining the effects of all forms of assessment.

Bourdieu (1991) alerts us to the need to understand the game, but his preoccupation with it as an inevitable process of domination generates its own problematic. Having understood this process, we seem to be left with a choice of either revolution or pessimism with its own forms of quietism. Neither of these, on Bourdieu's analysis, will actually eliminate the game of domination in which assessment plays a key role. An alternative is, on the basis of understanding this inevitability, to ask what different assessments can and do construct. What precisely is and could be made real (or denied reality) by assessments? Answers to this question might offer some basis for choice and improvement.

In the following discussion of two Australian ESL assessment frameworks, I pursue this question. I first examine how state policies, procedures, and ideologies created realities in which these frameworks had roles to play. In the final section, I explore the realities expressed in the frameworks themselves.

ASSERTING NATIONAL LEADERSHIP IN AUSTRALIAN EDUCATION

A Political Struggle: The Laborist Displacement of a Pluralist Vision

In the previous section I argued that a focus on educational standards appears to offer state authorities a means of system control that meets contemporary demands to do more for less. In Australia from 1987 onwards, system control through state-mandated standards in school and post-school education was vigorously pursued by the Hawke-Keating federal Labor government (1983–1996). The person who in 1987 became education minister (Dawkins) and a colleague trade unionist (Costello) expressed Labor's aspirations as follows:

> [T]hese two great themes, the need to take control of our own economic destiny and the need to give expression to our vision of a just and equal society provide the settings in which the education policies of the federal Labor government have been conceived. By their very nature, these objectives require of the Labor government that it provides new forms of national leadership in education. This is a task which goes beyond the provision of grants of money to schools, school authorities and tertiary institutions. It requires the national government to be concerned with the objectives of education and the structures through which it is provided and with the adequacy of our total educational efforts. (Dawkins and Costello 1983, 68, cited in Lingard, Porter, Bartlett, and Knight 1995, 44)

The inclusion of "social justice" as a "great theme" distinguished Labor from New Right governments, although it shared many of their other priorities and their interventionist stance. All policy-making was subordinated to the goal of "economic restructuring" directed toward opening the nation to global competition while attempting to offset its effects, particularly on employment. The Dawkins and Costello paper clearly set out Labor's goal of steering education within this framework. It also signaled budget cuts made to the public sector in the 1980s, including to education and ESL.

The most significant feature distinguishing the Labor government from its conservative counterparts was its linkages with the union movement. However, in place of its previous antagonism to business and industry, Labor opened new formal and informal lines of communication, using its trade union linkages to advantage. A series of "accords" between the government and unions reduced strikes, regulated wages and, until the 1990–1991 recession, lifted employment levels in return for improved working conditions and lower inflation. The achievements made through "consensus politics" were the foundation of Labor's claim to govern.

Yeatman (1990), using Beilharz (1987), describes these politics in terms of "the discourse of laborism" (p. 158). Drawn from traditional Marxism but dispensing with its oppositions, laborism constructed the interests and understandings of workers (represented by unions), employers, and government as natural sources of policy (p. 158). Although social justice was given prominence, it is "specifically for those whom laborist discourse *excludes* from mainstream modes of participation and distribution" (p. 158, italics added). She argues that social justice was "a strategy which maintains, and even *develops* . . . the exclusions which are built into the dominant laborist discourse" (p. 158, italics added here too). Those judged as "disadvantaged" did not contribute to policy-making but became "objects" of policy intervention (p. 158). As objects, their own ways of naming themselves, understanding their realities, and staking their claims were denied legitimacy. This ideology contributed to the content and processes of the ESL assessment frameworks that I will discuss in the next section.

Similar to Yeatman (1990), Lingard, Knight and Porter (1993) describe policy-making under Hawke as changing to "a game played primarily inside the state and its peak organizations" (p. viii). They point out that "corporatist" policy-making "cut off the politics of policy making from civil society, and from the pluralist and democratic process enshrined at the national level under the earlier Whitlam Labor Government (1972–1975)" (p. viii).

The differences between the Whitlam and Hawke Labor governments played an important strategic role in the latter's claim to govern. Also reformist, the Whitlam government had unleashed the pressures from 23 years of previous conservative rule, opening Australia to social change and pursuing policies to redress inequalities. It had promoted Aboriginal and immigrant rights in a variety of arenas, vigorously celebrated diversity, and promoted multiculturalism in place of as-similationism. These reforms, together with unorthodox economic policies, made Whitlam's experience in government brief and tumultuous. His prime ministership was ignominiously terminated by the Governor General to resolve a deadlock caused by the conservative upper house's denial of the budget, and Labor suffered a massive defeat at the polls. The Hawke government was determined to learn from this experience, which they blamed on inept economic management and radical interest groups' undue influence.

Paradoxically, Whitlam's policies for immigrants had been continued and strengthened by the incoming Liberal (conservative) prime minister Fraser and his government (1975–1983), although the emphasis was redirected from "rights" toward "social cohesion" (Lo Bianco 1988). Mobilization of immigrant groups under Whitlam had made "the migrant presence" a potent force in Australian politics (Martin 1978). Fraser sought the policy high ground with these groups by reendorsing multiculturalism and instituting the most comprehensive and substantive assistance for immigrants to that point (Australia 1978). This move effectively brought broad bipartisan agreement at the federal political level on immigrant issues.

Thus, from the early 1970s until the end of the 1980s, a starting point for social policies, albeit developed somewhat differently and contested by fringe elements, was the foundational assertion that linguistic and cultural pluralism contributed to the social good: to individuals and their communities and hence to a vibrant and harmonious society (Foster and Stockley 1984; Lo Bianco 1988; Ozolins 1991; Rizvi 1993). The unquestioned and unassailable dominance of English as the language of public life and institutions can be seen as a backdrop allowing pluralist aspirations to flourish. Federal and state policies focused on access to English while maintaining and promoting the use of "community languages" in education, health, the media, the law, and other arenas. In education, research indicating the advantages of bilingualism and mother tongue literacy (e.g., Peal and Lambert 1962; Cummins 1978; Swain and Cummins 1979) became a cornerstone of ESL teacher development and of advocacy to communities, bureaucrats, and politicians. Leadership in the ESL profession rejected its previous assimilationist image and agenda and, in schools, promoted ESL as one of a number of interdependent aspects of the bilingual child's development. ESL teachers were key advocates for bilingual programs, community languages in the mainstream curriculum, and linguistically and culturally inclusive practices. These ideals were given coherent statement and formal endorsement the 1987 National Policy on Languages (henceforth NPL; Lo Bianco 1987). Under the auspices of this policy, the National Languages and Literacy Institute of Australia (henceforth NLLIA) was created, whose charter was to "contribute to improving the quality and relevance of language education in keeping with Australia's social, economic and cultural needs" (Australian Advisory Council on Language and Multicultural Education [AACLAME] 1990, 20). This body commissioned one of the ESL frameworks that I shall describe.

Dawkins' contribution to "national leadership" as minister of the newly created Department of Employment, Education and Training (henceforth DEET) began a far-reaching reversal of these developments and assumptions, although the dramatic effects of laborist ideology on language and cultural issues did not become fully apparent until after 1991, when the NPL was replaced by the Australian Language and Literacy Policy (Australia 1991; henceforth ALLP). In line with laborist ideology, the new policy reconfigured the NPL's pluralism into two main themes: English literacy for those disadvantaged in the labor market and foreign language learning as a means of assisting overseas trade (Moore 1996b).

The Minister's first move was in line with the corporatist strategies that Lingard and associates (1993) describe earlier. He abolished existing semi-autonomous educational advisory bodies, which represented providers and professional, parent, and community groups. New structures ensured greater ministerial and bureaucratic power and gave stronger representation to business, unions, and state/territory bureaucrats. Where previously educators and those they served had generated much of the knowledge on which the Whitlam and Fraser governments' social policies were based, Minister Dawkins and his department now saw them as self-interested pressure groups whose claims inflated public spending.

Yeatman (1990) supports my earlier analysis of the contemporary culture of system control in her description of Labor's reforms to the public sector as emphasizing "technique" (p. 9). A set of top-down controls to institute "efficiency" and "effectiveness" were

> designed to offset and limit the influence of "content," namely, commitments and loyalties which are tied to particular departmental or agency portfolios and *which acquire authority through the development of specialized experience and links to client groups. . . .* For those of us oriented to change, it is a situation which maintains the *status quo* precisely because it undermines the stability of networks and local connections between people on which any genuinely workable change is dependent. (Yeatman 1996, 9; italics added)

In the next section, I describe how these controls and distrust of the knowledge produced by educational networks lay at the heart of the struggle over the ESL assessment projects.

In Broadfoot's (1996) terms, the Minister pursued educational reform through measures (in all educational sectors) that more closely tied together assessment's roles in attesting competence, providing certification, motivating individuals, and monitoring systems. However, the Australian constitution, which allocates responsibility for schools to the states, ensured a slow start to his agenda and gave prominence to the theme of "collaboration" in policy documents.[3] Lingard, Porter, Knight, and Bartlett (1995) point out that, in the Australian political context:

> The term "collaboration" has a high semantic overload: it has been used by the Commonwealth in an attempt to incorporate the States into its own agenda; it has also been used by the States to resist this process and to assert their primacy in determining schooling policy. (p. 48)

The Minister chose as his forum the Australian Education Council (henceforth AEC), consisting of federal and state/territory education ministers and the CEOs of state/territory education authorities. The politics of this body became the driving force in the reform process. In April 1991, the AEC agreed that guidelines for eight key learning areas in schools would be produced.[4] In June 1992, to bring the work (which always faced the danger of stalling) to conclusion, the AEC Curriculum and Assessment committee (known as CURASS) abolished the individual steering committees for each learning area and appointed a full-time secretariat consisting of high-profile educators who were closely connected to or working for state bureaucracies. This secretariat, according to a CURASS member in a book on this process, "became quite prescriptive, in the interests of quality control, and insisted on specific procedures and guidelines to be followed closely by all project teams" (Marsh 1994, 110). Throughout 1993, two sets of publications appeared: eight curriculum *Statements*, which set out frameworks for syllabus development, and eight *Profiles*, which specified levels and descriptors for reporting student achievement (AEC 1994, iii). The two ESL assessment frameworks whose formation I next describe came about in the context of these developments.

Competing ESL Assessment Guidelines: Struggles for Steering Control[5]

Moves to create an ESL-specific assessment framework resulted from a coalescence of agendas that came to a head in 1991. Notable among these was pressure from federal funding bodies, especially DEET, for quantifiable data to justify expenditure on school ESL, which, in turn, was partly a response to persistent claims from ESL professionals that sizable cuts made to school ESL in 1986 should be reversed. Assessment experts also felt that the time was ripe to complement an assessment tool used in adult ESL with one for schools (Wylie and Ingram 1985). Two such experts (Griffin and Ingram) had submitted a proposal in 1988 to the advisory body for the implementation of the NPL, which was subsequently taken up by the NLLIA. Both of these bodies were headed by Jo LoBianco, the author of the NPL. A national ESL curriculum development project, published in 1991, laid the ground for a more fully developed assessment framework (McKay and Scarino 1991), as did also a DEET-funded report on school ESL (Herriman 1991). The 1991 ALLP promised a proficiency measure for schools, and by the end of that year DEET had allocated funds to the NLLIA to manage production of "bandscales." These were to allow assessment and reporting of learner progress in ESL along a continuum of descriptors, divided into bands or developmental levels.

Tensions were present from the project's outset, one occurring within the project itself and another originating from the national curriculum. In Yeatman's (1990) terms, both arose from struggles between technocratic approaches, aiming at limited but supposedly clear goals, and the diverse concerns of ESL teacher networks. The project team was headed by one of the authors of the submission just mentioned (Griffin). He had considerable expertise in devising frameworks, known as "scales," for describing learner performances in terms of graduated levels. He had developed several of these, including literacy scales for Victorian government schools and another commissioned by DEET for national use in adult literacy. The first phase of his development procedure used teacher workshops to generate descriptors of student achievement. These descriptors were then turned into observational checklists of learning outcomes ("can do" statements), and trialled in classrooms; the results were statistically calibrated to provide orders of difficulty (Griffin 1990; Griffin and Nix 1991).

Although some teachers welcomed their role in the development process, the workshops and initial trialling generated considerable resistance from others, particularly those trained and knowledgeable in ESL. Project team members were also critical, especially the principal officer, a former ESL teacher. She had coauthored the ESL curriculum guidelines mentioned earlier and had previously been a team member in a related project in curriculum for languages other than English (Scarino, Vale, McKay, and Clark 1988). Both these projects had been devised and completed in the climate of assumptions that had generated the NPL and before the effects were felt of the Dawkins reforms. Criticisms of the scale procedures were that the descriptors were atheoretically and randomly derived from the teacher workshops, too much influenced by the need for statistical treatment, and assumed that learner behaviors could be assessed independently of contextual factors, such as pedagogic setting, task content, interlocutor support, and the learner's age and educational experience.

After several months, the NLLIA steering committee decided in favor of a more eclectic approach, and management of the project was revised accordingly. In its final form, the project encompassed four components, aimed at providing a comprehensive framework for assessing and reporting ESL development in all curriculum areas and in social interactions within and beyond the classroom (McKay, Hudson, Sappuppo, Lumley, Minchem, and Raso 1994). First, a set of staged descriptions of ESL development or "bandscales" were derived, partly from the previous teacher workshops, but also from a well-known theoretical model of language competence (Bachman 1990) and the project team's own intuitions, beliefs, and insights, together with feedback from extensive teacher trialling. Second, "Exemplar Assessment Activities" showed how assessment might function in the context of classroom activities across the curriculum. A third component was "Observation Guides and Reporting Formats" for use in reporting assessments within schools and to parents. Finally, specially commissioned baseline research on school-age ESL development was documented.

The other major tension surrounding the project was its relationship to the concurrently developing CURASS work. The NLLIA was a semi-autonomous body funded by DEET and had no representation within the AEC-CURASS management structure. However, the potential of the

NLLIA project became obvious when the drafts for the CURASS English *Statement* and *Profile* appeared in early 1992. These met with considerable criticism from ESL teachers and other educators, for, among other things, their inadequate treatment of the needs of bilingual students, conflating their learning with that of younger English native speakers. Meetings were held between the NLLIA project group and a representative from CURASS but, since the CURASS work was still in a considerable state of flux, the implications for the NLLIA project were difficult to determine. Recognizing the NLLIA project within the national guidelines seemed a logical way forward, and in April 1992 CURASS agreed that "band scales for ESL students based on work undertaken by the NLLIA" should proceed (Marsh 1994, 127).

However, with the appointment of the CURASS secretariat in June 1992, issues of control became critical. A specific outcomes-based format had been agreed upon for the *Profiles* for all learning areas in "early 1992" (Marsh 1994, 127). The secretariat determined that, since the NLLIA project did not follow the required format, a separate project aligned to the English profile was required. In late 1992, a CURASS project team was chosen, consisting of curriculum consultants from within three state government education ministries. Among them were a group who were producing ESL scales for the Victorian government and who included personnel from the previous literacy scales project (DSE 1993). The Victorian project had begun after the original NLLIA project coordinator had discontinued in this position to become a consultant to both the NLLIA project and the Victorian ESL Scales teams. In the event, the Victorian ESL Scales project was replaced by the new CURASS project.

As the body authorized by federal and state/territory hierarchies to bring the national statements and profiles to fruition, the CURASS secretariat was vigorous in its pursuit of control. Although the completed NLLIA ESL project was handed to DEET in January 1993, copies were suppressed for over twelve months, while the NLLIA was pressured to abandon publication on the grounds that its existence would confuse teachers. Threat of public scandal appears to have secured its release in 1994, shortly before the launch of the CURASS ESL Scales. The NLLIA project became available on a "user pays" basis from the NLLIA (based at a university in Queensland). The project is reported to be in use in two government systems (Queensland and Western Australia) and four Catholic school systems (Derewianka 1997, 43).

As the product of a joint Commonwealth-states venture, the CURASS ESL Scales were published in somewhat more glossy form by the National Curriculum Corporation, jointly owned by the Commonwealth and the states and responsible for developing materials held to be a priority (Marsh 1994, 49). All state ministries of education except that of Queensland endorsed the CURASS Scales for ESL assessment and reporting, although in four states/territories, they were not actually adopted but became the basis for the state's/territory's own ESL assessment and reporting system. In these adaptations, and often at the insistence of local ESL professional associations, features of the NLLIA bandscales were also incorporated.

Yeatman (1990) argues that, in corporate managerialist discourse, the emphasis on efficiency and cost-effectiveness has a political function: It accommodates the rhetoric of small government and limits demands for state resources (p. 6). However, neither efficiency nor cost-effectiveness is ensured, but rather bureaucratic interventions are liable to increase (p. 6). The extraordinary duplication and willingness to abandon a publicly funded project that I have just described support these claims. It is clear that, for state authorities in Australia, achieving "steering capacity" in schooling was a priority that had little to do with cost efficiency.

The politics of Australian federalism that led to the reworking of the national guidelines in several states/territories (and the development of supplementary material in others) also illustrates that steering capacity is ephemeral. State-level projects made the 1992 nonnegotiable CURASS format a thing of the past by 1996. These rapid changes suggest that, although battles may be fought over the content that is to deliver system control, *actual* content is probably an irrelevance from the system control perspective. It is the power to exercise this control that is the object of contest.

Steering capacity is ephemeral because the contest for control is ongoing. It occurs between state authorities and other groups but also within state authorities, who themselves are not one body or even one group within a given body. Power brokers and the shifting alliances accompanying them have crucial interests in disparaging their predecessors and establishing the supposed need for new or counter-initiatives. This process puts into constant flux *who* is steering and *what* they decide constitutes control.

The perspective is different for educators and students caught up in these processes and working with the resultant mandates, which often require considerable time to make intelligible. Often this process is overtaken by new struggles for new versions of steering capacity, which generate their own new mandates. The wastage, confusion, and emotional pain generated by these processes are evidence that people see high stakes in the assessment game and the realities it produces, whether their interests be long or short term. Often the game is won in such a way that only one reality is apparent for a given period of time. The NLLIA and the CURASS ESL frameworks provide a unique opportunity to examine *competing* views of the same phenomenon in the same time frame. In the final part of this chapter, I contrast what counts as real in each. A further step in this investigation would explore how these realities play out in classrooms where such frameworks are used (see, for example, Breen et al. 1997; Leung and Teasdale 1997).

TWO VIEWS OF ESL DEVELOPMENT

The realities described and implied in the NLLIA ESL project and the CURASS ESL Scales are very different. In what follows, I first compare how teachers are asked to consider what learners "are," that is, the *learner* and *learning characteristics* seen as relevant to ESL development. I then discuss what each project supposes and requires of the *environment* in which learning takes place, using Bourdieu (1991) somewhat loosely, how each situates the people and structures that bear on what learners "have to be." In each section, I begin by describing the NLLIA project and then turn to the CURASS Scales for relevant comparisons. Table 15.1 (next page) summarizes the features I discuss and illustrate.

What ESL Learners Are: Maturity, Experience, L1, and the Particularities of L2 Learning

What learners have validated as real about themselves and their learning and what is excluded are crucial stakes in the assessment game. Material and symbolic consequences follow for learners, classroom processes, and valued educational outcomes. These consequences also motivate or alienate learners, telling them (and others) what they can or cannot be.

The NLLIA ESL project gives considerable attention to what Wolf and associates (1991) earlier call "the capacities children bring to school." Learner maturity is seen as crucial. For this reason, the bandscales consist of three sets of separate but parallel descriptors for three broad phases of schooling: Junior Primary, Middle/Upper Primary, and Secondary.[6] For each phase, eight levels of ESL development are separately described. Related considerations are listed as the learner's previous education, informal exposure to English, prior literacy development in both English and other languages,[7] and particular learning difficulties (p. A19). This list is elaborated for each schooling phase. These descriptions construct ESL learners as complex and various in their experiences, abilities, and needs. Teachers are encouraged to acknowledge this complexity and to inquire into it, if they are to teach and assess their students appropriately.

At each ESL development level (1–8), Listening, Speaking, Reading, and Writing skills are separately described. These descriptors are organized as a general statement (an overview of the level); skills/strategies and features of second language acquisition ("the process dimension"); features

Table 15.1 *How the NLLIA ESL Project and the CURASS ESL Scales Describe Learners and the Learning Environment*

	The NLLIA ESL Project	The CURASS ESL Scales
What learners are seen to be • **maturity and experience brought to the task of learning another language and in another language.**	Three sets of descriptors, one each for Junior Primary, Middle/Upper Primary and Secondary phases of schooling.	One set of descriptors spanning grades K - 10.
	8 levels of ESL development within each of these phases.	8 levels of ESL development aligned with age-appropriate grade level in English (i.e. the higher the appropriate grade level for the learner, the higher the ESL level required).
	Descriptors include attention to how learners' English varies according to: • "knowledge of the world in L1 and English;" • previous education in Australia and overseas; • informal exposure to English; • literacy development in L1 and/or English; • particular learning difficulties.	Scales consist of outcome statements framed strictly in terms of learner behaviors. Introduction states that age, grade and literacy background affect rate and level of achievement but not ESL outcomes themselves.
	Descriptors for each schooling phase: • are parallel but vary in length, complexity and tasks according to phase; • cover interactional skills and all curriculum areas. Descriptors for the Secondary phase: • separate *academic* from *personal, social and general school* uses; • draw attention to learners with a strong background in specific subjects but low levels of English; • describe beginning ESL learners with prior schooling separately from those with limited schooling and literacy.	Descriptors: • match lower ESL levels to early schooling, and higher ESL levels to later schooling; • are aligned with the CURASS English *Profile*. • describe learners beginning literacy in terms of grade K - 1 behaviors.
	Listening descriptors are separate from speaking, allowing: • separate assessment of each; • range of behaviors appropriate to each to be included.	One strand for "Oral Interaction," following the English *Profile*. Hence: • listening levels are equated with speaking levels; • listening behaviors are limited to interactional contexts. Listening behaviors are also sometimes described in terms of speaking behaviors.
What learners "have to be" **situating gatekeepers:**		
• **programs and teaching**	Demands in both mainstream and ESL classes described.	Outcomes in ESL/English learning contexts described.
		Learners' ESL needs appear to cease when they achieve outcomes in age-appropriate English *Profile*.
• **assessment and learning**	Exemplar assessment activities show how ESL assessment can be incorporated in topics across the curriculum.	No exemplar assessment activities. (Subsequently developed at State/Territory level).
	Exemplars show assessment in the context of but separate from learning activities.	Outcomes specifications provide a *de facto* ESL syllabus.
• **interlocutors**	The learner's performance frequently described in relation to how interlocutors (teachers and peers) can provide (or withhold) support.	Learner behaviors only are described.
		Teacher positioned as judge. Interlocutors invisible.
	Learner difficulties and approximations are described, which provides teachers with more fine-grained language for understanding and observing progress.	"Can do" statements allow only for yes/no judgments as whether learners achieve outcomes.

of language performance (discourse, vocabulary, syntax, pronunciation); higher-level features (e.g., use of idiom, precision); and notes on specific learner groups, implications for placement (McKay et al. 1994, A27). For each schooling phase, each level description incorporates more developmental features appropriate to age and schooling and hence is longer and more complex (for example, Level 4 for Junior Primary is described in under four pages, whereas Level 4 Secondary is six). The descriptors at Junior Primary and Middle/Upper Primary Levels include general social contexts and classroom activities across all curriculum areas. The Secondary descriptors take account of students' potentially more independent and diverse encounters with English and literacy in both L1 and L2 and also include separate sections on academic demands.

Although these features are difficult to illustrate without the complete texts, Extracts 1 and 2 give some indication. These are extracts from *Level 4 Reading* for Middle/Upper Primary and Secondary respectively (McKay et al. 1994, C21, D32). The General Statements for both schooling phases direct the teacher to consider the learner's "knowledge of the world" in L1 and English, drawing attention to potential differences between learners according to how their knowledge is mediated by each language and by varying degrees of literacy in each language. Middle/Upper Primary learners are described as "expanding" their reading range, since they are learning English and literacy concurrently. Likewise, in Extract 1 the process descriptors for Middle/Upper Primary match primary classrooms and interactions, whereas those for Secondary in Extract 2 encompass a greater range of text types, more independent learning styles, and more complex demands. Possible learner differences are also signaled by qualifications to "can" statements with words such as "tend to," "may," and "if."

Extract 1

Middle & Upper Primary Reading, Level 4[8]

General statement

Expanding reading range based on their growing proficiency in English: drawing on knowledge of the world in L1 and English language and literacy (to varying degrees).

Process features
- Can read for pleasure simply structured stories which do not contain too many cultural references. Can retell a story read in English, but tend to include all details rather than summarize.

- Can acquire factual information from a growing range of texts on familiar topics but still need specific teacher guidance (e.g., selection of texts avoiding density of information and language complexity) and visual support. Comprehension on non-teacher-selected texts (i.e., texts for mainstream learners) expected to be read within a time frame for native-speaking readers, will break down or will be piece-meal.

Extract 2

Secondary Reading, Level 4

General statement

Becoming confident in English and in learning through English: drawing on L1 and L2 literacy (to varying degrees) and knowledge of the world in L1 and L2.

Process features

Language ability across a Range of Personal, Social And General School Contexts
- Can get essential information and sometimes fully comprehend straight-forward factual texts, popular newspaper and magazine articles with familiar content and (though not essential) some visual support. Can handle these texts if they do not require significant cultural knowledge.
- Can read for pleasure simply structured prose and literature and other texts which do not assume significant cultural knowledge, an ability to handle complex discourse structure, or a specialist register.
- Can extract main ideas from above straight-forward texts. May use bilingual dictionary extensively (if able to do so). . . .

Application And Extension To Academic Contexts

Can comprehend straight-forward structured factual mainstream text extracts on familiar topics. Can locate main ideas (headings etc.) and from these predict basic content.

The diversity of older learners is further noted. Students "with strong subject background knowledge in a specific subject area" may have a higher reading proficiency in that subject than with other content (p. D33). Teachers' attention is also drawn to learners with special difficulties and to the differences between those ESL learners in the Secondary phase coming directly from overseas and those with experience of Australian primary schools.

Whether or not older learners have experience of literacy in other language(s) is a crucial influence on their English learning (Cummins 1978). The bandscales provide separate descriptors for ESL beginners in Secondary who have developed literacy through their "L1 schooling" and those who have not. This allows teachers to appropriately monitor the progress of these very different types of learners. The reading descriptors for ESL beginners with previous schooling in L1 include those shown in Extract 3 (p. D27).

Extract 3

Learner Group A: L1 School Literacy Background Learners

Reading in English
- Are able to recognize their name, and language related to the immediate environment (e.g., name of school, international logos). May be able to recognize and name letters of the Roman alphabet. . . .

Reading in L1
- Are likely to be able to comprehend the varieties and registers encountered in their personal, social, and school life. Are similarly sensitive to the implications of the variety and register used.

The parallel reading descriptors for ESL beginners with little or no L1 schooling are quite different (p. D28), and include considerable attention to the kinds of support these learners require (Extract 4).

Extract 4

Learner Group B: Low Literacy Background Learners

Reading in English
- Are unable to read in English, and there may be little or no match between their reading ability in L1 and the expected ability in reading for their chronological age. Will need to develop concepts of literacy, and to pass through a range of steps in early literacy (depending on their L1 literacy experience) before they move to Level 2. . . .
- Will be bringing to their learning a range of knowledge, understandings, skills, and attitudes which will affect their approach to learning.
- Will be restricted in their ability to gain meaning from written text until their literacy concepts are established and until an initial familiarity with English is gained (e.g., will have insecure grasp of sound-symbol relationships in L1, which will affect transfer to reading in English).
- Will benefit from bilingual assistance, most particularly at early levels of literacy development in English. (Bilingual assistance will benefit all groups, but may be critical for literacy development in English for this group). . . .

Reading in L1
- Will have limited (if any) L1 reading skills.
- Will be unable to operate in L1 in literacy contexts.

Like the NLLIA project, the introduction to the CURASS ESL Scales lists various learner factors relating to previous educational experience and exposure to English (AEC 1994, 2). However, it also states that these issues do not affect outcomes but rather learner speed and level of attainment:

> The scales assume that the particular nature and order of outcomes will apply to all ESL learners regardless of age, grade and language and literacy background. Differences in learners will be reflected in their rate of attainment of outcomes and the outcome levels they ultimately attain. (AEC 1994, 8–9)

The outcomes specified in the CURASS ESL Scales lead towards the age-appropriate outcomes in the English *Profile*. This construct allows age and other developmental features to be accounted for as follows:

> In general, younger students will reach a level of proficiency in English that will enable them to successfully participate in mainstream curriculum more quickly than older students. In reporting the English development of younger students, therefore, teachers will find that they can be described through the English *Profile* sooner and at lower levels than older students. Older students need to reach higher levels of proficiency in English in order to deal with more linguistically demanding curriculum at their appropriate age and grade level. (Saker 1994, 14)

Thus a learner for whom Year 10 English is age-appropriate is described as needing to pass through the full range of levels (1–8). Younger learners pass through fewer ESL levels on the way to their age-appropriate English outcomes. For beginning reading, a single set of descriptors covers all age levels, although the behaviors described (Extract 5) seem to have been modeled on young speakers of English as a mother tongue preparing to enter grade 1 of school (AEC 1994, 29).

Extract 5

Beginning Level Reading and Responding

Strategies

At level B1, a student:

Interacts with texts, focusing on visual support to gain meaning.

Evident when students, for example:

- Demonstrate reading-like behavior (look at books in own time, retell a story to others).
- Focus on and join in group or individual reading (by sitting at desk, by repeating key words and phrases with class).
- Concentrate during a reading activity.
- Choose known books to "read."
- When "reading" a book, derive understanding of the sequence of events by focusing on the illustrations.

Teachers are to extrapolate these descriptors to older learners as they see fit. This raises the same problems ESL teachers identified in regard to the draft English *Profile*. Compared with Extract 4, from the NLLIA Bandscales, these descriptors seem limited and infantilizing.

In justifying the exclusion of learner characteristics necessitated by the CURASS outcomes format, a member of the CURASS project team demonstrated how this definition steered views of ESL development away from considering the potential role of learners' other languages:

> [T]he ESL Scales are concerned with students' English development and don't attempt to describe first language achievement or development. It is impossible to cross reference a student's development in two, or possibly more, different languages through a document whose main concern is with mapping the development of English as a second language. To suggest that this can be done is to gravely simplify the complexity of interaction between the students' developing languages. (Saker 1994, 11).

This rationale conflates *mapping development in a language* with *the relations between learners' languages*. It demonstrates how the logic of outcomes frames languages (and other learning) in isolation. When learners' other languages are not invisible in the CURASS ESL Scales, the focus is on the problems they create for English. Their communicative value lies only in trivial exchanges that are seen, in any case, as more effective in English, as in the suggestion that the learner may "Speak to first-language peers in English, in certain contexts ('Don't take that book!') so that the teacher will be aware of what is happening" (AEC 1994, 82). In contrast, the NLLIA Bandscales describe L1 as a legitimate and crucial means of communication and learning, for example, in observing that the learner "May choose to explore more complex ideas in L1 with L1 peers" (McKay et al. 1994, B13).

Following the English *Profile* format, the CURASS ESL Scales treat listening and speaking as a unified construct—"Oral Interaction."

Within "Oral Interaction," considerably greater emphasis is given to speaking, which follows from the focus on "outcomes" since productive skills are more directly observable. At Level 4, for example, there are twenty "communicative" descriptors and seven "receptive" ones. The seven receptive descriptors are shown in Extract 6 (AEC 1994, 82–83).

Extract 6

Receptive pointers (from Oral Interaction, Level 4)
• Understand teacher questions on familiar topics or themes by responding with phrases or sentences.
• Understand the differences between suggestions and directives.
• Extract basic information from an announcement (in assembly).
• Respond to different registers appropriately (match a formal response to a formal request).
• Respond appropriately in different classroom activities.
• Acquire new English from sources other than the classroom (the media, friends, family).
• Attend to spoken English (listen to the conversation of others).

These pointers are limited and misleading criteria for judging listening skills. They are almost entirely confined to immediate reactions in spoken interactive contexts. Three pointers direct teachers' attention to irrelevant features of learners' spoken language: Understanding is judged by responses "with phrases or sentences," "formal requests" are to be matched by "formal responses," and "in different classroom activities" the learner must "respond appropriately."

The conflation of listening and speaking as Oral Interaction also assumes inappropriate native-speaker norms. The gap between capabilities in listening and speaking is more significant for second-language learners than native speakers (although it exists for both). Research shows overwhelmingly that second-language receptive skills do not necessarily translate into equal productive skills (Swain 1985, 1995). Research in Australian schools also shows that listening skills contribute separately to ESL students' success (McQueen and Aldous 1993, cited in McKay 1994b, 10). In distinguishing listening from speaking, the NLLIA Bandscales draw on this literature and allow us to see what the CURASS ESL Scales obscure. For example, comparing just some of the NLLIA Level 4 listening descriptors in Extract 7 with their counterparts in the CURASS example, Extract 6, we can see that separate listening descriptors do not confine outcomes to those manifested in learners' spoken interactions and that they encompass more diverse listening activities, including extended listening (McKay et al. 1994, D7).

Extract 7

Listening (Secondary, Level 4)
- Can follow the gist and many details of careful speech and questions on familiar topics. Are less dependent on face-to-face contact and are beginning to understand context-reduced spoken texts (i.e., are less reliant on immediate contextual support such as pictures). Have severe comprehension problems with highly concentrated information (e.g., radio, TV news) and lengthy discourse.

The bandscales' separate speaking descriptors also illustrate how far apart listening and speaking proficiency levels can be. For example, a learner's listening ability to "follow the gist and many details of careful speech" (as in extract 7) has no necessary relation to the speaking skills described at the same level, as in Extract 8 (McKay 1994a, D18).

Extract 8

Speaking (Secondary, Level 4)
- Able to participate in expanded interactions with supportive interlocutor (e.g., interview with school counselor) and can handle with confidence giving detailed autobiographical information and describing past and present events, though this may be in short rather than longer utterances. May attempt to express complex thoughts and feelings in English, but rely on attentive interlocutor asking for clarification, etc., to do so successfully.

These differences between listening and speaking capabilities must be discarded if both are treated at one level of oral interaction, as is done in the CURASS scales' more impoverished and monolingually oriented reality.

As can also be seen in Extract 6, the CURASS ESL Scales descriptors frame outcomes as a checklist of observable learner behaviors, whereas the NLLIA examples are more discursively expressed and eclectic in content. This was precisely the point at issue in the NLLIA project's initial procedures, when ESL educators argued that assessments should incorporate contextualized understandings about learners. Their convictions drew from what were earlier described as specialist local knowledge (Yeatman 1990, 158) and teachers' "lived experience" (Pusey 1981, 99). The descriptors in the final project validated this knowledge and experience in attending to learner diversity and by incorporating contextual concerns.

However, the NLLIA descriptors also violated the CURASS "outcomes" format, which was the reason given for the decision that the bandscales were unsuitable for inclusion in the national guidelines. The descriptors in the CURASS ESL Scales reflect the initial procedures of the NLLIA project, which reduced teacher descriptions of ESL development to checklists for trialling and statistical treatment. Although ESL educators felt that these atomized descriptors fragmented and distorted their knowledge of their students, CURASS were committed to outcomes statements that were codified and countable. In the light of my previous discussion, this commitment is not surprising. It was authorized by an expert technique in developing assessment tools and simultaneously met managerial expectations described earlier that "the fine grain of educational practice can and should be more closely structured" (Pusey 1983, 405). It also reflects Broadfoot's (1996) description of the relentless pressure to quantify "value." The technical and managerial priorities that overrode the realities that teachers understood were justified by appeal to "the absolute dictates of scientific efficiency" (Broadfoot 1996, 22).

Just as Broadfoot (1996) describes, the norms governing the CURASS ESL Scales were hidden "in the guise of a bland neutral technology" (p. 233). These norms were managerially and technically stated and motivated: that the format be consistent and that the ESL scales be an adjunct to the English *Profile* (AEC 1994, 2). These managerial requirements privileged monolingual assumptions, invalidated information that could counter these assumptions, and *created* the entirely circular logic that the "particular nature and order of outcomes" applied to all ESL learners. This is an example of what Dorothy Smith calls an "ideological circle," that is, a practice that sustains its own procedures, descriptions, and theoretical edifices (1990, 35–45). Despite the fact that the CURASS ESL Scales incorporated material from the NLLIA Bandscales and claimed the same theoretical sources, the CURASS definition of outcomes specifically mandated the exclusion of attention to learners' previous education, experience, literacy and L1, and the multiple and messy complexities that, in contrast, the complex and eclectic language of the NLLIA project sought to accommodate.

These managerial requirements also had consequences for the way educators could interact with the two projects. Whereas the NLLIA project was open to challenge and critique from educators and researchers, and indeed explicitly invites this (McKay et al. 1994, A26), the constraints placed on the CURASS scales ruled out of order the very criticisms that many ESL professionals had already made. Despite unmet criticism, managerial power authorized the CURASS outcomes as self-evident, supported by scientific methods, and derived from nationally representative consensual processes. This same authority ensured widespread distribution of the CURASS document and marginalization of the NLLIA project.

The differences between the NLLIA and CURASS approaches demonstrate how criterion-referenced, performance-based assessment can make learner characteristics visible or invisible. Each legitimates what it is about the learner and learning that can claim the teacher's attention. The learner's other languages, his or her experience and maturity, and the complexities of the learning process can either be part of what is real in ESL classrooms or an irrelevance, even an annoyance or something to eradicate.

In building its realities, the NLLIA project drew from multiple sources. It acknowledges learners' interdependent and variable repertoires of languages, knowledge, and skills and makes them relevant to learning English. It sees second-language learning as a particular kind of challenge. Its insistence on learner diversity and complexity invites teachers to consider new questions about their ESL learners and to observe and work with them as diverse, complex knowers and doers. In these respects, it embodies a pluralist vision.

By eliminating contextual concerns and silencing its critics, CURASS marginalized what Whitlam had set loose in education: the affirmation and valuing of diversity and use of the complex and messy knowledge that teachers, educational reformers, and community groups produce. The laborist and corporatist political process by which CURASS operated excluded educators' experience in assessing ESL learners and constrained the knowledge that could be brought to bear. Instead, this process prioritized technique and laborist system control. In the resultant ESL assessment framework, learner capabilities are made real only in relation to their rate of attainment of English outcomes whose normative basis is inexplicit, monolingually biased, and technically determined. Other capabilities slide from view or are constructed as disadvantages, thus reinforcing the "divisive and inegalitarian educational experience" that Broadfoot (1986b) earlier describes. From the standpoint of the CURASS guidelines, ESL students' failures are likely to become their most salient feature.

What Learners Have to Be: Exclusion or Access? Who Is Responsible?

For Bourdieu (1991), symbolic and material domination occurs in processes whereby gatekeepers "produce the need for . . . [their] own services and . . . products" (p. 61). These processes inevitably entail exclusion from the benefits that dominant groups enjoy. Gatekeepers depend entirely on the scarcity value of the material and cultural capital they control and purport to offer to others. Educational assessment is crucial to these processes. It is used to ration but simultaneously necessitate gatekeepers' "services" and "products" and thus maintains the disparities between the dominant and the dominated (p. 64). The dominant may "condescend" toward those they dominate by appearing to offer help and to ignore their superior position. But these strategies do not change dominating relations; instead, they strengthen them (p. 68).

On this view, ESL teaching establishes and maintains the domination of English over speakers of other languages. Such a view is illuminating. But ESL raises important questions: Are educational endeavors that seek to give immigrants access to the dominant language and culture always simply condescension that keeps people in their place? Or are *exclusionary* practices worse for immigrants and their children than dominating ones, for example, when access to English is denied, made difficult, or not assisted? How are we to acknowledge that gaining high levels of English while maintaining their other languages and cultural perspectives constitute high stakes for immigrants and impact substantively on their material and spiritual well-being? And what are the processes by which genuine access might be made possible?

Bourdieu (1991) does not name or explore access except as part of the game of domination. This view blunts our capacity to distinguish between processes that heighten exclusion from valued material and symbolic resources and those that lessen it. A focus on domination occludes the options that gatekeepers have and that affect what the dominated can achieve.

The NLLIA and CURASS projects exemplify some of these options. The previous section has shown that we can either deny or affirm ESL learners' existing knowledge and previous experiences, including their other languages. Likewise, we can deny, neglect, or facilitate their access to English. In the same way as the NLLIA project situates learners, it also contextualizes gatekeepers and gatekeeping, most notably in its attention to programs, classroom interaction, and the place of assessment.

In regard to programming and teaching, each level description concludes with recommendations for suitable teaching and for placing students in ESL and mainstream programs. Thus the descriptors provide a concrete basis for arguing the need for specialist ESL teaching to assist learners' access to English, which was one of the factors I described as motivating the project. However, the descriptors do not presuppose the existence of separate ESL programs or that learners are separated from other classes until achieving the highest ESL level. Rather, they attempt to describe "the tasks and texts of the context which the ESL students must deal with (whether they have the necessary level of ability or not)" (McKay 1994b, 9). As can be seen from the preceding extracts (1–4, 7–8), reference is made to non-ESL classroom contexts, personal/social contexts, and academic ones. The exemplar assessment activities are drawn from the national curriculum key learning areas of Science, Mathematics, English, Technology & Computers, and Society & Environment. Thus, the NLLIA project directs specialist ESL teachers to "across the curriculum" concerns and assists both ESL and mainstream teachers to observe and promote ESL in other subjects.

At the microlevel of interaction, the descriptors in the NLLIA Bandscales emphasize the role of learners' interlocutors, both teachers and classmates, as seen in Extracts 1 and 8 (e.g., "need specific teacher guidance," "rely on attentive interlocutor"). All the examples demonstrate how attention is given, not only to what learners can be expected to do, but also the difficulties they are likely to experience (e.g., "can read . . . simply structured stories which do not contain too many cultural references"; "have severe comprehension problems with highly concentrated information"). By attending to interlocutor roles and learner difficulties, the descriptors place the onus on all teachers to meet ESL students' needs for support. They alert teachers to what can be achieved when this support is given and indicate unreasonable expectations.

The NLLIA project also confronts the power of alternative forms of assessment to penetrate classroom interaction. The exemplar assessment activities suggest how teachers may informally observe much of what students do, but they also place a clear boundary, evident to both teacher and student, around planned assessment. The exemplars show how opportunities can be provided for rehearsal of what is to be assessed, thereby demarcating those contexts where the focus is on *assisting learning* from those where learners *act intentionally* to have their learning recognized. Thus, although the NLLIA project allows for considerable penetration of teaching and learning by assessment, it does not entirely collapse one into the other.

As we have seen, the overriding contextual concern for the CURASS ESL Scales were the outcomes and the format of the national English *Profile*. As with the scales' normative assumptions about learners, those regarding programs, classroom interaction and assessment, and the sites of gatekeeping and the roles of gatekeepers are also inexplicit and inchoate.

The CURASS descriptors refer predominantly to teaching points in ESL and English classrooms. Despite statements to the contrary (Saker 1994, 11), McKay (1994b) points out that the descriptors appear to imply a self-contained, sequential, albeit reduced, ESL curriculum preliminary to the English one. Since the descriptors were atheoretically derived from teachers' descriptions of learner progress, it is not surprising that they relate to teaching points, since no other subject matter was to hand. The scales offer teachers a de facto syllabus and simultaneous assessment checklist, deskilling them into the role of monitoring the production of an impoverished and technicist reality.

Like the NLLIA Bandscales, the CURASS ESL Scales provide a basis for arguing the need for specialist ESL programs to assist greater access to English, since, as I have discussed, their format relates directly to norms that were determined as age-appropriate for native English speakers (Michel, personal communication, January 15, 1995). In fact, neither state-authorized indicators of ESL need, such as the CURASS ESL Scales, nor the NLLIA Bandscales have prevented further reductions in funding for ESL beyond beginners' levels. The political reality is that more than demonstrated need is required for adequate funding to be forthcoming or even for existing levels to be maintained. The implicit reliance on a self-contained ESL curriculum leaves the scales unable to cope with this particular reality, in contrast to the NLLIA project, whose across-the-curriculum perspective indicates ways of both challenging prevailing funding levels and working within them.

The other side of this coin is that the convergence of the CURASS ESL Scales with the English *Profile* implies that, once learners achieve the age-appropriate outcomes for English and enter mainstream classes, special attention to their needs is not required (McKay 1994b, 11; Williams 1994, 21). This makes invisible ESL teachers' responsibilities to take account of the mainstream curriculum and the role of other teachers in charting and promoting ESL learners' development. It perpetuates the common belief that ESL students should somehow be "fixed up" before they enter mainstream classes, absolving teachers from responsibility for the ongoing processes that exclude learners from access to English.

At the microlevel of interaction, the CURASS ESL Scales are likewise silent. The outcomes statements for each level are framed as tasks that learners should successfully perform (McKay 1994b, 9). Learners are seen as responsible for their performance, while teachers make judgments as to whether they meet the stated criteria. When no indication is given of what might be done to assist (or undermine) learners, as occurs in the NLLIA Bandscales, the teacher's role as gatekeeper is as Bourdieu (1991) describes, namely, to maintain the disparities that make learners dependent upon them. Moreover, although the outcomes statements require yes/no judgments, learner progress is frequently not translatable into this form (for example, how should a gain from a 30% to a 70% success rate in achieving a given task be judged?). This problem makes teachers' judgments arbitrary, further increasing learners' dependence on them.

Whereas the NLLIA project produces knowledge about ESL development that requires responses from teachers and institutions, the CURASS ESL Scales create a self-contained, self-referencing reality that maps the learner's success or failure to match this. At both institutional and interpersonal levels, the NLLIA project is focused on issues of access. *It deals with what gatekeepers, as much as learners, must do for change to happen.* It makes visible gatekeepers and their responsibilities for diverse learners and learning needs. Although the CURASS ESL Scales can be used to document student needs in relation to its norms, they have nothing to say about the changes required in individuals' and institutions' relations to ESL students. This silence is compliant not just in processes of domination, but in the day-to-day exclusion of ESL learners from the benefits of education.

CONCLUSION

Foregrounding assessment as a domination game brings into focus the spurious claim that alternatives to standardized tests and examinations liberate students from the hegemony of norms, statistical or otherwise. All forms of assessment play a role in the game of attesting competence, regulating competition, and controlling individuals and systems. These roles necessarily entail the imposition of social norms.

Alternatives to tests and examinations have the potential to realign these roles in powerful ways and therefore require as much critical scrutiny as any other assessment type. Although they undoubtedly have the potential to influence teaching and learning for the better, by the same token they can dominate the classroom—and learners—as relentlessly, if not more so, than tests and examinations ever could.

If the imposition of social norms through educational assessment is an inescapable process, we need to explore and evaluate the particular norms that are imposed. I hope to have shown how these norms are not self-contained but are constructed and contested across different sites, flowing between state ideology, government agendas, advisory and expert bodies, the sources and techniques used to develop assessment tools, and the resources provided to teachers and students. The details of the Australian experience indicate that this flow is not deterministic but contingent, although these examples are also illustrative of a general trend for the content and values of system control to subvert other concerns.

Bourdieu's (1991) analysis of how dominant relations are reproduced is deterministic. It does not take my inquiry further than seeing ESL teaching as inevitably inculcating English as a dominant language. It would have us ignore the differences between the two assessment tools I have described. A pluralist stance would be irrelevant and impossible in the practice of ESL. This is precisely the logic of the CURASS project. To fail to attend to what is at stake here would be to accept this logic.

A pluralist society is one that makes space for diverse groups to make and pursue their claims (Yeatman 1994). The NLLIA project shows what might be meant by pluralism within ESL teaching and learning. It demonstrates how ESL practice can stake quite precise claims for, on the one hand, the recognition and development of non-dominant groups' linguistic and cultural resources in the dominant society and, on the other, their access to what this society values. In contrast, the CURASS project demonstrates how corporatist managerial processes and the ideology of outcomes can produce a self-reifying technicist logic that is antagonistic to pluralism.

The NLLIA project joins a growing body of work showing how ESL curriculum, methodologies, and classrooms are crucial sites for opening up our views of immigrant children, what they are and are capable of being (e.g., Genesee 1994b; Lucas and Katz 1994; Pease-Alvarez and Winsler 1994). They are also sites that require intensive scrutiny of the role gatekeepers play in promoting what is possible for learners and schools. As ESL teachers have learned, far from ESL being irrelevant, it is central to how linguistic and cultural diversity is addressed or suppressed.

ESL is not only an important site in which the dominant society makes clear its responses to diversity. It is also one of struggle. The Australian experience is particularly telling, since it illustrates what can be won and lost in such struggles. The fact that ideologies antagonistic to dominated groups are currently in the ascendant can be used to support Bourdieu's (1991) view that domination is inevitable. However, this experience also demonstrates that alternatives are possible. It remains to be seen whether and how the multiple realities recognized in the pluralist vision will be (re-)asserted from within and beyond Australian classrooms, as the inadequacies of the corporatist monolith create a crisis of legitimacy.

ACRONYMS USED IN THIS CHAPTER

AEC	Australian Education Council
AACLAME	Australian Council on Language and Multicultural Education
ALLP	Australian Language and Literacy Policy
CEO	Chief Executive Officer
CURASS	Curriculum and Assessment Committee and Secretariat
DEET	Department of Employment, Education and Training
ESL	English as a Second Language
NLLIA	National Languages and Literacy Institute
NPL	National Policy on Languages

NOTES

1. This chapter is an extensively revised and updated version of "Telling what is real: Competing views in assessing ESL development," which first appeared in *Linguistics and Education*, 8(2), 1996. My grateful thanks to the following for particular insights and/or comment on previous drafts: Chris Davison, Andy Hargreaves, Monica Heller, Jo Lo Bianco, Tom Lumley, Brian Lynch, Penny McKay, and Alan Williams. The material here is entirely my own responsibility.

2. Neither criterion-referenced nor performance-based assessment is new (Lynch and Davidson 1997; McNamara 1997). What is new is their increasingly common use and the intersection and expansion of their content.

3. Funding for schools comes entirely through transfer grants from the Commonwealth to states/territories. (There are no school boards, as in North America, or local authorities, as in Britain.) It therefore has some leverage, although the states/territories jealously guard their powers over schooling. In return for the states' cooperation, a number of specially designated (or tied) Commonwealth grants were untied.

4. The eight key learning areas were: The Arts, English, Health and Physical Education, Languages Other Than English, Mathematics, Studies of Society and Environment, Science, and Technology.

5. Much of the information in this section is derived from interviews with various players in these processes, to whom I am very grateful. The interpretation of this information is, of course, my own.

6. Schooling in Australia generally consists of kindergarten plus 12 years prior to university entry. Primary schools cater for years K–6 and secondary schools for years 7–12, with separate secondary colleges for the final years of schooling in some states/territories.

7. Many ESL learners have previous schooling and literacy in languages other than English that are not their mother tongues. "L1" will be used as shorthand for these languages.

8. In the interests of clarity, the format of extracts slightly alters the originals and adds headings. Most of the descriptors in both the NLLIA or the CURASS scales are at least a page in length for each level. Examples are mostly from Level 4 descriptors in each document, in order to allow a more complete picture of at least one level.

REFERENCES

Apple, M. (1986). *Teachers and texts: A political economy of class and gender relations in education.* New York: Routledge and Kegan Paul.

Apple, M. (1993).The politics of official knowledge: Does a national curriculum make sense? *Discourse, 14(1),* 1–16.

Auerbach, E. (1986). Competency-based ESL: One step forward and two steps back? *TESOL Quarterly, 20(30),* 411–429.

Australia, Department of Employment, Education and Training. (1991). *Australia's language: The Australian language and literacy policy* (Vols. 1 and 2). Canberra: Australian Government Publishing Service.

Australian Advisory Council on Languages and Multicultural Education (AACLAME). (1990, May). *The National Policy on Languages, December 1987–*

March 1990: Report to the Minister for Employment, Education and Training.
Canberra: AACLAME Secretariat.

Australian Education Council (AEC), Commonwealth of Australia. (1994). *The ESL Scales.* Carlton, Victoria: Curriculum Corporation.

Australian Government. (1978). *Migrant services and programs. Report and Appendices.* 2 vols. Review of Post-Arrival Programs and Services for Migrants (Chair: F. Galbally). Canberra: Australian Government Publishing Service.

Bachman, L. (1990). *Fundamental considerations in language testing.* Oxford: Oxford University Press.

Ball, S. (1990). *Politics and policy-making in education: Explorations in political sociology.* London: Routledge.

Bamforth, J., and Grieve, E. (1996). *From implementation to continuation: A case study of the institutionalization of a curriculum innovation.* Sydney: National Centre for English Language Teaching and Research, Macquarie University.

Baron, J. (1990). *Blurring the edges of assessment, curriculum, and instruction.* Paper presented at the Institute on New Modes of Assessment, Cambridge, Mass., July.

Beilharz, P. (1987). Reading politics: Social theory and social policy. *Australian and New Zealand Journal of Sociology, 23,* 388–407.

Birenbaum, M., and Dochy, F. J. R. C. (Eds.) (1996). *Alternatives in the assessment of achievements, learning processes, and prior knowledge.* Dordrecht, Netherlands: Kluwer Academic Publishers.

Block, F., Cloward, R. A., Ehrenreich, B., and Fox Piven, F. (1987). *The mean season: The attack on the welfare state.* New York: Pantheon.

Bourdieu, P. (1991). *Language and symbolic power.* Cambridge, Mass.: Harvard University Press.

Boycoff Baron, J., and Palmer Wolf, D. (Eds.). (1996). *Performance-based student assessment: Challenges and possibilities.* 95th Yearbook of the National Society for the Study of Evaluation, Part 1. Chicago: University of Chicago Press.

Breen, M. P., Barratt-Pugh, C., Derewianka, B., House, H., Hudson, C., Lumley, T., and Rohl, M. (1997). *Profiling ESL children.* Canberra: Department of Employment, Education, Training and Youth Affairs.

Brindley, G. (Ed.). (1995). *Language assessment in action.* Sydney: National Centre for English Language Teaching and Research, Macquarie University.

Brindley, G. (1998). Outcomes-based assessment and reporting in language learning programs: A review of the issues. *Language Testing, 15(1),* 45–85.

Broadfoot, P. (1984). From public examinations to profile assessment: The French experience. In P. Broadfoot (Ed.), *Selection, certification and control: Social issues in educational assessment,* (pp. 199–219). London: Falmer Press.

Broadfoot, P. (Ed.). (1986a). *Profiles and records of achievement: A review of issues and practice.* London: Holt, Rinehart and Winston.

Broadfoot, P. (1986b). Assessment policy and inequality: The United Kingdom experience. *British Journal of Sociology of Education, 7(2),* 205–224.

Broadfoot, P. (1996). *Education, assessment and society: A sociological analysis.* Buckingham and Philadelphia: Open University Press.

California Assessment Program. (1990a). *The California assessment program: A position paper on testing and instruction.* Sacramento, Calif: Author.

California Assessment Program. (1990b). *Guidelines for mathematics portfolios.* Sacramento, Calif: Author.

Cerny, P. (1990). *The changing architecture of politics: Structure, agency and the future of the state.* London: Sage.

Cummins, J. (1978). Educational implications of mother tongue maintenance in minority language groups. *Canadian Modern Language Review, 34*, 855–883.

Cummins, J., and Swain, M. (1986). *Bilingualism in education*. London: Longman.

Dale, R., and Ozga, J. (1993). Two hemispheres—both New Right?: Education reform in New Zealand and England and Wales. In B. Lingard, J. Knight, and P. Porter (Eds.), *Schooling reform in hard times* (pp. 63–87). London: Falmer Press.

Darling-Hammond, L. (1994). National standards and assessments: Will they improve education? *American Journal of Education, 102(4)*, 478–510.

Darling-Hammond, L., and Ancess, J. (1996). Authentic assessment and school development. In J. Boycoff Baron and D. Palmer Wolf (Eds.), *Performance-based student assessment: Challenges and possibilities* (pp. 52–83). 95th Year-book of the National Society for the Study of Evaluation, Part 1. Chicago: University of Chicago Press.

Davies, A. (1995). *Introduction: Measures and reports. Melbourne Papers in Language Testing*. Working Papers of the NLLIA Language Testing Research Center, Department of Linguistics and Applied Linguistics, University of Melbourne (ISSN 1327-0311), 4(2), 1–11.

Davies, A. (Ed.). (1997). Special issue: Ethics in language testing. *Language Testing, 14*, 3.

Dawkins, J., and Costello, R. (1983). Education: Progress and equality. In J. Reeves and K. Thomson (Eds.), *Labor essays 1983* (pp. 67–79). Melbourne: Dove Publications.

Derewianka, B. (1997). National developments in the assessment of ESL students. In M. P. Breen, C. Barratt-Pugh, B. Derewianka, H. House, C. Hudson, T. Lumley, and M. Rohl, *Profiling ESL children*, (pp. 15–65). Canberra: Department of Employment, Education, Training and Youth Affairs.

Directorate of School Education (DSE), School Services Division. (1993). *Victorian ESL Profiles Project*. Melbourne: Directorate of School Education.

Foster, L., and Stockley, D. (1984). *Multiculturalism: The changing Australian paradigm*. Clevedon, England: Multilingual Matters.

Foucault, M. (1977). *Discipline and Punish*. London: Penguin.

Genesee, F. (1994a). Assessment alternatives. President's Message. *TESOL Matters, 4(5)*, 3.

Genesee, F. (Ed.). (1994b). *Educating second language children: The whole child, the whole curriculum, the whole community*. Cambridge: Cambridge University Press.

Gipps, C. (1994). *Beyond testing: Towards a theory of educational assessment*. London: Falmer Press.

Griffin, P. (1990). Profiling literacy development: Monitoring the accumulation of reading skills. *Australian Journal of Education, 43(3)*, 290–331.

Griffin, P. (1997, 18 September). *Developing assessment in schools and workplaces*. Inaugural professorial lecture. Dean's Lecture Series. Melbourne: Faculty of Education, University of Melbourne.

Griffin, P. and Nix, P. (1991). *Educational assessment and reporting: A new approach*. Sydney: Harcourt Brace Jovanovich.

Habermas, J. (1976). *Legitimation crisis*. London: Heinemann (1975, original work published by Beacon Press, Boston).

Hamayan, E. V. (1995). Approaches to alternative assessment. *Annual Review of Applied Linguistics, 15*, 212–226.

Hamp-Lyons, L. (1997) Ethics in language testing. In C. Clapham and D. Corson (Eds.), *Encyclopedia of language and education: Volume 7. Language testing and assessment* (pp. 323–333). Dordrecht, Netherlands: Kluwer Academic Publishers.

Hargreaves, A. (1989). *Curriculum and assessment reform*. Milton Keynes: Open University Press.

Harp, J. (1993). *The crisis in contemporary education: Alternative models of reform*. Working Papers, Muni Frumhartz Centre for Research on Education, Carleton University.

Herriman, M. (1991). *Review of the English as a second language curriculum in government schools*. Western Australia: Ministry of Education.

Jones, L., and Moore, R. (1993). Education, competence and the control of expertise. *British Journal of the Sociology of Education, 14(4)*, 385–397.

Kane, M. B., and Mitchell, R. (Eds.). (1996). *Implementing performance assessment: Promises, problems, and challenges*. Mahwah, N.J.: Lawrence Erlbaum Associates.

Knight, J., Lingard, B., and Porter, P. (1993). Restructuring schooling towards the 1990s. In B. Lingard, J. Knight, and P. Porter (Eds.), *Schooling reform in hard times* (pp. 2–22). London: Falmer Press.

Leung, C., and Teasdale, A. (1997). What do teachers mean by speaking and listening? A contextualised study of assessment in multilingual classrooms in the English National Curriculum. In A. Huhta, V. Kohonen, L. Kurki-Suonio, and S. Luoma (Eds.). *Current developments and alternatives in language assessment* (pp. 291–324). Finland: University of Jyvaskyla.

Lingard, B. (1990). Accountability and control: A sociological account of secondary school assessment in Queensland. *British Journal of the Sociology of Education, 13(2)*, 171–188.

Lingard, B., Knight, J., and Porter, P. (Eds.). (1993). *Schooling reform in hard times*. London: Falmer Press.

Lingard, B., Porter, P., Bartlett, L. and Knight, J. (1995). Federal/State mediations in the Australian national education agenda: From the AEC to MCEETYA 1987–1993. *Australian Journal of Education, 39(1)*, 41–66.

Linn, R. L., and Baker, E. L. (1996). Can performance-based assessments be psychometrically sound? In J. Boycoff Baron and D. Palmer Wolf (Eds.), *Performance-based student assessment: Challenges and possibilities* (pp. 84–103). 95th Yearbook of the National Society for the Study of Evaluation, Part 1. Chicago: University of Chicago Press.

Lo Bianco, J. (1987). *The national policy on languages*. Canberra: Australian Government Printing Service.

Lo Bianco, J. (1988). Multiculturalism and the national Policy on Languages. *Journal of Multicultural Studies, 9(1)*, 25–39.

Lucas, T., and Katz, A. (1994). Reframing the debate: The roles of native languages in English-only programs for language minority students. *TESOL Quarterly, 28(3)*, 537–561.

Lynch, B. K., and Davidson, F. (1994). Criterion-referenced language test development: Linking curricula, teachers and tests. *TESOL Quarterly, 28(4)*, 727–743.

Lynch, B. K., and Davidson, F. (1997). Criterion referenced testing. In C. Clapham and D. Corson (Eds.), *Encyclopedia of language and education: Vol. 7. Language testing and assessment* (pp. 263–273). Dordrecht, Netherlands: Kluwer Academic Publishers.

Marsh, C. (1994). *Producing the national curriculum: Plans and paranoia*. St. Leonard's, Australia: Allen and Unwin.

Martin, J. (1978). *The migrant presence*. Sydney: Allen and Unwin.

Masters, G. (1990, May). *Subject profiles as frameworks for assessing and reporting student achievement*. Paper presented to the Management Committee of the Australasian Cooperative Assessment Project, Perth.

McKay, P. (1994a). Two ESL scales at the national level? What has happened and why? *Australian Language Matters, 2(2)*, 1, 18.

McKay, P. (1994b). A response to the ESL Scales. *Victorian Association of TESOL and Multicultural Education (VATME) Newsletter, 54*, 8–11.

McKay, P., Hudson, C., Sappuppo, M., Lumley, T., Minchem, L., and Raso, E. (1994). *ESL development: Language and literacy in schools project*. Vol. 1: Teachers' Manual—Project overview, The ESL Bandscales, The ESL Assessment Activities, The Reporting Format. Vol. 2: Report and Documents. Canberra: National Languages and Literacy Institute.

McKay, P., and Scarino, A. (1991). *The ESL Framework of Stages: An approach to ESL learning in schools, K–12*. Carlton, Victoria: Curriculum Corporation.

McGaw, B. (1997). Towards outcomes-based education: National and school perspectives. Keynote paper, *Forum on national statements and profiles in Australian schools*. Department of Training and Education Coordination, New South Wales (NSW).

McNamara, T. F. (1997a). Interaction in second language performance assessment: Whose performance? *Applied Linguistics, 18*, 446–466.

McNamara, T. F. (1997b). Performance testing. In C. Clapham and D. Corson (Eds.), *Encyclopedia of language and education: Vol. 7. Language testing and assessment* (pp. 131–139). Dordrecht, Netherlands: Kluwer Academic Publishers.

McQueen, J., and Aldous, C. (1993). *Assessment of newly arrived secondary students—a solution*. Hawthorn, Victoria: Australian Council for Education Research.

Moore, H. (1996a). Why has competency-based training become the "solution"? *Prospect, 11(2)*, 28–46.

Moore, H. (1996b). Language policies as virtual reality: Two Australian examples. *TESOL Quarterly, 30(3)*, 473–497.

Nespor, J. (1997). *Tangled up in school: Politics, space, bodies, and signs in the educational process*. Mahwah, N.J.: Lawrence Erlbaum Associates.

Norton, B. (1997). Accountability in language testing. In C. Clapham and D. Corson (Eds.), *Encyclopedia of language and education: Vol. 7. Language testing and assessment* (pp. 313–322). Dordrecht, Netherlands: Kluwer Academic Publishers.

Nuttall, D. (Ed.). (1986). *Assessing educational achievement*. London: Falmer Press.

Nuttall, D., and Stobart, G. (1994). National curriculum assessment in the U.K. *Educational Measurement: Issues and Practice, 13(3)*, 24–39.

Organization for Economic Cooperation and Development (OECD). (1992). *The OECD international educational indicators: A framework for analysis*. Paris: OECD.

Ozolins, U. (1991). National language policy and planning: Migrant languages. In S. Romaine (Ed.), *Language in Australia* (pp. 329–348). Cambridge: Cambridge University Press.

Ozolins, U. (1993). *The politics of language in Australia*. Cambridge: Cambridge University Press.

Peal, E., and Lambert, W. E. (1962). The relation of bilingualism and intelligence. *Psychological Monographs: General and Applied, 76(546)*, 1–23.

Pease-Álvarez, L., and Winsler, A. (1994). Cuando el maestro no habla español: Children's bilingual language practices in the classroom. *TESOL Quarterly, 28(3)*, 507–535.

378   Voices of Authority: Education and Linguistic Difference

Pusey, M. (1981). The control of education in the 1980s. *Politics, 16,* 223–224.
Pusey, M. (1982). Assessment education policy. In R. Young, M. Pusey, and R.
Bates (Eds.), *Australian education policy issues and critique.* Geelong, Victoria,
Australia: Deakin University Press.
Pusey, M. (1983). The control and rationalization of schooling. In R. Browne and
L. Foster (Eds.), *Sociology of education.* Melbourne: Macmillan.
Rizvi, F. (1993). Multiculturalism, social justice and the restructuring of the
Australian state. In B. Lingard, J. Knight, and P. Porter (Eds.), *Schooling
reform in hard times* (pp. 120–138). London: Falmer Press.
Saker, J. (1994, April/May). A "Profile" of our own. *Victorian Association for
TESOL and Multicultural Education (VATME) Newsletter,* 10–15.
Scarino, A. D., Vale, D., McKay, P., and Clark, J. (1988). *The Australian Language
Levels Guidelines.* Canberra: Curriculum Development Center.
Shavelson, R., Baxter, G., and Pine, J. (1992). Performance assessment: Political
rhetoric and measurement reality. *Educational Researcher, 21(4),* 22–27.
Shohamy, E. (1994). The use of language tests for power and control. In J. Alatis
(Ed.), *Georgetown University Roundtable on Language and Linguistics* (pp.
57–72). Washington, D.C.: Georgetown University Press.
Silver, H. (1990). *Education, change, and the policy process.* London: Falmer Press.
Smith, D. (1990). *The conceptual practices of power: A feminist sociology of knowledge.*
Toronto: University of Toronto Press.
Smith, D., and Smith, G. (1990). Re-organizing the jobs-skills training relation:
From "human capital" to "human resources." In J. Muller (Ed.), *Education
for Work, Education as Work: Canada's Changing Community Colleges* (pp.
171–196). Toronto: Garamond Press.
Smith, M. (1990). *State roles in improving instruction.* Paper presented at the
meeting of the Commission of Chief State School Officers, Clearwater, Fla.
Swain, M. (1985). Communicative competence: Some roles of comprehensible
input and comprehensible output in its development. In S. Gass and C.
Madden (Eds.), *Input and Second Language Acquisition,* (pp. 235–253). Rowley, Mass.: Newbury House.
Swain, M. (1995). Three functions of output in second language learning. In G.
Cook and B. Seidlhofer (Eds.), *For H. G. Widdowson: Principles and practice
in the study of language. A festschrift on the occasion of his 60th birthday* (pp.
125–144). Oxford: Oxford University Press.
Swain, M., and Cummins, J. (1979). Bilingualism, cognitive functioning and
education. *Language Teaching and Linguistics Abstracts, 12(1),* 4–18.
Tollefson, J. (1986). Functional competencies in the U.S. refugee program: Theoretical and practical problems. *TESOL Quarterly, 20(4),* 649–664.
Torrance, H. (1994). *Evaluating authentic assessment: Problems and possibilities in
new approaches to assessment.* Buckingham: Open University Press.
Victorian Association of TESOL and Multicultural Education (VATME). (1994).
Exploring the English Curriculum Statement and Profile for Australian
Schools. *VATME Newsletter, 50,* 15–24.
Wall, D. (1997). Impact and washback in language testing. In C. Clapham and
D. Corson (Eds.), *Encyclopedia of language and education: Volume 7. Language
testing and assessment* (pp. 291–302). Dordrecht, Netherlands: Kluwer Academic Publishers.
Williams, A. (1994). A profusion of profiles: Assessment and reporting for ESL
students in schools. Where do we go from here? *Victorian Association of
TESOL and Multicultural Education (VATME) Newsletter, 54,* 18–22.

Wolf, D., Bixby, J., Glenn, J., III, and Gardner, H. (1991). To use their minds well: Investigating new forms of student assessment. In G. Grant (Ed.), *Review of research in Education* (pp. 370–378). Washington, D.C.: American Educational Research Foundation.

Wylie, E., and Ingram, D. (1985). *Australian Second Language Proficiency Ratings (ASLPR): General proficiency version for English.* Nathan, Qld., Australia: Centre for Applied Linguistics (CALL), Griffith University.

Yeatman, A. (1990). *Bureaucrats, technocrats, femocrats.* Sydney: Allen and Unwin.

Yeatman, A. (1994). *Postmodern revisionings of the political.* New York: Routledge.

16

Legitimate Language in a Multilingual School

Monica Heller[1]

INTRODUCTION

In the spring of 1993 I received a phone call from a reporter newly assigned to the Toronto office of a U.S. newspaper. He was covering the contest for the leadership of the Progressive Conservative party (the party in power at that time). He wanted to know why people cared so much about whether the different candidates were bilingual and why they seemed to judge the bilingual proficiency of some candidates by a different yardstick than others.

I won't develop here a disquisition on Canadian politics, but that reporter was onto something worth contemplating. Ever since the Canadian federal government symbolically invested in French-English bilingualism as a counterbalance to Quebec francophone nationalism, aspiring politicians must be considered bilingual in order to have any legitimacy as leaders on the national stage. But while some people, like Pierre Trudeau or Brian Mulroney, had to be so bilingual as to constitute walking matched-guise tests, others, like Mulroney's short-lived successor, Kim Campbell, only had to have a passable knowledge of French in order to be taken seriously (Campbell's rise and fall may have been meteoric, but it wasn't her French that was her downfall). The reason for this is that Trudeau and Mulroney are from Quebec, the source of the menace to the federal government, whereas Campbell is from British Columbia, far from the fray.

In Canadian political life, and in most other aspects of our life as well, there are complex sets of expectations regarding bilingual proficiency, which depend greatly on your position in Canadian society and which have an impact on the extent to which people are prepared to listen to you and to believe what you say. We use these judgments constantly in daily life, and it is no surprise that the legitimacy of a candidate's quest for power should repose, at least in part, on his or her ability to manipulate the codes of authority, that is, French and English, in ways that are consonant with other aspects of who that candidate is. Who we are constrains to whom we can speak, under what circumstances, and, most important for my purposes here, *how*.

This, of course, is the essence of Bourdieu's concept of "legitimate language," which he formulates thus:

> [W]e can state the characteristics which legitimate discourse must fulfill, the tacit presuppositions of its efficacy: it is uttered by a legitimate speaker, i.e. by the appropriate person, as opposed to the impostor (religious language/priest, poetry/poet, etc.); it is uttered in a legitimate situation, i.e. on the appropriate market (as opposed to insane discourse, e.g. a surrealist poem read in the Stock Exchange) and addressed to legitimate receivers; it is formulated in the legitimate phonological and syntactic forms (what linguists call grammaticalness), except when transgressing these norms is part of the legitimate definition of the legitimate producer (Bourdieu 1977, 650)

The key elements of legitimate language (or discourse) from Bourdieu's perspective include being a legitimate speaker, addressing legitimate interlocutors, under specific social conditions, in language that respects specific conventions of form. While Bourdieu's notion of form seems restricted to things like phonology and syntax, I want to enlarge it here to include language *choice*. I also want to consider how examining language *use*, that is, the deployment of language forms in social interaction, reveals the relationship among the different dimensions of legitimate language.

My purpose here is to use this concept of legitimate language to examine some important aspects of the role of language in bilingual (or multilingual) educational contexts. First, I want to explore how specific kinds of language practices are legitimized (and for whom and under what circumstances). Second, I want to take a look at how legitimizing those practices helps advance or marginalize the interests of different groups in such contexts, groups that are distinguished from each other in terms of their actual linguistic repertoires and in terms of the linguistic repertoires people think they should have. Finally, I want to examine what this tells us about the development of relations of power among such groups through the process of bilingual or multilingual education.

In other words, I want to argue that certain language practices and language forms are considered legitimate in educational settings while others are not. Generally, these "others" are not utterly suppressed (although I suppose they may be) but instead form an object of more-or-less painful, more-or-less serious struggle. Our job is to understand why some language is legitimate and some is not, and what that means for the participants in the setting. Of course, much of this problem the way I have stated it holds for any kind of linguistically variable setting; my interest here, however, is limited to the kinds of bilingualism and multilingualism that increasingly characterize educational settings in Europe and North America.

I have become interested in this issue over many years of watching the ways in which the manipulation of French and English is used in Canada to advance the interests of francophones and anglophones occupying a variety of social positions. I have become concerned with the ways these processes unfold in education, an institutional context of great political and social significance especially for francophones, who have invested in it nothing less than the mission of preserving French language and culture in a society dominated by English-speakers.

In order to explore these issues here I will draw on my experience in French-language minority education in Ontario, Canada's largest province and one in which English, although by no means the only language spoken, is still clearly the dominant one. The context in which I work does not correspond to most orthodox definitions of "bilingual education," in that it is actually *monolingual* education, but a monolingual education that takes place in a bilingual and frequently multilingual context and that in fact aims at achieving individual bilingualism through institutional monolingualism (cf. Heller 1994a).

My discussion is based on the ethnographic work in a French-language high school in the Toronto area and will focus on data collected from the fall of 1991 to the spring of 1993. Here I will call the school École secondaire Samuel de Champlain, or simply Champlain. (Samuel de Champlain was one of the major figures in the seventeenth-century French colonization of North America.) However, before turning to an examination of the legitimization and contestation of language practices at Champlain, I will first briefly describe the nature of Franco-

Ontarian education and provide some background regarding this particular school.

FRANCO-ONTARIAN SCHOOLS AND CULTURAL DIVERSITY

Education has been a particularly significant arena in the fight waged by the francophone minority of Canada, particularly outside Quebec, for their rights. Francophones have fought long and hard for the right to have schools in which French is the language of instruction. They argue that without those schools as institutions of cultural reproduction, they will disappear, their children assimilated forever into the anglophone majority, as many indeed have been already. The rate of assimilation of francophones outside Quebec, especially since World War II, has remained fairly high. Over the course of the nineteenth and twentieth centuries, provincial governments gained increasing control over education and have hence become the principal interlocutors of militant francophones, especially since the late 1960s.

The Franco-Ontarian school system is principally designed to maintain the French language and culture in Ontario, to resist the crushing domination of English. But the nature of francophone militancy since the 1960s has raised some paradoxes regarding this mission. First, the principal purpose of political mobilization has been to facilitate francophone access, as francophones, to mainstream provincial, national, and international political and economic processes. Of course, these processes unfold mainly in English. Thus francophone resistance to English has nothing to do with rejecting it, with building an alternative francophone world, but instead is about creating a francophone space from which to more easily enter the anglophone world. This has worked best for middle-class francophones who are now in their forties and fifties, who participated in the early struggles of the 1960s and 1970s, and many of whom now occupy jobs made necessary by successful mobilization, for example, teaching or other professional or paraprofessional positions in newly created French-language educational institutions; civil service positions in governments that have accepted, since Trudeau in the 1960s, the ideology of bilingualism and of francophone minority rights; or administrative positions in francophone lobbying or cultural organizations (cf. Welch 1988; Frenette and Gauthier 1990).

Most of the teachers and many of the parents at Champlain have lived these experiences, occupy these positions, and see the world in this way. For them, the resolution of the paradox lies in the principle that francophones can only successfully enter the modern world as equals if they can fall back on institutions that are monolingual and belong to them.

They focus on the struggle of francophones, seen as a unified group with a common history, turned outward against but simultaneously in collaboration with the anglophone majority, seen also as a unified and undifferentiated group.

Some students in the school also take this position, mainly those who grew up in Quebec (this is especially strong since many of these students are in Ontario, as it were, against their will, dragged there because of a parent's employment or search for employment or by family break-ups and other traumas). But many students in the school live a different reality, one in which English is part of their everyday world. French-language schools attract assimilated francophones and middle-class anglophones no less interested in the valuable resource of bilingualism than are middle-class francophones; there are therefore students in those schools whose English is much better than their French. As immigration to Canada, particularly to Toronto, has increased over the past 10 or 15 years, many others have come from places where French is a majority language or a prestigious second language (Poles, Iranians, Vietnamese, Somalis, etc.); they are not used to having to struggle against the stigmatization of French (indeed, many look down on the "inferior" variety of French that they are surprised to encounter in Canada). Many of these students are coping with the realities of having immigrated to what is, in the end, an English-dominated city; they are much less worried about losing their French than they are about learning English. Finally, the very success of francophone mobilization has transformed and widened the gulf between the new professional and public sector élite and the working class. This diversity raises the second paradox, which pits real heterogeneity and inequality against the imagined uniformity that supposedly underlies francophone solidarity and legitimates the existence of French-language minority schools.

Most Franco-Ontarian schools have no choice but to accept such a wide range of students; in some cases, there are legal rights to access, and in many cases there is a strong feeling of moral obligation, but in any case the schools need the numbers. Thus schools that legitimate their separate existence on the grounds of a uniform and distinct cultural reality and set of needs and on the grounds that only autonomous institutions can provide egalitarian access to social mobility, in fact serve an increasingly diversified and stratified clientele.

LANGUAGE PRACTICES AT L'ÉCOLE CHAMPLAIN

With these issues in mind, two years ago I undertook an ethnographic study of l'École Champlain. It is a small school, with about 400 students from grade 7 through to the end of high school (roughly ages 12 to 18).[2] In 1992–1993, the major groups of students (accounting for about half the school population) included French Canadians (mainly from Quebec, Ontario, and New Brunswick), Toronto-born children of mixed marriages or anglophone background, and (mainly ethnic Somali) students from Somalia, Ethiopia, and Djibouti (most of whom had arrived within the previous three years). There were also significant numbers of francophone Europeans, Iranians, Lebanese, and Haitians, as well as many other groups. Some of these students had been in the Franco-Ontarian school system since elementary school (indeed, some had known each other since kindergarten); some went to immersion schools; many others were schooled elsewhere before moving to Toronto. The class backgrounds of the students were quite varied, although many of the francophones with long roots in Canada (Franco-Ontarians, Québecois, and Acadiens) were of working-class background, and most of the English-dominant students were middle class. My sense is that many of the Somali students were members of their country's elite. The school structure, consonant with that of the rest of the Ontario system, is stratified by what are known as "levels of difficulty"; in other words, the system is streamed. The levels that are important for my purposes here are the university-preparatory "advanced" level, and the vocational training–oriented "general" level. Most of the working-class French-Canadians and most of the Somalis and Haitians found themselves in the lower levels at the time to which I refer here.

In the course of this study, I have been asking two questions, both focusing on the role of language in the processes central to the school's mandate and legitimacy. The first has to do with the link between the forms of language valued at school, the linguistic repertoires of the students, and the verbal performances that are evaluated as part of the process of achieving school success. The second has to do with the role of language in the construction of cultural identity, in the context of the school's investment in *la francitude*. In other words, I am interested in the ways in which what the students can offer as verbal performance in the classroom is evaluated in academic as well as in cultural terms by the representatives of school authority. I am also interested in the ways in which the students themselves construct their cultural identity on the basis of their experiences at school and elsewhere. The questions are linked because they both speak to a central concern of minority education, the question of *whom* that education is for. Who has a right to be in this school? Whose needs are to be considered paramount? Whose interests are to be served?

In order to examine how these questions are linked in practice, I will use the lens of the concept of legitimate language to explore two specific aspects of communicative processes at Champlain: language choice and turn-taking in the classroom. Language choice is primarily a question of form, of the *how* of speaking (as opposed to the "who" or the "under what circumstances"). Turn-taking is a question both of "how" and of "who," a question of legitimate users of the legitimate forms using those forms as they should. Turn-taking is one of the aspects of language use that show how different dimensions of legitimate language interact. Both turn-taking and language choice are central to the norms that allow us to understand the ideological content of life at school and that we can use to explore to whom they apply and under what conditions.

Language choice and turn-taking are particularly pertinent examples in the context of Franco-Ontarian education for several reasons. First, in the context of a school that defines itself principally in terms of language of instruction and whose historical and legal existence is predicated on an opposition of language communities, language choice is clearly an important matter. In addition, the characteristics of the student population, as I have described them, mean that language choice is actually not such a simple question. It is not possible to take for granted that French will be uncritically adopted and accepted as the sole language of communication at school when English is such an important and powerful part of everyone's experience and when so many students actually feel more comfortable in many ways in English than in French. It is also not simply a question of French versus English; many other languages are included in the linguistic repertoires of the students, the teachers, and their families. And, finally, it is also not simply a question of French versus other languages; it is also a question of *what* French, or perhaps more accurately *whose* French. The forms of language that are considered legitimate in the classroom context must thus be seen as something to be constructed, worked at, even struggled for or against. The different forms of language present in classroom discourse represent different repertoires, different kinds of speakers, and hence different sets of interests with respect to what one wants out of Franco-Ontarian education and eventually different sets of possibilities in terms of what one is actually likely to get.

Turn-taking is, of course, somewhat more complex. My assumption here, shared with many other sociolinguists, is that turn-taking is a window onto interlocutors' struggles to be heard, to have their point of view represented in public discourse (granting always that both speaking and keeping silent can be manifestations of both power and powerlessness; cf. Watts 1991; Gal 1989). In the classrooms of Champlain, as in most of the classrooms of Europe and North America, the regulation of turn-taking is a way to structure verbal displays of knowledge, and this regulation plays an important role in how teachers teach and in how they evaluate their students. While language choice is about using the right form of language, turn-taking is about using that form in the right way. It is not enough, then, to master the legitimate forms of French; you have to display those forms in the right ways in order to have them count in the eyes of the school. Turn-taking in the classroom is one of the major categories of the rules of the game of doing school; it is about learning who has the right to define other rules, as well as about what can and cannot be said, by whom, to whom, and under what circumstances.

LANGUAGE CHOICE

At Champlain, as at any other Franco-Ontarian school, language choice is a highly charged domain. Obviously, the use of French is considered extremely important, both by representatives of school authority and by many parents. At the same time, it is generally held to be true that many students actually prefer to speak English. Indeed, this belief has held in every Franco-Ontarian school in which I have ever set foot and is reflected in official discourse in any number of ways. One that stands out is the amount of time and money devoted by the Ontario Ministry of Education and many school boards to analyzing the extent to which French is actually spoken in French-language minority schools and to developing strategies to promote the use of French in those schools (Heller 1994b). Underlying all these preoccupations is a concept of bilingualism as a pair of fully developed monolingualisms, as distinct from a unified form of competence drawing from a range of language varieties.

Consequently, at Champlain, as at many other schools, teachers work on the creation of institutional monolingualism as a component of this idea of bilingualism and therefore spend a fair amount of time exhorting or imploring, in shouts and in whispers, *"Parlez français!"* I argued earlier that this use of French in school is an essential element of the school's legitimacy and of the ability of the school's supporters to advance their interests through the school. If students do not speak French at school, there are no grounds to claim a distinct set of resources and a distinctive credential of value in the middle-class symbolic and material marketplaces. Of course, the students' relatively infrequent free choice of French also legitimizes the maintenance of a state of panic; we *must* strengthen our schools if we are not to lose our children—children who, we can demonstrate by a stroll through the corridors, are in severe danger of assimilation.

Students are thus surrounded by manifestations of the school's (and by extension, parents') will that they speak French. The use of French becomes a symbol of the acceptance of school authority. Significantly, English then becomes available as a means of contesting that authority (and only English, as the symbol of the dominant society whose hegemony Franco-Ontarian schools exist to resist). I have seen students calmly answer a teacher's question in English, provoking anger, acquiescing by repeating themselves in French. I have heard them argue that the French-only rule doesn't apply until the bell rings, carving out an autonomous space for themselves in the temporal organization of the school day. Most of the students who consistently use English on the floor of public, institutional discourse in fact end up leaving the school.

Students from outside Canada who speak no English learn the powerful significance of English very quickly. For example, Mohamud, a Somali boy newly arrived in Canada, spent most of his first semester struggling against his placement in the general-level Français course. Every day, he argued against the teacher's choice of pedagogical content, interrupted her, failed to turn in his homework, came to class late, and in other ways displayed his anger and resistance. All of the talk between the teacher, Lise, and Mohamud surrounding this process was in French (and indeed Mohamud was proud of his skills in that language), while discussions between Mohamud and other Somalis in the classroom took place in Somali. However, one day the running disputes between Mohamud and Lise came to a head, and Lise decided she had to send Mohamud to the school office for discipline. Mohamud's last rejoinder to Lise was suddenly in English, as he stormed out of the class, slamming the door behind him.

While in many ways the school tries to suppress the use of English, school staff members also often recognize it as a reality in the lives of many of their students. While this is rarely acted on in advanced-level Français classes, presumably because of the importance of these classes in fulfilling goals related to the prevailing ideology of institutional monolingualism, it may be acted on with varying frequency in general-level Français classes and in other subject areas, where teachers are more often confronted with various kinds of contradictions between values accorded to French and English and have less invested in maintaining classroom monolingualism. When such teachers encounter communication difficulties or when they need to refer to students' outside experience to make a point, they generally assume that they should do so with reference to English. In one advanced-level science class, for instance, the teacher dictated notes on natural fibers, instructing the students where and how to list materials such as wool, silk, cotton, and linen (Extract 1). Students are most likely to have run into these items at home or in stores, buying clothes, and therefore might be expected to be more familiar with the English than the French forms:

Extract 1

à côté de coton et lin on n'a pas du tout (xxx) produit naturel le lin <u>*linen*</u> *en anglais okay donc ajouter le lin dans votre liste de fibres naturels le lin* <u>*linen*</u> *en anglais*	(next to cotton and linen we have absolutely no (xxx) natural product *"le lin"* <u>linen</u> in English okay so add linen to your list of natural fibres *"le lin"* <u>linen</u> in English)

The discourse surrounding language choice in the classroom thus supposes a fundamental opposition between French and English and also is built on the expectation that those two languages form the totality of the linguistic repertoires of the student body. That reality, as we have seen, has changed, and students speak in fact many other languages. Teachers' tendency to explain things with reference to English can be mystifying to the many new students who speak no English. Lise once engaged a Somali student in the conversation shown in Extract 2.

Extract 2

Student: *qu'est-ce que ça veut dire "indice"?*	(what does *"indice"* mean?)
Lise: *indice (pause) mon Dieu comment est-ce qu'on traduit "indice"?* index *en anglais (xxx) une façon une façon de (xxx)*	(*"indice"* [pause] my God how do you translate *"indice"* "index" in English[xxx] a way a way to [xxx])

Lise recognized that a translation to English was not going to help, and so found a way to paraphrase.

At the moment, though, only one other language, Somali, is really spoken by sufficient numbers of students to make a difference (although there have occasionally been pockets of Farsi-speakers here and there in the school). The preference for Somali-speakers to use their language among themselves even in the classroom, while at one level rather unsurprising, does create dilemmas for the teachers. Many of them understand that speaking Somali is as important to those students as speaking French is for them, and yet to countenance use of that language while suppressing the use of English by other students seems unjust. Lise faced this problem in her general-level Français class, populated as it was by students of French Canadian origin who preferred to speak English (the forbidden language) and Somalis, who always talked to each other in Somali.

One student remarked on a similar dilemma in the English as a Second Language class, the student population of which was made up of Somalis and newly arrived French Canadians. This student, a francophone from Quebec, asked the teacher why she allowed the Somalis to speak Somali to each other when she continually asked the francophones to stop speaking French. Well, she replied, it's their (the Somalis') mother tongue. The francophone protested that French was *his* mother tongue. Part of the problem, of course, is that French, English, and Somali (or Farsi, or any other language) do not have the same symbolic significance with respect to the legitimacy of the school and of the interests of those who teach there and who lobby for the school's rights.

French is the language of the school, English the loved and hated, respected and feared language of the dominant society (while often also the students' mother tongue). Other languages have no part to play in this script and instead introduce a new dynamic for which Franco-Ontarian education has been largely unprepared, the problem of internal relations of power. Focused intently on internal solidarity, Franco-Ontarian education lacks the means to attend to this question. Because little attention has been devoted to this problem, it has to be dealt with on a case-by-case basis; each teacher has to decide what she or he wants to do about students speaking other languages in the classroom, for instance. The strong province-wide convention symbolized by the eternal cry of *"Parlez français!"* has as its subtext "Don't speak English"; it is in the province's classrooms that people have to work out the relationship between French and languages other than English.

At least as much attention is devoted to the form of French to be used as is devoted to assuring the language's presence in the school. One salient characteristic of Canadian francophone political mobilization has been the development of a Canadian standard French, which establishes a new terrain of legitimate language, distinct both from the old imperialist-imposed standard of European French and the still-stigmatized Canadian French vernaculars. This process does not radically alter the basic notion of what it means to be a francophone in Canada; it accepts the idea that a standard variety is necessary and reinforces the notion that the only good kind of bilingualism is one in which people speak multiple monolingual linguistic varieties. The new standard is as harsh in its judgments of interference from English as was the old one. The major difference lies in who has control of the definition of legitimate form, and here the purpose is clearly to place that control in the hands of the new, educated, and mobilized elite (and more particularly in the hands of professionals of language: language planners and terminologists, translators and teachers). Schools are important sites for the construction of this standard and for its deployment in gatekeeping and credentialing.

In Champlain's classrooms, one sees reflections of these processes. In classes where French is taught as a subject matter, particularly in

392	Voices of Authority: Education and Linguistic Difference

advanced-level classes, care is taken to teach this standard form. *Anglicismes* are identified as such and corrected, whether in texts or in the stream of speech. In one advanced-level French class, for example, the exchange shown in Extract 3 took place.

Extract 3

Teacher: *pourquoi lit-on?*	(why do we read?)
Student: *pour relaxer*	(to relax)
Teacher: *pour se détendre, "relaxer"*	(to *"se détendre"* [relax], *"relaxer"*
c'est anglais	is English)

In a course on French for business purposes, a section of the textbook (written and published in Quebec) was devoted to *anglicismes*, and the presentation both in the text and in class assumed knowledge both of English and of the "erroneous" forms in question. Teachers also take pains to substitute standard variants for forms that spring from Canadian vernaculars (such as *vue* [movie] instead of *film*; *à cause que* [because] instead of *parce que*; and so on). (Competing European regional forms, such as the distinctive Swiss and Belgian numeral system, are also corrected, but with greater tolerance.) Even distinctively Canadian pronunciation is muted, internationalized. The effect is to value the verbal displays of students who come from middle- or upper-class well-educated backgrounds, especially those who grew up in areas where French is a majority language. Students in one class consistently explained the success of one of their peers with the comment, "Well, of course, he's from France." It also permits the relative success of students who have learned their French mainly at school and who can produce good academic French, although their skills at using French in social interaction may be weak. Finally, it devalues any number of authentic but regional vernaculars and any form that too strongly betrays the speaker as a second-language learner of French.

In the general-level classes, where Canadian French vernacular and contact variety speakers are to be found, along with Haitians and Somalis used to European French, there is less clarity of purpose. The general-level Français class was oriented towards the preparation of students for the use of French as a language of basic communication in the workplace, based on the assumption that most students would already possess similar skills in English. This was, of course, only true of one segment of the class. The Somali students, for the most part, had little or no knowledge of English and little interest in vocational training. Indeed, many looked down on the Canadian French they encountered in the school. (In one exchange, a Somali student in this class practiced a *dictée* read by the teacher, in which the word "fax" appeared.

He was unfamiliar with it, and asked for an explanation and the spelling. It came out that the word "fax" is actually from English. "Oh," said the student, laughing, "so it's not real French!" "Well," the teacher had to grudgingly admit, "it's a borrowing.") The French Canadians were either struggling with the stigmatization of their language or had given up on it entirely and were waiting patiently (or not so patiently) to get parental permission to transfer to an English school.

Less overt attention is paid in verbal interaction in other classes to the mastery of standard French, but it frequently remains important in the evaluation of written work. Interestingly, many students consider that such concerns are legitimate in French class but not in, say, history or biology, where, they feel, their mastery of the content of the subject should be the only concern. One student complained that a poor mark in a social science class reflected her errors in French and not her understanding of her subject; she felt that that was unreasonable. Extract 4 shows what graduating student had to say, in fractured French, in the yearbook next to his picture:

Extract 4

"Je m'exkuze pour leuh kalité de lengue, mais kum vous savé tousse, la frensaix ne fue jammait une çujais dent lakel je sui d'ouwer"	(Excuse the quality of my language, but as you all know, French was never a subject in which I am gifted)

French for him is a *subject*, not the language of life at Champlain, even less *his* language in any way. This is a self-mockery, of course, but also a mockery of the school's linguistic standards. He knows enough about French to know what an egregious mistake is, and he can make it on purpose, as his send-off, once he has his diploma in hand.

I take the examples I have just given as evidence of three sorts of contradictions:

1. contradictions between an emphasis on the development of some form of standard monolingual-variety French as a hallmark of the school and the concrete possibility that one can at least graduate from Champlain without actually mastering that French;
2. contradictions between the construction of a French Canadian identity and the valuing, on the one hand, of European French and the devaluing, on the other, of Canadian French vernaculars; and
3. contradictions between Somali and Haitian students' valuing of European French and inability to speak English, and their placement in general-level classes oriented toward Canadian French vernacular and contact-variety speakers.

At Champlain, legitimate language is French. This is unambiguously true for written work and for public and official discourse. In classroom interaction, French is preferred and English dispreferred, and hence any use of English must be seen as a direct contestation of the legitimacy of French and by extension of the teacher's authority. It is not clear yet how the school feels about the language of its own minorities. Further, only Canadian and European standard forms of French are accepted; consistent production of anything else has consequences for streaming and for marks and even for teachers' assessment of whether a student belongs in this school at all.

As long as this definition of legitimacy is accepted in the classroom in direct, public interactions with the teacher, other forms of language can be tolerated. Students can speak English in whispered asides to each other; if called upon to place their utterances on the common, public floor, they typically rephrase what they have to say in French or deny having said anything at all. They can speak English in the hallways to each other, but not to a teacher or even to a visitor. They can speak Somali, they can speak Arabic, they can speak Farsi, they can speak Haitian Creole; they can codeswitch and play with language as much as they like, as long as it is to each other and not on the school's official floor. To do otherwise is to risk conferring the status of impostor on either the school or the student speaker.

TURN-TAKING, LEGITIMATE LANGUAGE, AND LEGITIMATE SPEAKER-HEARERS

A brief examination of turn-taking in the classroom provides another way to look at the construction of legitimate language. I will focus on the significance of two models of turn-taking that compete in Champlain's classrooms. The first is a model of sequential turn-taking on a unified floor. It is the one that best typifies our expectations of what classrooms are like: Each person takes the floor in turn, and everyone participates in the same conversation. Usually, but not necessarily, the teacher selects the speakers. This is the model that Champlain teachers use, a model that structures the public, official, on-record, French floor of classroom talk. The competing floor is multivocal and nonsequential. Many people can talk at once or may overlap. This is the typical form of off-the-record talk, which usually takes place in a language other than French and over which the teacher exerts no control. As long as the two are kept separate, there is little problem; it is clear which format has official sanction. Occasionally, however, the two collide. This happens most clearly in classrooms with significant numbers of Somali students, who appear to favor this format, and was inadvertently reinforced in at least one classroom.

In the general-level Français class, a great deal of emphasis is placed on oral language skills. Lise, the teacher, took this up by trying to give students greater control of talk, even rearranging chairs and desks into a circle or a U-shape instead of keeping them in rows. However, she inevitably ended up frustrated at what appeared to be the students' inability to stick to a topic and to listen to each other. Instead of the sequentiality and unified floor that she had hoped to map onto group discussion, what she got was lots of people talking more or less at the same time, on floors that shifted both in terms of topic and in terms of participants. In the end, she always put the students back into their rows, and over time she felt obliged to define explicit codes of conduct and to introduce more teacher-oriented transmission-type teaching than she felt intellectually comfortable with.

For Lise, the theme of the semester eventually became the theme of "*le respect.*" In many ways, the reason has to do with Mohamud's explicit challenges to her authority. But through various interactional episodes, including these challenges and Lise's and other students' responses to them, we can see the outlines of the relative importance and interplay of the various dimensions of legitimacy.

In one episode, Lise organized student presentations. She began by circulating an evaluation sheet. Extract 5 gives the exchange that followed.

Extract 5

Lise: *on vous laisse deux minutes pour vous préparer puis après ça on commence*

(you have two minutes to prepare yourselves and after that we start)

Leila: *d'accord*

(okay)

Abdul: *Leila et Abdi*

Lise: *Zahra (xxx) feuille Abdul tu lui as donné à à*

(Zahra [xxx] sheet Abdul you gave it to to)

Abdul: *oh e (speaks in Somali)*

Lise: *(xxx) aujourd'hui vous parlez en Français*

([xxx] today you speak French)

Abdul: *d'accord je vais parler Français*

(okay I'll speak French)

Lise: *okay alors on écoute Leila et Abdi*

(okay so we listen to Leila and Abdi)

Student: *chut*   (shh)

Student: shut up   (shut up)

Lise: *okay on recommence quand on*   (okay we start again when we do
fait une présentation orale ou un   an oral presentation and exposé
exposé on s'attend vraiment à ce que we really expect people to listen...)
à ce que les gens écoutent...

The episode goes on in this vein for another few minutes, but this extract is sufficient to show how Lise uses her position to take the floor and uses the floor to make explicit what will count as legitimate language (French, not Somali) and to reinforce the conventions of turn-taking. She defines the situation as a *"présentation orale,"* and she states that in such a situation the speakers speak and everyone else listens. She does not let the episode begin until that has been established.

Lise has privileged use of interruptions and self-selections when she is not in fact the designated speaker and addressee, because she is the teacher (and so she is always a legitimate speaker or hearer). She uses this position to make other communicative conventions clear.

Among the conventions she defined, one says that no foul language is allowed (Extract 6).

Extract 6
(Mohamud is participating in the question period following another student's oral presentation of an imaginary machine.)

Mohamud (to the other student):   (how does it work, your piece of
comment elle marche, ta saloperie? shit?)

Lise: *pardon Mohamud, ça ne marche*   (sorry, Mohamud, that won't
pas   work; that is, that is not
                                       acceptable)

Note here that while *"saloperie"* may not be polite language, it does betray an impressive command of French vocabulary. This aspect of Mohamud's proficiency is, however, ignored.

Another convention that Lise makes explicit is that students call other students by their first names (Extract 7).

Extract 7
(Mohamud is trying to get another student's attention.)

Mohamud: *Larose!*

Lise: *c'est Stéphane son nom*   (Stéphane is his name Mohamud)
Mohamud

A final example: Students stick to the subject as defined by the teacher. In Extract 8, the class is discussing whether or not chewing gum in class is a sign of disrespect:

Extract 8

Lise: *okay t'allais faire un commentaire Zahra*	(okay you were going to make a comment Zahra)
Zahra: *non j'ai déjà (xxx)*	(no I already [xxx])
Lise: *Mohamud*	
Mohamud: *j'avais toujours su Madame de faire ce qu'il me plaît*	(I have always known Madame how to do what I like)
Lise: *parle de la gomme sur le sujet on parle de la gomme*	(talk about gum on the topic we're talking about gum)

At another moment, Lise asks the students to put their desks in a U-shape and organizes a discussion on the meaning of the word *"respect."* The episode is too long to reproduce here; for my purposes there are two essential elements. The first is Lise's statement that respect means listening quietly when someone else talks (*"lorsqu'(il y a) une personne qui parle tu dois apprendre à te taire"* [when a person (who) talks you have to learn to be silent]). The second is the form that the discussion takes; throughout Lise attempts to exert control by selecting speakers and by enforcing precisely what she wants to teach, namely, that others should listen when one person has the floor. In fact, however, there are often numerous discussions going on at once, and student talk often overlaps. (Sometimes such overlapping talk might be characterized as collaborative, in that there is a shared topic and mutual addressing of turns; at other times, speakers are ignored, and competing topics with different sets of interlocutors are opened up simultaneously with someone else's ongoing talk. This last happens more when some students take the floor than others, and I take this to be an index of the legitimacy of the speakers.)

The importance of the interplay of different aspects of legitimacy is revealed in another episode (Extract 9) a few days later. Here, Mohamud's challenge to Lise has been taken up. Lise has decided that if Mohamud is unhappy with what she is doing in class, then she will briefly turn the class over to him. He has decided to do what is for him a more credible activity than group discussions and pen-and-paper exercises, namely, a good old-fashioned *dictée*. He follows this with a lecture on the relations between men and women in Somalia. Throughout this episode, however, Mohamud has trouble acting and being taken seriously in the teacher role. First, he breaks the "no foul language" rule:

Extract 9

Mohamud: *on commence à la ligne le vingt janvier*	(we begin new line January 20th)
Abdul: *est-ce qu'on écrit vingt en lettres?*	(do we write twenty in letters?)
Mohamud: *tout ce que tu veux j'en ai rien à foutre (rires, Mohamud inclus) virgule la plupart des zé des ces infortunés ne se sentirent pas la force de se*	(whatever you want I don't give a shit [laughter, including Mohamud] comma most of the zé of the these unfortunates didn't have the strength to)

Then, the other students start giving him a hard time, interrupting him, complaining about the comprehensibility of his speech and asking questions (Extract 10). Anne, one of the French Canadian students, mocks his intonation.

Extract 10

Zahra: *doucement attend*	(slowly wait)
Abdul: *infortunés*	(unfortunates)
Mohamud: *de ces infortunés la plupart de ces infortunés ne se sentirent pas la force de quitter leur lit*	(of these unfortunates most of these unfortunates didn't have the strength to get out of bed)
Anne: *ne sent quoi?*	(didn't feel what?)
Mohamud: *ne se sen ti rent pas la force de qui-tter leur lit*	(did not have the strength to get out of bed; said with exaggerated separation of syllables)
Anne: *je peux pas com-pren-dre (rires)*	(I do not un-der-stand [laughter])

These problems continue throughout the *dictée*, and in comments afterwards students (including other Somalis) complain that they could not understand him. During his lecture, the Somali women in the class interrupt him and challenge his affirmations about Somali marriage practices. Mohamud is not allowed to do what Lise does (admittedly not always successfully) in terms of using the floor to establish control; he is not a legitimate speaker. He may partly disqualify himself by using foul language, but likely he is prevented by other students from taking on a role he does not rightly have a claim to simply because he is, like them, a student. Interestingly, however, the challenges to Mohamud are phrased not in terms of his status but in terms of his mastery of the legitimate forms of language (we can't understand you, you have an accent, you talk too fast).

This examination of turn-taking in Lise's Français général class shows us how important the conventions of legitimate form are (speak polite French). But it also shows that form is not everything; form must be used appropriately (in a unified floor by designated speakers). In the end, this dimension of language use is nothing less than *"respect."* But there is more: Being a designated speaker is not the same as being a legitimate speaker. Mohamud is a designated speaker, but he does not get the *"respect"* that Lise does. Lise often can take the floor despite not being a designated speaker, because her authority as a teacher is invested in that kind of control over turns at talk (hers and everyone else's). (This is also why Mohamud's contestation is so effective; it aims directly at the legitimacy of Lise's control over turns at talk and over topics).

The turn-taking conventions of the classroom reinforce the teachers' control of the situation, including therefore their ability to define and maintain the definition of legitimate language. Through controlling the shape of classroom talk, they can control its form, and they can also control who count as legitimate speakers and hearers. Finally, the external shape of talk, its deployment in interaction, may be as important as its structure, its internal form. Possessing the legitimate variety may not get you anywhere if you cannot or do not use it according to the rules of the game. Looking at turn-taking allows us to see who the legitimate speakers are of what legitimate forms and how they use those forms to regulate both access to knowledge and displays of knowledge.

CONCLUSION

At Champlain, the processes of interaction in the classroom, as I have presented them here, reveal some profound contradictions that, in the end, serve the interests of some participants better than they serve others. While the value of French and of specific varieties of French, as well as of francophone identity, is clear, there is no simple correlation between possessing those varieties and identities and doing well at school or being seen as a central player there. Some students speak and write standard French, identify themselves as francophones, and do well. But others can do fairly well despite not fully mastering standard French or identifying themselves as francophones. These students have North American mainstream class-based knowledge about how to do school, including knowledge of how to use language, which appears at least as important as their knowledge of certain linguistic structures. (Also, the school needs to maintain a certain level of enrollment, and the presence of English-dominant students is part of the basis of the justification for francophone militancy.) In addition, some students who identify themselves as francophones but who speak the vernacular do poorly, in part because the stigmatization of their linguistic skills overrides their authenticity. Further, other students (notably the Somalis) encounter difficulties because their lack of knowledge of the school's expectations of how to use language overrides their mastery of linguistic structures. Legitimacy is thus both more and less than mastery of the forms of standard French, although it is always defined with reference to standard French. It is also knowing when and how to use them and being a member of a group with the right to use them or not to use them, depending on the circumstances.

Underlying these facts is the fundamental contradiction of a school made for people who speak French and English and aspire to professional careers that finds itself faced with many other kinds of students. In the end, the school serves the interests of the bilingual, francophone politically mobilized middle class that fought so hard for its creation and, ironically, also the interest of anglophones who have managed to acquire academic French. These are the two groups for whom French-English bilingualism is important and for whom the school represents a crucial source of valued linguistic capital. In the struggle, the cultural dimensions of Franco-Ontarian education are marginalized and folklorified, icons of a reality long gone and perhaps always an invention. New participants fight for a way into this game, but find frequently that they have to learn more than just French in order to be allowed to play.

Looking at bilingual classroom discourse thus allows us to see how people draw on their linguistic resources to accomplish their aims. It allows us to understand the different dimensions of legitimate language and, behind that, how legitimacy gets defined and by whom. It allows us to see where there are struggles over that definition and what the consequences of definitions and struggles over definitions are for different kinds of students. It allows us to see what people are after in bilingual classrooms, what valuable resources are there for them, and how they formulate and act on their interests.

Bilingual education is therefore about more than simply maintaining and learning a language. It is about constructing the value of the different languages in a community repertoire and about defining who has the right to use them under what circumstances. What goes on in classroom interaction teaches students about their position both in the school and in the community and shows them what their chances are of being able to acquire the forms of language that count. It also gives them a chance to see how successful any challenges to school authority are likely to be and what their options are outside of collaboration.

The analysis of bilingual classroom discourse, seen in this light, becomes a window onto the opportunities and obstacles that bilingual education presents to different kinds of students, as well as a glimpse at the strategies teachers and students use to deal with them. By understanding what constitutes legitimate language in a bilingual classroom, we can see whose interests are favored and whose are marginalized and how bilingual education contributes to the welfare of minority groups.

NOTES

1. This chapter is a revised version of the plenary address given at a seminar on bilingual classroom discourse organized as part of the Occasional Seminar Series of the British Association of Applied Linguistics, Lancaster University, July 22–24, 1993. It is based on research supported by the Social Sciences and Humanities Research Council of Canada and the Ontario Ministry of Education Transfer Grant to the Ontario Institute for Studies in Education. I am grateful to Laurette Lévy, who played an important role in data collection and analysis, as well as to subsequent project personnel who have contributed significantly to discussions of this data, notably Mark Campbell and Phyllis Dalley.

2. However, significant numbers of refugee or immigrant students are older, having lost a few years of schooling along the way or having been required to make up courses that are part of the obligatory Ontario curriculum, as well as older Canadian-born students who had dropped out of school and are now returning.

REFERENCES

Bourdieu, P. (1977). The economics of linguistic exchanges. *Social Science Information, 16(6)*, 645–668.

Frenette, N., and L. Gauthier. (1990). Luttes idéologiques et cultures institutionnelles en éducation minoritaire: Le cas de l'Ontario français. *Revue Éducation canadienne et internationale, 19(1)*, 16–31.

Gal, S. (1989). Between speech and silence: The problematics of research on language and gender. *Papers in Pragmatics, 3(1)*, 1–38.

Heller, M. (1994a). *Crosswords: Language, education and ethnicity in French Ontario.* Berlin, N.Y.: Mouton de Gruyter.

Heller, M. (1994b). La sociolinguistique et l'éducation franco-ontarienne. *Sociologie et sociétés, 26(1)*, 155–166.

Watts, R. (1991). *Power in family discourse.* Berlin, N.Y.: Mouton de Gruyter.

Welch, D. (1988). *The social construction of Franco-Ontarian interests towards French–language schooling.* Unpublished Ph.D. thesis, Graduate Department of Education, University of Toronto.

17

Youth, Race, and Resistance: A Sociolinguistic Perspective on Micropolitics in England

Ben Rampton

INTRODUCTION

This chapter focuses on interethnic interaction in which adolescents of Asian descent put on strong Indian English accents when addressing Anglo teachers and adults, and it discusses the extent to which these codeswitchings constitute acts of resistance within a racist society. The chapter recognizes the ambiguity in the relationship between resistance and just "messing about" (Gilroy and Lawrence 1988, 136–137); but rather than invalidating a political interpretation, detailed interaction analysis reveals subtleties in oppositional meaning that make the term "resistance" seem rather crude. Codeswitching into Indian English conjured a very specific political problematic; it could even lead to the consolidation of amicable Black-White pupil-teacher relations counterposed to wider patterns of race stratification.

The chapter looks at how interpretive sociolinguistic analysis can contribute to sociological discussions about youth, race, and resistance, and it concentrates on the way that British-born adolescents of Indian and Pakistani descent sometimes spoke to teachers and adults in second-language learner Indian English, even though, in reality, they were fluent speakers of vernacular English.[1] When British Asian adolescents put on strong Indian accents ("stylized Asian English" [SAE]) in talking to white adults, how far and in what ways were they engaged in acts of resistance?

There are six sections in the chapter. After a brief outline of the database, the chapter begins with a sketch of what adolescents themselves reported in interviews. It then turns to an interaction in which this kind of codeswitching actually happened. What actually happened turns out to be more complicated than what got reported. That may be not be very surprising in itself, but at least at first sight, it does present quite a problem for extrapolations about resistance. Closer inspection, however, reveals ways in which a political interpretation of stylized Asian English remains relevant. In the last three sections of the chapter, I try to show how the term "resistance" is actually too crude to do justice to the subtle political processes achieved through this kind of codeswitching. (More-extensive discussion of these issues can be found in Rampton 1995, which also provides much fuller empirical evidence.)

THE DATABASE

The chapter draws on two years of fieldwork in one neighborhood in the South Midlands of England; field methods centered around radio-microphone recordings, interviews, participant-observation, and retrospective participant commentaries. The informant core comprised twenty-three 11- to 13-year-old informants of African-Caribbean, Anglo, Indian, and Pakistani descent in 1984, and about sixty-four 14- to 16-year-olds in 1987 (two-thirds male, one-third female). My analysis took "language crossing" as its central focus: the use of Panjabi by black and white youngsters, the use of Creole by whites and Asians, and the use of stylized Indian English by all three. Three significantly different situational contexts were identified: interaction with adults, interaction with peers, and performance art. The present discussion is based on the examination of about forty episodes in which adolescents used SAE in interaction with adults. Before turning to representative examples, it is worth briefly considering what adolescents themselves had to say about this kind of codeswitching.

INTERVIEW REPORTS OF SAE

The black, white, and Asian informants I interviewed often reported SAE being used to adults in authority. From what they said, the typical situation appeared to be in class, either with a new teacher or with a teacher on temporary supply. The teacher would address a question or request to a pupil of Asian descent, and the pupil would reply in a strong Indian accent with something like **"excuse me Miss me no understanding," "what you talking about," "what did you say."**

Overall, these reports seemed to invite four inferences.

1. Firstly, SAE seemed to involve a rejection of the teacher's attempt to elicit the show of active commitment to some task or topic of the teacher's deciding.
2. Second, this rejection was superficially mitigated by the remedial politeness encoded in the disguise: terms of formal address (Miss) and an excuse in terms of personal inability (Goffman 1971; Heritage 1984).
3. Third, it is easy to infer an element of political testing. There was a general consensus among informants that, at least on the surface, there wasn't much racism in the locality, but that you'd find a lot of it in the areas beyond. I was quite often told that "you find (racism with) some teachers who come from villages outside" [17-year-old male of Indian descent]. In this light, stylized Indian English looks like some kind of trap. The persona it projected reflected racist stereotypes inherited from the days of the British Empire: specifically, it invoked images about Asians being polite but incompetent in English (cf. Yule and Burnell 1886/1985; Goffe 1985). If this was how a new teacher saw these pupils, then they'd be drawn into pedagogic ineffectuality, the victims of their own prejudice.
4. Last, both black and white peers found this an entertaining stratagem, and I was even told of one white boy who tried it out himself (not very successfully).

From these interview reports of pupils using SAE to teachers, it does look rather like a form of resistance, which is the interpretation that Parmar puts on comparable reports in an influential publication from the Birmingham Center for Contemporary Cultural Studies (1982). Indeed, this is an interpretation that made some sense to informants themselves (cf. Rampton 1992, 33–46). Even so, interview reports are often rather idealized, which becomes clearer if we turn now to some interactional data in which it is rather more complicated to attribute political significance to SAE.

SAE IN SPONTANEOUS INTERACTION WITH TEACHERS

Extract 1 involved two teachers and four boys—one Anglo and three Asian—and was recorded during a dinnertime detention.

Extract 1

Participants: Asif (15, male, Pakistani descent, wearing radiomicrophone), Alan (15, male, Anglo descent), Salim (15, Male, Pakistani descent), Kazim (15, Male, Pakistani descent), Mr. Chambers (25+, Anglo descent), Ms. Jameson (25+, Anglo descent)
Setting: Asif and his friend Alan are in detention for writing on desks during lessons. They are being temporarily supervised by Mr. Chambers, standing in for Ms. Jameson, who has gone to try to find the head teacher about something else. Round about lines 31 or 32, their friends Salim and Kazim arrive at the door, at roughly the same time as Ms. Jameson returns.

1	Asif:	there's loads of writing on this table (2.0) I just
2		wrote two: words on there and then she put me in
3		detention [ ] (.)
4	Alan:	ENNIT (1.0) guess what I put
5	Mr. C:	what were they ( )
6	Alan:	I put M R
7	Asif:	((laughs)) I wrote mister right
8	Mr. C:	( ) (.)
9	Asif:	that's it (1.0)
10	Alan:	ennit that's it ( )
11	Mr. C:	what ( ) was there?
12	Asif:	what?
13	Mr. C:	what ( )
14	Asif:	yeh I know Alan wrote them
15	Alan:	don't be silly
16	Asif:	((louder)): eh don't be silly now
17		((half laughing:)) look you're in

```
18            detent ⌈ ion so tell the truth
19  Alan:           ⌊ you can't blame it on me now
20  Asif:   ((loud)): tel l the truth Alan (2.0)
21  Asif:   she goes I don't trust you (.) she goes ⌈ well I
22  Mr.C:                                          ⌊ (neither
23          do I Asif) (.)
24  Asif:   what?
25  Mr.C:   I don't tr ⌈ ust (you )
26  Asif:              ⌊ I don't trust YOU (.)
27          ((half laughing)) I tell you straight right (7.0)
28          ((?Mr. C? whistles for 4.0 secs))
29  Asif:   nobody trusts a cowboy (1.5)
30  Mr. C:  (what?)
31  Asif    ((laughing quietly)): (      ) (.)
32  Mr. C:  (      )
            ((Kazim and Salim arrive at the door about now))
33  Alan:                      ⌈ (     )
34  Asif:   ((f)):    Kaz      ⌊ [ethe ɾo ethe ɾo]
                            ((Panj: stay here stay here))
35  Mr. C:  (            see you messing    around      )
36  Alan:                   ⌈ (    )
37  Asif    ((chants)): ⌊ 'te'ri _____'a:ˌdi:ˌdi:]
            ((ff))
                    ((Panj: your + (obscenity) + nonsense)?
38  Ms J:   'after' you
39  Asif:   'after' you::ˋ
            [ʌftə juʊu]
40  Sal:    ((at a higher pitch)): 'after' you::ˋ
                                    [ʌftə juʊu]
```

41 Mr.C: (   )(1.0)

42   ((door bangs shut))

43 Ms J: ((f)) have we got another cloth?

44 Sal.:   ((f)) alright (   )

45   ((a lot of loud laughter))

46 Asif: ((f)) Kazim you want to help us?

47 Kaz: pardon

48 Mr. C: you want another cloth do you

49 Asif: ((f)) yeh yeh say yeh   [ɑː ɑː ɑː ɑː]

                                      ((Panj: yes yes yes yes

50 Ms J: (   )

51 Sal.:   yeh I might   (   )

52 Mr. C: (   )

53 Asif: yeh

54 Kaz: I'll help 'em

55 Sal.:   yeh we'   ll help 'em

56 Ms J: no you won't (.) out

57 Kas: ((1)) come on 'en

58 Sal.:   ((1)) come on

59 Ms J: OUT (2.0)

60 Kaz: ((1)) we're not joking

61 Asif: ((laughs))

62 Ms J: disobedient yes

63 Kaz: I know but I (don't)

64 Mr. C: ((1)) come on Salim

65 Kaz: ((f)) so what you doing here anyway

66 Ms J: ((f)) thank you   very much

67 Sal: ((f)) you you try to chat her up

68		ennit ( )
69	Ms J:	thank you very much
70		((Salim and Asif (start to) leave about now))
71	Asif:	can I go now
72	Ms J:	no, I want ⎡these desks
73	Asif:	⎣WHAT YOU ON ABOUT UUH
74	Alan	⎡Miss
75	Asif:	⎣two words wrote (.) you sa- is this half hour job

In some respects, the use of stylized Asian English in Asif and Salim's **'after you'** seemed to back up the interview reports.

1. It involved a stereotyped politeness, but this obviously could not be taken at face value. Among other things, the split between the words uttered and the speaker's usual selves was indicated by a sharp change from normal pitch, tune, and accent.
2. SAE was also quite clearly inserted within the micropolitics of pupil-teacher interaction: Skirmishing over the assertion of authority became overt in lines 56–64, and plainly a system of wider institutional sanctions was at stake throughout (detention as punishment for misconduct).

On these grounds, SAE does indeed appear to serve as a double-edged instrument of resistance in institutionally asymmetrical cross-ethnic negotiation. But if one looks more closely, the bald term "resistance" doesn't really capture the spirit of this encounter.

1. Contrary to what interview reports suggested, the teachers involved here were well known to these youngsters. On several occasions, youngsters spoke favorably about the minor adventures into multiracial playground Panjabi made by Mr. Chambers, and when they were later left alone, there was quite a lot of relatively amicable conversation between Ms. Jameson, Alan, and Asif.
2. More significant, the switch to stylized Asian English in lines 39 and 40 occurred within a sequence of *reciprocal* kidding that was actually *initiated* by Ms. Jameson. In line 38, Ms. Jameson's own "after you" was falsely polite, equivalent to saying, "please, do come and join us in detention." It was this that made the first move away from straight, untransformed talk. Once this initial shift from normal politeness had been made, it was easier for Asif and Salim to increase the nonliteral framing of the exchange by adding false accents (Goffman 1974, 159). Normally, one would expect a

gradually attenuating sequence "after you—thanks (—my pleasure)", but now the interlude promised to develop into an immobiliz-
ing spin of reciprocal deference—what Goffman calls "After you,
Alphonse" (Goffman 1971, 143–44). It is not clear from the recording
who entered the classroom first, but a nonliteral frame carried on
after the use of stylized Asian English. Both teachers participated up
until their bluff was called, and Ms. Jameson tried to bring things
down to earth in lines 56 and 59.

Taken as a whole, this episode undoubtedly did involve conflict, with
the boys probing away at the limits of authority. But in view of the two
teachers' conduct, couldn't this interaction be just as easily characterized as some kind of "sport"? After all, when they invited Salim and
Kazim into detention, it was the teachers themselves who transgressed
the basic features of detention as an event where attendance is both
involuntary and made by prior arrangement. And in the end, Kazim
and Salim left the scene, and Alan and Asif carried on with detention.
Doesn't this episode simply illustrate the kind of interactive juggling
between play and seriousness that has been well documented as a
popular and enlivening feature of the teacher's professional experience
(cf., e.g., Pollard 1985; Edwards and Westgate 1987)? Indeed, does the
difference between resistance and messing about just boil down to the
analyst's ideological preference? No, it doesn't, and to see why not, it
is worth looking at two other incidents (extracts 2 and 3), in which the
element of interpersonal conflict was virtually nonexistent.

SAE AND INTERACTIONAL BOUNDARY
NEGOTIATION

Extract 2

As I was going down the stairs into the gym at the youth club, a small
Asian boy (about 12 years old) was walking down in front of me. Jim Cook,
the school caretaker, was at the bottom by the doors. He held them open
for us and as the boy went through, he turned to Jim as he passed and said
in a very strong Panjabi accent (not subsequently maintained in ordinary
talk): 'how are you doing Mr. Cook'. As I passed through after him,
without any hint of annoyance Jim said something like 'might as well keep
the doors open all the time', which he did. [fieldnotes]

Extract 3

I was standing behind the snack bar. Ishfaq (15, male, Pakistani descent)
came into the club soon after it opened and in our first exchange of the
evening, he came up to me at the counter and said in a strong Panjabi

accent: **'Ben Rampton can I help you'**. Though it was me doing the serving, I sustained the joke and asked for 20? Mojos (chews). Then in his ordinary voice he placed an order for 10 Refreshers. 'Is this a party' I asked (etc.) [fieldnotes]

In these two extracts, SAE was being used in opening encounters. In both, a Panjabi youngster walked toward a white adult and the use of SAE marked the beginning of a period of heightened contact between them, even if the contact was only very brief.

To understand what was going on in these exchanges, it is worth considering opening encounters in a bit more detail. Normally, people open encounters with what Goffman calls "access rituals." Access rituals (for example, "hello," "how are you," "fine") have primarily phatic function, and, in Laver's words,

> they allow [interactants] the opportunity to explore, in a tentative way, the social identity and momentary state of mind of the other participant, in order to be able to define and construct an appropriate role for themselves in the rest of the interaction . . . [access rituals defuse] potential hostility . . . [and] allow the participants to cooperate in getting the interaction comfortably under way, using emotionally uncontroversial communicative material, and demonstrating by signals of cordiality and tentative social solidarity their mutual acceptance of the possibility of an interaction taking place. (Laver 1975, 218–219, 220, 221; see also, e.g., Firth 1972; Laver 1981; Ferguson 1981, 23–24; Kendon 1990, Ch. 6)

Goffman (1971, 78) identified two stages in opening encounters:

1. internal "cognitive recognition," in which each participant places the other within some framework of personal and/or social information about them, and
2. communicated "social" recognition, which overtly welcomes the approach, shows that further communication is permissible, and acknowledges the participants' specific personal and/or social identities and their membership in a shared relationship (see Goffman 1971, Ch. 7, and Schiffrin 1977 for a more differentiated account).

In Extracts 2 and 3, from my data, the youngsters seemed to be playing with the interactional structure of opening encounters. By using SAE in their first turn, they communicated an identity that contradicted the kind of cognitive recognition that the adults might be expected to make in the circumstances. It foregrounded a *social* category membership ("Asian who doesn't speak vernacular English") at a moment when the adults would normally be setting themselves up for interaction with an individual known to them in a primarily *personal/*

biographical capacity. In doing so, SAE promised to *destabilize* the transition to comfortable interaction, to the working consensus that phatic activity normally facilitates.

In what ways can these uses of SAE in access rituals be called "political"?

POLITICAL SYMBOLISM

In spite of the absence of any overt conflict between these participants, these switches into SAE had political meaning in at least two ways. First and fairly obvious, through the symbolic connotations of linguistic code itself. As already suggested, stylized Asian English was often associated with racist stereotypes of "babu." The potentially problematic character of these symbolic associations was partly attested to by the fact that white adolescents generally avoided using SAE to target Asian friends (Rampton 1995). In this light, rather more seems to have been involved in the switches we have examined than just the ruffling of interactional transition. Performing them, adolescents also made Anglo-Asian domination relevant as a larger interpretive framework. SAE evoked social knowledge about problematic intergroup relations, and it generated the potential significance of a "worst case" scenario in which one of the participants might be seen as a white racist believing in babu stereotypes or the other as an incompetent Asian (or both).

In addition to the symbolism of the code itself, SAE's specific location in interactional structure also invites a political interpretation. The micro-interactional positioning of switches into SAE seemed to dramatize the central macropolitical issues surrounding limited proficiency in English. At the microlevel, SAE was quite frequently used at moments when adolescents were negotiating participation in interactional enclosures in which a white adult would have some control or influence over them. Switches to SAE occurred

- at the threshold of activities like detention or basketball,
- on occasions when Asian adolescents asked white adults for goods or services,
- when teachers tried to institute question-answer exchanges, and
- when interviewers asked for more concentrated attention.

The key elements were boundaries, transition, and access on unequal terms; in this regard, switches to SAE bore a remarkable formal correspondence to the *institutional* issues raised by limited proficiency in English, both locally and nationally, in England. Locally and nationally, debate about second-language learners of English has been overwhelmingly concerned with the problems of marginality and with transition into the mainstream. Admittedly, this was not the sum total of debate about cultural pluralism, and with Panjabi, the emphasis was far more on the *development* of differences that were *positively* valued (cf. Rampton 1995, Ch. 4). But with ESL, the emphasis was very much on the eradication of negatively valued difference, and there was a remarkable formal correspondence between, for example, the marginal position of ESL learners struggling to gain a decent foothold in school on the one hand and, on the other, the microsocial relationships made salient by SAE. Overall, it is as if knowledge of the precarious institutional position of relatively recent migrants acted as a cognitive template that sensitized adolescents to particular micro-interactional moments, which they then marked out with SAE. Equally, the interactional organization of switches into SAE kept the institutional integration of L2 users alive as an issue on the implicit agenda of local adolescent social life. By switching into symbolic voices that inevitably evoked connotational fields that stretched beyond the matter on hand, adolescents invited participants to "read acts as symptoms" and to reinterpret particular interactional boundary negotiations in terms of the wider political domination of one group by another.

THE DEVELOPMENT OF POLITICAL SENSIBILITIES IN MULTIETHNIC FRIENDSHIP GROUPS

In concluding, two points need to be made, both of them about the development of political sensibilities in multiethnic friendship groups like the one I studied.

The microsocial arrangements and processes emerging around SAE instantiated a larger problematic in majority-minority relations. It seems quite likely that interactions like these could help sensitize black and white observers to the political concerns of their Indian and Pakistani friends; interactions like the ones described here can be seen as small but significant building blocks in the political socialization of non-Panjabis. But in saying that, it is worth emphasizing the way that these kinds of process differ from orthodox accounts of classroom socialization.

There are now quite a lot of studies looking at how school-students are socialized into different roles and attitudes, and more recent interactionist approaches have shown that there is more involved than just the dominating influence of schools, subjects, and teachers. Pupils themselves play an active role in shaping both the classroom environment and their own socialization within it (e.g., Mehan 1980; Cook-Gumperz and Corsaro 1986). By providing teachers with subtle (and

not always progressive) guidance about how to do their jobs (cf. Mc-
Dermott and Gospodinoff 1981; Pollard 1985; Cazden 1986), kids are
seen as "teaching teachers how to teach them."

In interactions like the ones discussed in this chapter, adults in
positions of relative authority were an indispensable presence; in that
regard, there was much in common with classroom interaction studies.
But here the primary pedagogic relationship wasn't between adults and
adolescents, and the knowledge at issue wasn't defined by the school
curriculum. Teachers (and other adults) had a crucial role, but not as
principal pedagogic agents. Instead, they functioned much more as
instructional objects, focal components to be observed in interactional
experiments run by one set of adolescents for the potential edification
of others. Of course, teachers could themselves learn from their participation (see later discussion); but in this kind of political education, the
main pedagogic relationship existed between peers, and the "lesson
content" derived not from the adult but from adolescent knowledge and
experience.

The second point about interethnic socialization underlines the
value of sociolinguistic discourse analysis. As sociolinguists are well
aware, the response that an utterance elicits plays an important part
in shaping that utterance's meaning. Responses not only display the
recipient's understanding, they also retrospectively affect the first
speaker's own interpretation of the significance of what he or she
has said. In fact, the recipient's contribution to meaning may be
particularly important in utterances that have a high symbolic loading
(cf. Sperber and Wilson 1986; Blakemore 1992), and so it is essential
to reckon with the kinds of *response* that stylized Asian English made
possible and elicited.

I have already suggested that SAE was designed to disturb smooth
interactional transition and that to do so, it conjured awkward social
knowledge about intergroup stratification. But of course the reactions
of white adult recipients could vary. The recipient might flounder,
embarrassed, unable to decide on the frame or footing that was being
offered (Goffman 1974, 423). If the subsequent interaction was uncomfortable, then this could affirm the problematicity of Anglo-Asian relations, nudging the participants towards opposite sides. On the other
hand, the recipient could also play along with SAE, take it in stride, and
process it in the context of other safer and more bonding identity
relations. If subsequent interaction went well, the participants could
gain some reassurance that although it couldn't be ignored, knowledge
of ethnic stratification wasn't dangerous or threatening for their particular relationship. More than that, for people who knew how to give or
to take it, these uses of stylized Asian English could themselves become
ritual emblems of community.

This is not, I think, a perspective that fits in with studies of resistance produced in the sociologies of race and youth in the 1970s and early 1980s. One of the problems with these studies of resistance was their use of the social, subcultural, or ethnic group as the basic unit of analysis (e.g., Willis 1977). This produced an overdetermined view of who stood where politically: An individual's political stance was fixed in his or her allocation to different analytic categories, and political positions were much too easily interpreted in terms of the shaping influence of gross variables such as ethnic background, lifestyle, network, or cultural orientation. Teachers were teachers, and pupils were either "lads" or "ear' oles."

More recently, though, scholars have become much more skeptical of this kind of determinism. In the study of race relations, absolutist ideas about ethnic essences about people being fundamentally African-Caribbean, Anglo, Indian, and so on, are being replaced by an interest in the emergence of much more dynamic and mixed identities. Hall, for example, talks about new ethnicities, and he argues that these engage in a politics

> which works with and through difference.[This is a politics] which is able to build forms of solidarity and identification that make common struggle and resistance possible *without* suppressing the real heterogeneity of interests and identities.[2] (Hall 1988, 28; see also Gilroy 1987)

This is an idiom that recognizes that in certain contexts and on certain issues, black pupils can share common cause with white teachers (see the articles in Donald and Rattansi 1992). It is an important theoretical expansion in the literature. This chapter is intended as a contribution to this expansion by showing

1. that situated interaction is the best place to investigate these processes empirically,
2. that sociolinguistic discourse analysis provides the best set of tools, and
3. that in the way that people used stylized Asian English to activate, neutralize, or transform race division, we can glimpse one of the processes involved in the emergence of new ethnicities and mixed solidarities.

TRANSCRIPTION SYMBOLS AND CONVENTIONS

Prosody

ˎ	low fall	ˈ	high stress
ˏ	low rise	ˌ	low stress
ˋ	high fall	‖	very high stress

´	high rise	‖	very low stress
ˇ	fall rise	⌐	pitch register shift upwards
ᴧ	rise fall	∟	pitch register shift downwards
		↑	extra pitch height

Segmental phonetics
[   ]   IPA phonetic transcription (revised to 1979)

Conversational features

⌈
| overlapping turns
⌊

=   two utterances closely connected without a noticeable overlap, or different parts of a single speaker's turn

(.)   pause of less than one second

(1.5)   approximate length of pause in seconds

l.   Lenis (quiet) enunciation

f.   Fortis (loud) enunciation

(( ))   'stage directions'

( )   speech inaudible

(text)   speech hard to discern, analyst guess

Bold   instance of crossing of central interest in discussion

NOTES

1. There has in fact been quite a lot of interpretive/interactional sociolinguistic research on communication between people of Anglo, African-Caribbean, and South Asian descent in contemporary Britain (e.g., Gumperz, Jupp, and Roberts 1979; Gumperz 1982a, 1982b; Roberts, Davies, and Jupp 1992). But these have been generally concerned with workplace interactions involving adults, who have been brought up both inside and outside Britain, who are unfamiliar with one another, and who occupy different positions of institutional power. The gist of these studies is to show how, despite initial goodwill, hidden differences in participants' communicative resources disrupt straight discussion, generate negative social categorizations, and result in the reproduction of racism. In contrast (following Hewitt 1986), much of my own research is concerned with the recreational interaction of British-born adolescents who know each other well and whose institutional positions are roughly similar. These youngsters recognize and even exaggerate the differences in their communicative repertoires in a set of stylized and often playful interactions that, up to a point at least, constitute a form of anti-racism.

The approach taken in the earlier interpretive sociolinguistic studies has much to offer. They generally study sites where interactional discourse and institutional processes come together (interviews, advice sessions, committee meetings); by analyzing face-to-face processes that result in decisions that critically affect a person's access to knowledge or material resources, they have revealed dimensions of discrimination that have been unrecognized hitherto. They also contest legitimating official ideologies that blame the victim, and challenge, for example, language-teaching orthodoxies by stressing the inadequate social and communicative practices of monolinguals in authority.

Nevertheless, even though they are no longer seen as exclusively responsible for their own failure, there is no fundamental break with the "blacks as victims" idea that Gilroy (1987) identifies as a cornerstone in the discourses of racism. Specifically surveying interactional sociolinguistics, Singh, Lele, and Martohardjono (1988) pick up on this, and they also argue that interactional sociolinguistic studies of "cross-cultural" communication have been too concerned with language as an instrument for assimilation to the demands of capitalist bureaucracy. They suggest that rather than studying "joyless [managerial] formalisms," ethnic resistance needs to be recognized and "understood in light of the human sense for the joyfulness of speech" (1988, 45). There is much in this to key with Hewitt 1986; Gilroy 1987; and my own approach.

2. "We are beginning to see constructions of . . . a new conception of ethnicity: a new cultural politics which engages rather than suppresses difference and which depends, in part, on the cultural construction of new ethnic identities. . . . What is involved is the splitting of the notion of ethnicity between, on the one hand the dominant notion which connects it to nation and 'race' and on the other hand what I think is the beginning of a positive conception of the ethnicity of the margins, of the periphery . . . this is not an ethnicity which is doomed to survive, as Englishness was, only by marginalising, dispossessing, displacing and forgetting other ethnicities. This precisely is the ethnicity predicated on difference and diversity." (Hall 1988, 29)

REFERENCES

Blakemore, D. (1992). *Understanding utterances*. Oxford: Blackwell.

Cazden, C. (1986). Classroom discourse. In M. Merlin and C. Wittrock (Eds.), *Handbook of research on teaching* (3rd ed.) (pp. 432–463). New York: Macmillan.

Center for Contemporary Cultural Studies (C.C.C.S.). (1982). *The empire strikes back*. London: Hutchinson.

Cook-Gumperz, J., and Corsaro, W. (1986). Introduction. In J. Cook-Gumperz, W. Corsaro, and J. Streeck (Eds.), *Children's worlds and children's language*. (pp. 1–11). Berlin: Mouton de Gruyter.

Donald, J., and Rattansi, A. (Eds.). (1992). *"Race," culture and difference*. London: Sage.

Edwards, A., and Westgate, D. (1987). *Investigating classroom talk*. Lewes: Falmer Press.

Ferguson, C. (1981). The structure and use of politeness formulas. In F. Coulmas (Ed.), Conversational routine (pp. 21–35). The Hague: Mouton.

Firth, R. (1972). Verbal and bodily rituals of greeting and parting. In J. S. La Fontaine (Ed.), *The interpretation of ritual* (pp. 1–38). London: Tavistock.

Gilroy, P. (1987). *There ain't no black in the Union Jack*. London: Hutchinson.

Gilroy, P., and Lawrence, E. (1988). Two-tone Britain: White and Black youth and the politics of anti-racism. In P. Cohen and H. Bains (Eds.), *Multiracist Britain* (pp. 121–155). Basingstoke: Macmillan.

Goffe, A. (1985, September 19). Black and brown in Brum. *The Guardian*.

Goffman, E. (1971). *Relations in public*. London: Allen Lane.

Goffman, E. (1974). *Frame analysis*. Harmondsworth: Penguin.

Gumperz, J. (1982). *Discourse strategies*. Cambridge: Cambridge University Press.

Gumperz, J. (Ed.). (1982). *Language and social identity*. Cambridge: Cambridge University Press.

Gumperz, J., Jupp, T., and Roberts, C. (1979). *Crosstalk: A study of cross-cultural communication*. Southall, Middlesex: National Centre for Industrial Language Training.

Hall, S. (1988). New ethnicities. *ICA Documents, 7*, 27–31.

Heritage, J. (1984). *Garfinkel and ethnomethodology*. Oxford: Blackwell.

Hewitt, R. (1986). *White talk, Black talk*. Cambridge: Cambridge University Press.

Kendon, A. (1990). *Conducting interaction*. Cambridge: Cambridge Univesity Press.

Laver, J. (1975). Communicative functions of phatic communion. In A. Kendon, R. Harris, and M. R. Key (Eds.), *Organisation of behaviour in face-to-face interaction* (pp. 215–238). The Hague: Mouton.

Laver, J. (1981). Linguistic routines and politeness in greeting and parting. In F. Coulmas (Ed.), *Conversational routine* (pp. 289–304). The Hague: Mouton.

McDermott, R., and Gospodinoff, K. (1981). Social contexts for ethnic borders and school failure. In H. Trueba, G. Guthrie, and K. Au (Eds.), *Culture and the bilingual classroom* (pp. 212–230). Rowley, Mass.: Newbury House.

Mehan, H. (1980). The competent student. *Anthropology and Education Quarterly, 11*, 131–152.

Parmar, P. (1982). Gender, race and class: Asian women in resistance. In Centre for Contemporary Cultural Studies, *The Empire Strikes Back* (pp. 236–275). London: Hutchinson.

Pollard, A. (1985). *The social world of the primary school*. New York: Holt, Rinehart and Winston.

Rampton, B. (1995). *Crossing: Language and ethnicity among adolescents*. London: Longman.

Rampton, M. B. (1992). Scope for "empowerment" in sociolinguistics? In D. Cameron, E. Frazer, P. Harvey, B. Rampton, and K. Richardson (Eds.), *Researching language: Issues of power and method* (pp. 29–64). London: Routledge.

Roberts, C., Davies, E., and Jupp, T. (1992). *Language and discrimination*. London: Longman.

Schiffrin, D. (1977). Opening encounters. *American Sociological Review, 42(5)*, 679–691.

Singh, R., Lele, J., and Martohardjono, G. (1988). Communication in a multilingual society: Some missed opportunities. *Language in Society, 17(1)*, 43–59.

Sperber, D., and Wilson, D. (1986). *Relevance*. Oxford: Blackwell.

Willis, P. (1977). *Learning to labour*. Aldershot: Saxon House.

Yule, H., and Burnell, A. (1886). *Hobson Jobson: A glossary of Anglo Indian colloquial words and phrases*. Reprinted 1985. London: RKP.

18

Conclusion: Education in Multilingual Settings: Stakes, Conditions, and Consequences

Monica Heller and Marilyn Martin-Jones

The chapters in this collection show how complex the issues surrounding education in multilingual settings can be. Educational choices in such settings, whether regarding structures, programs, practices, or materials, are clearly much more than choices about how to achieve linguistic proficiency. They are choices about how to distribute linguistic resources and about what value to attribute to linguistic forms and practices. They are choices that are embedded in the economic, political, and social interests of groups and that have consequences for the life chances of individuals as well as for the construction of social categories and relations of power.

These chapters make possible a number of generalizations and raise a number of questions. In this conclusion to the book, we sketch out what we see as the main lessons to be learned from the cases presented, as well as some areas that remain poorly understood or little explored.

The first theme to emerge from the studies reported here concerns the ritualized ways in which participants in educational encounters draw on linguistic resources to collaborate with, or to contest, the interactional and institutional order of the school or other settings. These more-or-less ritualized practices have consequences for the construction of social categories and for the use of those categories as ways of organizing the distribution of resources through education. We still need to ask under what conditions we find strategies of collaboration or contestation and under what conditions these strategies may be more or less successful and for whom.

The second theme concerns the extent to which the interactional and institutional orders of education in multilingual settings are in fact unified. Both may be traversed by a number of different, possibly competing, possibly contradictory, sets of interests and ideological orientations. Communicative and organizational practices in such complex settings may be primarily focused on coping with tensions. Such tensions might include those between the authority of the dominant language and the solidarity of the vernacular; between pedagogical commitments to group work and assessment pressures to monitor student performances; between valuing community-based knowledge and facilitating access to school-based knowledge; and so on.

The third important theme concerns the relationship between what happens in educational settings and what happens elsewhere, in other arenas. We would argue that it is necessary to link the interaction and institutional order of schools and other educational institutions to the social order of communities and therefore to link the consequences of practices in educational settings to other social categories and processes.

In most of the multilingual settings considered here, especially postcolonial and neocolonial ones, the language of instruction does not correspond to the language of the learners (although one could argue that this is a general principle for any socially differentiated community). This is not necessarily a problem in and of itself: Lin's chapter on Hong Kong, Ndayipfukamiye's chapter on Burundi, and Bunyi's chapter on Kenya all show that middle-class or elite members of society have the symbolic and material resources for investment in the language of instruction outside and inside school. They also have an interest in doing so: Their class position is linked to the use of multilingual resources that permit them to link to sources of power outside their own communities and also to control local production and distribution of resources. The use of a former colonial language as a language of instruction in these settings is a way of maintaining privileged access to linguistic resources and to educational credentials.

What happens to those who are located farther from the sources of power in their communities ? Many of the papers in this collection show that ritualized practices produce what Hornberger and Chick refer to as "safetalk," that is, ways of conducting classroom interaction that give the appearance of constructing knowledge under conditions that actually make it impossible for such teaching and learning to occur. Safetalk can be constructed through codeswitching and through fixed sequential interactional structures that include the use of a unified floor and of sequential turn-taking controlled by teachers, especially of Initiation-Response-Evaluation sequences that permit the close monitoring and evaluation of student performances. Safe spaces can also be constructed by employing code contrast to distinguish between "front" and "back-stage" performances and through keying and footing. These interactional practices are generally meant to help students gain access to school knowledge. We see them in a substantial proportion of the studies reported in this volume. (See the chapters by Arthur, Bunyi, Camilleri, Hornberger and Chick, Lin, Martin-Jones and Saxena, and Ndayipfukamiye). Ironically, they have the effect of erecting a barrier between the students' lifeworld and the world of the school, by signaling clearly what counts as legitimate knowledge and what does not. Safetalk further has the perverse effect of masking the real marginalization processes that can go on in such situations, precisely because it does make it seem as though teaching and learning are occurring. It is here that we can see symbolic domination working most clearly.

However, many papers here also show that the advancement or marginalization of interests in the context of social hierarchization is usually not a matter of simple dichotomous oppositions. The elites of Burundi, Hong Kong, Jaffna, Malta, or northern Québec and other sites retain their position also through the legitimacy accorded by the mastery of the local, authentic variety. So they must, in some ways, deal with the contradictions flowing from their ambivalent position with respect to local and colonialist varieties. They do this in part through structural, institutional arrangements such as the separation of Chinese-medium and English-medium schools (Hong Kong), ignoring the persistence of English in what is meant to be Tamil-medium education (Jaffna), or the use of the local variety in the early years of schooling (Botswana, Burundi, northern Québec).

Dominant groups in immigration settings may also display ambivalence about multilingual resources in settings characterized by postcolonial and neocolonial labor migration. The chapters by Moore, Martin-Jones and Saxena, and Mondada and Gajo all show how attempts to grapple with the realities of student multilingual repertoires are rife with contradictions. As Moore indicates, in Australia the ambivalence emerges clearly in the ideological debates underlying conflicts over English-language assessment procedures. In the British and Swiss cases, while in some ways educational arrangements explicitly recognize the linguistic resources of students who are acquiring the language of instruction, such resources tend to be marginalized, through institutional arrangements and interactional practices.

Similarly, marginalized groups may feel ambivalent about the value of languages that represent social advancement as opposed to those that may be stigmatized but are at the same time sources of solidarity and potential sources of alternative power bases. Cavalcanti's discussion of the Guarani teacher education program signals such possible ambivalence regarding Portuguese and Guarani in Brazil; the same may be said for the case of Corsica described by Jaffe, or of Hong Kong as described by Lin. Here, ambivalence must be manifested in ways other than in structural arrangements, since such groups have no control over institutions. In the case of the Guarani, we see an attempt to turn institutional opportunities to their own ends through the subversion and appropriation of the interaction order. In Hong Kong, such ambivalence may be manifested through codeswitching in the day-to-day communicative practices of teachers and learners. It is through the interaction order, then, that it is possible to act with regard to interests and positionings constrained by institutional and social orders beyond the control of actors.

This point emerges most clearly in the cases in which marginalized groups attempt to contest the dominant order of the school. The cases described by Rampton, Heller, and Roberts and Sarangi show how students can actively contest the dominant values accorded to linguistic varieties or the ways the school has positioned them (as minority students), either by refusing to comply with the interaction order or by appropriating linguistic practices in ways that infuse them with new, subversive, social meanings.

The chapters here have focused mainly on processes of social stratification and social categorization (in particular, who counts as a legitimate speaker of a legitimate language or languages) and on the ways in which these processes unfold in daily life. For this reason, it is harder to see clearly what their consequences may be for what happens in other arenas, for individual life trajectories or for long-term social structuration. Nonetheless, it is possible to see that there are cases where contestation rarely occurs and therefore where social and cultural reproduction is likely, while there are others where tensions and contradictions may destabilize the reproduction process unless they are effectively contained, and still others where there is at least the possibility of alternative visions, whether or not they ever get beyond the local.

There are a number of dimensions of categorization that also remain relatively unexplored here. We have seen how participants in educational settings are positioned, or try to position themselves, with respect to the legitimacy of languages and speakers. The chapters by Heller and by Roberts and Sarangi point to some ways in which students are categorized as legitimate learners or are evaluated in those terms, both through structural provisions (streaming and other special programs for those considered to be low achievers) and through interactional ones. These chapters also point to the linkages made between educational achievement categories and social organizational principles ("immigrants," "refugees," class, race), although how these linkages are actually constructed requires further study. These and other chapters begin to illuminate the ways in which linguistic legitimacy is tied to the definition of nation, state, and citizenship, since legitimate participation in the school entails legitimate participation in an institution of the state. However, we have yet to examine deeply how this kind of categorization is tied to the construction of categories such as class, race, or ethnicity. We catch glimpses of how gender is implicated in these processes, for example, in the representation of men and women among educators and policy-makers of different status, or in the relative legitimacy of male and female exploitation of interactional practices, or in gendered struggles for the floor. There may well be other categories that are locally, or even widely, relevant; in order to discover them, it would be necessary to broaden the lens of school ethnography and also to link schooling to other arenas of social life.

This book has privileged spoken-language practices as a way of understanding the central issues addressed here. However, it is clear that other forms of communication are equally implicated in multilingual educational settings, indeed, in ways that are closely intertwined. The regulation of turns at talk, for example, is not simply a question of verbal bids; it is also a question of paralinguistic phenomena (pitch, loudness, intonation) and of nonverbal ones (eye gaze, body orientation, gesture). In addition, written language is an essential element of communication, and educational practice tends to be highly oriented to text. Performances may be written as well as spoken, and what is done in spoken language may or may not be the same as what is done in writing (for example, one way in which ambivalence regarding multilingual resources can be manifested can be in the monolingualism of one channel and the multilingualism of the other). More broadly, spoken language is tied to the use of time and space and of material resources.

Much is at stake for educators and learners in multilingual settings. Access to valued linguistic resources is tied to access to educational credentials, and educational practice can challenge or reinforce the construction of social categories and of relations of power. Struggles over what counts as legitimate language in education are struggles over who count as legitimate speakers and over who can do what and under what conditions. If we fail to take this into account, we risk reproducing unintentionally the very relations of inequality we are striving to overcome.

Author Index

Page numbers in italic are in chapter references.

Subject Index

119, 135–136, 142–143, 159–162,
194–195, 197, 201, 208, 214, 221–
225, 233, 277, 280, 292, 302–303,
313, 351
language politics, 18, 196–197, 210,
290, 314, 383–385
language purists, 140–141, 197,
219, 232
language repertoires, 60–61, 65, 69,
217, 235, 240, 261, 367, 383, 386–
387, 390, 416, 421
language values, 2, 15–16, 19, 20–
22, 24, 43, 57, 59–60, 82, 87, 98,
101–103, 135, 144–145, 152, 155,
163, 197, 208, 213, 218–219, 221,
224, 232, 276
language-related pedagogies, 32, 45–
52
large classes, 13, 42, 70, 103
legitimate language, 2–3, 7, 9–11, 13,
15, 20, 24–26, 68, 82, 99, 141, 157,
174–175, 178, 187–188, 269, 281,
291, 294, 298, 302, 363, 381–402,
422, 424
lifeworld(s), 19, 21, 144–145, 155,
157–158
linguistic capital/symbolic
capital/linguistic resources, 2–3,
8–12, 15, 20, 48, 57, 87–89, 97, 99,
104, 136, 138, 143–146, 151, 155,
158, 160–164, 173–174, 176, 178,
196, 235–243, 247, 251, 261, 298–
299, 303, 312–313, 329, 368, 372
linguistic/symbolic market(s), 16,
19, 82, 143–144, 161–162, 173–177,
182, 295, 298, 308, 310–311, 313,
382, 388
literacy/literacies, 15, 40, 43, 45–46,
52, 84–85, 88–89, 272, 298, 302, 313,
351, 333–355, 359–362, 366, 372
London, 171–192

Malta/Maltese (language), 19, 213–
233, 421
metalanguage, 9, 181, 189, 243–244,
260, 287
migrants/migration, 2, 7, 16, 20, 118–
119, 235–241, 245, 252, 260–261,

263, 335, 337, 350, 368, 372, 382,
385, 413, 421, 423
missionaries, 209, 218, 300–301, 320
meritocracy, 15, 77–78, 173

new pedagogies, 14, 32, 45, 52–53

Panjabi, 10, 16, 25, 118–136, 404, 409–
411, 413
parents, 15, 22, 83–89, 99, 103, 120,
122, 142, 144–145, 158–159, 161–
164, 218–219, 222, 239–240, 246,
273, 276, 280–281, 285, 289, 294,
297, 299, 311–312, 337, 343, 347,
354, 384, 388
Peru, 13, 15, 35–42, 45–47
Portuguese
as a first language, 2, 20, 235–268
as a second language, 2, 23, 317–
333, 422
post-colonial contexts, 3, 7, 13, 16,
19, 31–55, 57–75, 77–100, 101–115,
139–168, 193–212, 213–234,
420–421
prescriptivism, 62, 273, 353
primary schools, 35–42, 57–75, 77–
100, 101–115, 117–138, 235–268
private schools/private tuition, 47,
144, 218–219, 222–223, 225, 228

Québec
Arctic Québec/*Nunavik*, 22, 297–
314
Québec francophone nationalism,
300–301, 381
Quechua, 10, 13–14, 31–32, 25, 41–42,
45–47

racism/discrimination, 25, 32, 47–48,
120, 173, 178, 236–237, 403, 405,
412, 416–417
reading
doing in–class 'reading,' 40–46, 89–
97, 200, 224, 301, 324
reading abilities, 46, 84, 272, 287,
312, 322
reading aloud, 84, 93, 161, 202,
206–207, 226, 392

About the Contributors

Jo Arthur is a Scot by birth. In the 1980s, she worked for six years in Botswana as a teacher trainer. She drew on this experience for her Ph.D., which she completed at Lancaster University in 1995. Since then, she has maintained an interest in issues of educational language policy and practice in former colonial settings. She has also recently begun research into linguistic and cultural values among Somali speakers in Liverpool. She currently teaches at Edge Hill University College, in the Northwest of England, specializing in language and education and in bilingualism.

Grace Bunyi teaches courses in curriculum studies, with a special focus on bilingual education, in the Department of Educational Administration, Planning and Curriculum Studies at Kenyatta University in Nairobi, Kenya. She completed a doctorate in education at the Ontario Institute for Studies in Education, Toronto. Her emerging interest is in gender in education, particularly as regards language and the curriculum.

Suresh Canagarajah taught English language and literature at the University of Jaffna for about ten years before joining the City University of New York (Baruch College) in September 1994. He has taught postcolonial literature, applied linguistics, and ESL academic writing. His publications include *Resisting Linguistic Imperialism in English Teaching* (Oxford University Press, 1999) and papers in *TESOL Quarterly, Language in Society, Written Communication, World Englishes, Journal of Multilingual and Multicultural Development*, and *Multilingua*. His research focuses on codeswitching (in classroom and community contexts), bilingual communicative strategies, and academic literacy.

Marilda C. Cavalcanti completed her Ph.D. at Lancaster University in the United Kingdom in 1983. She is currently associate professor in the Department of Applied Linguistics at the State University of Campinas (UNICAMP), Brazil. She is the former president of the Association for Applied Linguistics in Brazil. For the last decade, she has been conducting research in Brazil on bilingual education, with a focus on native Brazilian teacher education. Most recently, she was the overall coordinator of a research project entitled "Schools of the Rain Forest and Indigenous Teacher Education." Most of her publications have appeared in Portuguese in Brazil. She has also published in English and in Spanish in a number of international journals.

J. Keith Chick is professor and chair of linguistics at the University of Natal in Durban, South Africa. His specialist interests include sociolinguistics (especially interactional sociolinguistics), intercultural communication, cross-cultural pragmatics, critical discourse analysis, language educational planning, applied linguistics, and language teaching. His writing in these areas has been published in South African and international journals, including *Language in Society* and the *Journal of Multilingual and Multicultural Development*.

Laurent Gajo (Ph.D.) currently works as a lecturer and researcher in linguistics at the Universities of Lausanne and Neuchâtel. He has contributed to a number of research projects in sociolinguistics, language acquisition, and language teaching/learning in Switzerland, Canada (Toronto), Italy (Aoste), and France (Grenoble). His research interests lie in the development of bilingualism, bilingual education, and classroom interaction and, in particular, in the acquisition of minority languages and the linguistic issues arising in the context of migration. His doctoral research was on immersion education, encompassing pedagogic issues, the interactional order of the classroom, and the wider socio-political order.

Antoinette Camilleri Grima studied linguistics and education at the University of Malta and applied linguistics at the University of Edinburgh. She graduated with an M.Sc. and Ph.D. from the University of Edinburgh with a thesis on bilingual education. She has published a book entitled *Bilingualism in Education: The Maltese Experience* (1995, Verlag). She has also published other books on the teaching of Maltese as a first language and as a foreign language and on learner autonomy in teacher education. She is a senior lecturer in applied linguistics at the Institute of Linguistics and the Faculty of Education of the University of Malta. She also works for the European Centre for Modern Languages of the Council of Europe as consultant on modern languages, bilingual education, and learner autonomy.

Monica Heller is a professor at the Department of Sociology and Equity Studies and the Centre de recherches en éducation franco-ontarienne, Ontario Institute for Studies in Education, University of Toronto. She specializes in ethnographic sociolinguistic research on bilingualism, social difference, and social inequality, with an emphasis on French and English in Canada. Her publications include an edited volume, *Codeswitching: Anthropological and Sociolinguistic Perspectives* (Mouton de Gruyter, 1988), and two books on French in Ontario: *Crosswords: Language, Education and Ethnicity in French Ontario* (Mouton de Gruyter, 1994) and *Linguistic Minorities and Modernity: A Sociolinguistic Ethnography* (Longman, 1999). She has also published articles in journals such as *Multilingua, Language in Society, Langage et société, Sociologie et sociétés, Journal of Sociolinguistics, Linguistics and Education*, and *The Anthropology and Education Quarterly*.

Nancy H. Hornberger is professor of education and director of educational linguistics at the University of Pennsylvania Graduate School of Education, Philadelphia. She specializes in sociolinguistics, language planning, and bilingual education, with special attention to educational policy and practice for language minority populations in South America and the United States. Recent publications include edited volumes: *Research Methods in Language and Education* (Kluwer, 1997, coedited with D. Corson), *Indigenous Literacies in the Americas* (Mouton, 1996), and *Sociolinguistics and Language Teaching* (Cambridge, 1996, coedited with S. McKay).

Alexandra Jaffe has done research in Corsica since 1988. She received her Ph.D. from Indiana University in 1990 and taught at Bryant College and SUNY-Cortland before moving to the University of Mississippi in 1996. Her interests revolve around issues of language ideology and the politics of linguistic representation. In Mississippi, she and a colleague have been involved in the study of voice and stance in orthographic representations of stigmatized Southern speech varieties. She returned to Corsica in the year 2000 to conduct an extended ethnography of an experimental bilingual primary school. She is the author of a recent book entitled *Ideologies in Action: Language Politics on Corsica* (Mouton, 1999).

Angel M. Y. Lin is a doctoral graduate from the Ontario Institute for Studies in Education, University of Toronto. Her research interests are in classroom discourse analysis, bilingual education, and sociocultural studies of language learning. She is currently assistant professor in the Department of English at the City University of Hong Kong. Her publications include *Teaching in Two Tongues: Language Alternation in the Foreign Language Classroom* (City Polytechnic of Hong Kong, Research Report No. 3, 1990) and a number of articles in local and international journals.

Marilyn Martin-Jones is professor of bilingualism and education at the University of Wales, Aberystwyth. Before taking up that post in 1998, she taught for fifteen years in the Department of Linguistics at Lancaster University. Her main areas of interest are bilingualism, codeswitching in bilingual discourse, multilingual literacy practices, education, linguistic difference, and inequality. Most of the research that she has conducted over the last twenty years has been of a sociolinguistic and ethnographic nature and has been based in multilingual urban contexts in England—in classrooms and in local community contexts. Her research has been written up in articles for edited volumes or for journals such as *International Journal of the Sociology of Language, Journal of Multilingual and Multicultural Development, Applied Linguistics,* and *Linguistics and Education.* She was one of the authors of *The Other Languages of England* (Routledge, 1985), and she is coeditor (with Kathryn Jones) of a recent book entitled *Multilingual Literacies: Reading and Writing Different Worlds* (John Benjamins, 2000).

Lorenza Mondada has a Ph.D. in linguistics and now works as assistant professor of French linguistics at the University of Basel. She works on areas of language in social life such as conversation analysis, the explorations of the links between grammar and interaction, the analysis of scientific practices and of the interactive construction of knowledge, the organization of talk at work, the organization of urban polyphonies, and the description of acquisitional processes accomplished through social interaction. She has published articles on these topics in both English and French.

Helen Moore has worked in various contexts with teachers of English to speakers of other languages since 1971. Most of this time she has been based in the Graduate School of Education at La Trobe University in Melbourne, Australia, but she has also worked in the Netherlands, England, and China. She is currently completing her Ph.D. at the Ontario Institute for Studies in Education at the University of Toronto. Her research topic is the intersection of bureaucratic and educational agendas in Australian ESL curriculum development.

Lin Ndayipfukamiye completed his Ph.D. at Lancaster University in 1993. The main focus of his research was on the use of French and Kirundi in primary classrooms in Burundi (Central Africa). His interests include bilingualism and the teaching and learning of foreign languages in multicultural settings. He contributed to the volume *Teaching and Researching Language in African Classrooms* (ed. by C. Rubagumya, Multilingual Matters, 1994). He was formerly a lecturer at the University of Burundi. He now lives in Canada, where he teaches in French immersion and French programs.

Donna Patrick is an assistant professor in the Department of Applied Language Studies at Brock University in St. Catharines, Ontario. Her research focuses on aboriginal languages in Canada. More specifically, it considers the relation between language and nationhood in the aboriginal context and the political, economic, and social issues related to the maintenance of the aboriginal languages.

Ben Rampton is a reader at the School of Education, King's College, University of London. His current research focuses on language, discourse, and ethnicity in urban education. He is the author of *Crossing: Language and Ethnicity among Adolescents* (Longman, 1995), and a coauthor of *Researching Language: Issues of Power and Method* (Routledge, 1992).

Celia Roberts is senior research fellow at the School of Education, King's College, University of London. Her research interests include urban sociolinguistics with particular reference to gatekeeping interviews, classroom ethnography, issues related to ethnographic methods more generally, and the social aspects of second language development. Her publications include: *Language and Discrimination* (Longman 1992, with Davies and Jupp); *Achieving Understanding* (Longman 1996, with Bremer et al.), and *Talk, Work and Institutional Order: Discourse in Medical, Mediation and Management Settings* (Mouton, 1999, with Srikant Sarangi).

Srikant Sarangi is reader at the Centre for Language and Communication Research, Cardiff University. His research interests are discourse analysis and applied linguistics, language and identity in public life, institutional and professional discourse (e.g., bureaucracy, health, social welfare, education), genetic counseling and general practice, intercultural pragmatics, and racism and ethnicity in multicultural societies. His publications include *Language, Bureaucracy and Social Control* (Longman, 1996, with Stef Slembrouck); *Talk, Work and Institutional Order: Discourse in Medical, Mediation and Management Settings* (Mouton, 1999, with C. Roberts); *Discourse and Social Life* (Longman, 2000, with Malcolm Coulthard); and *Sociolinguistics and Social Theory* (Longman, 2000, with Nikolas Coupland and Chris Candlin). He is currently coeditor, with John Wilson, of *Text: An Interdisciplinary Journal for the Study of Discourse*.

Mukul Saxena has just taken up an appointment as a senior lecturer at the Department of English Language and Applied Linguistics at the University of Brunei Darussalam. Prior to this, he worked in Britain for fifteen years, at the University College of Ripon and York St. John, at Lancaster University, and at York University. In Britain, he was involved in research in a number of areas of sociolinguistics: bilingual classroom interaction, language maintenance and shift, multilingual literacies, and forensic linguistics.